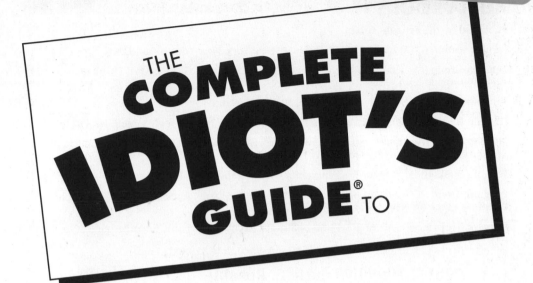

THE COMPLETE IDIOT'S GUIDE® TO

American Literature

by Laurie E. Rozakis, Ph.D.

ALPHA

A member of Penguin Group (USA) Inc.

ALPHA BOOKS

Published by the Penguin Group

Penguin Group (USA) Inc., 375 Hudson Street, New York, New York 10014, U.S.A.

Penguin Group (Canada), 10 Alcorn Avenue, Toronto, Ontario, Canada M4V 3B2 (a division of Pearson Penguin Canada Inc.)

Penguin Books Ltd, 80 Strand, London WC2R 0RL, England

Penguin Ireland, 25 St Stephen's Green, Dublin 2, Ireland (a division of Penguin Books Ltd)

Penguin Group (Australia), 250 Camberwell Road, Camberwell, Victoria 3124, Australia (a division of Pearson Australia Group Pty Ltd)

Penguin Books India Pvt Ltd, 11 Community Centre, Panchsheel Park, New Delhi—110 017, India

Penguin Group (NZ), cnr Airborne and Rosedale Roads, Albany, Auckland 1310, New Zealand (a division of Pearson New Zealand Ltd)

Penguin Books (South Africa) (Pty) Ltd, 24 Sturdee Avenue, Rosebank, Johannesburg 2196, South Africa

Penguin Books Ltd, Registered Offices: 80 Strand, London WC2R 0RL, England

Copyright © 1999 by Laurie E. Rozakis

International Standard Book Number: 0-02-863378-4
Library of Congress Catalog Card Number: 99-64167

07 06   11 10 9 8

Interpretation of the printing code: The rightmost number of the first series of numbers is the year of the book's printing; the rightmost number of the second series of numbers is the number of the book's printing. For example, a printing code of 99-1 shows that the first printing occurred in 1999.

Printed in the United States of America

Most Alpha books are available at special quantity discounts for bulk purchases for sales promotions, premiums, fund-raising, or educational use. Special books, or book excerpts, can also be created to fit specific needs.

For details, write: Special Markets, Alpha Books, 375 Hudson Street, New York, NY 10014.

Alpha Development Team

Publisher
Kathy Nebenhaus

Editorial Director
Gary M. Krebs

Marketing Brand Manager
Felice Primeau

Development Editors
Phil Kitchel
Amy Zavatto

Assistant Editor
Georgette Blau

Production Team

Development Editor
Amy Bryant

Tech Editor
Dolace McLean

Production Editor
Mark Enochs

Copy Editor
Fran Blauw

Cover Designer
Mike Freeland

Photo Editor
Richard H. Fox

Illustrator
Brian Mac Moyer

Book Designers
Scott Cook and Amy Adams of DesignLab

Indexer
Larry Sweazy

Layout/Proofreading
Angela Calvert
Mary Hunt

Contents at a Glance

Contents

Foreword

For better or worse, the literature that influenced me most as a reader, writer, and player in the great human narrative has always been American—the domestic stuff. I'm not sure why it should be that way. Maybe because, compared to the parts of the world that turned out the *Bible*, *Beowulf*, and the *Kama Sutra*, we're still such a young society that every story told in the United States isn't merely a story, but another stab at our noisy, ongoing national struggle to figure out who we are.

Then again, maybe it's because, especially in those years before multiculturalism went mainstream, we were given the impression in grade school that the homegrown crop (along with the major British imports, of course) made up the bulk of the stuff worth reading—something that now strikes me as about as duplicitous and amusing an idea as trying to pass off ketchup as a vegetable in public school lunches. (Not to malign ketchup, of course.)

Whatever the real reason, I, like a lot of people who grow up and become published authors, was a solitary adolescent who read too much (and yes, in a suburban world dominated by TV and sports, such a thing really did seem possible, and faintly suspect).

Now, as anyone who read too much as a solitary adolescent will tell you, characters on a page can have a way of becoming more real than the real people around you—or at least of shaping your world view in vast disproportion to those with whom you exist daily in three-dimensionality. In tenth grade, I never had a real-life friend who understood my loathing for bourgeois conformity and blithe hypocrisy better than my soulmate Holden Caulfield. It didn't matter that Holden was, in the end, just a collection of words on a page; if anything, never having met him made it all the easier for me to pretend that J.D. Salinger had prophesied my coming—that, indeed, I was the real-life Holden Caulfield, complete with a bad attitude and ear-flapped hunting cap, and that *The Catcher in the Rye* had been written expressly for—or *to*—me.

And as for that all-important adolescent matter of coolness—suffice it to say I formed my whole teenage identity as much on novels as I did on music, movies, or clothes. How else, before I discovered Cole Porter or Man Ray, could I have yearned to relive the impudent excesses of the 1920s without Jay Gatsby and his countless silk shirts? Why would I ever have longed to someday live in Greenwich Village if it hadn't been for the drop-dead hip world evoked by Jack Kerouac and James Baldwin, Allen Ginsburg and Gregory Corso—all of whom I knew intimately long before I'd even seen my first Jackson Pollock or heard my first Charlie Parker? Novels weren't just schoolbag ballast, time-killers, or sober morality tales; they were indispensable guides to the life well-lived, even if it was still a far cry from my own.

Fiction is just that—*fiction*, made-up stuff—and yet I, as a dangerously curious teenager who'd hardly been anywhere, met anyone, or done anything, called on its raucous cast of made-up characters to light a path for me through the so-called "real world," which always seemed more coherently illustrated through novels than through newspapers or the TV news. Ten years—and perhaps a smidge of experience—later, I think I can safely say my fellow travelers lighted me a reliable, instructive, and companionable path through the dark brambles of my youth.

All the friends of my youth—and many new ones—are here in this terrific book that makes browsing your way through a few centuries of great American storytelling as sensational, entertaining, and just plain F-U-N as the original storytellers meant it to be—no matter how successfully certain teachers in your past (or present) might have convinced you otherwise. Whether you're getting reacquainted with these characters or meeting them for the first time, you'll probably agree to this: With as diverse a cast as Huck and Jim; Scarlett and Rhett; Lewis' Babbitt and Updike's Rabbit; the Hardy Boys and Holly Golightly; Boo Radley and Bigger Thomas—and oh, how the list goes on! All they have in common is their American-ness. But in a country whose Big Story is really just a gloriously messy scrapbook of smaller, overlapping stories—well, that's actually saying quite a lot.

—Timothy Murphy

Timothy Murphy is a novelist, freelance writer, and editor. His books include the novels *Getting Off Clean* (St. Martin's 1997) and *The Breeders Box* (Little, Brown UK, 1998), as well as the nonfiction work *A Literary Book of Days* (Crown, 1994). He lives in New York City.

Introduction

It's Friday night and you're in the mood for a *real* book. Your soul is crying out for a novel with some meat on its bones. You've read too much *schlock* lately. It's time for a book that will stick to your ribs, a book that everyone else seems to have already read, a book that has weight and significance.

So you head down to the local library or bookstore and scan the American Literature section. What should you choose? To make sure you cover all the bases, you pick out an armload of titles you dimly remember from your high school American English class.

Flash forward two months. The books remain where you plunked them down that night, all unread. (The dust on the stack is pretty impressive, though.)

Time passes. A lot of time. You know it's all over when you find yourself unplugging your phone for the *Planet of the Apes* film marathon. You feel cheap in the morning.

Or maybe the date of your dreams believes his life changed forever when he read *Leaves of Grass.* So, to align yourself more fully with this dreamboat's soul, you decide to suck up the works of Walt Whitman. You *could* spend a week in the library trying to figure out what Walt was saying. Or, you could spend an hour with *The Complete Idiot's Guide to American Literature* and use the rest of your time impressing the love of your life with your knowledge of Whitman and his poetry.

Having washboard abs and a body-fat count lower than the inflation rate will get you only so far in life. You also need to know the basics of American literature to have a well-rounded education. That's why you bought this book.

Reading every American novel in the library isn't the answer. Wading through study guides is about as exciting as watching reruns of *Gilligan's Island* or *Green Acres.* Besides, you want more than a surface skim; you want the inside skinny from an expert.

You know you need to:

➤ Find out which American books, novels, and short stories are considered the most important—and why.

➤ Get the gist of key works in American literature, including the plot, characters, and themes.

➤ Evaluate each author's reputation and find out how the authors stand in relation to each other.

➤ Understand the major literary movements, such as *realism, romanticism,* and *transcendentalism.*

➤ Learn about each author's life and times.

➤ Read excerpts from the original works.

What You'll Learn in This Book

Success-conscious Americans understand the importance of knowing their country's literature. You know that if you want to get ahead in almost any business or profession, you must have a solid grounding in the major writers and novels, the people and books that everyone quotes and discusses. That's what this book can help you achieve.

You'll learn that American literature is not a mysterious entity that only a handful of people understand and know.

Rather, after you finish this book, you'll come away with a handle on the major themes and crucial connections that make great American literature great. You'll learn what all the fuss is about—and you'll appreciate the wonderful writers who form our unique literary heritage.

This book is divided into six sections that teach you all about American literature. You'll soon understand why certain writers and books are ranked at the very top. Most of all, you'll finish this book convinced that American literature is not only useful and important but also enjoyable—even fun. Here's what you'll find in each section:

Part 1, "A New Land, a New Literature (1607–1840)", introduces the writers who laid the foundation of American literature: the Puritans William Bradford, Anne Bradstreet, Edward Taylor, Cotton Mather, and the decidedly un-Puritan adventurer John Smith.

Next comes a look at the literature of the Revolutionary Period, including Abigail Adams' letters, J. Hector St. John de Crèvecoeur's essays, Benjamin Franklin's *Autobiography* and *Poor Richard's Almanac,* Thomas Jefferson's Declaration of Independence, and Thomas Paine's incendiary pamphlets.

Then you'll learn how Washington Irving and James Fenimore Cooper put England's isolated colony (that's us!) on the international literary map. Part 1 concludes with a discussion of Edgar Allan Poe. You'll learn that he invented the modern short story, detective story, and horror tale. By the end of this section, you'll understand how America started forming a national literary and political identity.

Part 2, "The New England Renaissance (1840–1855)," probes one of the most fertile times in American letters. You'll read all about the *transcendentalists,* philosophical idealists who believed that the human mind was the ultimate source of all knowledge and that each person must be true to his or her unique inspiration. You'll delve into the life and accomplishments of Ralph Waldo Emerson, Henry David Thoreau, Nathaniel Hawthorne, and Herman Melville.

Part 3, "The War Between the States (1855–1865)," explores the writing that came from America's most painful and divisive period. You'll see how Harriet Beecher Stowe helped catapult America into the Civil War with her polemic novel, *Uncle Tom's Cabin,* how former slave Frederick Douglass worked for abolitionism, and how Walt Whitman and Emily Dickinson revolutionized American poetry.

Part 4, "Realism and the Frontier (1865-1915)," traces how America transformed from an agricultural backwater into an industrial nation. You'll find out how the best novels of the period, including Stephen Crane's *Maggie: A Girl of the Streets,* Jack London's *Martin Eden,* and Theodore Dreiser's *An American Tragedy,* depict the damage that economic forces and alienation wreak on the weak or vulnerable. And you'll see how the survivors, like Twain's Huck Finn, made it through luck, pluck, and strength. There are also chapters on Henry James, Edith Wharton, and the so-called "local colorists."

Part 5, "Modern Literature (1915-1945)," explains how World War I, the Great Depression, and World War II significantly changed the tone of American literature. Those literary giants Ernest Hemingway, F. Scott Fitzgerald, John Steinbeck, and William Faulkner are included here. You'll also learn about the startling literary innovations that took place during this time, including the stream-of-consciousness technique, which pushed the envelope of written expression. At the same time, the African-American writers of the Harlem Renaissance burst forth with an extraordinary outpouring of creativity. We end on a laugh, with a jolly section on the humorists of the era.

Part 6, "Contemporary Literature (1946-Present)," probes what's happening today in American literature. Together, we'll survey the tremendous diversity of current writing, focusing on the writing of John Cheever, John Updike, Truman Capote, Mary Gordon, Stephen King, and Joyce Carol Oates. But lots of other heavy hitters are touched on, too, including Joan Didion and John Irving.

Lastly, there's a timeline of key literary, social, and political events; a list of important American writers and their main works; and a bibliography, with critical studies and Web sites where you can get even more information about American literature and the writers covered in this book.

More for Your Money!

In addition to all the explanation and teaching, this book contains other types of information to make it even easier for you to learn about American literature. Here's how you can recognize these features:

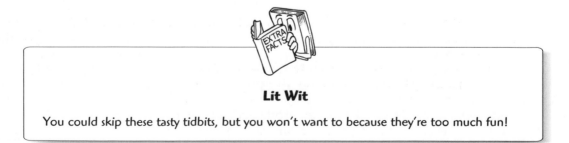

Lit Wit

You could skip these tasty tidbits, but you won't want to because they're too much fun!

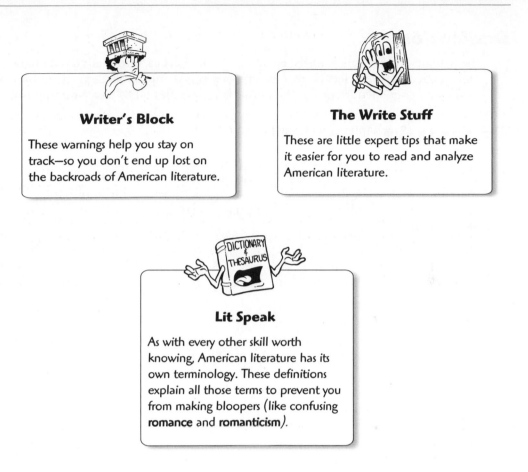

Writer's Block

These warnings help you stay on track—so you don't end up lost on the backroads of American literature.

The Write Stuff

These are little expert tips that make it easier for you to read and analyze American literature.

Lit Speak

As with every other skill worth knowing, American literature has its own terminology. These definitions explain all those terms to prevent you from making bloopers (like confusing **romance** and **romanticism**).

Special Thanks

"The moral is that the flower of art blooms only where the soil is deep, that it takes a great deal of history to produce a little literature, that it needs a complex social machinery to set a writer in motion."

—Henry James

My thanks to all the wonderful people at Alpha Books who have helped my art flower by providing deep soil and a great deal of encouragement. My special thanks especially to Kathy Nebenhaus, Gary Krebs, Richard Fox, and Amy Zavatto. In the Indiana office, Mike Thomas has offered his valuable assistance time and time again. I'm very fortunate to be working with such clever, capable, and caring people.

Dedication:

To Barbara and Dennis Bengels, Elizabeth, Emily, Jessica, and Melinda. Barbara, you are one of the finest teachers I have—in so many ways. The whole Bengels clan are beloved and cherished friends of the Rozakis. We are blessed to have you in our lives.

Trademarks

Part 1
A New Land, a New Literature (1607–1840)

"Our Fathers were Englishmen which came over this great ocean, and were ready to perish in this wilderness."

—William Bradford, Of Plymouth Plantation

Our journey opens with a look at the writers who laid the foundation of American literature: the Puritans William Bradford, Anne Bradstreet, Edward Taylor, Cotton Mather, and the decidedly un-Puritan adventurer John Smith.

Next comes a look at the literature of the Revolutionary Period, including Abigail Adams' letters, J. Hector St. John de Crèvecoeur's essays, Benjamin Franklin's Autobiography *and* Poor Richard's Almanac, *Thomas Jefferson's* Declaration of Independence, *and Thomas Paine's incendiary pamphlets. By the end of this chapter, you'll understand how America began forming a national identity.*

Chapter 4 explores the Big Daddy of American Literature, Washington Irving, and shows you how he put us on the literary map. In Chapter 5, you'll discover how James Fenimore Cooper did the same for the American novel. Part 1 concludes with a discussion of Edgar Allan Poe. You'll learn that he invented the modern short story, detective story, and horror tale.

By the end of the 19th century, America was well on her way to real American literature.

Chapter 1

America the Beautiful— and Talented

In This Chapter

➤ The characteristics of American literature

➤ The creation of American literature

➤ America's writers and writing

➤ American literature and the 21st century

➤ Terms used to describe literature

"Literature must spring from an impression or perception pressing enough to have made the writer write…. It should magnetize the imagination and give pleasure."

—novelist Elizabeth Bowen

We read American literature for a number of reasons. First, great books shape our goals and values by clarifying our own identities, especially our identities as Americans. Further, reading American literature enables us to develop perspectives on events occurring both locally and globally. Last but certainly not least, literature is one of the shaping influences of life.

Literature stimulates our imagination. By increasing our capacity to imagine, great literature makes our lives larger. Great writing becomes the voice that is great within us. Why American literature? Because it is grand and because it is our national voice.

In this chapter, you'll probe the characteristics of American literature, especially what makes it different from the literature of all other nations. You'll learn why American literature is important to *you,* especially as we move into the 21st century. Finally, you'll look at the terms you need to know to understand and discuss literature with intelligence and discernment.

What's So *American* About American Literature?

"Believe me, my friends, that men, not very much inferior to Shakespeare, are this day being born on the banks of the Ohio. And the day will come when you shall say, 'Who reads a book by an Englishman that is modern?'"

—Herman Melville, 1850

In the late 1700s, a French mapmaker named J. Hector St. John de Crèvecoeur came to America to find out what made the wild new country so different from his seasoned, civilized France. Crèvecoeur liked what he saw so much that he settled in for the long haul, becoming an alfalfa farmer in New York.

Lit Wit

Despite his fondness for the American way of life, when the Revolution came, Crèvecoeur's sympathies were with England. Crèvecoeur's unpopular position made life difficult, so he left for France to wait out the war. After the Revolution, Crèvecoeur returned to America, only to discover that his home had been burned to the ground and his wife was dead. He spent the next seven years as French consul, working to increase commerce between America and France. In 1790 he took a leave of absence, sailed for Europe, and never returned.

After years of close observation, Crèvecoeur was able to define the odd new creature called an *American*. You'll find his definition in Chapter 3, "Don't Tread on Me: The Revolutionary Period (1750–1800)." Crèvecoeur would have found it much harder to define *American literature*, however, because it was still in the making in his lifetime. During the 18th century, American literature was a pale imitation of its British model.

Copycats

"No author, without a trial, can conceive of the difficulty of writing a romance about a country where there is no shadow, no antiquity, no mystery, no picturesque and gloomy wrong, nor anything but a commonplace prosperity in broad and simple daylight, as is happily the case with my dear native land."

—Nathaniel Hawthorne, 1850s

For nearly 200 years, American readers had looked to Europe, mainly Great Britain, for most of their reading material (other than Bibles, almanacs, newspapers, and magazines). The Scottish writer Robert Burns and the English writers Sir Walter Scott, Lord

Byron, Percy Bysshe Shelley, and John Keats held sway in the New World. Shakespeare was still a hit, too. As a writer of the time commented, "There is hardly a pioneer's hut that does not contain a few odd volumes of Shakespeare."

By the early 19th century, readers on this side of the ocean hungered for a "national literature." This meant writing that relied on uniquely American themes, avoiding the slavish imitations of European styles that had previously guided the world of American letters. Two New Yorkers—Washington Irving and James Fenimore Cooper—were among the earliest homegrown wordsmiths of note. Each writer adapted the flavor of the times to the circumstances of the newly born frontier nation.

Staking Our Claim

"We have it in our power to begin the world over again. A situation, similar to the present, hath not appeared since the days of Noah until now. The birthday of a new world is at hand."

—Thomas Paine's *Common Sense*

Irving and Cooper lived in New York and so made that state the nation's first literary capital, but in truth exciting new writers flourished all across America. For example, New England would give rise to the transcendental writers, such as Ralph Waldo Emerson, who defined American poetry. His verse, celebrating ordinary experience rather than epic themes, was more concerned with fact than eloquence.

Meanwhile, Emily Dickinson, hiding in her room in Amherst, Massachusetts, was writing poetry on the themes of death, immortality, and the purpose of life. Her rich visual imagery, unique style, and unusual metaphors paved the way for modern American poetry.

Nathaniel Hawthorne created "allegories of the heart," such as his famous novel *The Scarlet Letter*. Working from the heritage of his Puritan ancestors, Hawthorne raised sin and guilt to an art form. This strain of fault, intermixed with the Puritan self-denial and sense of moral superiority, has permeated American literature ever since. No other national literature shows this dual heritage. America has other great novels as well.

In *The Adventures of Huckleberry Finn,* Mark Twain created a mythic tale of death, rebirth, freedom, and human bondage as an emblem for the universal themes of institutionalized injustice and social

The Write Stuff

Check out Chapter 7, "The Sage of Concord: Ralph Waldo Emerson (1803–1882)," to learn all about Emerson's influence on American life and letters.

Lit Speak

Dialect is the way people speak in a certain region or area.

bondage. Besides achieving these lofty aims, however, Twain also captured the diverse dialects of American English. He unerringly re-created the rhythms, vocabulary, and tone of regional speech to set American literature off even further from European, Asian, and African writing.

Singular Sensation

"I too am not a bit tamed, I too am untranslatable,
I sound my barbaric yawp over the roofs of the world."

—Walt Whitman, "Song of Myself"

America's cultural independence did not come easily—but it *did* come, and the world has never been the same. America's literature reveals our cultural and ethnic richness. It captures our unique history and experiences. Our poets, playwrights, novelists, and essayists express our special voice, different from any voice on earth.

Some of our classics, such as Henry David Thoreau's *Walden*, provide a blueprint for American living. *Walden* is a layman's guide for living an honorable, wholesome life. Other seminal works, such as John Steinbeck's *The Grapes of Wrath,* revealed the despair at dark periods in our national history. And still others, such as Upton Sinclair's *The Jungle,* effected great social change. But every classic American work of literature challenges our way of thinking and opens new vistas onto the world.

Lit Wit

The Jungle, a story so shocking that it launched a government investigation into the meat-packing industry, re-creates a startling chapter in American history. Jurgis Rudkis, a young Lithuanian immigrant who arrives in America fired with dreams of wealth, freedom, and opportunity, discovers instead the dark side of the American Dream. With him, readers discover the astonishing truth about Packingtown, the flourishing—and filthy—Chicago stockyards, where new-world visions perish in a jungle of human suffering. Sinclair, master of the muckraking novel, explores in this novel the workingman's lot at the turn of the century.

Write Away

America is a country that seems to have written itself into existence—first by Europeans persuading other Europeans to invest in a trip across the Atlantic, then by these same explorers trying to persuade whomever they brought to stay, and then by still others writing back to Europe inviting more people to join them. And, of course, a little later than that, the story was revised by Africans brought here as slaves. Even more recently, the Native American stories that were already here (before America was "discovered") have become part of our literary consciousness.

If the writing of Thomas Jefferson, Abraham Lincoln, and Martin Luther King amply demonstrates the previously unimagined literary power of the political document, James Fenimore Cooper, Harriet Beecher Stowe, and Ralph Ellison equally demonstrate the overtly political power of American literature. The result is a fascinating mix of national and political ideology that has influenced readers around the world. Literature can offer us even more, however.

Armchair Traveler

"I know what the psychologists say, that a fellow can't comprehend a condition that he has never experienced… Of course, I have never been in a battle, but I believe that I got my sense of the rage of conflict on the football field, or else fighting is a hereditary instinct, and I wrote intuitively."

—Stephen Crane

Literature allows readers to traverse the realms of American culture without moving from their chairs. American books, short stories, and poems provide a rich account of the nation's beauty and bounty.

Living in America, it's difficult to imagine the impact our literature has on other nations. A British writer named Eric Glasgow traced the effect American literature had on his life in a look back to his experiences studying American literature in Cambridge University during World War II. With the British professors away at the front, the universities imported American teachers. Glasgow thus had the chance to study American literature with American teachers—all without ever leaving England. "America's books and novels provide rich accounts of America's bounty and its people's renowned way of life," he notes in the article "My American Dreams."

American literature is clearly important in terms of understanding the past, but it's equally important to the future. Read on to find out why we need American literature more than ever as we approach the millennium.

Future Shock

Our world is changing in exciting—and frightening—ways. The 21st century promises to bring radical changes in the way we work, live, and even think. Check out these numbers:

➤ *One* daily edition of the *New York Times* contains more information than an educated 16th-century person assimilated in his entire lifetime.

➤ More information has been produced in *the last 50 years* than in the *previous 5,000*.

➤ The amount of information available doubles every *five* years. By the year 2000, the amount of information available will double in *less than two years.*

It might seem that everyone will be so busy coping with the information deluge that no one will have time for novels, short stories, or poems. Not so, as a recent announcement of the 100 best English-language novels of the 20th century reveals.

When Random House released its list, people were in an uproar. And not just teachers, scholars, and professors. The list was the talk of the town, from bars to late-night talk shows. There was considerable skepticism, if not outright hostility, about the choices the Random House editors made. Some people noted the absence of African American or Canadian authors, the scarcity of women, and the predominance of older writers over young ones. Others questioned the methods used to select the "winners."

The outcry was so great that a number of important newspapers invited readers to submit their own choices for the best novels of the 20th century. An avalanche of Great American Novel nominations poured in, including *Gone with the Wind, Look Homeward Angel, To Kill a Mockingbird, A Tree Grows in Brooklyn, East of Eden, The Source, The Stand, One Flew Over the Cuckoo's Nest, Gravity's Rainbow, The Maltese Falcon,* and *On the Road.*

This incident just goes to show that great American literature will be as important in the 21st century as it is today, if not more so, because it provides the moral touchstone we need to stay grounded in an age of dizzying change.

Writer's Block

The 21st century begins January 1, 2001, not January 1, 2000. But don't cancel the party on my account.

The Write Stuff

Traditionally, poems had a specific rhythm and rhyme, but modern poetry such as *free verse* does not have a regular beat, rhyme, or line length. It's still considered poetry, though.

Words to the Wise

Computer mavens chat about *bits* and *bytes;* printers have *highlap folios* and *prepress blues.* In the same way, literature has its own jargon—the words and phrases we use to talk about what we're reading. The term *literature,* for example, refers to the whole enchilada, because it's the umbrella term we use to refer to a type of art expressed in writing. Literature includes poetry, fiction, nonfiction, and drama.

When we narrow it down a notch, we get *genre*—a term that refers to a major literary category. The three primary genres are *prose, poetry,* and *drama:*

➤ *Prose* is all written work that is not poetry, drama, or song. Articles, autobiographies, biographies, novels, essays, and editorials are prose.

➤ *Poetry* is a type of literature in which words are selected and strung together for their beauty, sound, and power to express feelings.

➤ *Drama* is a piece of literature intended to be performed in front of an audience. The actors tell the story through their words and actions.

Like people, prose comes in different shapes and sizes. Here are some nifty types of prose you'll soon be seeing.

Types of Prose

➤ *Autobiography:* A person's story of his or her own life.

➤ *Biography:* A story about a person's life, written by another person.

➤ *Essay:* A brief writing on a particular subject or idea.

➤ *Fable:* A short, easy-to-read story that teaches a lesson about people. Fables often feature animals that talk and act like people. (We use the word *personification* when referring to this technique.)

➤ *Fiction:* Writing, such as novels and short stories, that tells about imaginary events and characters. Fiction that seems very similar to real life is called *realistic fiction.*

➤ *Folktale:* A story that has been handed down from generation to generation, such as a fable, fairy tale, legend, tall tale, or myth.

➤ *Legend:* A story that explains how or why something in nature originated. Legends are sometimes based on historical facts, but they often contain exaggerated details and characters.

➤ *Humor:* Parts of a story that are amusing. Humor can be created through sarcasm, word play, irony, and exaggeration.

➤ *Memoir:* A first-person writing about an event.

➤ *Myth:* A story from ancient days that explains certain aspects of life and nature.

➤ *Novel:* A long work of fiction with one main plot and several subplots.

➤ *Short story:* Narrative prose fiction, shorter than a novel, which focuses on a single character and a single event. Most short stories can be read in one sitting and convey a single overall impression.

➤ *Tall tale:* A folktale that exaggerates the main events or the characters' abilities. Tall tales came from the oral tradition, as pioneers sitting around the campfires at night tried to top each other's outrageous stories.

Let's not forget about poetry! What follows are the most common types of poetry. Knowing these categories can help you recognize the different poems you'll read and analyze later in this book.

Types of Poetry

➤ *Ballad:* A story told in song form. Since ballads were passed down by word of mouth from person to person, the words are simple and have a strong beat. Ballads often tell stories about adventure and love.

➤ *Lyric poem:* Brief, musical poems that convey a speaker's feelings. Way back when, people sang lyrics as they played string-like instruments called *lyres.*

➤ *Narrative poem:* A story in poetic form. As with a narrative story, a narrative poem has a plot, characters, and theme.

➤ *Sonnet:* A 14-line poem with a set rhythm and rhyme scheme.

Since this book focuses on prose and poetry, why not review some of the key terms you'll encounter as we work our way through our national literature? We'll start with terms used to describe prose.

Terms Used to Analyze Prose

➤ *Antagonist:* The force or person in conflict with the main character (the *protagonist)* in a work of literature. An antagonist can be another character, a force of nature, society, or something within the protagonist.

➤ *Conflict:* A struggle or fight. Conflict makes a story interesting because readers want to find out the outcome.

➤ *Plot:* The arrangement of events in a work of literature. The *exposition* introduces the characters, setting, and conflict. The *rising action* builds the conflict and develops the characters. The *climax* shows the highest point of the action, and the *denouement* resolves the story and ties up all the loose ends.

➤ *Point of view:* The position from which a story is told. In the *first-person point of view,* the narrator is one of the characters in the story. In the *third-person omniscient point of view,* the narrator looks through the eyes of all the characters and is all-knowing. In the *third-person limited point of view,* the narrator tells the story through the eyes of only one character.

➤ *Protagonist*: The main character in a work of literature, usually the hero.

➤ *Flashback:* A scene that breaks into the story to show an earlier part of the action, fill in missing information, explain the characters' actions, and advance the plot.

Lit Speak

There are two kinds of conflict. In an **external conflict**, characters struggle against a force outside themselves. In an **internal conflict**, characters battle a force within themselves, such as guilt. Stories often contain both external and internal conflicts.

➤ *Foreshadowing:* Clues that hint at what will happen later on in the story. Foreshadowing creates suspense and links related details.

Here are a handful of the most common terms used to describe poetry. Learning these terms can help you understand and appreciate what you read.

Terms Used to Analyze Poetry

➤ *Blank verse:* Unrhymed poetry. Blank verse is popular with poets, because it captures the natural rhythm of speech.

➤ *Foot:* A group of stressed and unstressed syllables in a line of poetry.

➤ *Free verse:* Poetry that does not have a regular beat, rhyme, or line length. Walt Whitman wrote free verse.

➤ *Meter:* The beat or rhythm of a poem, created by a pattern of stressed and unstressed syllables.

➤ *Refrain:* A line or a group of lines repeated at the end of a poem or song. Refrains reinforce the main point and create musical effects.

➤ *Rhyme:* The repeated use of identical or nearly identical sounds. Poets use rhyme to create a musical sound, meaning, and structure.

➤ *Rhyme scheme:* A regular pattern of words that end with the same sound.

➤ *Rhythm:* A pattern of stressed and unstressed syllables that create a beat, as in music.

➤ *Scan:* The process of reading a poem to figure out its *meter* (pattern of stressed and unstressed syllables).

➤ *Stanza:* A group of lines in a poem. Lines of poems are grouped into stanzas, just as sentences of prose are grouped into paragraphs.

➤ *Verse:* A stanza.

Lit Speak

The most common meter in English poetry is called **iambic pentameter**. It's a pattern of five **feet** (groups of syllables), each having one unstressed syllable and one stressed syllable.

Lit Speak

End rhyme occurs when words at the end of lines of poetry have the same sound. **Internal rhyme** occurs when words within a sentence share the same sound, such as "Each narrow cell in which we dwell." *Cell* and *dwell* have internal rhyme because they share the same sound, and one of the words that rhymes is set in the middle of the line.

The Write Stuff

When you read a poem, use the punctuation and capitalization in each line to help you decide where to pause and what words to stress to make the rhythm clear.

Share and Share Alike

Here's a list of terms used to describe both poetry and prose. These terms are so handy that both genres use them!

➤ *Allusion:* A reference to a well-known place, event, person, work of art, or other work of literature. Allusions enrich a story or poem by suggesting powerful and exciting comparisons.

Lit Speak

In **verbal irony**, there is a contrast between what is stated and what is suggested. In **dramatic irony**, there is a contrast between what a character believes and what the audience knows is true. In **irony of situation**, an event reverses the readers' or characters' expectations.

Writer's Block

Don't confuse the speaker with the author. They are not the same.

➤ *Image:* A word that appeals to one or more of our five senses: sight, sound, taste, touch, or smell.

➤ *Irony:* When the opposite of what is expected occurs.

➤ *Mood* (or *atmosphere):* The strong feeling created within a literary work.

➤ *Speaker:* The personality the writer assumes when telling a story.

➤ *Style:* An author's distinctive way of writing. Style includes word choice, sentence length and structure, figures of speech, and tone.

➤ *Suspense:* The feeling of tension or anticipation created in a work.

➤ *Symbol:* A person, place, or object that represents an abstract idea. A dove may symbolize peace, for example, or a rose may symbolize love.

➤ *Theme:* The work's main idea—a general statement about life. The theme can be stated outright in the work, or readers can infer it from details.

➤ *Tone:* The writer's attitude toward his or her subject matter (cheerful, bitter, enthusiastic, frightened).

The Least You Need to Know

➤ American literature shapes our goals and values by clarifying our own identity, stimulating our imagination, and making our lives larger.

➤ American literature is relevant to the future as well as the past.

➤ Learning the terms used to describe and analyze literature can help you understand and appreciate it more.

Chapter 2

In the Beginning: America's First Writers (1607–1750)

In This Chapter

➤ The Puritans and their beliefs

➤ William Bradford, *The Mayflower,* and Massachusetts Bay

➤ Anne Bradstreet, America's first published poet

➤ Edward Taylor, America's best Puritan poet

➤ Cotton Mather, minister and witchcraft authority

➤ The Salem witchcraft trials

➤ John Smith, ad man extraordinaire

Sherlock Holmes and Watson were camping in the forest. They had gone to bed and were lying beneath the night sky. Holmes said, "Watson, look up. What do you see?"

"I see thousands of stars," Watson replied.

"And what does that mean to you?" Holmes asked.

"I suppose it means that of all the planets in the universe, we are truly fortunate to be here on Earth. We should struggle every day to be worthy of our blessings. What does it mean to you, Holmes?"

"To me, it means someone has stolen our tent," Holmes replied.

Reality was just as crystal clear to the Puritans. As you'll discover in this chapter, the famous Puritan writers—William Bradford, Anne Bradstreet, Cotton Mather, and

Edward Taylor—also saw God's hand in every single aspect of life. And then we have feisty John Smith, but he's a whole different ball of wax. Let's see what our literature was like when we were the new kids on the block.

Saints and Strangers

The date: Late 16th century to early 17th century

The place: England

The times were religious—and angry. King Henry VIII had split with the Catholic Church over the sticky issue of divorcing his wife and marrying a handful of other women (one at a time, of course). The kingly creator of serial monogamy promptly established his own church, the Church of England (also called the Anglican Church), with himself and all future kings as its leader. By the early 1600s, most Englishmen and women belonged to the Church of England. Except for the issues of control and leadership, the Catholic Church and the Church of England were pretty much alike—although they hated and persecuted each other.

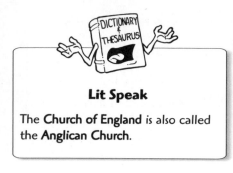

Lit Speak

The **Church of England** is also called the **Anglican Church.**

A small group of Anglicans felt that Henry just hadn't gone far enough when he outlawed the Catholic Church. Since they wanted to "purify" the Anglican Church of all traces of Roman Catholicism, they were generally referred to as "Puritans." They called themselves "Saints." Some people called them "Separatists." Others just called them troublemakers.

Lit Wit

Puritans (also called Saints or Separatists) wanted to rid the Anglican Church of all its Roman Catholic trimmings—stained glass, incense, fancy priestly robes, and so on.

King James I was very clear on this point: Attend the Church of England or take up residence in the local jail. To escape life in the Big House, some of the Separatists headed to Holland. After reading John Smith's action-packed *A Description of New England* (more on this later), the Separatist Pilgrims boarded the Mayflower for New England in 1620. (They were actually headed for Virginia, but they hit some killer headwinds.) Of the 102 people on board the Mayflower, about half were called Saints and the other half were called Strangers. The Strangers were mainly out for adventure, while the Saints were out to escape hanging.

Fire and Ice: The Puritans

"In Adam's Fall, we sinned all."

—Bay Psalm Book

Once they landed in America and got settled, the Pilgrims developed their New World vision: They were soldiers in the war against Satan—the Arch-Enemy—who planned to ruin the kingdom of God on earth (the Plymouth colony) by sowing discord among those who professed to be Christians.

Since virtually all early American literature was steeped in Puritanism, you'll need a primer on their beliefs. And here it is:

Puritanism: Sin and Guilt 101

1. **Total depravity:** Through Adam's fall, every human is born sinful. This is the concept of "original sin."

2. **The doctrine of election:** God would freely choose those He would save and those He would damn eternally. No one knows if they are damned or saved.

3. **Predestination:** Only a few are selected for salvation.

4. **Limited atonement:** Jesus died for the chosen only, not for everyone.

5. **Irresistible grace:** God's grace is freely given. It cannot be earned or denied.

6. **Perseverance of the "Saints":** Those elected by God have full power to interpret the will of God. This meant they freely told others how to live their lives. (The Saints were the elect—they did not have to be ministers.)

Now you know where all that baggage you carry around comes from! Puritanism is still in the air, an indelible part of American culture. The ingrained American sense of responsibility, moral superiority, and nagging guilt all come from our Puritan heritage. So clean your room, finish everything on your plate, and call your mother already.

Lit Speak

To a Puritan, **grace** is defined as the saving and transfiguring power of God.

The Devil Made Me Do It

"O sinner! Consider the fearful danger you are in: it is a great furnace of wrath, a wide and bottomless pit, full of the fire of wrath, that you are held over in the hand of that God, whose wrath is provoked and incensed as much against you, as against many of the damned in Hell. You hang by a slender thread, with the flames of divine wrath flashing about it, and ready every moment to singe it, and burn it asunder and you have nothing…to induce God to spare you one moment."

—Jonathan Edwards, 1703—58, *from his sermon*
"Sinners in the Hands of an Angry God"

In the black-and-white world of the Puritan, writing had a clear purpose: To glorify God. This means that you're now going to learn about:

➤ Sermons

➤ Religious poems

➤ Religious tracts

➤ Interpretation of God's doings on Earth

➤ Diaries and journals about religious experiences

William Bradford (1590–1657)

William Bradford was the first leader of Plymouth Colony. And, apparently, a darn good governor as he was reelected to the position 30 times. Bradford epitomizes the determination and self-sacrifice that come to mind when we imagine the stern and stiffly starched black-clad Pilgrims gathered around that first Thanksgiving table, with the stalwart and friendly Native Americans hovering dimly in the background.

The Mayflower Compact

Bradford is also famous for being one of the authors and signers of the "Mayflower Compact" (1620), which was the Pilgrims' constitution. The document shaped the politics, religion, and social behavior of the first settlers. It eventually influenced the shape, style, and content of the U.S. Constitution as well. It's short, so I'll lay the whole thing on you:

Mayflower Compact

"In the name of God, Amen. We, whose names are underwritten, the Loyal Subjects of our dread Sovereign Lord King James, by the Grace of God, of Great Britain, France, and Ireland, King, Defender of the Faith, & etc. Having undertaken for the Glory of God, and the advancement of the Christian Faith, and the Honour of our King and Country, a Voyage to plant the first Colony in the northern parts of Virginia; do by these Presents, solemnly and mutually in the Presence of God and one another, covenant and combine ourselves together in a civil body politick, for our better ordering and preservation, and of the ends aforesaid: and by virtue hereof do enact, constitute, and frame such just and equal laws, ordinances, acts, constitutions, and offices, from time to time, as shall be thought most meet and convenient of the general good of the Colony; unto which we promise all due submission and obedience. In witness whereof we have hereunto subscribed our names at Cape Cod, the eleventh of November, in the reign of our Sovereign Lord King James of England, France, and Ireland, the eighteenth, and of Scotland, the fifty-fourth. Anno Domini 1620."

History of Plymouth Plantation

Bradford's greatest contribution to early writing is his *History of Plymouth Plantation, 1620–1647.* Not published until 1856, Bradford's journals recount his voyage to the New World, the founding of Plymouth Plantation, and the Pilgrims' experiences during the early years of the colony's existence. The *History of Plymouth Plantation* contains the famous story of the first Thanksgiving.

The following anecdote from the *History of Plymouth Plantation* illustrates Bradford's deep, unswerving Puritan beliefs. In it, he recounts the fate of a blasphemous sailor during the *Mayflower's* voyage to America:

"And I may not omit here a special work of God's providence. There was a proud and very profane young man, one of the seamen, of a lusty [strong], able body, which made him the more haughty; he would always be contemning [condemning] the poor people in their sickness and cursing them daily with grievous execrations; and did not let [hesitate] to tell them that he hoped to help to cast half of them overboard before they came to their journey's end, and to make merry with what they had; and if he were by any gently reproved, he would curse and swear most bitterly. But it pleased God before they came half seas over, to smite this young man with a grievous disease, of which he died in a desperate manner, and so was himself the first that was thrown overboard. Thus his curses light on his own head, and it was an astonishment to all his fellows for they noted it to be the just hand of God upon him."

Lit Wit

John Winthrop, a founder of another colony, the Massachusetts Bay Colony, arrived in 1630 aboard the flagship *Arbella.* As governor of the Colony, he established the center of government at Boston. Winthrop began writing his *Journal* in 1630 and continued it until his death. On board the *Arbella,* he prepared his famous sermon, "A Model of Christian Charity."

Anne Bradstreet (1612–1672)

Anne Bradstreet is assured literary immortality as America's first published poet. Bradstreet's *The Tenth Muse Lately Sprung Up in America* was published in London in 1650. Bradstreet didn't know the book was being published: Her brother-in-law took it to England to be set in type as a surprise. Don't you wish you had in-laws like that?

Despite criticism from a number of men who claimed that a woman's hand "fits a needle better" than a pen, history has judged Bradstreet to be a good (if not great) poet whose struggles with the difficulties of life on the frontier and with the Puritan faith put a personal face on a fascinating period in American literary history. Like the other Puritans, Bradstreet believed she should lead a life guided by the principles of grace, plainness, and divine mission.

In England, Bradstreet and her family had enjoyed the advantages of wealth. Bradstreet was fond of learning, and when she was about seven years old, several tutors were hired to teach her dancing, music, and languages, among other subjects. When she was 16, Anne married Simon Bradstreet, the son of a Puritan minister.

At age 18, Bradstreet's family was among the hundreds of English Puritans who sailed for America. Anne's household was influential in the new land: Both Anne's father, Thomas Dudley, and her husband, Simon, were active in the governmental affairs of Massachusetts Bay Colony; both served several terms as governor of the colony.

Writer's Block

So what about the Native Americans? Don't they rate as our first writers? Unfortunately, since the Native Americans didn't have a written language, their songs and stories changed with each speaker, so we don't have any fixed versions of their works. However, myths and stories do survive (see Chapter 31, "Native-American, Latino-American, and Asian-American Literature" for more coverage of Native American literature).

Love Me Tender, Love Me True

All of Bradstreet's poetry is infused with Puritanism; nonetheless, much of it shows her very real passion for her husband. A well-known example of her poetry follows. Notice how her love shines through the Puritan overlay:

> *"To My Dear and Loving Husband"*
> *If ever two were one, then surely we.*
> *If ever man were lov'd by wife, then thee;*
> *If ever wife was happy in a man,*
> *Compare with me ye women if ye can.*
> *I prize thy love more than whole Mines of gold,*
> *Or all the riches that the East doth hold.*
> *My love is such that rivers cannot quench,*
> *Nor ought but love from thee, give recompense.*
> *Thy love is such I can no way repay,*
> *The heavens reward thee manifold, I pray.*
> *Then while we live, in love let's so persevere,*
> *That when we live no more, we may live ever.*

In addition to the love for her husband, the poem conveys the Puritan idea that heaven is a paradise and that the Elect are rewarded in the afterlife.

Home Sweet Home

Some of Bradstreet's poems were written as prayers in the midst of the events of her active family life, but many came out of the pain of being a settler in a wild new land. Such is the case with "Verses Upon the Burning of Our House, July 10, 1666," written when her house burned to the ground. The ending shows her firm faith in God:

"Verses Upon the Burning of Our House, July 10, 1666"

Thou hast an house on high erect,
Fram'd by that mighty Architect,
With glory richly furnished,
Stands permanent though this be fled.
It's purchased, and paid for too
By him who hath enough to do.
A Price so vast as is unknown,
Yet, by his Gift, is made thine own.
There's wealth enough, I need no more;
Farewell my Self, farewell my Store.
The world no longer let me Love,
My hope and Treasure lies Above.

The message: The paltry treasures of this world don't amount to a hill of beans when compared to God's treasures in heaven. Now, there's a *house.*

Lit Wit

Minister Michael Wigglesworth's poem *The Day of Doom* (1662) is the first American best-seller. It contains an expression of the basic Puritan beliefs and describes the end of the world.

Edward Taylor (1645–1729)

The minister Edward Taylor is considered to be the finest Puritan writer, hands down. But since Taylor considered his poetry a form of personal religious worship, he allowed only two stanzas from one of his poems to be published during his lifetime. As a result, few people knew about his work until it was published in 1939, more than two centuries after his death.

Lit Speak

A **conceit** is an extended metaphor that compares two startlingly different subjects.

Taylor's poetry captures the attitudes of the second-generation Puritans in its emphasis on self-examination, particularly in an individual's relations to God. His poetry is marked by *conceits,* which are elaborate and unusual comparisons between two startlingly different subjects. Taylor's poetry is important today chiefly for its influence on T.S. Eliot, Ezra Pound, and the other modern "metaphysical" poets who picked up on his conceits. See Chapter 23, "Three Big Deals: Ezra Pound (1885–1972) T.S. Eliot (1888–1965), and John Steinbeck (1902–68).

Here's the first stanza from Taylor's well-known poem "Huswifery," which expresses the poet's wish to serve and praise God. The conceit of a spinning wheel shows the speaker's desire to be part of God's plan—a device through which the "material" of God is transmitted.

"Huswifery"

"Make me, O lord, Thy spinning wheel complete.
Thy holy word my distaff [staff] make for me.
Make mine affections [emotions] Thy swift flyers neat
And make my soul Thy holy spoole to be.
My conversation make to be Thy reel
And reel the yarn thereon spun of Thy wheel."

Cotton Mather (1663–1728)

A member of the powerful Mather family, Cotton Mather produced more than 450 volumes of written work. Yes, you read that right, the man wrote 450-plus books. Mather was clearly a type-A personality: He entered Harvard at age 12 and received his bachelor's degree when he was 15. He got his master's degree just three years later.

Although Mather's writing is didactic, moralistic, and filled with references to the Bible, it reveals important information on the history and society of his time, especially the attitude toward witches. Mather's best-known work is the *Magnalia Christi Americana* (1702), which gives an insight into his views on Puritan society.

A Puritan minister, Mather is most famous for being the scribe at the Salem witchcraft trials. Cotton and his father Increase helped stir up the Salem witchcraft trials with their inflammatory writings.

Witchy Women

"And we have now with Horror seen the Discovery of such a Witchcraft! An Army of Devils is horribly broke in upon—our English Settlements: and the Houses of the Good People there are fill'd with the doleful Shrieks of the Children and Servants."

—Cotton Mather

During Puritan times (and before), the whole world believed in witches—there was nothing new about that. In 1515 alone, more than 500 "witches" were burned at the stake in Europe. In the colonies, men and women were routinely hanged or drowned for being witches, but what happened in Salem, Massachusetts, in 1692 was different from the usual enchanted entertainment.

It all began when a handful of little girls and their West Indian servant Tituba conjured some spirits to while away the long winter evenings. The Reverend Samuel Parris, the father of one of the girls, became alarmed—especially when the girls began barking like dogs, crying out spirits, (claiming to see spirits) and having fits during the Sunday church services.

Lit Wit

The Puritans' attempts to eradicate the evil of a community by identifying and eliminating certain individuals for collusion with the Devil has fascinated the American imagination ever since. Indeed, the term "witch hunt" is commonly heard today applied not only to religion but also to politics—any search for a scapegoat who can be blamed for society's problems. In the early 1950s, Senator Joseph McCarthy conducted such a witch hunt for communists—whom he called "pinkos." In the process, he shattered the lives of many innocent and talented people. In 1953, American playwright Arthur Miller set his tragedy *The Crucible* in colonial Salem during the witchcraft hysteria, but his audience knew the play was really about the McCarthy witch hunts of the 1950s. The continued success of *The Crucible* indicates how relevant the Puritan era is today.

Before you could twitch your nose and say, "Oh, Darren," Salem went mad with witch fever. The girls may have been pretending at the start of the hysteria, but by its tragic culmination, they seemed as convinced as everyone else that the witches were real. More than 100 people were tried as witches; 19 people and two dogs were put to death.

Spin Doctors

In part because of the Salem witchcraft trials and probably because of all that heavy black clothing, the Puritans have gotten a bum rap today. We tend to think of them as narrow-minded, bigoted, judgmental, self-righteous, and hypocritical. That's not the whole picture.

The Puritans tried to do right in what they saw as an evil world. They left Europe because they didn't want their children seduced by an evil society—but society followed them to the New World. The problem for people who were utterly convinced that they knew the ultimate truth was how to deal with reality when the "truth" seemed untrue. The witchcraft issue was a real problem. How could good women, upright women, moral wives and mothers, be secret witches? Ditto on the persecution and expulsion of scores of dissenters. Why didn't they see the light?

Let's not be quite so harsh on the Puritans. After all, our society has inherited quite a bit of their bigotry, harshness, and sanctimoniousness. We also have their determination, strength of purpose, and strong will. It's our legacy, folks.

John Smith (1580–1631)

An enemy called John Smith "An Ambityous unworthy and vayneglorious fellowe," and he wasn't alone in his opinion.

Halfway through the voyage to Jamestown, the captain clapped Smith into custody and accused him of concealing an intended mutiny. At the next stop, the captain offered to hang Smith, and actually got as far as hammering together the gallows. Before his fellow settlers threw him out of Virginia 32 months later, they would again propose to stretch Smith's neck, banish him, and even murder him.

In his 51 years, Smith was a compiler and writer of exuberant travelers' tales, an explorer, a mapmaker, a geographer, a soldier, a governor, a trader, a sailor, an admiral, and the editor of a seaman's handbook. He was also famously commanding and crotchety.

I Get Around

Enormously energetic, Smith's adventures and travels touched Europe, Africa, and America, and matched the boldest exploits of fearless knights. Smith's admirers credited him with almost single-handedly preserving the first English Virginians from the ravages of their own sloth as well as from the hostility of their native neighbors. Except for his pen, chapters of America's earliest history would be lost, since much of what we know about Jamestown comes from him. As an assembler of other men's accounts and a writer of his own, Smith is responsible for five swashbuckling descriptions of the colony and its struggles. He produced seven other volumes and helped bring to the press a still-stunning map of Virginia.

Lit Wit

Smith's two most famous works are *A Description of New England* (1616) and *The General History of Virginia, New England, and the Summer Isles* (1624). If you read nothing else of his, try to check out these two books. They're worth the time!

Too Close for Comfort

Smith's trip down the Chickahominy River gave rise to the famous Pocahontas legend. Smith made his way first in a barge and then in a canoe, scattering his company in his wake. Indian women ambushed two indiscreet soldiers, while braves killed a third who guarded the canoe. Marched to Powhatan, the "emperor" of the Tidewater tribes, Smith was promised his freedom in four days. As he told it in his *Generall Historie*, however, the next day he was summoned to Powhatan's house. Smith's account:

"At his entrance before the King, all the people gave a great shout… [A] long consultation was held, but the conclusion was, two great stones were brought before Powhatan: then as many as could laid hands on him, dragged him to them, and thereon laid his head, and being ready with their clubs, to beat out his brains, Pocahontas the King's dearest daughter, when no entreaty would prevail, got his head in her arms, and laid her own upon his to save him from death."

Powhatan decided he would instead regard Smith as a son, make him a tributary *werowance*—as headmen were called—and bestow on him a territory just downriver. Remember, however, that Smith wrote this account of his adventures. No fool, Smith enlarged the story, making it more dramatic and spicing up his role in events. Smith added the little extra sparkle that created an irresistible story. People back in England read Smith's account, passed it around to their friends, and a myth was born.

It was an oddly assorted group that established the foundations of American literature: the Puritans with their preoccupation with sin and salvation and the Southern Planters with their tales of wild adventure. Indeed, much of the literature that the colonists read was not produced in the colonies at all—it came from Europe. Yet by 1750 there were clear beginnings of an American literature, an authentic voice that would one day be honored throughout the English-speaking world.

The Least You Need to Know

➤ The *Puritans* were a group who separated from the Anglican Church.

➤ The *Pilgrims* were the Puritans who traveled via the *Mayflower* to Plymouth, Massachusetts, in 1620.

➤ The Puritans believed in original sin, the doctrine of election, predestination, limited atonement, irresistible grace, and perseverance of the "saints."

➤ William Bradford, the first leader of the Plymouth Colony, was the Alpha Puritan. He's famous as one of the authors and signers of the "Mayflower Compact" (1620), the Pilgrims' constitution, and his *History of Plymouth Plantation,* 1620–1647.

➤ Anne Bradstreet was the first published American poet.

➤ The minister Edward Taylor is known as the finest Puritan poet.

➤ Cotton Mather is a famous Puritan minister and supporter of the Salem witchcraft trials.

➤ Our first huckster, John Smith, was short in stature but larger than life. His writing helped lay the foundation for American literature.

Chapter 3

Don't Tread on Me: The Revolutionary Period (1750–1800)

In This Chapter

➤ John and Abigail Adams

➤ Abigail Adams' letters

➤ J. Hector St. Jean de Crèvecoeur's *Letters from an American Farmer*

➤ Ben Franklin's *Autobiography* and *Poor Richard's Almanac*

➤ Thomas Jefferson and the *Declaration of Independence*

➤ Thomas Paine's *The American Crisis*

Like their Puritan counterparts, educated men (and even a few women) who lived in 18th century America did a great deal of writing. Unlike the private soul-searching of the Puritans, however, much of the writing produced from 1750–1800 was intended for a public audience. Almost all the writing produced in America during this time was influenced by the revolutionary spirit, the flavor of the new nation.

In this chapter, you'll read about the lives and careers of the influential American writers of the colonial period: John and Abigail Adams, J. Hector St. Jean de Crèvecoeur, Benjamin Franklin, Thomas Jefferson, and Thomas Paine. I've included key excerpts from their work, too, so you'll better understand how their words shaped the American consciousness.

The Dream Team

John Adams (1735–1826) definitely had the power career in the family—he was not only the first vice president of the United States and its second president, but he was also a member of the First and Second Continental Congresses, helped draft the Declaration of Independence, and served with Benjamin Franklin as a diplomatic representative in Europe. However, it was his wife, Abigail Adams, who made a greater mark on early American letters.

Lit Wit

By the end of the Revolutionary War, America was already a literate nation. Nearly 50 newspapers and 40 magazines had been established in America's coastal cities. Almanacs were big-time sellers all over the country.

Remember the Ladies

Born in 1744 in Massachusetts, Abigail Adams had no formal schooling. But her curiosity spurred her keen intelligence, and she avidly read all the books she could—the Bible, history, sermons, philosophy, essays, and poetry. Adams would become one of the most well-read women in America and among the most influential women of her day.

By the time Abigail was 17 years old, she and 26-year-old John were exchanging love letters. They married two years later. Making history keeps you on the road a great deal, so Abby had some time on her hands while John was off establishing a new nation. She used it well. Aside from the usual female duties—raising a future president (John Quincy Adams) and all that—she campaigned for women's rights in a series of brilliant letters. On March 31, 1776, she urged Congress:

"Remember the Ladies, and be more generous and favorable to them than your ancestors. Do not put such unlimited power into the hands of Husbands. Remember all Men would be tyrants if they could. If particular care and attention is not paid to the Ladies, we are determined to foment a Rebellion, and will not hold ourselves bound by any Laws in which we have no voice, or Representation."

Her rational, measured tone belied a strong and unique message for its day.

Special Delivery

Abigail knew that she was ranging far outside the conventional role for women in her day. Writing to her mother on February 3, 1815, Abigail explained:

"I think sometimes, my dear Mother, that you must smile at my warmth in politics, but when the interests of our Country are at stake, I feel too warmly concerned to stand as silent spectator of the scene, and I generally write what is uppermost in my thoughts."

Many of Abigail Adams's letters still exist, informing and delighting readers today while providing rich clues to the past. Reading them, we learn about customs, habits, and day-to-day family life of colonial times. Her words help us better understand the history of our nation.

Lit Wit

There's no Easter Bunny, Twinkies really *do* have calories, and George Washington never chopped down a cherry tree. Nor did he ever utter the famous sentence, "Father, I cannot tell a lie." The tale was invented by a Maryland book salesman. Although the fruit-tree story is mythical, Washington's reputation for integrity was real. Shy and modest, he confessed that taking office gave him "feelings not unlike those of a culprit... going to the place of his execution." And while we're on the subject, Washington's famous false wooden teeth were actually made of cow's teeth, ivory, and metal. He's also the only American president who never lived in the White House. Why? Because it wasn't built until 1800, a year after his death.

J. Hector St. Jean de Crèvecoeur (1735–1813)

A Frenchman who spent more than half his life in the New World, Crèvecoeur contributed two important concepts to the American consciousness:

➤ The *American Adam*—the idea that there is something different, unique, special, or new about these people called "Americans."

➤ The *melting pot*—that America's unique identity transcends ethnic, cultural, or religious backgrounds.

Both ideas have had a strong impact on American culture. Here's how Crèvecoeur himself phrased it in *Letters from an American Farmer:*

From Letter III: What is an American?

"…What then is the American, this new man? He is either an European, or the descendant of an European, hence that strange mixture of blood, which you will find in no other country. I could point out to you a family whose grandfather was an Englishman, whose wife was Dutch, whose son married a French woman, and whose present four sons have now four wives of different nations. He is an American, who leaving behind him all his ancient prejudices and manners, receives new ones from the new mode of life he has embraced, the new government he obeys, and the new rank he holds. He becomes an American by being received in the broad lap of our great Alma Mater. Here individuals of all nations are melted into a new race of men, whose labors and posterity will one day cause great changes in the world. Americans are the western pilgrims, who are carrying along with them that great mass of arts, sciences, vigor, and industry which began long since in the east; they will finish the great circle. The Americans were once scattered all over Europe; here they are incorporated into one of the finest systems of population which has ever appeared, and which will hereafter become distinct by the power of the different climates they inhabit. The American ought therefore to love this country much better than that wherein either he or his forefathers were born. Here the rewards of his industry follow with equal steps the progress of his labor; his labor is founded on the basis of nature, self-interest; can it want a stronger allurement?"

For many years, Crèvecoeur was the most widely read commentator on American life. His reputation was further increased in the 1920s when a bundle of his unpublished English essays was discovered in an attic in France. These were brought out as *Sketches of Eighteenth Century America, or More Letters from an American Farmer* (1925). And then we have Ben Franklin, who didn't so much comment on the American character as help create it!

Benjamin Franklin (1706–1790)

Which of the following inventions are credited to Ben Franklin?

➤ Bifocals
➤ The Franklin stove
➤ The first flexible urinary catheter
➤ The *armonica* (a musical instrument)
➤ Watertight bulkheads for ships
➤ The lightning rod
➤ Swimming fins
➤ The one-armed desk chair
➤ The first fire insurance company
➤ The first odometer

Writer's Block

In 1752, Franklin flew a kite in a thunderstorm and showed that a metal key tied to thread would charge a Leyden jar. This resulted in his invention of the lightning rod. The next two people who attempted the experiment were killed in the effort. Don't try this at home.

➤ The long arm (a tool to reach high books)
➤ Daylight Saving Time

Yup, Franklin invented them all—and more. He also founded the first public library, the first city hospital, and the University of Pennsylvania. An American inventor, printer, politician, diplomat, and scientist, Benjamin Franklin is also one of our greatest colonial writers.

B-B-B-Benny

The fifteenth of 17 children, Benjamin Franklin was born and raised in Philadelphia, Pa. He left school at 10. Two years later, he was apprenticed to his brother James, a printer. Hating the work, Franklin stayed five years out of courtesy (and law) and then hit the road, going first to New York and then to Philadelphia.

After a number of hard years, Franklin set up a printing shop, married, and became active in community affairs. Wise investments enabled Franklin to retire when he was 44 years old and devote his time to inventing and experimenting. His findings established him as the leading scientist in the Western Hemisphere.

It's only natural that a man of Franklin's talent should be sought out for public service. By 1770, he was the chief spokesman for the colonies; in 1757, he was elected to the Second Continental Congress. Later that year, he was appointed commissioner to France. Franklin's immense popularity helped the colonies gain the support of France and Spain, the decisive factor in our victory in the American Revolution. Even though he was in his eighties by then, Franklin served as president of the Commonwealth of Pennsylvania and as a member of the Constitutional Convention.

Benjamin Franklin.

Dear Diary

Although Franklin never considered himself a serious writer, his *Autobiography* is considered among the greatest autobiographies produced in Colonial America and one of the greatest autobiographies of the world. The following well-known excerpt describes Franklin's arrival in Philadelphia:

> *"Then I walked up the street, gazing about till near the market-house I met a boy with bread. I had made many a meal on bread, and, inquiring where he got it, I went immediately to the baker's he directed me to, in Second Street, and asked for biscuit, intending such as we had in Boston; but they, it seems, were not made in Philadelphia. Then I asked for a three-penny loaf, and was told they had none such. So not considering or knowing the difference of money, and the greater cheapness nor the names of his bread, I made him give me three-penny worth of any sort.*

> *He gave me, accordingly, three great puffy rolls. I was surpriz'd at the quantity, but took it, and, having no room in my pockets, walk'd off with a roll under each arm, and eating the other. Thus I went up Market-street as far as Fourth-street, passing by the door of Mr. Read, my future wife's father; when she, standing at the door, saw me, and thought I made, as I certainly did, a most awkward, ridiculous appearance.*

> *Then I turned and went down Chestnut-street and part of Walnut-street, eating my roll all the way, and, corning round, found myself again at Market-street wharf, near the boat I came in, to which I went for a draught of the river water; and, being filled with one of my rolls, gave the other two to a woman and her child that came down the river in the boat with us, and were waiting to go farther.*

> *Thus refreshed, I walked again up the street."*

Words to the Wise: Poor Richard's Almanac

> *"A little neglect may breed mischief:*
> *for want of a nail the shoe was lost;*
> *for want of a shoe the horse was lost;*
> *for want of a horse the rider was lost.*
> *For want of a rider the battle was lost.*

—Benjamin Franklin

From 1732–1757, Franklin published *Poor Richard's Almanac,* one of his most successful books. In addition to advice on crops, the tide, and dandruff, he offered aphorisms that have since become an indelible part of the American consciousness.

Here are some of his now familiar words to live by:

➤ "Early to bed, early to rise, makes a man healthy, wealthy and wise."

➤ "God helps those who help themselves."

➤ "Little strokes fell great oaks."

➤ "Three may keep a secret if two of them are dead."

➤ "Where there's marriage without love, there will be love without marriage."

➤ "There will be sleeping enough in the grave."

➤ "Never leave that till tomorrow which you can do today."

➤ "Fools make feasts, and wise men eat them."

➤ "The sleeping fox catches no poultry."

➤ "There are no gains without pains."

➤ "He that lives upon hope will die fasting."

➤ "Fish and visitors smell in three days."

Lit Speak

Aphorisms are clever, memorable sayings.

No other American better embodied the promise of America than Benjamin Franklin. Through hard work, dedication, and ingenuity, Franklin was able to rise out of poverty to become wealthy, famous, and influential. Although he had little formal education, Franklin made significant contributions to many fields, including literature, science, education, diplomacy, and philosophy.

The Write Stuff

Franklin achieved much of his characteristic style from imitating the writing in *The Spectator*, Joseph Addison and Richard Stelle's famous periodical of essays. Like them, Franklin favored parallel structure, vivid details, and strong verbs.

Thomas Jefferson (1743–1826)

Speaking of his famous grandfather, namesake grandson Thomas Jefferson Randolph recalled that:

> "Mr. Jefferson's hair, when young, was of a reddish cast; sandy as he advanced in years; his eye, hazel... Mr. Jefferson's stature was commanding—six feet two-and-a half inches in height, well formed, indicating strength, activity, and robust health; his carriage erect; step firm and elastic, which he preserved to his death; his temper, naturally strong, under perfect control; his courage cool and impassive...it was remarked of him that he never abandoned a plan, a principle, or a friend."

The third president of the United States, the "Sage of Monticello" was also a diplomat, an architect, a musician, a scientist and inventor, a strong supporter of religious freedom, and an early advocate of public education. He was also one of America's finest writers.

Lit Wit

Arguably, Jefferson's most notable achievement during his presidency was his purchase of the Louisiana Territory from France in 1803. The acquisition of this vast land, lying between the Mississippi River and the Rocky Mountains, doubled the area of the United States.

Take That, You Tyrant

Drafted by Jefferson between June 11 and June 28, 1776, the Declaration of Independence is at once America's most cherished symbol of liberty and Jefferson's most enduring monument. In ringing language, Jefferson expressed the American determination to be free. Since you probably haven't read the Declaration since Miss Schimmeldorf's fourth-grade class, why not take another look at it now?

"The unanimous Declaration of the thirteen united States of America,

When in the Course of human events, it becomes necessary for one people to dissolve the political bands which have connected them with another, and to assume among the powers of the earth, the separate and equal station to which the Laws of Nature and of Nature's God entitle them, a decent respect to the opinions of mankind requires that they should declare the causes which impel them to the separation.

We hold these truths to be self-evident, that all men are created equal, that they are endowed by their Creator with certain unalienable Rights, that among these are Life, Liberty and the pursuit of Happiness.—That to secure these rights, Governments are instituted among Men, deriving their just powers from the consent of the governed, —That whenever any Form of Government becomes destructive of these ends, it is the Right of the People to alter or to abolish it, and to institute new Government, laying its foundation on such principles and organizing its powers in such form, as to them shall seem most likely to effect their Safety and Happiness. Prudence, indeed, will dictate that Governments long established should not be changed for light and transient causes; and accordingly all experience hath shewn, that mankind are more disposed to suffer, while evils are sufferable, than to right themselves by abolishing the forms to which they are accustomed. But when a long train of abuses and usurpations, pursuing invariably the same Object evinces a design to reduce them under absolute Despotism, it is their right, it is their duty, to throw off such Government, and to provide new Guards for their future security.—Such has been the patient sufferance of these Colonies; and such is now the necessity which constrains them to alter their former Systems of Government. The history of the present King of Great Britain is a history of repeated injuries and usurpations, all having in direct object the establishment of an absolute Tyranny over these States. To prove this, let Facts be submitted to a candid world.

He has refused his Assent to Laws, the most wholesome and necessary for the public good.

He has forbidden his Governors to pass Laws of immediate and pressing importance, unless suspended in their operation till his Assent should be obtained; and when so suspended, he has utterly neglected to attend to them.

He has refused to pass other Laws for the accommodation of large districts of people, unless those people would relinquish the right of Representation in the Legislature, a right inestimable to them and formidable to tyrants only.

He has called together legislative bodies at places unusual, uncomfortable, and distant from the depository of their public Records, for the sole purpose of fatiguing them into compliance with his measures.

The Write Stuff

The Declaration's political philosophy wasn't new; its ideals of individual liberty had already been expressed by John Locke and the Continental philosophers. Jefferson summarized this philosophy in "self-evident truths" and set forth a list of grievances against the King in order to justify before the world the breaking of ties between the colonies and the mother country.

He has dissolved Representative Houses repeatedly, for opposing with manly firmness his invasions on the rights of the people.

He has refused for a long time, after such dissolutions, to cause others to be elected; whereby the Legislative powers, incapable of Annihilation, have returned to the People at large for their exercise; the State remaining in the mean time exposed to all the dangers of invasion from without, and convulsions within.

He has endeavored to prevent the population of these States; for that purpose obstructing the Laws for Naturalization of Foreigners; refusing to pass others to encourage their migrations hither, and raising the conditions of new Appropriations of Lands.

He has obstructed the Administration of Justice, by refusing his Assent to Laws for establishing Judiciary powers.

He has made Judges dependent on his Will alone, for the tenure of their offices, and the amount and payment of their salaries.

He has erected a multitude of New Offices, and sent hither swarms of Officers to harass our people, and eat out their substance.

He has kept among us, in times of peace, Standing Armies without the Consent of our legislatures.

He has affected to render the Military independent of and superior to the Civil power.

He has combined with others to subject us to a jurisdiction foreign to our constitution, and unacknowledged by our laws; giving his Assent to their Acts of pretended Legislation:

For Quartering large bodies of armed troops among us:

For protecting them, by a mock Trial, from punishment for any Murders which they should commit on the Inhabitants of these States:

For cutting off our Trade with all parts of the world:

For imposing Taxes on us without our Consent:

For depriving us in many cases, of the benefits of Trial by Jury:

For transporting us beyond Seas to be tried for pretended offenses:

For abolishing the free System of English Laws in a neighboring Province, establishing therein an Arbitrary government, and enlarging its Boundaries so as to render it at once an example and fit instrument for introducing the same absolute rule into these Colonies:

For taking away our Charters, abolishing our most valuable Laws, and altering fundamentally the Forms of our Governments:

For suspending our own Legislatures, and declaring themselves invested with power to legislate for us in all cases whatsoever.

He has abdicated Government here, by declaring us out of his Protection and waging War against us.

He has plundered our seas, ravaged our Coasts, burnt our towns, and destroyed the lives of our people.

He is at this time transporting large Armies of foreign Mercenaries to complete the works of death, desolation and tyranny, already begun with circumstances of Cruelty & perfidy scarcely paralleled in the most barbarous ages, and totally unworthy the Head of a civilized nation.

He has constrained our fellow Citizens taken Captive on the high Seas to bear Arms against their Country, to become the executioners of their friends and Brethren, or to fall themselves by their Hands.

He has excited domestic insurrections amongst us, and has endeavored to bring on the inhabitants of our frontiers, the merciless Indian Savages, whose known rule of warfare, is an undistinguished destruction of all ages, sexes and conditions.

In every stage of these Oppressions We have Petitioned for Redress in the most humble terms: Our repeated Petitions have been answered only by repeated injury. A Prince whose character is thus marked by every act which may define a Tyrant, is unfit to be the ruler of a free people.

Nor have We been wanting in attentions to our British brethren. We have warned them from time to time of attempts by their legislature to extend an unwarrantable jurisdiction over us. We have reminded them of the circumstances of our emigration and settlement here. We have appealed to their native justice and magnanimity, and we have conjured them by the ties of our common kindred to disavow these usurpations, which, would inevitably interrupt our connections and correspondence. They too have been deaf to the voice of justice and of consanguinity. We must, therefore, acquiesce in the necessity, which denounces our Separation, and hold them, as we hold the rest of mankind, Enemies in War, in Peace Friends.

Lit Wit

One of the most famous stories in American literature concerns the relationship of John Adams and Thomas Jefferson. On July 4, 1826, former Presidents John Adams and Thomas Jefferson lay on their deathbeds—Adams in Quincy, Massachusetts; Jefferson at Monticello. Both men, friends and collaborators early in life, then political enemies, and finally reconciled in the end, were determined to live to see the 50th anniversary of the *Declaration of Independence*—and to outlive the other.

The spirit of competition lingered until the very end. Jefferson died shortly before 1:00 p.m. Adams lived a few hours longer, his last words purported to have been, "Does Jefferson still survive?"

We, therefore, the Representatives of the united States of America, in General Congress, Assembled, appealing to the Supreme Judge of the world for the rectitude of our intentions, do, in the Name, and by Authority of the good People of these Colonies, solemnly publish and declare, That these United Colonies are, and of Right ought to be Free and Independent States; that they are Absolved from all Allegiance to the British Crown, and that all political connection between them and the State of Great Britain, is and ought to be totally dissolved; and that as Free and Independent States, they have full Power to levy War, conclude Peace, contract Alliances, establish Commerce, and to do all other Acts and Things which Independent States may of right do. And for the support of this Declaration, with a firm reliance on the protection of divine Providence, we mutually pledge to each other our Lives, our Fortunes and our sacred Honor."

Lit Speak

Broadsides were extremely popular during colonial times. A **broadside** is a single sheet of paper printed on one or both sides, dealing with a current topic. One of the most popular broadsides was a ballad called "The Dying Redcoat," supposedly written during the Revolutionary War by a British sergeant as he lay dying. He realizes, too late, that he's on America's side:

"Fight on, America's noble sons,
Fear not Britannia's thundering guns:
Maintain your cause from year to year,
God's on your side, you need not fear."

Writer's Block

Don't confuse Thomas Paine with Patrick Henry. Patrick Henry is the one who declared, "Give me liberty or give me death" at the end of his March 23, 1775 "Speech in the Virginia Convention."

From the Pen of the Master

Jefferson took Benjamin Franklin's words, "Rebellion to tyrants is obedience to God," to heart. In fact, this idea is woven into the fabric of the Declaration of Independence. But it's not just Jefferson's content that makes the Declaration of Independence so moving, it's also his style. The stylistic elements that make the Declaration such a successful document are…

➤ Parallel structure (the repeated use of phrases, clauses, or sentences that are similar in structure)

➤ Rhythm

➤ Forceful and direct language

➤ Loaded words (words that carry strong emotional overtones), such as *tyranny, liberty, justice,* and *honor.*

Thomas Paine (1737–1809)

A humble corsetmaker turned grocer, Paine didn't make it to our shores until he was 37 years old. His passage was paid by Ben Franklin, who called Paine an "ingenious, worthy young man." Franklin's investment in Paine paid off: In America, Paine quickly came into his own as a pamphleteer.

Paine's first pamphlet, *Common Sense,* appeared in January 1776, a time when most Americans still hoped the quarrel with England could be resolved amicably. *Common Sense* sold 500,000 copies and is credited with getting the colonists to see the "advantage, necessity, and obligation" of breaking with Britain. It was followed by a series of pamphlets, collectively called *An American Crisis.*

A Royal Paine

Hoping that Paine's words would inspire his soldiers to fight with passion, George Washington ordered Paine's pamphlets read aloud to his troops a few days before they crossed the Delaware River to attack the British at Trenton. The pamphlets were read, the soldiers fought like pit bulls, and the ensuing victory marked a turning point in the war.

The following excerpt from Paine's most famous pamphlet, *Common Sense*, has become part of our national fabric:

> *"THESE ARE THE TIMES THAT TRY MEN'S SOULS. The summer soldier and the sunshine patriot will, in this crisis, shrink from the service of their country; but he that stands it now, deserves the love and thanks of man and woman. Tyranny, like hell, is not easily conquered; yet we have this consolation with us, that the harder the conflict, the more glorious the triumph. What we obtain too cheap, we esteem too lightly: it is dearness only that gives every thing its value. Heaven knows how to put a proper price upon its goods; and it would be strange indeed if so celestial an article as FREEDOM should not be highly rated. Britain, with an army to enforce her tyranny, has declared that she has a right (not only to TAX) but "to BIND us in ALL CASES WHATSOEVER," and if being bound in that manner, is not slavery, then is there not such a thing as slavery upon earth. Even the expression is impious; for so unlimited a power can belong only to God."*

> —December 23, 1776

To Arms!

Not all American colonists supported succession from England. American Tories were so passionate in their support of Great Britain that more than 55,000 of them enlisted in the British army in the Revolutionary War!

Hence the need for Paine's rhetoric. Here's why his writing worked so well:

➤ He appealed to emotion as well as reason.

➤ He contrasted weak, self-centered people with courageous patriots.

➤ He used loaded language to emphasize British tyranny.

➤ He included his own view of the validity of the cause.

➤ He pledged God's support.

Lit Speak

During the Revolutionary War, a **Tory** was a person who supported the British cause—a loyalist. Today, a Tory is a member of the Conservative party in Great Britain or Canada.

The (Cultural) State of the Union

As you've probably gathered by now, it was a turbulent era and a time of action. But the legacy of the Revolutionary era was cultural as well as political. Guided by her writers, America was building a cultural identity. For example,

➤ Theaters were built from New York to Charleston, Virginia.

➤ A number of new colleges were built after the Revolutionary War, especially in the South.

➤ Painting flourished: John Singleton Copley, Gilbert Stuart, John Trumbull, and Charles Willson Peale were the leading artists of their time.

Nonetheless, there were not yet any American novels or plays of importance, and the modern short story had yet to be invented. However, the raw materials for a great national literature were at hand, waiting to be used. As America stood poised on the brink of a stunning territorial and population explosion, American literature would soon burst forth with a power that would have astonished even the most farsighted founders of America.

The Least You Need to Know

➤ The writing produced from 1750–1800 was public rather than private. It consisted of letters, pamphlets, declarations, speeches, and essays.

➤ In her letters, Abigail Adams campaigned for women's rights and provided a fascinating look at life in the Revolutionary period.

➤ J. Hector St. Jean de Crèvecoeur's *Letters from an American Farmer* helped establish our national identity by coining the term "melting pot" and giving us the notion that there's something special about "Americans."

➤ Ben Franklin became the symbol of success gained by hard work and common sense. His *Autobiography* and *Poor Richard's Almanac* portrayed Americans as ambitious but agreeable.

➤ Thomas Jefferson is considered to be the finest writer of the era, as the Declaration of Independence demonstrates.

➤ Thomas Paine's *The American Crisis,* which helped propel us into war, remains a model of effective propaganda.

Chapter 4

The Big Daddy of American Literature: Washington Irving (1789–1851)

In This Chapter

➤ American literature in the 19th century

➤ Washington Irving's life

➤ Washington Irving's contribution to American literature

➤ Irving's "Rip Van Winkle"

➤ Irving's "The Legend of Sleepy Hollow"

➤ Irving's "The Devil and Tom Walker"

Question: What do the following people have in common?

➤ Geoffrey Crayon

➤ Jonathan Oldstyle, Gent.

➤ Anthony Evergreen, Gent.

➤ Diedrich Knickerbocker

Answer: They're all the same man—Washington Irving, the Father of American Literature. Irving was 50 years old before his real name appeared on any of his books, but you really can't blame him—before Irving came along, no self-respecting writer would *ever* admit that he *was* an American. Why the shame about being an American writer? That's one of the things you'll learn in this chapter.

You'll also find out all about Irving's three most famous stories: "The Legend of Sleepy Hollow," "Rip Van Winkle," and "The Devil and Tom Walker." By the end of the chapter, you'll understand exactly what Irving did to put America on the international literary map.

Always a Bridesmaid, Never a Bride

"In the four quarters of the globe, who reads an American book, or goes to an American play, or looks at an American picture or statue?"

—Washington Irving

In 1820, the British writer Sydney Smith taunted Americans with this vicious jab at their provincialism. Let there be no mistake; the jibe cut deeply because it was true.

Lit Wit

Before Washington Irving and James Fennimore Cooper, the best-selling writers in America were all English or Scottish: Charles Dickens, Sir Walter Scott, Percy Bysshe Shelley, John Keats, and Lord Byron.

Writer's Block

Don't confuse *Washington* Irving with *John* Irving. The latter is the American novelist and short-story writer who established his reputation in 1978 with *The World According to Garp* (film, 1982). Both Washington and John share more than a last name, however: they both have a talent for engaging story lines, colorful characterization, and macabre humor.

In the early 1800s, America was still a sleepy little backwater, devoid of real culture. Our tastes in books, music, and fashion were all shaped by Europe, and aspiring American writers would have been well-advised not to give up their day jobs. As you read in previous chapters, many important figures of the Early National period were outstanding writers, but none made literature his profession. Jefferson, for instance, was a statesman; Franklin, a printer, statesman, and inventor. In the early 1800s, Americans already had Mom and apple pie, but still no real *American* literature.

Further, until the end of the century, American printers routinely stole the work of English writers, paying nothing, nada, and zip for books by the likes of Charles Dickens and Sir Walter Scott. American readers loved the situation because they could get the best British books very cheaply, but American writers suffered: If they were to receive royalties, their books had to sell at higher prices than British novels. It was not until 1891 that an international copyright law was enforced on both sides of the Atlantic.

Before 1891, American writers of the time just couldn't make the cut with book buyers. To this day, books from scores of writers from the Early National period are as dead as disco: Charles Brockden Brown, James Paulding, Fitz-Green Halleck, Caroline Kirkland, and N.P. Willis all fell to the literary wayside. Then along came Washington Irving.

A Declaration of Independence

Washington Irving was born in New York City on April 8, 1783, the last of 11 children. (Now you know how people spent their nights before television.) Like most famous writers, he was judged a cement-head as a child, but it was plain early on that the kid understood how to play the game: Irving wrote classmates' compositions in exchange for math assignments.

When Irving was 14 years old, he tried to run away to sea, having spent a year sleeping on the floor and eating slimy salt pork in preparation. His plans were thwarted by his parents, and Irving was forced to stay in school until he was 16 and then sent to study law.

In 1804, Irving, suffering from a bout of tuberculosis, embarked on a two-year tour of Europe in hopes of a cure. The change in scenery, it was felt, would strengthen him. On his return, Irving passed the bar exam in 1806 and served in a minor capacity at former vice president Aaron Burr's trial.

Lit Wit

Aaron Burr (1756–1836), the third vice president of the United States, began his career in the Continental Army and was admitted to the New York bar in 1782. From there it was straight up to attorney general and senator. In 1800, Burr served as vice president, but four years later he failed to win renomination because of Alexander Hamilton's opposition. Seriously annoyed, Burr killed Hamilton in a duel and became an instant political pariah. Washed up, he went for hung-out-to-dry by getting involved in a wild scheme to invade Spanish Territory. Arrested, Burr was denounced for treason but was acquitted in 1807 after a six-month trial.

Around the same time, Washington's brother William founded a satirical magazine called *Salmagundi* (a spicy hash) and enlisted his baby brother's help in filling the pages. Vowing to "instruct the young, reform the old, correct the town, and castigate the age," the brothers took their work seriously. When not playing leapfrog in the office or hoisting a few in the local tavern, they even wrote a little. When they finished making fun of everyone they knew, the dynamic duo suspended publication, and Irving was once again on his own. The magazine had lasted a year, from 1807-1808.

Top of the Charts

In 1809, Irving created his first great triumph, *A History of New York,* a wickedly funny spoof of various well-known figures, including then-President Thomas Jefferson. Irving launched the book in one of the cleverest hoaxes in publishing history:

First, the *Evening Post* noted the disappearance of "a small elderly gentleman by the name of Knickerbocker," adding that there were "some reasons for believing that he is not entirely in his right mind." Three months later, another article revealed that Knickerbocker's landlord had found a "very curious kind of written book" in his rooms, which he intended to sell to pay the back rent. At last the book appeared, credited to "Diedrich Knickerbocker."

Begun as a parody of a New York guidebook, Irving ended by writing a comic history of New York under Dutch authority. Fact is interspersed with exaggeration, burlesque, and biting sarcasm. *A History's* combination of mock solemnity and extravagant irreverence laid the foundation of style for many subsequent American humorists, notably Mark Twain and Will Rogers. *A History of New York* made Irving a celebrity on both sides of the Atlantic.

Writer's Block

A History was hysterical in its day, but like all topical humor, it hasn't held up. To modern readers, the jokes are virtually meaningless.

Nonetheless, it still didn't dawn on Irving that he was the Real Thing, a Genuine Talent. As a result, he spent the next 10 years toiling away at the family hardware business, traveling, and editing a bit here and there. When the family business went belly-up in 1818, Irving finally turned to his pen to make a buck. Lucky for us.

Setting Up Shop

Using old German folk tales as his base, Irving created a series of remarkable stories. In 1820 he published his first groundbreaking collection, *The Sketch Book of Geoffrey Crayon, Gent,* under the pen name Geoffrey Crayon. Two stories in particular, "Rip Van Winkle" and "The Legend of Sleepy Hollow," catapulted him to fame.

Irving's next two books, *Bracebridge Hall* (1822) and *Tales of a Traveler* (1824), were savaged by the critics. Irving then tried his hand at biography and history. He accepted an invitation to join the American legation in Spain and produced a number of fine books there, including *History of the Life and Voyages of Columbus* (1828) and *The Alhambra* (1832). The latter was nicknamed "the Spanish *Sketch Book.*"

While in Spain, Irving made many devoted friends. This wasn't unusual for Irving, since his talent for friendship was equal to his talent for writing.

Lit Wit

Clement Clarke Moore, a New York Biblical scholar, gained lasting fame with a poem he wrote for his family. The poem was called "A Visit from St. Nicholas." A relative of Moore's gave a copy of the poem to a newspaper editor in Troy, New York, who published it in 1823. The poem? "Twas the Night Before Christmas."

After a 17-year absence, Irving returned to New York in 1832. Several years later, Irving set down roots when he purchased and refurbished a charming house called Sunnyside near Tarrytown, New York. Lifestyles of the rich and famous get old fast, however, so in 1842 Irving accepted an appointment as minister to Spain. Upon his return to America in 1846, the Father of American Literature wrote a biography of the Father of his Country, George Washington. Irving died just after finishing the last volume, on November 28, 1859.

Lit Wit

More than 500 people marched in Irving's funeral procession; the church floor sank slightly under the unaccustomed weight of those who crowded in for the service.

The Big Kahuna

Years before his death, Irving was acknowledged for putting American literature on the map. He was a master of style as well as substance. Here's a little proof:

➤ Both Henry Wadsworth Longfellow and Nathaniel Hawthorne were inspired by Irving's *Sketch Book,* and their writing owes much to his influence.

➤ Herman Melville paid homage to Irving's genius in his poem "Rip Van Winkle's Lilacs."

➤ In a number of public speeches, the best-selling British authors Charles Dickens and Sir Walter Scott acknowledged their debt to Irving's writing.

➤ From Irving, Mark Twain learned how to use realistic details of rural life in America.

➤ The "local color" school of fiction (described in detail in Chapter 18, "Color My World: The Local Colorists 1865-1930") got its start with Irving.

When he was not busy inspiring writers by his work, Irving was helping them in person: Generous to younger writers all his life, Irving promoted Herman Melville and William Cullen Bryant, among others.

By the 1850s, there was an elusive quality in the air about the country's new literature that was unmistakably American. Not only were Irving's stories set on American soil, but they spoke to the American soul: Rip Van Winkle captured the American trauma of dealing with rapid change and repeated physical uprooting. Rip also helped Americans overcome a sense of underachievement and failure. His success at living his life on his own terms became a model for our own. Even Irving, a master patriot, could not have imagined that one day America would be the leader of the free world.

Let's look at Irving's most famous stories, starting with "The Legend of Sleepy Hollow."

Pumpkin Head

Icabod Crane, the main character in "The Legend of Sleepy Hollow," is...

"...tall, but exceedingly lank, with narrow shoulder, long arms and legs, hands that dangled a mile out of his sleeves, feet that might have served for shovels, and his whole frame most loosely hung together. His head was small, and flat at top, with huge ears, large green glassy eyes, and a long snipe nose, so that it might have been mistaken for a weathercock perched upon a spindle neck, to tell which way the wind blew. To see him striding along the profile of a hill on a windy day, with his clothes bagging and fluttering about him, one might have mistaken him for the genius [image] of famine descending upon the earth, or some scarecrow eloped from a cornfield."

Now meet the rest of the gang...

➤ *Gunpowder:* Icabod's borrowed bag-of-bones horse.

➤ *Katrina Van Tassel:* A rosy-cheeked rustic heiress.

➤ *Mynheer Van Tassel:* Katrina's father, a colonial Daddy Warbucks.

➤ *The Headless Horseman:* The legendary Hudson Valley ghost, supposedly of a Hessian cavalryman whose head had been shot off by a cannonball.

➤ *Abraham Van Brunt (Brom Bones):* The leading man of the crowd, in love with Katrina.

Fright Night

The folks who inhabit Sleepy Hollow believe their village is bewitched. The primary ghost is the Headless Horseman, rumored to be a Hessian soldier who had lost his noggin to a stray cannonball.

Icabod Crane arrives in town to become the local schoolmaster for the village children. As was the custom back then, Icabod boards with each of his pupils for a week at a time. Icabod meets Katrina Van Tassel, a looker whose substantial physical charms are augmented by her father's substantial bank account. But Abraham (Brom) Van Brunt, an 18th-century stud also in love with Katrina, makes a formidable rival for poor, gaunt Icabod. Since it was tacky in the 18th century to physically assault a school-teacher, Brom resorts to playing practical jokes on his rival.

The entire village is invited to a party at Mynheer Van Tassel's prosperous farm. Icabod has a wonderful time dancing with Katrina, telling ghost stories, and eating himself into a stupor.

Heads Up

The night is dark and scary. On his way home, Icabod is shadowed by the headless horseman. Icabod races for the church bridge, where legend has it that the specter will vanish in a flash of fire and brimstone:

> *"'If I can but reach that bridge,' Icabod thinks, 'I am safe.'"*

But the creature breaks with tradition and throws his head at the terrified schoolmaster:

> *"Icabod endeavored to dodge the horrible missile, but too late. It encountered his cranium with a tremendous crash—he tumbled headlong into the dust, and Gunpowder, the black steed, and the goblin rider, passed by like a whirlwind."*

The next morning a shattered pumpkin is found near the bridge with Icabod's horse grazing nearby—but Icabod himself is never seen again. According to tradition, Brom Bones "always burst into a hearty laugh at the mention of the pumpkin; which led some to suspect that he knew more about the matter than he chose to tell."

The Big Sleep

"Rip Van Winkle," which Irving published in 1819, has become an American legend, in large part because of its main character. "The great error in Rip's composition was an insuperable aversion to all kinds of profitable labor," the narrator notes. OK, so the guy wasn't a ball of ambition, but dogs and kids liked him. A descendent of an old and hard-working Dutch family, he falls asleep in the Catskill Mountains for 20 years.

Here's the rest of the gang:

➤ *Dame Van Winkle:* Rip's temperamental wife—no wonder the man headed for the hills.

➤ *Wolf:* Rip's pooch.

➤ *Judith Van Winkle:* Rip's daughter.

➤ *Hendrick Hudson:* Leader of the little people who visit once a year to party.

Bowling, Anyone?

Good-humored Rip Van Winkle, a kind of Norm Peterson of the Catskill set, prefers to warm the barstool at the village inn rather than work. Although very adept at dodging his wife's messages, occasionally Rip slips up and Dame Van Winkle comes after him in person. When he glimpses her formidable fists, Rip heads for the hills. There, he can relax in peace.

One night on the way home from his mountain refuge, Rip is accosted by Hendrick Hudson, a strange little man in old-fashioned clothing who asks him to help carry a keg of liquor to the top of the mountain, where Rip finds a band of little men playing ninepins. Our hero takes a few snorts from the cask and, like sports fans the world over, falls asleep watching the game.

Lit Wit

Bowling, also called "tenpins," is one of the most popular games in the world. A variant of the game, called "ninepins" or "skittles," is played in the Netherlands and Germany, where it seems to have originated. Dutch settlers brought the game to America, where it then moved indoors. In 1875, the National Bowling League was established in America, but the rules of the game weren't standardized until 1895, when the American Bowling Congress was created. There are 10 frames in the modern version of the game, and the highest possible score is 300.

The Write Stuff

Here's the mark of real success: Disney made both "Rip Van Winkle" and "The Legend of Sleepy Hollow" into animated movies that are still shown today. *The Legend of Sleepy Hollow* is shown on the Disney channel every October for Halloween.

When Rip awakens, the little men have disappeared, his gun is rusty, and his dog is gone. Rip returns to town, but no one seems to know who he is, and his home lies in ruins. To his astonishment, Rip realizes that he has been asleep for 20 years. When he learns that his wife has died, Rip breathes a sign of relief and lives happily ever after, regaling the locals with his strange tale of Henrick Hudson and the little men playing ninepins.

Born in the USA

"When I first wrote 'The Legend of Rip Van Winkle,'" Irving said, "my thoughts had been for some time turned toward giving a color of romance and tradition to interesting points of our national scenery which is so generally deficient in our country." Irving succeeded so well in creating a genuine American tale that translators have always had a hard time with the story.

Why is "Rip Van Winkle" such a seminal American story?

Thanks to Irving…

➤ Henpecked husbands, overbearing wives, and mysterious apparitions have become standard fictional elements in American literature.

➤ The laid-back antihero balances the dour, Puritanical hero.

➤ Rip Van Winkle marks the beginning of the "local color" school of writing, in which authors use vivid details to re-create a specific place.

Going to the Devil

"The Devil and Tom Walker," from Irving's *Tales of a Traveler,* is based on a German folktale about a man who sells his soul to the devil. Irving made the tale distinctly American by switching the setting to New England in 1727, at the time that the Puritan belief that life should be devoted to God was being replaced by materialism.

The story has only three characters:

➤ *Tom Walker:* Makes Dickens's Scrooge look like a humanitarian.

➤ *Mrs. Walker:* A dragon with attitude.

➤ *The Devil:* A devil of a fellow.

Beam Me Down, Scotty

It's 1727. A few miles from Boston, Mr. and Mrs. Tom Walker live in wedded misery. Mrs. Walker is a shrew who's not above aiming the plates and her right hook at her hubby. But Tom's no prize, either; he's at least as miserly and vicious as his spouse.

One day Tom takes a shortcut through a swamp and accidentally uncovers a skull. Suddenly, a large sooty man appears and orders Tom to leave his property. Tom refuses to be intimidated and quickly realizes that he's shooting the breeze with the devil himself. Having lived so long with his strong-willed wife, Tom finds the devil pleasant company and they strike a deal: Tom will help the devil in exchange for the treasure of a famous pirate named Kidd.

Tom foolishly tells his missus about his strange encounter of the devilish kind, and Mrs. Walker sets out to visit the devil and get a cut of the action. The devil won't deal, so she returns with the family's silver as a bribe. Several nights pass, and Mrs. Walker doesn't return. Tom grows increasingly uneasy when he realizes that the silver is also missing. A practical man, he decides, "Let us get hold of the property, and we shall endeavor to do without the woman."

Searching the woods, he finds nothing but her heart and liver tied in her apron. Tom consoles himself for the loss of his silver with the cheerful news that he has lost his wife as well. Tom then does the devil's work as a moneylender, gleefully foreclosing and dispossessing.

Lit Speak

Gothic refers to the use of medieval, wild, or mysterious elements in literature. Gothic literature features mysterious and gloomy settings and horrifying events. Edgar Allan Poe is generally regarded as the American master of Gothic writing.

Happy years pass. Sensing the end is near, Tom embraces religion as a shield to damnation. This works out well until he shouts out, "The devil take me if I have made a farthing (cent)." The devil, an obliging sort, calls in his chit.

What Becomes a Legend Most?

"The Devil and Tom Walker" satirized hypocritical Puritans who used their social standing in the community to amass wealth. As with all of Irving's best stories, "The Devil and Tom Walker" starts off gently humorous and builds to a fearful climax. Irving's use of Gothic props—the devil, the dank forest, the grisly murder— in a bucolic American setting creates a uniquely American slant on the supernatural.

The Least You Need to Know

➤ Washington Irving (1783–1859) is called "the Father of American Literature" because he proved that memorable fiction could feature both American settings and American "types."

➤ Irving became the first American writer to achieve an international reputation and was the central figure in the American literary scene between 1809 and 1865.

➤ Irving wrote short stories, travel books, and satires. His most famous works are the short stories "The Legend of Sleepy Hollow," "Rip Van Winkle," and "The Devil and Tom Walker."

➤ The man who missed his wake-up call, Rip Van Winkle, created success from failure, becoming an American antihero.

➤ The Headless Horseman of Sleepy Hollow has terrified generations of American children.

➤ "The Devil and Tom Walker" presents an American twist to the traditional encounter-with-the-devil folktale.

Chapter 5

HEY, WHERE IS EVERYONE?

Father of the American Novel: James Fenimore Cooper (1789–1851)

In This Chapter

➤ Cooper's life story and personality

➤ Cooper's literary reputation

➤ *The Leatherstocking Tales*

➤ *The Last of the Mohicans*

➤ *The Deerslayer*

➤ Cooper's "literary offenses"

On his deathbed, Cooper begged his family not to allow any account of his life to be published. No doubt Cooper feared that posterity might not overlook his insufferable snobbery, litigious nature, and general crankiness when praising his genius.

During his long life, Cooper managed to insult an astonishingly wide range of people on both sides of the Atlantic. Arriving in London, for example, he announced that the majestic Thames river was "a stream of trivial expanse." At home he spent his nonwriting time suing and slandering his neighbors. He was, as the 20th-century British writer D.H. Lawrence put it, "A gentleman in the worst sense."

Read on to find out how this first-class crank became a first-class writer, creating the first American adventure story, the first American novel of manners, and the first American novel of the sea. Thanks to all these accomplishments, Cooper became the first successful American novelist.

The father of the American novel.

From an engraving, by J. B. Forrest, of a miniature by H. Chilton.)

Green Acres Is the Place for Me

When Cooper was a little more than a year old, his affable and astute father moved his considerable brood from Burlington, New Jersey, to the shores of Ostego Lake in central New York. Flatly refusing to leave civilization for the wilderness, Mrs. Cooper committed herself to her armchair. Mr. Cooper hoisted her, armchair and all, into the wagon and headed north. William Cooper settled his wife, her armchair, and their seven children on more than a million acres. With characteristic family modesty, he named his spread Cooperstown.

Although a wealthy country squire of the first order, Cooper senior had the common touch, settling arguments with friendly wrestling matches and spreading around the beer in lieu of cash. Under his father's good-natured guidance, young Cooper flourished.

Cooper was such an outstanding student, in fact, that he entered Yale University in 1803, when he was only 13 years old. Although he was a "fine, sparkling" lad, as one of his professors noted, young Cooper was not above playing a prank or two. School officials turned the

Writer's Block

Don't be mislead by the number of Coopers that moved. At the time of their relocation, the Cooper brood did indeed number seven, but it eventually grew to 13.

50

other cheek when Cooper blew off a classmate's door with gunpowder. They were able to forgive the huge debts he ran up in fashionable shops, too. They did have a bit of a problem ignoring the donkey that Cooper taught to sit on the professor's chair—*that* stunt landed him on the street. He had no choice but to return to the family mansion.

Lit Wit

Although we in the lit biz like to think that Cooperstown, NY, is famous as the home of James Fenimore Cooper, the grim reality is that our man in the forest has been overshadowed by the national pastime. While devoted literature majors trek to Cooperstown to soak in the leftover ink, most traffic in this cute tourist trap can be attributed to a nonliterary landmark, the National Baseball Hall of Fame and Museum. In 1839, while Cooper was inventing the American novel, Abner Doubleday invented baseball.

Six Days, Seven Nights

Correctly surmising that he was a little lax in the discipline department, Cooper's father decided that his youngest son needed a firmer hand, and so promptly sent him off to sea. In October 1806, Cooper set sail aboard the *Stirling*, a small merchant ship bound out of New York for England. They carried a load of flour.

Barely 17 years old, Cooper took his place on the deck next to kindly old salts screaming with delirium tremens in the end stages of alcoholism. The voyage was uneventful—the usual pursuit by a heavily armed pirate ship, attempted impressment by the British Navy, and various men overboard. Two years later, Cooper had learned the ropes well enough to get his midshipman's certificate, signed by Thomas Jefferson.

Cooper was hot to check out the beaches and nightlife in the warmer climates, and so was bitterly disappointed when he was assigned to an inactive bomb ketch laid up for repairs in New York Harbor. Things got even worse with his next assignment: Oswego, a frontier village in Lake Ontario, 200 miles from the sea.

Down for the Count

Fate intervened, and Cooper abandoned his first love, the sea, for his second, Susan DeLancey, an heiress who was winsome as well as wealthy. During their courtship, Cooper's father died, leaving James the enormous sum of $50,000 and a share in the $750,00 estate. James and Susan married in 1811, only after he promised to give up his naval career.

At first the marriage was happy as well as prosperous, producing four daughters. But in the depression following the War of 1812, the Cooper family fortune collapsed. To make matters worse, Cooper's five profligate brothers died between 1813 and 1819, leaving Cooper to support their large families. As the head of the household, he begged and borrowed in a vain attempt to keep the clan afloat.

Anything You Can Do, I Can Do Better

According to the Cooper family legend, in 1821, James was reading a new novel from England when he threw it aside and exclaimed, "I could write a better book than that myself!" Wife Susan challenged him to make good of his boast; never one to turn down a dare, the following year he produced *Precaution,* a novel about high society.

The critics weren't bowled over. They realized that the novel was little more than another echo of English fiction, and a dull one at that. Undaunted, Cooper tried again. This time he struck pay dirt, producing two undeniably American novels: *The Spy* (1821), the first important historical romance of the American Revolution, and *The Pioneers,* a story of the frontier. *The Pioneers* (1823) was a runaway bestseller; more than 3,500 copies flew off the shelves the very day it was printed. And Cooper was just getting started.

Lit Wit

During Cooper's boyhood, there were few backwoodsmen left and fewer Indians; the information he used as the basis for his novels was secondhand, from older people and books.

Scott Free

Next Cooper churned out *The Pilot,* the first of his 11 influential novels of the sea. This one finally impressed the critics, a tough lot in general. They gave him the highest praise they had, calling him "the American Scott," comparing his thrilling yarns to the equally spellbinding stories of England's Sir Walter Scott. Although neither writer liked the comparison, it did move the merchandise. Cooper's money problems were over.

The Ugly American

In 1826, Cooper added the "Fenimore" to his name to honor his mother's family, set off for Europe with his clan, and set up shop for the next seven years. In addition to seeing the sights, Cooper alienated most of the civilized world and wrote a series of good novels. These included *The Prairie* (1827) and *Notions of the Americans* (1828). An equal-opportunity scold, he spread around his bad cheer; few people or places could complain that they had been overlooked by his contentious nature. He was especially fond of suing his friends and neighbors and insulting everything from their appearance to their behavior. In addition, he was especially vain about his writing, feeling it was vastly superior to everyone else's.

Of course, Cooper's enemies struck back with a vengeance. In an attempt to defend himself from personal attacks by the press and public, Cooper published *A Letter to His Countrymen.* No dice; this only added fuel to the fire.

When Cooper returned to America, he continued to write and arouse even more bad feelings. Trouble started from the moment he got off the boat: He refused to attend a dinner planned in his honor. He also began a series of lawsuits against his neighbors for picnicking on his land. His awesome literary productivity and litigation continued unabated through the years, as he wrote and sued until he could no longer hold a pen. All told, Cooper brought approximately 40 libel suits, winning about one-third of them.

Cooper died in 1851. His reputation declined in the end of the 19th century, but revived in the 1920s. Today, his work continues to be a strong presence in American fiction.

Bumpp and Grind

Although he wrote both tales of the sea and novels of manners, Cooper's fame rests largely on *The Leatherstocking Tales,* a series of five novels about the frontiersman, Natty Bumppo. Here's a list of them:

➤ *The Pioneers* (1823)

➤ *The Last of the Mohicans* (1826)

➤ *The Prairie* (1827)

➤ *The Pathfinder* (1840)

➤ *The Deerslayer* (1841)

Each of the five novels traces a phase in the life and times of Natty Bumppo, the last action hero of the New World. Raised by Native Americans, Bumppo is a deer-clad Superman, faster than a speeding bullet, more powerful than a locomotive, and able to race-walk 50 miles without stopping to take a breath. He also has a nice body and great hair. But I digress.

Since the books were written out of chronological order, here's a crib sheet you can use to keep the "Nattys" straight.

Writer's Block

Make no mistake about it: Cooper will never be considered a major literary artist on the scale of say, Emily Dickinson and Herman Melville. Nonetheless, he will always be a key source for the foundation of American literature.

The Write Stuff

Strong echoes of *The Last of the Mohicans* can be heard in Nathaniel Hawthorne's *The Scarlet Letter* (Chapter 9) and Herman Melville's *Moby Dick* (Chapter 10). All three novels treat the American wilderness, Native Americans, and complex heroes.

Title	Date of Publication	Date of Action	Name	Age
The Pioneers	1823	1793	Natty or Leatherstocking	70s
The Last of the Mohicans	1826	1757	Hawkeye	mid-30s
The Prairie	1827	1804	The Trapper or The Old Man	late 70s to mid-80s
The Pathfinder	1840	1759	Pathfinder	late 30s
The Deerslayer	1841	1740s	Deerslayer	mid-20s

My Hero: *The Last of the Mohicans*

America's most famous fictional frontiersman, Natty Bumppo, stands "about six feet in his moccasins" and has a "comparatively light and slender" muscular body. Although not handsome, he's known for truth, justice, and the American way. He was educated by the Delaware Indians, who gave him his name (Hawkeye) because of his "quick eye" in spotting a deer and his "actyve foot" in chasing it.

Meet the entire gang:

➤ *Natty Bumppo (Hawkeye):* The long, lean hunk straight out of the pages of *Field and Stream.*

➤ *Chingachgook*: The courageous and loyal Mohican chief: Hawkeye's main man.

➤ *Uncas:* The last of the Mohicans, Chingachgook's son, who falls for Cora, and she for him.

➤ *Major Duncan Heyward:* Like nearly all the men in this book, he's handsome, intelligent, and brave.

Writer's Block

Don't confuse Cooper's noble frontiersman Hawkeye with Alan Alda's noble doctor in the movie/TV show M*A*S*H. Cooper's is the original; Alda's, the tribute.

➤ *Magua:* The handsome, intelligent, brave, Huron chief who seeks revenge on Colonel Munro by turning his feisty daughter Cora into a servile squaw.

➤ *Cora Munro:* The dark-haired daughter of Colonel Munro, equally handy with a flintlock and a frying pan.

➤ *Alice Munro:* Cora's half-sister, a blond babe who clings like a cheap suit. She's Duncan's beloved.

➤ *Colonel Munro:* The English general in charge of defending Fort Williams. He eventually is forced to surrender the Fort to the French when backup troops cannot provide military support.

➤ *David Gamut:* The only wuss of the group, a singing teacher.

➤ *The Marquis de Montcalm:* The enterprising French general who captures Fort William Henry and allows the Hurons to massacre the English.

➤ *General Webb:* Fort Edward's incompetent commander.

What I Did over My Summer Vacation

Time: 1757

Place: Near Lake George, in New York Colony, during the war between the British and the French

When the novel opens, Cora and Alice, the two beautiful daughters of Colonel Munro, commander of Fort William Henry, are trekking through the wilderness toward their father's headquarters. They are accompanied by Major Duncan Heyward, a young British officer from Virginia, and David Gamut, a Connecticut singing-master. Their guide through the woods is a treacherous Huron Indian named Magua, who claims that he knows the shortcut to their destination. Hawkeye (a.k.a. Natty Bumppo, a.k.a Leatherstocking) and his two Delaware Indian friends Chingachgook and his son Uncas join the group and casually mention that Magua has been leading them in a circle.

Lit Speak

The **Hurons** are also called the **Iroquois**.

Realizing that the jig is up, Magua heads for the hills. Hostile Huron warriors attack. Wild pursuit! Hairbreadth escape!

Hawkeye and Chingachgook's Excellent Adventure

Under Hawkeye's guidance, the good guys hide in a cave. Their ammunition all used up, Cora takes charge and insists that Hawkeye and his two Indian friends escape and seek help. Major Heyward and David remain behind. With Our Hero gone, Magua and his men capture the good guys and gals. Cora is promptly tied to a stake in preparation for torture.

Hawykeye comes to the rescue! He blasts the Indians with his trusty rifle (called "Killdeer") and saves the day. In the melee, Magua escapes. The gang (Hawkeye, Chingachgook, Cora, Uncas, Alice, David, and Duncan) pass through the French fort to get to Fort William. A guard stops them and questions them, but Duncan fools them by replying in French that they are friends of the French crown. The guard buys their ruse, and then Chingachgook goes back to scalp the guard.

The English surrender the fort, and more than 2,000 Iroquois Indians (a.k.a. Hurons) massacre the women and children of the defeated garrison. Magua grabs Alice and Cora and heads for the hills. Hawkeye and his buddies set off to rescue them.

Hawkeye and his buddies reach the Huron camp and meet David the singing-master, who reports that Alice is in the Huron camp nearby and Cora is with a tribe of Delaware Indians some distance away. Aided by Hawkeye, Duncan saves his Alice, who he is in love with.

The Delawares, led by Uncas, Hawkeye, and Chingachgook, defeat the Iroquois, but Cora is fatally stabbed by a Huron, and Magua kills Uncas. Hawkeye and his noble sidekick, Chingachgook, survive for the sequel.

So Why Not Just Watch the Movie?

Invariably, *The Last of the Mohicans* has spawned a number of film versions. Its most recent incarnation (1992, Twentieth Century Fox) transforms the jolly adventure tale into a jolly good romance. Daniel Day-Lewis plays Hawkeye and romances his Cora, Madeleine Stowe, amid lots of blood and scenery. It's a very good hair day in this version. My personal favorite is still the 1936 version starring Randolph Scott as Hawkeye and Binnie Barnes as the virginal Alice. It has lots more blood and thunder. With two good filmed versions to pick from (and several not-so-good ones), why slip on the reading glasses and open the book? Here's why:

➤ The novel, unlike the movie versions, shows how Cooper interprets the American experience and elevates it to epic level.

➤ In the book, Unca's death illustrates the tragedy of the Native American encounter with white civilization.

➤ Cooper's characters show the qualities that define America: bravery, self-reliance, democracy.

➤ The novel better illustrates the true grandeur of the frontier.

➤ The book is cheaper than a movie ticket and less fattening than all that buttered popcorn.

Son of a Bestseller: *The Deerslayer*

Paradoxically, in the last of the Leatherstocking novels, Natty Bumppo is the youngest: When we first meet him in this book, he's about 23 years old. Here's the whole cast:

➤ *Natty Bumppo* (here called *Deerslayer*):

➤ *Chingachgook:* The trusted sidekick.

➤ *Hurry Harry March:* A greedy frontiersman. He'd make a good inside trader nowadays.

➤ *Tom Hutter:* Yo-ho-ho and a bottle of rum; former pirate, current trapper.

➤ *Judith Hutter:* Tom's daughter and babe-o-rama.

➤ *Hetty Hutter:* Judith's sister, a girl with such Christian simplicity that she awes even the Native Americans into granting her safe passage. (She's also one taco short of a combination plate.)

➤ *Hist-ho!-Hist* or *Wah-ta!-Wah:* Chingachgook's significant other, she's called by either name.

➤ *Captain Warley:* The cavalryman to the rescue.

➤ *Rivernoak:* The enemy Iroquois chief, fierce but honorable.

Lights! Camera! Action!

Time: 1740s

Place: The northern New York Colony

The novel opens with Deerslayer (Natty Bumppo) and Hurry Harry traveling to meet Chingachgook at Lake Glimmerglass, located in the northern part of the New York Colony. At Muskrat Castle (near a British fort), Hurry puts the moves on Judith, but she's got a thing for a British officer. Of course, this is a no-no, since the Brits are the enemy.

Against Deerslayer's wishes, Hurry Harry and Hutter want to harvest some Native American scalps for which they hope to be given a bounty (money) by the colony and for which they are unsuccessful. The two white men are captured by the Mingos (a.k.a. Hurons or Iroquois), which serves them right. Deerslayer cools his heels waiting for Chingachgook, who's trying to rescue Hist from the enemy Iroquois. Deerslayer meets with the Iroquois chief Rivernoak to ransom Hurry Harry and Hutter. That evening, Hutter and Hurry are exchanged for a ransom of ivory chessmen.

The Write Stuff

Lake Glimmerglass is Cooper's fictional name for the real Lake Otsego. It's located in Cooperstown, New York.

Lit Wit

The Iroquois Confederacy included five tribes—Mohawk, Onondaga, Cayuga, Oneida, and Seneca—known as the "Five Nations." A complex and stable political organization, combined with skill in warfare, enabled the Iroquois to become very powerful during the 1600s. By the early 1700s, they had conquered almost all the tribes from the Atlantic to the Mississippi, and from the St. Lawrence to the Tennessee rivers.

When Deerslayer and HH reach Gimmerglass, they find that the Mingos have already arrived at the scene. Deerslayer races off to help Chingachgook rescue Hist. After some running around, their quest is successful, which naturally gets the Mingos seriously annoyed. To make their anger quite clear, the Mingos take Natty prisoner. Hutter and HH are recaptured while seeking scalps and in a delicious bit of irony, Hutter himself is scalped and shuffles off this mortal coil.

Truth or Consequences

From old letters, Judith learns that Daddy Dearest was not Daddy Dearest after all, but rather a reformed pirate whom their mother married after being deserted by the father of Judith and Hetty. Setting the letters aside, Judith puts the moves on Deerslayer, but he doesn't take the bait.

Deerslayer rejoins the Iroquois and is promptly tortured by tomahawks, knives, and rifles. Chingachgook comes to the rescue!

The cavalry thunders down the hill, stirs up a lot of dust, and massacres all the Indians. Hetty is wounded and dies.

Judith hot-foots it to merry old England as a mistress of a British officer who seduces her.

Fifteen years later, Deerslayer and Chingachgook return to Glimmerglass to find the castle in ruins.

So What's It All About?

The Deerslayer is an edge-of-your-seat adventure tale. It's also got a heavy message: Natty Bumppo becomes the representative hero of a culture that blends qualities the Europeans brought to the New World with qualities of the frontier. Without this message, the novel would run the risk of being just another wonderfully diverting wild ride.

Judith is the model for the fallen woman. Cooper's influence was strong: Judith comes back as the straight-A student Hester Prynne in Nathaniel Hawthorne's *The Scarlet Letter* and later as Charlotte Stant, the ruthless adventuress in Henry James' *The Golden Bowl*.

The Broken Twig Series

➤ "Cooper is the greatest artist in the domain of romantic fiction yet produced in America." —[British novelist] Wilkie Collins

➤ "...One of the very greatest characters in fiction, Natty Bumppo..." — Professor Brander Matthews

➤ "The defects in both these tales are comparatively slight. They were pure works of art." —Professor Lounsbury

So the jury's in… or is it?

In his famous essay, "Fenimore Cooper's Literary Offenses," Mark Train (Samuel Clemens) asserts that Cooper's writing has some defects. Well, maybe more than *some*. "In one place in *Deerslayer*, and in the restricted place of two-thirds of a page, Cooper has scored 114 offenses against literary art out of a possible 115. It breaks the record," Twain claims.

Here are five of Cooper's major literary offenses, according to Twain:

1. "They require the personages in a tale shall be alive, except in the case of corpses, and that always the reader shall be able to tell the corpses from the others. But this detail has been overlooked in the *Deerslayer* tale."

2. "Use the right word, not its second cousin."

3. "That a tale shall accomplish something and arrive somewhere. But the *Deerslayer* tale accomplished nothing and arrives in the air."

4. "They require that the episodes of a tale shall be necessary parts of the tale, and shall help to develop it. But as the *Deerslayer* tale is not a tale, and accomplishes nothing and arrives nowhere, the episodes have no rightful place in the work, since there was nothing for them to develop."

5. "They require that crass stupidities shall not be played upon the reader as 'the craft of the woodsman, the delicate art of the forest,' by either the author or the people in the tale. But this rule is persistently violated in the *Deerslayer* tale.

While Cooper's novelistic shortcomings are clear—awkward, stilted language; illogical plots, and lame attempts at humor—so are his very real achievements. Cooper opened up new American scenes and themes for fiction. He spread the word, too, by establishing the Bread and Cheese Club, where he became the center of a group of influential writers and artists. What Washington Irving did for the short story, James Fenimore Cooper did for the novel. He put America on the world literary map, gentle reader.

The Least You Need to Know

➤ James Fenimore Cooper (1789–1851) was America's first successful novelist.

➤ He created the first American adventure story, the first American novel of manners, and the first American novel of the sea.

➤ He raised the American frontier experience to epic proportions and helped define the American character as we know it today.

➤ His most famous character was Natty Bumppo, a.k.a. Deerslayer, Hawkeye, and Leatherstocking, one of the most popular characters in literature.

Chapter 6

Life on the Ledge: Edgar Allan Poe (1809–1849)

In This Chapter

➤ Poe's Life

➤ Poe's reputation

➤ "The Raven"

➤ "The Philosophy of Composition"

➤ "The Cask of Amontillado" and the single effect

➤ "The Gold Bug" and the detective story

Edgar Allan Poe is dead. He died in Baltimore the day before yesterday. This announcement will startle many, but few will be grieved by it. The poet was known, personally or by reputation, in all this country; he had readers in England, and in several of the states of Continental Europe; but he had few or no friends; and the regrets for his death will be suggested principally by the consideration that in him literary art has lost one of its most brilliant but erratic stars.

—The *New York Tribune*, October 9, 1849

So wrote Edgar Allan Poe's supposed "friend" and literary executor, Rufus Wilmot Griswold.

In this chapter, you'll find out how the original hard-luck kid managed to create the modern short story, the detective story, and write some landmark poetry—despite being dealt a really bad hand in the game of life.

A Rocky Start

Poe was born to two struggling actors who lived in a Boston apartment so small they had to go into the hall to change their minds. Poverty aside, Poe didn't have a good start: His mother died of tuberculosis and his father of alcoholism before Poe was out of diapers. The orphan was then adopted by John and Frances Allan of Richmond, Virginia. John was a prosperous merchant.

Frances bonded immediately with the lad, but John kept his distance. Nonetheless, John gave Edgar the finest education, sending him to topnotch schools in America and Europe. Edgar excelled at both sports and studies. Even though he was viciously taunted because of his lowly birth, he made a number of close friends.

When he was 17, Poe enrolled in the University of Virginia. Within a day of his arrival, Poe managed to gamble away his entire term's allowance. Just a few months later, he owed $2,500 in gambling debts. The skill Poe lacked in cards he more than made up with in drinking, and he managed to stay drunk for the entire semester. Astonishingly, he aced his classes, earning the University's highest distinction.

Unimpressed with Edgar's extracurricular activities, John Allan yanked his drunken cardsharp son out of college faster than you can say "Deal 'em and pour me a stiff one." Soon after, Edgar left home for Boston.

Beat It to Beantown

Boston was then America's center of publishing, and Poe was determined to write the Great American Novel or Something. At his own expense, Poe published *Tamerlane and Other Poems*. Since he didn't have a whole lot of spare change, only 50 copies were printed. Unfortunately, the book didn't even make a ripple in the literary pond. Desperate, Poe enlisted in the Army. He was 18 years old.

Although he did well soldiering, Poe soon realized that he was not cut from khaki. Logic demanded a different tack, so Poe decided to enter West Point. It was July 1830. Within six months, Poe knew he had made a bad career move. After getting himself court-martialed for his drinking and gambling, Poe headed for the Big Apple, where he managed to get a book of poems published at someone else's expense. Like his previous attempt, this book sunk as fast as the Titanic. He took off to Baltimore to continue writing stories.

Getting the Short End of the Stick

After months of living in a style to which no one would like to become accustomed, Poe won $50 and some recognition for his poetry. He also fell in love with his preteen cousin Virginia. Virginia was pale, dark-haired, and as dumb as toast. In 1835, when Poe was 26, he married Virginia, who had just turned 13.

Meanwhile, John Allan had died, leaving Poe completely out of his will. For the rest of Poe's life, his family (now including Virginia's mother as well as his child bride) shuttled back and forth among New York, Philadelphia, Baltimore, and Richmond, surviving mainly on bread and molasses as Poe tried to make it as a writer. His astonishing talent secured him a number of jobs as an editor and critic for magazines and newspapers; his equally astonishing inability to hold his booze got him fired from them all.

Lit Wit

During a trip to see President John Tyler, Poe was reported to be so drunk that he wore his coat inside out. History does not record whether the President noticed.

The Sorrow and the Pity

That Poe managed to write anything at all is astounding; that he wrote so much of such value is nothing short of remarkable. Poe looked so bad when he personally submitted the manuscript of "The Raven" to *Graham's Magazine* that even though the editors rejected the poem, they took up a collection of $15 to give him (he eventually got $10 for "The Raven" from the *New York Mirror.)*

Virginia's death from tuberculosis in 1847 sent Poe into a drunken tailspin. Two years later, Poe decided to try drying out for awhile, but his good intentions lasted only a few hours. He fell off the wagon with such a resounding crash that he died three days later, in the gutter. His body wasn't claimed for several days.

"This death was a suicide," French poet Charles Baudelaire remarked, "a suicide prepared for a long time."

Lit Wit

Talk about hero worship: Playwright August Strindberg fantasized that because he was born in 1849, Poe's spirit must have passed on to him.

Great Balls of Fire

Given the circumstances of his life, it's not astonishing that Poe managed to screw up from beyond the grave. The man he appointed his literary executor, Rufus Griswold, wrote a vicious obit, claiming that Poe had been expelled from college, committed plagiarism, and drunk himself to death.

Poe's genius was never tangibly rewarded in his lifetime. In fact, he was barely tolerated by the literary establishment. For example:

➤ Uneasy with Poe's strong use of rhythm, the famous 19th-century philosopher Ralph Waldo Emerson dubbed him "the Jingle Man."

➤ Novelist Henry James thought an enthusiasm for Poe was "the mark of a decidedly primitive stage of reflection."

➤ Poet T.S. Eliot said Poe's intellect was that of a "highly gifted young person before puberty."

➤ Writer James Russell Lowell characterized Poe as "three-fifths genius and two-fifths sheer fudge."

➤ "To me, Poe's prose is unreadable—like Jane Austen's," Mark Twain said. "No, there is a difference. I could read his prose on salary, but not Jane's."

Slams aside, no other American writer, with the possible exception of Mark Twain, has been as influential as Poe on the American consciousness, especially in his use of the supernatural, strong rhythm, and striking images. Here are just a few of the writers whom Poe has influenced:

➤ New England poet E.A. Robinson

➤ Novelist Frank Norris

➤ Novelist Theodore Dreiser

➤ Southern writer William Faulkner

➤ British mystery writer Sir Arthur Conan Doyle

➤ Irish playwright and critic George Bernard Shaw

➤ Horror master Stephen King

The Write Stuff

Thinking of becoming a writer? Perhaps you should brush up on your penmanship: Poe probably had the best handwriting of any noted author. When he won a prize for his short story "MS. Found in a Bottle," Poe claimed he was helped "by the beauty of his handwriting."

We like Poe for his whiz-bang poems such as "The Raven," "Ulalume," and "The Bells," and his horror tales, including "The Black Cat," "The Fall of the House of Usher," "The Pit and the Pendulum," and "The Tell-Tale Heart." Scholars celebrate his literary criticism (the bulk of his writing), including his take-no-prisoners reviews and his ruminations on writing.

Even though Poe married jailbait and ingested every controlled substance short of plutonium, he still found time to create the modern short story and the detective story, and wrote some nifty poetry.

For the Birds: The Raven

The Raven

Once upon a midnight dreary, while I pondered, weak and weary,

Over many a quaint and curious volume of forgotten lore,

While I nodded, nearly napping, suddenly there came a tapping,

As of someone gently rapping, rapping at my chamber door.

'Tis some visitor,' I muttered, 'tapping at my chamber door—

> Only this and nothing more.'

Ah, distinctly I remember it was in the bleak December,

And each separate dying ember wrought its ghost upon the floor.

Eagerly I wished the morrow;—vainly I had sought to borrow

From my books surcease of sorrow—sorrow for the lost Lenore—

For the rare and radiant maiden whom the angels name Lenore—

> Nameless here for evermore.

Lit Wit

Poe's epitaph is *Quoth the Raven nevermore.*

"The Raven" is a ballad of 18 six-line stanzas that's about as subtle as Pamela Anderson. As these opening two stanzas hint, "The Raven" describes the nightmarish story of a young man mourning the death of his beloved (Lenore). As he mourns, he's driven mad by a raven. The bird is no motormouth—all it can say is "Nevermore"—so we know the narrator has a dicey grip on reality to begin with. Bet you're surprised. But hey, we're in Poe country now.

Lit Speak

A **stanza** is a group of lines in a poem, considered as a unit. Stanzas often function just like paragraphs do in prose (non-poetry).

Here's the breakdown:

➤ Stanzas 1 to 7 describe the eerie setting and the narrator's shaky grip on reality.

➤ Stanzas 8 to 11 show the narrator chatting up the bird, but all the bird says is "Nevermore."

➤ Stanzas 12 to 13 reveal how the narrator treats the bird like a feathered Ouija board, bombarding it with questions.

➤ Stanza 14 to 18 build to the climax. As his frenzy mounts, the narrator asks the bird if Lenore will return. The bird replies only, "Nevermore." The narrator then demands that the bird leave, our feathered friend refuses to budge, and the narrator slips off the track.

Here's the last stanza. Try reading this one late at night…
And the Raven, never flitting, still is sitting, still is sitting
On the pallid bust of Pallas just above my chamber door;
And his eyes have all the seeming of a demon that is dreaming,
And the lamplight o'er him streaming throws his shadow on the floor;
And my soul from out that shadow that lies floating on the floor
    Shall be lifted—nevermore!

Lit Wit

"The Raven" is often imitated, parodied, and lampooned. For example, the speaker in this version is a cat:

On a night quite unenchanting, when the rain was downward slanting,

I awakened to the ranting of the man I catch mice for.

Tipsy and a bit unshaven, in a tone I found quite craven,

Poe was talking to a raven perched above the chamber door.

"Raven's very tasty," thought I, as I tiptoed o'er the floor,

"There is nothing I like more…"

                                     —anonymous

The dramatic juxtaposition of the black bird perched on the white bust, central to the play of light and shadow, helps the poem move to its frenzied climax, the speaker's overwhelming sorrow and insane desperation.

The Philosophy of Composition

"The Raven" is Poe's most famous poem because he immortalized its creation in the pivotal essay "The Philosophy of Composition." In so doing, he set the ground rules for 19th-century poetry.

Poe's essay explains how the poem's subject and mood are underscored by its rhythm and rhymes. It also spells out Poe's belief that a poem's beauty is an end unto itself.

Poe's rules are clear:

1. First comes the *effect:*

   "I prefer commencing with the consideration of an effect... I say to myself, in the first place, "Of the innumerable effects, or impressions, of which the heart, the intellect, or (more generally) the soul is susceptible, what one shall I, on the present occasion, select?"

2. Then we get *length:*

   "The initial consideration was that of extent. If any literary work is too long to be read at one sitting, we must be content to dispense with the immensely important effect derivable from unity of impression—for, if two sittings be required, the affairs of the world interfere, and everything like totality is at once destroyed... I reached at once what I conceived the proper length for my intended poem—a length of about one hundred lines. It is, in fact, a hundred and eight."

3. Next comes *impression:*

   "My next thought concerned the choice of an impression, or effect, to be conveyed... That pleasure which is at once the most intense, the most elevating, and the most pure is, I believe, found in the contemplation of the beautiful."

4. Then *tone:*

   "My next question referred to the tone of its highest manifestation—and all experience has shown that this tone is one of sadness. Beauty of whatever kind in its supreme development invariably excites the sensitive soul to tears. Melancholy is thus the most legitimate of all the poetical tones."

The Write Stuff

In "The Philosophy of Composition," Poe also attacked two other long-standing poetic conventions:

➤ The *epic mania:* The notion that a poem has to be long to be good.

➤ The *didactic heresy:* The belief that a poem (or any work of literature) has to teach a lesson.

5. Finally, the *subject:*

"Now, never losing sight of the object... I asked myself—"Of all melancholy topics what, according to the universal understanding of mankind, is the most melancholy?" Death, was the obvious reply. "And when," I said, "is this most melancholy of topics most poetical?" From what I have already explained at some length the answer here also is obvious—"When it most closely allies itself to Beauty: the death then of a beautiful woman is unquestionably the most poetical topic in the world, and equally is it beyond doubt that the lips best suited for such topic are those of a bereaved lover."

The ideal poem, therefore, has a single effect, can be read in one sitting, concerns the contemplation of the beautiful, is sad, and deals with the death of a beautiful woman. Let's see how Poe put theory to practice in another of his well-known poems, "Annabel Lee."

Annabel Lee

"Annabel Lee" tells the usual Poe story—boy loves girl, girl dies, boy spends every night in a tomb lying next to her dead body. Keep in mind, Gentle Reader, that this girl has been dead for years (many and many a year ago, in fact). You can interpret this poem as either an admirable testimony to everlasting love or the rhyming ravings of a psychopath. Here's the poem: Judge for yourself.

Annabel Lee
It was many and many a year ago,
   In a kingdom by the sea,
That a maiden there lived whom you may know
   By the name of Annabel Lee;
And this maiden she lived with no other thought
   Than to love and be loved by me.

I was a child and *she* was a child,
   In this kingdom by the sea;
But we loved with a love that was more than love—
   I and my Annabel Lee;
With a love that the winged seraphs of heaven
   Coveted her and me.

And this was the reason that, long ago,
   In this kingdom by the sea,

A wind blew out of a cloud, chilling
   My beautiful Annabel Lee;
So that her highborn kinsmen came
   And bore her away from me,
To shut her up in a sepulchre,
   In this kingdom by the sea.

The angels, not half so happy in heaven,
   Went envying her and me—
Yes!—that was the reason (as all men know,
   In this kingdom by the sea)
That the wind came out of the cloud by night,
   Chilling and killing my Annabel Lee.

But our love it was stronger by far than the love
   Of those who were older than we—
   Of many far wiser than we—
And neither the angels in heaven above,
   Nor the demons down under the sea,
Can ever dissever my soul from the soul
   Of the beautiful Annabel Lee.

For the moon never beams, without bringing me dreams
   Of the beautiful Annabel Lee;
And the stars never rise but I feel the bright eyes
   Of the beautiful Annabel Lee;
And so, all the night-tide, I lie down by the side
Of my darling—my darling—my life and my bride,
   In her sepulchre there by the sea,
   In her tomb by the sounding sea.

"Annabel Lee" is famous for its haunting rhythms and lulling repetition. The rhymes capture the cadence of the ocean. Notice how the repetition of "sea," "Lee," and "me" induce sleep better than a mug of hot milk. Lines such as "But we loved with a love that was more than love" create a dreamy feeling with the gliding consonants *m, n, l,* and *s.*

The Write Stuff

This is probably the last poem that Poe wrote. In 1850, Poe's wife Virginia was fingered as the inspiration for Annabel Lee, an attribution that has met with much agreement.

69

"Annabel Lee" also fits Poe's standards for a successful poem, as the following chart shows:

Rule	Example
Single effect	Loss and sadness.
Read in one sitting	You just did.
Contemplation of beauty	Their rare love.
Melancholy tone	Boy, is it ever sad.
Death of a beautiful woman	"Chilling and killing my Annabel Lee."

Edgar Allan Poe's poetry was enough to put him on the literary landscape, but he also wrote extraordinary—and important—short stories. Let's see how Poe's short stories helped create what we know as "American Literature."

The Cask of Amontillado

"The thousand injuries of Fortunato I had borne as I best could, but when he ventured upon insult I vowed revenge. You, who so well know the nature of my soul, will not suppose, however, that I gave utterance to a threat. At *length* I would be avenged; this was a point definitively settled—but the very definitiveness with which it was resolved precluded the idea of risk. I must not only punish but punish with impunity. A wrong is unredressed when retribution overtakes its redresser. It is equally unredressed when the avenger fails to make himself felt as such to him who has done the wrong."

What's the crime? What's the difference? In a Poe story, it's the madness that matters. And along with the madness, readers get a generous dollop of white-knuckle suspense and some gorgeous writing. How does he do it?

Poe's Single Effect

By striving for a *single effect,* every character, detail, and incident in the story helps create the mood. "In the whole composition," Poe wrote in "The Philosophy of Composition," "there should be no word written, of which the tendency, direct or indirect, is not to the preestablished design." And it has to happen from the very beginning of the story. Poe asserted: If a writer's "very initial sentence tend not to the outbringing of this effect, then he has failed in his first step."

The Write Stuff

Poe explained his theory of the short story in a review of Nathaniel Hawthorne's *Twice-Told Tales.* It's worth the read.

More than any other writer, Poe is responsible for the emergence of the short story as a popular and respected literary form. Poe was the first writer to classify and define the short story as a distinct literary genre and argue that the short story deserves the same status as the poem and the novel. As you read the following excerpt from "The Cask of Amontillado," see how Poe instantly plunges us into the terrifying mind of a madman.

No More Mr. Nice Guy

"It was about dusk, one evening during the supreme madness of the carnival season, that I encountered my friend. He accosted me with excessive warmth, for he had been drinking much…

I said to him—'My dear Fortunato, you are luckily met. How remarkably well you are looking to-day. But I have received a pipe of what passes for Amontillado [a type of sherry], and I have my doubts.'

'How?' said he, 'Amontillado? A pipe? Impossible! And in the middle of the carnival!'"

To achieve his revenge, Montressor tricks his enemy Fortunato into a wine cellar by playing on his vanity about his knowledge of fine sherry. The story starts this way…

Drunk as a skunk, Fortunato falls for the bait and follows Montressor into the wine cellar/catacomb. Montressor lures him deeper and deeper into the damp cavern. When they reach the end of the tunnel, Montressor springs forward and chains Fortunato to the granite. Fortunato is too astounded to resist. In a flash, Montressor has uncovered the pile of stone and mortar he had conveniently stashed there earlier and with chilling industry walls his friend in.

By the time Montressor builds the second tier, Fortunato is moaning; by the fourth, he's screaming and clanking his chains. Nonetheless, Montressor keeps working. By midnight, he's just about finished. Right before he lays the last brick to entomb his "friend" alive, Fortunato screams out, *"For the love of God, Montressor!"* "Yes," Montressor replies, "for the love of God!"

The story ends…

"I hastened to make an end of my labor. I forced the last stone into its position; I plastered it up. Against the new masonry I re-erected the old rampart of bones. For the half of a century no mortal has disturbed them. In pace requiescat! ['May he rest in peace!']"

Poe didn't stop there. Remember that Poe invented the mystery story genre, too. Read on to find out how.

Lit Speak

The Edgar is a small bust of Edgar Allan Poe, presented by the Mystery Writers of America annually to the best writers of detective stories. Edgars are awarded in several categories, including best novel and best short story.

Gilt Trip: The Gold Bug

The story takes place on the imaginary Sullivan's Island. While looking for entomological specimens, William Legrand finds an entirely new insect, a gold bug. When he gets home, Legrand draws a picture of the bug for his friend, the narrator, to examine. When his friend mocks the drawing as resembling a skull, Legrand takes another look, pales, and shoves the sketch in his wallet. A month later, Jupiter, Legrand's servant, visits the narrator with the news that his master has gone 'round the bend.

Carrying the gold bug, which, it was discovered, actually existed, the narrator accompanies Legrand and Jupiter (hey, someone has to tell the story) around the island in search of the place where Legrand orginally found the gold bug. At this point, the gold bug seems saner than Legrand. Things don't get much better when Legrand suddenly orders Jupiter to climb a giant tulip tree.

Near the end of the seventh branch of the tree, Jupiter finds a human skull.

On Legrand's orders, Jupiter drops the gold bug through the skull's left eye socket. After completing a series of feverish measurements, Legrand begins to dig. Voilá! A treasure chest!

Legrand then explains how he solved the mystery, found the treasure, and lived happily ever after, even without his Captain America magic decoder ring. (You'll have to read the story yourself to find out the details!)

Dick Lit

The general lack of living entombments, screaming maniacs, and bloody limbs in "The Gold Bug" is rather strange, when you consider who the author is. There aren't any chains, decaying mansions, or thunderstorms, either. Was Poe finally taking the right medication? Nope. Instead, he was inventing a whole new genre: the detective story. He was 34 years old.

"The Gold Bug," one of Poe's best-known stories, belongs to a small group of stories he dubbed "tales of ratiocination," stories in which logic is used to solve a mystery. Other examples include

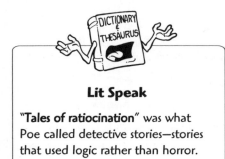

Lit Speak

"Tales of ratiocination" was what Poe called detective stories—stories that used logic rather than horror.

➤ "Murders in the Rue Morgue"

➤ "The Mystery of Marie Rog[ct]et"

➤ "The Purloined Letter"

These stories differ from Poe's horror tales in two key ways: language and plot. Here's a crib sheet:

Element	*Detective Stories*	*Horror Tales*
Language	Unemotional and rational	Emotional, shrill
Plot	Action in first part	Builds to climax

Lit Wit

Sir Arthur Conan Doyle's Sherlock Holmes was inspired by Edgar Allan Poe's amateur detective Monsieur C. Auguste Dupin, featured in several Poe tales, including "The Purloined Letter."

The Least You Need to Know

➤ Despite a lousy childhood and some serious substance-abuse problems, Poe wrote landmark criticism and memorable poetry.

➤ Poe also created the modern short story, with its unity of character, detail, and mood.

➤ Poe's psychotic murder stories paved the way for such pop-culture icons as Norman Bates and Freddy Kruger.

➤ Poe also created the detective story.

➤ Reviled in his day, Poe's fame is now secure.

Part 2
The New England Renaissance (1840–1855)

"When Nature has work to be done, she creates a genius to do it."

—*Ralph Waldo Emerson,* Nature

Elaborate theories have been devised to explain why sudden bursts of creativity occur at certain places and times. In New England from 1840 to 1855, a group of writers made an astonishing contribution to American letters. Their names loom large on our national consciousness: Ralph Waldo Emerson, Henry David Thoreau, Nathaniel Hawthorne, and Herman Melville.

Chapter 7

The Sage of Concord: Ralph Waldo Emerson (1803–1882)

In This Chapter

➤ Transcendentalism

➤ Ralph Waldo Emerson's life

➤ Emerson's "*Nature*"

➤ Emerson's "The American Scholar" speech

➤ Emerson's "Divinity School Address"

➤ Emerson's "Self-Reliance"

➤ Emerson's "Hymn Sung at the Completion of the Concord Monument, April 19, 1836"

How many of these quotations have you heard?

➤ "The only way to have a friend is to be one." —Emerson

➤ "To be great is to be misunderstood." —Emerson

➤ "Life only avails, not the having lived." —Emerson

➤ "That government is best which governs not at all." —Thoreau

➤ "If a man does not keep pace with his companions, perhaps it is because he hears a different drummer. Let him step to the music which he hears, however measured or far away." —Thoreau

➤ "The mass of men lead lives of quiet desperation." —Thoreau

Ralph Waldo Emerson and Henry David Thoreau contributed more than sound bites to our national consciousness. They created a new philosophy, *transcendentalism,* which is responsible for America's sturdy optimism and determined self-reliance. Add Thoreau's guidebook for life, *Walden,* and his handbook for rebellion, "Civil Disobedience," and you've got a giant step forward for American culture. In this chapter, you'll learn all about Emerson. I've saved his main man Henry for the next chapter.

Transcendentalism

"There are always two parties: the establishment and the movement."

—*from* Nature

The hoopla over transcendentalism started around 1820, when a group of young Unitarian ministers became agitated that the party line had become too rational and lacked the essentials of a religious experience—intuition, emotion, and mystery.

Transcendentalism didn't develop in a vacuum; a similar philosophical movement called *romanticism* had already occurred in England and Germany. The Romantic movement supported individual worth, the goodness of humanity, the glory of communion with nature, and individual freedom of expression. This appealed to Americans beginning to chafe at the restrictions of an already declining Puritanism.

> ### Writer's Block
>
> Emerson and his cohorts didn't coin the term "transcendentalism." Rather, the German philosopher Immanuel Kant (1724–1804) gets the credit.

Making the A List

Like Woodstock, the 1969 music love-in, the Transcendental movement was brief, messy, and influential out of proportion to its size. The Transcendental party kicked off in 1836 with the formation of the Transcendental Club in Boston. The core members were

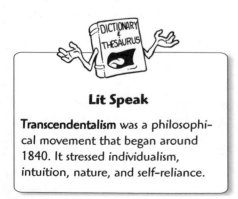

> ### Lit Speak
>
> **Transcendentalism** was a philosophical movement that began around 1840. It stressed individualism, intuition, nature, and self-reliance.

➤ Writer Ralph Waldo Emerson

➤ Writer/naturalist Henry David Thoreau

➤ Feminist writer and lecturer Margaret Fuller

➤ Unitarian preacher and social reformer Theodore Parker

➤ Educator Bronson Alcott

➤ Philosopher, minister, and author William Ellery Channing

➤ George Ripley, Unitarian minister, leader of the transcendentalists, and contributor to *The Dial*

➤ Elizabeth Palmer Peabody, publisher of *The Dial*

The group published a slender magazine, *The Dial,* and some of the members got a littler chummier at Brook Farm, a commune that set the pace for the co-ed dorms to follow.

Philosophy 101

So what *is* transcendentalism? A floor wax? A breath mint? A laxative? Actually, it's a philosophy. Here are the Big Three beliefs of the transcendentalists:

1. There's a direct connection or "correspondence" between the universe and the individual soul. As a result, Nature is where it's at. Nature is the gospel of the new faith. As Emerson wrote in his "Divinity School Address,"

    The first in time and the first in importance of the influences upon the mind is that of nature. Every day, the sun; and, after sunset, night and her stars. Ever the winds blow; ever the grass grows. Every day, men and women, conversing, beholding and beholden. The scholar is he of all men whom this spectacle most engages. He must settle its value in his mind. What is nature to him? There is never a beginning, there is never an end, to the inexplicable continuity of this web of God, but always circular power returning into itself. Therein it resembles his own spirit, whose beginning, whose ending, he never can find—so entire, so boundless. And, in fine, the ancient precept, "Know thyself," and the modern precept, "Study nature," become at last one maxim.

2. By contemplating objects in nature, people can transcend the world and discover union with the *Over-Soul* (also known as the *Ideal* or *Supreme Mind*) that unites us all.

    As Emerson said in *Nature,*

    …the currents of the Universal Being circulate through me,
    I am part or parcel of God.

3. Follow your own intuition and own beliefs, however divergent from the social norm they may be. Since all people are inherently good, the mantra ran, the individual's intuitive response to any given situation will be the right thing to do. Here's where we get our robust strain of self-reliance. As Emerson said (yes, also in *Nature*),

    "If the single man plant himself indomitably on his instincts, and there abide, the huge world will come round to him."

The transcendentalists were an equal-opportunity group. So what if some adherents saw transcendentalism as a single-minded commitment to improve the lot of the poor and oppressed? Not to worry; in the transcendentalists' democracy of intellect, you could interpret the movement any way you wanted. Emerson even had a slogan for it:

"A foolish consistency is the hobgoblin of little minds, adored by little statesman and philosophers and divines."

Since Emerson got the transcendental ball rolling and all, let's take a look at the inside skinny on this tremendously influential poet/philosopher.

Where's Waldo?

"Nothing great was ever achieved without enthusiasm."

— *from "Circles"*

Happily married, kind to dogs and kids, the kind of guy you'd call to help you unclog the storm drains, Emerson led a totally upright and conventional life. Nevertheless, this quiet, conventional man espoused ideas that were neither cautious nor conventional. Every American writer of Emerson's era—and every American writer to follow—had to come to terms with Emerson's belief that knowledge of fundamental reality was derived through intuition rather than through sensory experience.

Lit Speak

Unitarianism is the branch of Christianity that denies the doctrines of the Trinity, original sin, vicarious atonement, the deity of Christ, and everlasting damnation. So what's left? you may ask. Well, you have the Eucharist and baptism, but the transcendentalists felt there just wasn't enough meat left on those bones. Thus, a new –ism, trancendentalism, was born.

On the low end of the scale, Herman Melville mocked Emerson in his novel *The Confidence Man* as a philosophical fraud; on the other hand, Thoreau, Walt Whitman, and Emily Dickinson worshipped him as a fount of inspiration. So who was this man? What forces shaped his life?

Emerson was eight years old when his father, a Unitarian minister, died. Determined that her four sons would attend Harvard, the widow Emerson took in boarders to make the tuition money.

Emerson got into and through Harvard despite not being the strongest student (they clearly hadn't invented the SATs yet), earning a degree in divinity. Emerson celebrated his ordination at age 26 in 1829 by marrying his sweetie, Ellen Tucker. They were by all accounts a well-matched pair. Unfortunately, Ellen died of tuberculosis less than two years later. Grief-stricken, Emerson turned in his cassock and set off for Europe.

Nature

"He is great who is what he is from Nature, and who never reminds us of others."

—*from* Nature

When a legacy from his wife's estate granted him financial freedom, Emerson returned to Concord, Massachusetts from Europe. In 1834 he married Lydia Jackson and started writing.

His first work, *Nature*, did little to establish his literary reputation at first, at least in part because Emerson published it anonymously. The publication did become the unofficial manifesto of the Transcendental Club, founded in 1836, which kicked off the Transcendental party and eventually transformed the American identity.

This long essay is Emerson's I'm-okay-you're-okay hymn to individualism, in which he explains how Nature's green breast can restore our confidence and release our powers, as religion once did. The basic concept: Nature is God's work made visible to humanity. "The whole of Nature is a metaphor of the human mind," he wrote. "The relation between the mind and matter is not fancied by some poets, but stands in the will of God, and so is free to be known by all men."

In Emerson's own words:

"Crossing a bare common, in snow puddles, at twilight, under a clouded sky, without having in my thoughts any occurrence of special good fortune, I have enjoyed a perfect exhilaration. I am glad to the brink of fear. In the woods too, a man casts off his years, as the snake his slough, and at what period soever of life, is always a child. In the woods, is perpetual youth. Within these plantations of God, a decorum and sanctity reign, a perennial festival is dressed, and the guest sees not how he should tire of them in a thousand years. In the woods, we return to reason and faith. There I feel that nothing can befall me in life,—no disgrace, no calamity, (leaving me my eyes,) which nature cannot repair. Standing on the bare ground,—my head bathed by the blithe air, and uplifted into infinite space,—all mean egotism vanishes."

"I become a transparent eye-ball; I am nothing; I see all; the currents of the Universal Being circulate through me; I am part or particle of God. The name of the nearest friend sounds then foreign and accidental: to be brothers, to be acquaintances, — master or servant, is then a trifle and a disturbance. I am the lover of uncontained and immortal beauty. In the wilderness, I find something more dear and connate than in streets or villages. In the tranquil landscape, and especially in the distant line of the horizon, man beholds somewhat as beautiful as his own nature."

Emerson concluded that the way to God's truth is by communicating with nature, not through reason. This works especially well if you failed geometry but aced earth science.

The Write Stuff

What did Emerson mean by "...no calamity, (leaving me my eyes,)"? He had a deep fear of losing his vision, and so asserts it is the only tragedy he would fear.

The American Scholar

Emerson's 1837 speech to Phi Beta Kappa at Harvard, "The American Scholar," expressed the practical aspects of transcendentalism. The speech made a huge splash from the very start. Oliver Wendell Holmes, no slouch with a pen himself, called the speech "our intellectual Declaration of Independence," which is precisely what Emerson had in mind.

It was a call for American intellectuals to trust their individuality and act as noble representatives to the world. Its effect was not unlike that of God delivering the tablets to Moses, only these tablets helped establish a national consciousness, not a religion.

Lit Wit

Today, Emerson, Thoreau, Hawthorne, and Melville are considered to be the literary giants of the 1850s. At the time, however, physician/poet Oliver Wendell Holmes was the unofficial poet laureate of the New England intellectuals. Both in his poetry and prose, Holmes strove for a light, informal tone, charm, and humor. Many of his verses were *occasional*—that is, they were composed for reading aloud at graduations, reunions, birthdays, and other occasions. Other well-known writers of the day included Harvard professor and poet Henry Wadsworth Longfellow and journalist/essayist James Russell Lowell. Another celebrated writer of the day was John Greenleaf Whittier, a Quaker poet and antislavery crusader.

In his speech, Emerson prodded the students to become more confident in their abilities and to take pride in Americanism: "We have listened too long to the courtly muses of Europe… We will walk on our own feet, we will work with our own hands, we will speak our own minds."

The main influences on the scholar's education are nature, books, and action, Emerson declared. Scholars who are free and brave will be rewarded amply; their minds will be altered by the truths they discover.

Divinity School Address

In this oration, Emerson declared that true religion resides within the individual, not in Christianity or in the church. Emerson said, "It [the truth] cannot be received at second hand. Truly speaking, it is not instruction, but provocation, that I can receive from another soul."

According to Emerson, since everyone has equal access to the Divine Spirit, all that people need in order to validate religious truth is their inner experience. Here's how Emerson put it:

"Meantime, whilst the doors of the temple stand open, night and day, before every man, and the oracles of this truth cease never, it is guarded by one stern condition; this, namely; it is an intuition. It cannot be received at second hand. Truly speaking, it is not instruction, but provocation, that I can receive from another soul. What he announces, I must find true in me, or wholly reject; and on his word, or as his second, be he who he may, I can accept nothing."

Not surprisingly, this didn't sit well with a flock of freshly minted ministers who had just spent the best years of their lives locked in a stuffy classroom learning theology. Emerson was branded an infidel and barred from speaking at his alma mater for 30 years.

The Fame Game

"To be great is to be misunderstood."

—*from* "Self-Reliance"

Emerson's fame grew when *Essays* became famous in 1841 and made him the unofficial prophet from Massachusetts. "Self-Reliance" and "Hymn Sung at the Completion of the Concord Monument, April 19, 1836" hit the top of the charts, too, because they struck a chord in Americans who were eager to establish their national identity. Transcendental Clubs sprang up in New England; writers began to adopt Emerson's ideas. Let's look at these two works now.

Self-Reliance

"There is a time in every man's education when he arrives at the conviction that envy is ignorance; that imitation is suicide."

—*from* "Self-Reliance"

This essay further elaborates on the familiar Emersonian thesis—*Trust thyself* (because "every heart vibrates to that iron string" of intuition and confidence).

Emerson declared, "Whoso would be a man, must be a nonconformist." If nature reveals the moral truths of life, then people must focus on nature, humanity, and humanity's attitude toward nature.

Since "Nothing is at last sacred but the integrity of your own mind," people should "absolve you to yourself, and you shall have the suffrage of the world." Emerson continues....

"To believe your own thought, to believe that what is true for you in your private heart is true for all men,—that is genius… A man should learn to detect and watch that gleam of light which flashes across his mind from within, more than the luster of the firmament of bards and sages....

"There is a time in every man's education when he arrives at the conviction that envy is ignorance; that imitation is suicide; that he must take himself

The Write Stuff

Emerson's poems try to accomplish what his essays trumpet: the joining of people and nature. Although Emerson wrote relatively little poetry, he made up in impact what he lacked in bulk.

for better or for worse as his portion; that though the wide universe is full of good, no kernel of nourishing corn can come to him but through his toil bestowed on that plot of ground which is given to him to till. The power which resides in him is new in nature, and none but he knows what that is which he can do, nor does he know until he has tried…

"What I must do is all that concerns me, not what the people think. This rule, equally arduous in actual and in intellectual life, may serve for the whole distinction between greatness and meanness. It is the harder, because you will always find those who think they know what is your duty better than you know it. It is easy in the world to live after the world's opinion; it is easy in solitude to live after our own; but the great man is he who in the midst of the crowd keeps with perfect sweetness the independence of solitude."

"Self-Reliance" shows Emerson looking inward, but many of his poems and essays also look outward to explore how Transcendentalism applied to current events. The "Hymn Sung at the Completion of the Concord Monument, April 19, 1836," for example, is Emerson's reaction to a key event in American history.

Hymn Sung at the Completion of the Concord Monument, April 19, 1836

This is one of Emerson's most popular poems, probably because it's a real toe-tapper. Emerson wrote it for the dedication of a monument to those who fought at the Battle of Concord, so it has a predictable format:

➤ Opening: Why the poem was written

➤ Middle: Comment on the passage of time

➤ Close: Inspiring words to live by

Take a minute to read this classic gem of American literature:

"By the rude bridge that arched the flood,
Their flag to April's breeze unfurled,
Here once the embattled farmers stood,
And fired the shot heard round the world.

The foe long since in silence slept;
Alike the conqueror silent sleeps;
And Time the ruined bridge has swept
Down the dark stream which seaward creeps.

On this green bank, by this soft stream,
We set to-day a votive stone;
That memory may their deed redeem,
When, like our sires, our sons are gone.

Spirit, that made those heroes dare
To die, or leave their children free,
Bid Time and Nature gently spare
The shaft we raise to them and thee."

Emerson was the first to define what made American poetry American—it is verse that celebrates ordinary experience rather than the epic themes of the past. In addition, American poetry focuses on facts rather than eloquence. As a result, the poet of democracy should be equal parts prophet, oracle, visionary, and seer. Scorning imitators, the poet should create verse that is fresh and new. Emerson pointed the way to a unique "American" voice in poetry, but it was Walt Whitman (Chapter 13) who finished the job.

Lit Wit

To his credit, Emerson was one of the first established poets to support Whitman and his original verse. For a long time, he was the only mainstream supporter Whitman had.

Master of His Domain

"Life is not so short but that there is always time enough for courtesy."

—*from* "Letters and Social Aims"

Unlike Henry David Thoreau, Emerson's cantankerous homeboy and sometime handyman, Emerson was a jovial and generous fellow who enjoyed a wide circle of friends. Emerson was so well liked, for example, that when his house burned to the ground in 1877, his friends and admirers sent him on an all-expense-paid vacation to Europe and Egypt. The house was rebuilt in his absence—at his friends' expense.

Emerson's mind collapsed before his body, and he spent the last decades of his life in benign senility, beloved as a prophet of individualism, idealism, optimism, and self-confidence. I'll let his own words stand as his testimonial:

"Whatever you do, you need courage. Whatever course you decide upon, there is always someone to tell you that you are wrong. There are always difficulties arising that tempt you to believe your critics are right. To map out a course of action and follow it to an end requires some of the same courage that a soldier needs. Peace has its victories, but it takes brave men and women to win them."

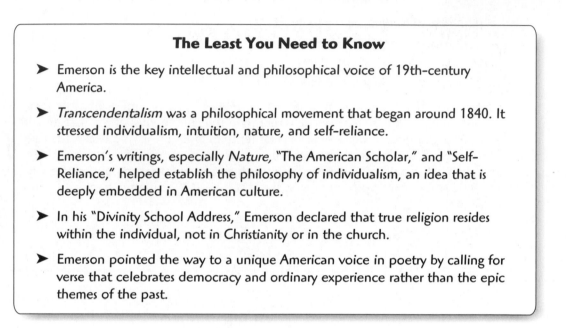

The Least You Need to Know

➤ Emerson is the key intellectual and philosophical voice of 19th-century America.

➤ *Transcendentalism* was a philosophical movement that began around 1840. It stressed individualism, intuition, nature, and self-reliance.

➤ Emerson's writings, especially *Nature,* "The American Scholar," and "Self-Reliance," helped establish the philosophy of individualism, an idea that is deeply embedded in American culture.

➤ In his "Divinity School Address," Emerson declared that true religion resides within the individual, not in Christianity or in the church.

➤ Emerson pointed the way to a unique American voice in poetry by calling for verse that celebrates democracy and ordinary experience rather than the epic themes of the past.

Nature Boy: Henry David Thoreau (1817–1862)

"There is no more fatal blunder than he who consumes the greater part of his life getting his living. All great enterprises are self-supporting."

—Thoreau, *from* "Life Without Principle"

To his neighbors in Concord, Massachusetts, Henry David Thoreau was a washout: a Harvard graduate who spent his days loafing around. When he wasn't wandering aimlessly through the woods, however, Thoreau was home writing; and every now and again, he'd help out at his father's pencil factory. After a brief stint teaching, he also did a little surveying. In 1842, Thoreau moved into Ralph Waldo Emerson's house, where he stayed for two years, doing odd jobs to pay his room and board.

Occasionally Thoreau earned a nominal fee for lecturing in small towns—charming audiences with his Yankee wit, instructing them on ecology, or lecturing them on the evils of slavery.

In 1849 at his own expense, Thoreau printed 1,000 copies of his first book, *A Week on the Concord and Merrimack Rivers;* 275 books sold, while the rest served as attic insulation. His second book, *Walden,* didn't make the best-seller list either when it was published in 1854: A total of seven copies sold, most of them to his mother. Even Emerson, his closest friend, thought Thoreau was drifting off-course. (However, Emerson did buy copies of both his books.)

Thoreau never married, and though he was briefly engaged to Ellen Sewall in 1840, he isn't known to have had a lover of either sex. So how did this seeming ne'er-do-well manage to snatch victory from the jaws of defeat? How did a rarely employed handyman become a major player in American literature? Read on to find out.

Oh Henry!

Thoreau wasn't drifting: Rather, his entire life was a deliberate effort to live precisely the way he wanted. While the world lived by one definition of success, Thoreau lived by quite a different one, and his writing won for itself a permanence that belied the scorn of his contemporaries.

Thoreau acted out the dictates of his conscience with a determination unsettling to those living more cautious and conventional lives. For example, while Emerson and most of the other transcendentalists were mum on the issue of slavery, Thoreau was helping runaway slaves escape to Canada. And Thoreau was the first American writer to speak on behalf of John Brown, delivering his fiery "Plea for Captain John Brown" in 1859.

Writer's Block

Watch what you say when you check out of this world for the next one: Thoreau's last words were "Moose. Indians." Disappointing, no? His next-to-last words, however, are worth quoting. When asked if he had made his peace with God, Henry replied, "I was not aware that we had ever quarreled."

Lit Wit

John Brown (1800–59) was actively hostile to slavery his entire life. In 1855, Brown followed his five sons to Kansas Territory, the epicenter of the slavery struggle. Under his leadership, the family took arms against marauding proslavery terrorists from Missouri who had murdered a group of abolitionists. On May 14, 1856, Brown and his sons avenged the murders by killing the proslavery agitators. Emboldened by his success, Brown plotted to free the slaves by armed forces. He launched his attack on October 16, 1859, by seizing the U.S. Arsenal at Harpers Ferry, Virginia. The militia, led by Robert E. Lee, marched in and killed 10 of Brown's 21 men. Convicted of treason and murder, Brown was hanged on December 2, 1859. An instant martyr, he became the subject of the federal soldiers' marching song, "John Brown," whose "body lies a-mouldering in the grave" but whose "soul goes marching on."

When Thoreau died of tuberculosis at the age of 44, his writing had received little notice. By the 1930s, however, Thoreau had gained the status of a major American writer; in the next decades, his reputation eclipsed that of Emerson's.

Today, Thoreau is revered by an astonishingly wide array of people, including social and political leaders and environmentalists.

A Travel Guide for the Mind: *Walden*

"I went to the woods because I wished to live deliberately, to front only the essential facts of life, and see if I could not learn what it had to teach, and not, when I came to die, discover that I had not lived a true account of it in my next excursion."

From 1845 to 1847, Thoreau lived near Walden Pond in a small cabin he built himself. To each his own, of course, but why not just join the Boy Scouts? Thoreau was very clear on this point:

"I wanted to live deep and suck out all the marrow of life, to live so sturdily and Spartanlike as to put to rout all that was not life, to cut a broad swath and shave close, to drive life into a corner, and reduce it to its lowest terms, and, if it proved to be mean, why then to get the whole and genuine meanness of it, and publish its meanness to the world; or if it were sublime, to know it by experience, and be able to give a true account of it in my next excursion."

Walden shows the reader how to live wisely in a world designed to make wise living impossible. Packed with brief fables, allegories, aphorisms, and puns, Walden demonstrates that happiness can be yours if you're willing to throw away the Rolex, the Armani wardrobe, the Mercedes, and grow your own beans.

Hello, I Came to Say...

Never one to overlook a chance to make a point, Thoreau moved to Walden Pond on July 4, 1845, the date representing his personal declaration of independence from society's numbing materialism. The move enabled him to commune with nature and devote more time to his writing. The book spans one year and was first published on August 9, 1854.

The Write Stuff

Although Thoreau's writing received little notice during his life, he is now recognized as a masterful prose stylist. The strength of Thoreau's writing results from his aphoristic sentences, his brief allegories, his striking metaphors, and his use of rhetorical devices such as repetition, parallelism, and rhetorical questions. Many of these stylistic techniques are evident in the excerpts included here.

Writer's Block

Thoreau chose a life of deliberate simplicity and relative poverty, but he had the benefit of a Harvard education and a well-off family. Don't forget that he had a good fall-back: the pencil business that his father had established.

Some believe that Thoreau went to live at Walden Pond because he was a hermit or a recluse, but it just ain't so.

Thoreau went to Walden to see if he could live deliberately and simply, to make the philosophy of transcendentalism into reality. He realized that…

"Our life is frittered away by detail. An honest man has hardly need to count more than his ten fingers, or in extreme cases he may add his ten toes, and lump the rest. Simplicity, simplicity, simplicity! I say, let your affairs be as two or three, and not a hundred or a thousand; instead of a million count half a dozen, and keep your accounts on your thumbnail."

And he meant every word of it.

I Cannot Stay

Thoreau lived at Walden Pond for two years, two months, and two days. The experiment completed, Thoreau decided it was time to move on. "I left the woods for as good a reason as I went there," he wrote.

"Perhaps it seemed to me that I had several more lives to live, and could not spare any more time for that one. It is remarkable how easily and insensibly we fall into a particular route, and make a beaten track for ourselves. I had not lived there a week before my feet wore a path from my door to the pondside; and though it is five or six years since I trod it, it is still quite distinct. It is true, I fear that others may have fallen into it, and so helped to keep it open. The surface of the earth is soft and impressionable by the feet of men; and so with the paths which the mind travels. How worn and dusty, then, must be the highways of the world, how deep the ruts of tradition and conformity! I did not wish to take a cabin passage, but rather to go before the mast and on the deck of the world, for there I could best see the moonlight amid the mountains."

Cream of the Crop

Walden is Thoreau's masterpiece, a unique blend of natural observation, social criticism, and philosophical insight. Now considered the treasure of the transcendental mother lode, *Walden* is also unquestionably one of the classics of American literature.

For example, in 1954, the essayist and children's book writer E.B. White wrote an article in honor of the 100-year anniversary of the publication of *Walden:*

"It may very well be the oddest of our distinguished oddities… Many think it is a sermon; many set it down as an attempt to rearrange society; some think it an exercise in nature-loving; some find it a rather irritating collection of inspirational puffballs by an eccentric showoff. I think it none of these. It still seems to me the best youth's companion yet written by an American, for it carries a solemn warning against the loss of one's valuables, it advances a good argument for traveling light and trying new adventures, it rings with the power of positive adoration, it contains religions feelings without religious images, and it steadfastly refuses to record bad news."

Imitation Is the Sincerest Form of Flattery

During Thoreau's life, his writings were known to only a small group of people. Today, however, his place in American letters is secure. Thoreau's account of his time at Walden Pond has inspired legions of people to try their hand at simplifying their lives and getting close to nature. Annie Dillard, for example, spent a year in a small cabin on Tinker Creek in West Virginia. She described her experiences in *Pilgrim at Tinker Creek,* which won a Pulitzer Prize in 1975.

"I propose," she announces in the first chapter, "to keep here what Thoreau called a 'meteorological journal of the mind,' telling some tales and describing some of the sights of this rather tamed valley, and exploring, in fear and trembling, some of the unmapped dim reaches and unholy fastness of which these tales and sights so dizzingly lead."

Another contemporary writer, Anne Morrow Lindbergh, also felt Thoreau's siren call to a simple life. In *The Gift from the Sea* (1955), Lindbergh says, "I mean to live a simple life, to choose an ample shell I can carry easily—like the hermit crab." Unlike Dillard, however, Lindbergh found such a life impossible in the modern world. "I find that my frame of life does not foster simplicity. The life I have chosen as wife and mother entrains a whole caravan of complications… For life today in America is based on the premise of ever widening circles of contact and communication… This is not the life of simplicity but the life of multiplicity that the wise men warn of. It does not bring grace; it destroys the soul."

The Write Stuff

Many scholars consider Thoreau to be the father of the American conservation and preservation movements. Thoreau laid out his ideas of conservation and preservation in his essay "Walking." There, he claims, "in Wildness is the preservation of the world."

On the Duty of Civil Disobedience

From 1846 to 1848, the United States had a nasty little spat with Mexico over the boundary between Mexico and Texas and Mexico's stubborn refusal to sell us those sweet states, California and New Mexico. Thoreau strongly objected to the war on several fronts, not the least being his belief that President James K. Polk had lit the powder keg before getting Congress' approval.

In 1846, the town constable asked Thoreau to pay his poll tax. Thoreau flat-out refused to ante up what he owed—$1.50—thus showing his disapproval of the war and the enforcement of slavery laws. Push came to shove, and Thoreau landed in jail. That evening, Henry's Aunt Maria Thoreau paid the bill, and Thoreau was forced to leave the joint. Enraged that he hadn't been allowed to continue his protest under lockdown, Thoreau turned to his pen.

The Last Straw

The result was what has become one of the most important political essays ever, "On the Duty of Civil Disobedience."

In that essay, Thoreau writes,

"I heartily accept the motto, 'That government is best which governs least'; and I should like to see it acted up to more rapidly and systematically. Carried out, it finally amounts to this, which also I believe—'That government is best which governs not at all'; and when men are prepared for it, that will be the kind of government which they will have.

Government is at best but an expedient; but most governments are usually, and all governments are sometimes, inexpedient. The objections which have been brought against a standing army, and they are many and weighty, and deserve to prevail, may also at last be brought against a standing government. The standing army is only an arm of the standing government. The government itself, which is only the mode which the people have chosen to execute their will, is equally liable to be abused and perverted before the people can act through it. Witness the present Mexican war, the work of comparatively a few individuals using the standing government as their tool; for in the outset, the people would not have consented to this measure."

Unjust laws exist; shall we be content to obey them, or shall we endeavor to amend them, and obey them until we have succeeded, or shall we transgress them at once?… I do not hesitate to say, that those who call themselves abolitionists should at once effectively withdraw their support, both in person and property, from the government of Massachusetts, and not wait till they constitute a majority of one, before they suffer the right to prevail through them… Moreover, any man more right than his neighbors, constitutes a majority of one already.

After all, the practical reason why, when the power is once in the hands of the people, a majority are permitted, and for a long period continue, to rule is not because they are most likely to be in the right, nor because this seems fairest to the minority, but because they are physically the strongest. But a government in which the majority rule in all cases can not be based on justice, even as far as men understand it. Can there not be a government in which the majorities do not virtually decide right and wrong, but conscience? —in which majorities decide only those questions to which the rule of expediency is applicable? Must the citizen ever for a moment, or in the least degree, resign his conscience to the legislator? Why has every man a conscience then? I think that we should be men first, and subjects afterward. It is not desirable to cultivate a respect for the law, so much as for the right. The only obligation which I have a right to assume is to do at any time what I think right…

Men, generally, under such a government as this, think that they ought to wait until they have persuaded the majority to alter them. They think that, if they should resist, the remedy would be worse than the evil. But it is the fault of the government itself that the remedy is worse than the evil. It makes it worse. Why is it not more apt to anticipate and provide for reform? Why does it not cherish its wise minority? Why does it cry and resist before it is hurt? Why does it not encourage its citizens to put out its faults, and do better than it would have them? Why does it always crucify Christ and excommunicate Copernicus and Luther, and pronounce Washington and Franklin rebels?"

Lit Wit

During Thoreau's lifetime most people viewed him as an extreme eccentric lacking both ambition and direction. However, Thoreau was undaunted by the scorn of others and continued to live his life exactly as he pleased. In the following excerpt from his essay "life without Principle, "Thoreau conveyed his belief in the need to assert one's individuality in the face of society's demands:

"If a man walks in the woods for love of them half of each day, he is in danger of being regarded as a loafer; but if he spends his whole day as a speculator, shearing off these woods and making the earth bald before her time, he is esteemed an industrious and enterprising citizen. As if a town had no interest in its forests but to cut them down!"

Power to the People

"Civil Disobedience" influenced some of the world's greatest leaders, including Mohandas "Mahatma" Gandhi, Martin Luther King, Jr., and Nelson Mandela. Here are a few examples of Thoreau's influence:

➤ In 1906, Mohandas Gandhi adapted Thoreau's ideas on civil disobedience as the core of his campaign for Indian independence from the British Empire.

➤ In 1955, the Reverend Martin Luther King, Jr. used Thoreau's ideas on civil disobedience to organize the Montgomery, Alabama, bus boycott. From this came the civil rights movement of the 1960s. The 1963 March on Washington alone drew 250,000 participants.

➤ The Salvadoran people transformed Thoreau's ideas on civil disobedience into stage occupations and sit-ins at universities, government offices, factories, and haciendas to achieve their civil rights.

➤ Opponents of the Vietnam War adapted Thoreau's ideas on civil disobedience as they burned draft cards, blocked induction centers, and demonstrated nonviolently.

➤ Since the 1970s, nonviolent civil disobedience actions have occurred at dozens of nuclear weapons research installations, storage areas, missile silos, test sites, military bases, corporate and government offices, and nuclear power plants.

➤ In the 1980s, Nelson Mandela led the South African anti-apartheid movement, using Thoreau's "Civil Disobedience" as a blueprint.

➤ Student activists in South Africa incorporated civil disobedience into their anti-apartheid protests, building shantytowns and staging sit-ins at administrator's offices. Their efforts resulted in the divestment of over 130 campuses and the subsequent withdrawal of over $4 billion from the South African economy.

➤ Nonviolent resistance has been an integral part of the lesbian and gay community since 1987, when ACT UP (AIDS Coalition to Unleash Power) was formed.

The Least You Need to Know

➤ Thoreau resisted materialism and chose a life of simplicity, close to nature.

➤ *Walden* is a guidebook for life, showing the reader how to live wisely in a world designed to make wise living impossible.

➤ "On the Duty of Civil Disobedience" has become a primer for nonviolent protest, used by Gandhi, King, Mandela, and many others.

Chapter 9

Nate the Great: Nathaniel Hawthorne (1804–1864)

In This Chapter

➤ Nathaniel Hawthorne's life

➤ Hawthorne's *The Scarlet Letter*

➤ Hawthorne's main themes: sin and guilt

➤ The "romance"

➤ Hawthorne's short stories

➤ "Young Goodman Brown"

"What do you think of my becoming an author and relying for support on my pen? Indeed, I think the illegibility of my handwriting is very author-like."

—Nathaniel Hawthorne *in a letter written while at college*

Nathaniel Hawthorne managed to scrape out a living as a writer. Along the way, he did for adultery what Poe did for death and gore, Thoreau for nature, and Melville for the sea. Obsessed with sin and guilt, Hawthorne was the first great American writer of psychological fiction.

In this chapter, you'll learn all about Hawthorne's life and influences. There's also a complete discussion of his masterpiece, *The Scarlet Letter,* and an explanation of the literary genre of romance. You'll also learn about his short stories by focusing on one of his most famous tales, "Young Goodman Brown." By the end of this chapter, you'll understand how Hawthorne raised sin and guilt to an art form.

Begin at the Very Beginning

Fellow novelist Henry James once described Nathaniel Hawthorne at a New York dinner party of literary people as looking like "a rogue who suddenly finds himself in a company of detectives." Henry was a good host, but even he couldn't have made Hawthorne feel comfortable with strangers, even those who plied the same trade. Perhaps Hawthorne's uneasiness came from his family, which had more skeletons than clothing in their closets.

Nathaniel Hawthorne's first American ancestor, William Hathorne, was a magistrate who once had a Quaker woman publicly whipped in the streets.

William's son, John Hathorne, inherited his father's kindly touch. As the infamous "Hanging Judge" of Salem, he presided over the 1692 witchcraft trials, during which an accused witch cursed him with the cry, "God will give you blood to drink!" Small wonder the Hawthorns added a *w* to the family name—can you blame them for wanting to put some distance between themselves and *these* relatives?

Hawthorne's childhood was no picnic. When Nathaniel was four, his seafaring father died while on a voyage to Surinam, Dutch Guinea. The family lived in genteel poverty. However, Hawthorne's mother's family came through with the tuition for Bowdoin College.

Lit Wit

Hawthorne made friends with a number of his classmates, many of whom went on to important literary and political careers, including writer Horatio Bridge, Senator Jonathan Ciley, writer Henry Wadsworth Longfellow, and President Franklin Pierce. The group stayed close, and when times got tough for Nate, his buddies pitched in with jobs on Uncle Sam's payroll.

Doing Hard Time

After graduating from college in 1825, Hawthorne returned home to become a writer. As so often happens, fame didn't come quickly: It took Hawthorne three years before he published his first book—and at his own expense, at that. The year was 1828; the book, *Fanshawe. Fanshawe* sank faster than a bowling ball. It took nine more years for Hawthorne to make an audible splash in the literary world: His collection of short stories, *Twice-Told Tales,* turned the trick.

In 1837, Hawthorne fell for Sophia Peabody, the 29-year-old girl next door. To earn enough money to marry, he took a job in 1839 at the Boston Custom House as salt and coal measurer, but lost his post in 1840 for political reasons.

Sophia drew Hawthorne into the transcendental movement, and in 1841 he invested $1,500 in the Brook Farm Utopian Community, moved in, but left disillusioned within a year.

Soon after, Nathaniel and Sophia married and moved to Concord. By all accounts, the marriage was idyllic, and his 1846 political appointment as surveyor of the port of Salem cemented his happiness. It's not surprising that Hawthorne was fit to be tied three years later when he was once again removed from office due to a change in political parties.

Writer's Block

Beware of publishing too soon—Hawthorne later formally withdrew most of this early work, discounting it as the work of inexperienced youth. He was right.

Revenge Is Sweet

This job loss prompted Hawthorne to return to writing, starting with a revenge essay he called "The Custom-House." The essay accomplished a dual purpose: It achieved his political revenge by depicting his enemies as dottering fools, while also serving as the prologue to *The Scarlet Letter*. The essay purports to explain how the narrator came to find a mysterious scarlet letter. Hawthorne wrote feverishly and completed *The Scarlet Letter* in a year. It was published in 1850.

The publishing company Ticknor & Fields agreed to publish *The Scarlet Letter* in 1850, and Hawthorne's powerful friends provided favorable reviews.

The novel was an immediate smash, selling 4,000 copies in the first ten days. Why the instant popularity? Because *The Scarlet Letter* addressed spiritual and moral issues from a uniquely American standpoint. (It's also not a bad read.) In 1850, adultery was a taboo subject, but because Hawthorne had the support of the New England literary establishment, the novel was released for public consumption.

Lit Wit

Franklin Pierce (1804–1869) was the fourteenth president of the United States and astonishingly undistinguished in the role.

On a roll, Hawthorne wrote and published *The House of the Seven Gables* (1851) and *The Blithedale Romance* (1852). They sold well. But despite his success, Hawthorne still didn't have enough cash to give up his day job, so when his college buddy Franklin Pierce, President of the U.S. at the time, offered him the American consulship in England, Hawthorne jumped.

The Hawthornes returned to America in 1860, and our hero set to work on another novel. But his strength was broken by poor health and his ideas just didn't come together. Hawthorne died of a heart attack in 1864 while on a walking tour of new Hampshire.

Nathaniel Hawthorne.

Gimme an A

The Scarlet Letter is Hawthorne's masterpiece and America's first true psychological novel. The novel represents the height of Hawthorne's literary genius and has held up over time as a classic tale with a universal theme.

As you learned earlier, *The Scarlet Letter* opens with "The Custom-House" essay, which describes how Hawthorne found in the Salem Custom House "a rag of scarlet cloth" shaped in "a letter 'A.'" It also explains how Hawthorne got information about Hester Prynne, the Puritan woman forced to wear an "A" for "Adultery." The "facts" about the "A" are as fictional as Hester herself, although history does record that some Puritans did carry on on the sly.

Meet the crowd:

➤ *Hester Prynne:* The proud, regal beauty who stands by her man and learns that love doesn't conquer all.

➤ *Roger Chillingworth:* Hester's chilly burger of a husband, who manages to wrest defeat from the jaws of victory.

➤ *The Reverend Arthur Dimmesdale:* Hester's lover.

➤ *Pearl:* The product of Hester's horizontal cha-cha with Dimmesdale.

➤ *Governor Bellingman:* His idea of a social program is putting up a new scaffold.

➤ *The Reverend Mr. John Wilson:* Would love to see the Inquisition catch on in the colonies.

➤ *Mistress Hibbins:* The governor's sister. She's a real witch—no kidding.

The Young and the Restless

As the story opens, a group of gossips are hanging around the jail, jeering at Hester Prynne, who has been convicted of the crime of adultery. The townspeople are furious that the court has been merciful toward Hester; instead of the promised public hanging, she has merely been condemned to wear a scarlet "A" on her chest and serve some jail time.

On this day, Hester and her infant Pearl (living proof of her sin) are forced to stand on the scaffold in shame. The word on the street is that Hester has been spared death only through the intercession of her minister, the Reverend Dimmesdale. Hester has refused to name her partner in pleasure, much to Dimmesdale's relief. On the edge of the crowd, there's an elderly, deformed man whom Hester recognizes—it's her husband! Two years earlier he had sent her alone to America, and she has never seen or heard from him since—until this moment.

Writer's Block

Wearing a letter wasn't actually the preferred punishment in colonial New England: Most adulterers, for instance, were branded, mutilated, or hanged for straying.

Have a taste of the novel for yourself. Here's how the story opens:

"I. The Prison-Door

A throng of bearded men, in sad-colored garments and gray steeple-crowned hats, intermixed with women, some wearing hoods, and others bareheaded, was assembled in front of a wooden edifice, the door of which was heavily timbered with oak, and studded with iron spikes.

The founders of a new colony, whatever Utopia of human virtue and happiness they might originally project, have invariably recognized it among their earliest practical necessities to allot a portion of the virgin soil as a cemetery, and another portion as the site of a prison. In accordance with this rule it may safely be assumed that the forefathers of Boston had built the first prison-house somewhere in the Vicinity of Cornhill, almost as seasonably as they marked out the first burial-ground, on Isaac Johnson's lot, and round about his grave, which subsequently became the nucleus of all the congregated sepulchers in the old church-yard of King's Chapel. Certain it is that, some fifteen or twenty years after the settlement of the town, the wooden jail was already marked with weather-stains and other indications of age, which gave a yet darker aspect to its beetle-browed and gloomy front. The rust on the ponderous iron-work of its oaken door looked more antique than anything else in the New World. Like all that pertains to crime, it seemed never to have known a youthful era. Before this ugly edifice, and between it and the wheel-track of the street, was a grass-plot, much overgrown with burdock, pig-weed, apple-pern, and such unsightly vegetation, which evidently found something congenial in the soil that had so early borne the black flower of civilized society, a prison. But on one side of the portal, and rooted almost at the threshold, was a wild rose-hush, covered, in this month of June, with its delicate gems, which might be imagined to offer their fragrance and fragile beauty to the prisoner as he went in, and to the condemned criminal as he came forth to his doom, in token that the deep heart of Nature could pity and be kind to him. This rose-bush, by a strange chance, has been kept alive in history; but whether it had merely survived out of the stern old wilderness, so long after the fall of the gigantic pines and oaks that originally overshadowed it, or whether, as there is far authority for believing, it had sprung up under the footsteps of the sainted Ann Hutchinson as she entered the prison-door, we shall not take upon us to determine. Finding it so directly on the threshold of our narrative, which is now about to issue from that inauspicious portal, we could hardly do otherwise than pluck one of its flowers, and present it to the reader. It may serve, let us hope, to symbolize some sweet moral blossom that may be found along the track, or relieve the darkening close of a tale of human frailty and sorrow."

The rosebush symbolizes Hester, the one spot of goodness and beauty in the bleak Puritan landscape.

What's Love Got to Do with It?

Soon after, Hester's husband demands that she reveal her lover's name. When she refuses, he vows revenge. He takes the name "Roger Chillingworth" to conceal his identity and swears Hester to secrecy. Hester and her daughter Pearl move to an isolated part of the village, where Hester earns their living sewing. No one will talk to her, but everyone lines up to buy her gorgeously embroidered items.

Hester dresses Pearl in outrageously gorgeous clothes, a clear nose-thumb at the town. The townspeople retaliate by declaring her an unfit mother and plan to take Pearl away to be raised by more suitable guardians. Dimmesdale again saves the day with a heartfelt appeal on Hester's behalf. Hester is allowed to keep her child.

Suspicious of Dimmesdale's motives, Chillingworth clings to him like a cheap suit. Dimmesdale is so consumed with guilt that he begins to physically decay. Shocked at

Dimmesdale's rapid decline, Hester tells him Chillingworth's identity. The lovers make plans to leave New England for Old England, but Chillingworth gets wind of their plans and books passage on the same boat.

A's not for Apple in This Town

Before the boat sails, Dimmesdale delivers the greatest sermon of his career, even though he looks like roadkill. After he finishes the speech, Dimmesdale calls Hester and Pearl to the scaffold with him, admits his guilt, tears aside his vestment, reveals his chest, and falls down dead. What's on his chest? Find out for yourself in this excerpt from Chapter XXIII, "The Revelation of the Scarlet Letter:"

> *"'People of New England!' cried he, with a voice that rose over them, high, solemn, and majestic,—yet had always a tremor through it, and sometimes a shriek, struggling up out of a fathomless depth of remorse and woe—'ye, that have loved me!—ye, that have deemed me holy!—behold me here, the one sinner of the world! At last—at last!—I stand upon the spot where, seven years since, I should have stood; here, with this woman, whose arm, more than the little strength wherewith I have crept hitherward, sustains me at this dreadful moment, from groveling down upon my face! Lo, the scarlet letter which Hester wears! Ye have all shuddered at it! Wherever her walk hath been—wherever, so miserably burdened, she may have hoped to find repose,—it hath cast a lurid gleam of awe and horrible repugnance round about her. But there stood one in the midst of you, at whose brand of sin and infamy ye have not shuddered!' ... Stand any here that question God's judgment on a sinner! Behold! Behold, a dreadful witness of it!'*
>
> *With a convulsive motion, he tore away the ministerial band from before his breast. It was revealed! But it were irreverent to describe that revelation. For an instant, the gaze of the horror-stricken multitude was concentrated on the ghastly miracle; while the minister stood, with a flush of triumph in his face, as one who, in the crisis of acutest pain, had won a victory. Then, down he sank upon the scaffold! Hester partly raised him, and supported his head against her bosom."*

So what *is* on Dimmesdale's chest? Some people swear there's a scarlet "A" burned into his breast; others dispute this. Chillingworth, deprived of his raison d'çetre, dies within the year. Hester and Pearl disappear, but years later Hester returns alone. It is thought that Pearl has married and moved to England. Hester lives quietly in her cottage until her death.

Once a sign of shame, by the end of the book (and Hester's saga), the "A" has become a symbol of mercy because of Hester's good deeds and great kindness. She nurses the sick, soothes the disconsolate, and comforts the lonely. At her death, Hester is buried beside Dimmesdale, their tombstone engraved with an "A."

Lit Wit

A creative group, the Puritans had letters of punishment for almost every crime. Those under the influence of Demon Rum got to stand in the town square with a large "D" (for "drunk") around their necks. Thieves were adorned with a big "T," and people who took the Lord's name in vain got a "B" for "blasphemy." But every now and again tragedy struck: Two crimes with the same initials would be committed! For example, since "I" was already taken for "incest," the Puritans were forced to improvise when some of their brethren did the nasty with Indians—they wore a cutout of an Indian on their arm for a year.

You Play, You Pay

The Scarlet Letter was praised for its "subtle knowledge of character" and "tragic power." Novelist Henry James (whom you'll meet in Chapter 19), called *The Scarlet Letter* "the finest piece of imaginative writing yet put forth in America."

The novel focuses on, you guessed it, sin and guilt, and their effect on the individual and society. For those of you who haven't tried on the Seven Deadly Sins for size, sinning isn't as simple as it seems: There are sins of passion and those of principle.

Dimmesdale understands the difference: "We are not, Hester, the worst sinners in the world. There is one worse than even the polluted priest! That old man's revenge has been blacker than my sin. He has violated, in cold blood, the sanctity of the human heart." Chillingworth is the true criminal because he has boldly gone where no one belongs—he violates another person's soul.

The Write Stuff

Poe, Hawthorne, and Melville are sometimes called the "dark romantics" for their bleak vision.

Hester, whose sin is revealed, grows through her suffering, comes to terms with her guilt, and reconciles herself with God. In contrast, Dimmesdale is tortured by secret guilt and cannot make peace with himself or with God. His guilt manifests itself physically, and it kills him.

What's the solution to secret suffering? Hawthorne tells us in Chapter XXIV, "Conclusion"—

"Among many morals which press upon us from the poor minister's miserable experience, we put only this into a sentence:—'Be true! Be true! Be true! Show freely to the world, if not your worst, yet some trait whereby the worst may be inferred!'"

Obsessed with the Puritan past, Hawthorne dallied with transcendentalism, but instead allied himself with the dark side of subjects. As a result, Hawthorne is closer in theme and tone to Herman Melville and Edgar Allan Poe than to Ralph Waldo Emerson and Henry David Thoreau.

Writing of his close friend Hawthorne, Herman Melville said, "…in spite of all the Indian-summer sunlight on the hither side of Hawthorne's soul, the other side—like the dark half of the physical sphere—is shrouded in blackness, ten times black."

Romancing the Novel

So how does Hawthorne get away with all the weirdness, like the "A" that appears (or doesn't appear) on Dimmesdale's chest, and other strange happenings? Easy—he doesn't claim to be writing a *novel*. Instead, he wrote a *romance*. So what's the difference?

Both novels and romances are works of imaginative fiction with multiple characters, but that's where the similarities end. Novels are realistic; romances aren't. In the 19th century, a romance was a prose narrative that told a fictional story that dealt with its subjects and characters in a symbolic, imaginative, and nonrealistic way. Typically, a romance deals with plots and people that are exotic, remote in time or place from the reader, and obviously imaginary.

The romance grants the author a certain leeway for melodrama and emotionality. In his preface to *The House of the Seven Gables*, Hawthorne wrote:

> *"When a writer calls his work a Romance, it need hardly be observed that he wishes to claim a certain latitude, both as to its fashion and material, which he would not have felt himself entitled to assume, had he professed to be writing a Novel. The latter form of composition is presumed to aim at a very minute fidelity, not merely to the possible, but to the probable and ordinary course of man's existence. The former… has fairly a right to present that truth under circumstances, to a great extent, of the writer's own choosing or creation."*

Lit Speak

A **narrative** is a story told in fiction, nonfiction, poetry, or drama. *Prose* is any writing that is not poetry or drama. A *prose narrative*, therefore, is a story told in the ordinary form of written language (rather than drama or poetry).

Short, but Not Sweet: Hawthorne's Stories

Today, *The Scarlet Letter* is firmly enshrined in America's soul as a classic of the first order, but Hawthorne's short stories deserve more than a passing nod.

His most famous short stories include

➤ "The Artist of the Beautiful"

➤ "The Birthmark"

➤ "The Celestial Railroad"

➤ "Ethan Brand"

➤ "Feathertop: A Moralized Legend"

➤ "The Minister's Black Veil"

➤ "My Kinsman, Major Molineux"

➤ "Rappaccini's Daughter"

➤ "Roger Malvin's Burial"

➤ "Young Goodman Brown"

Unlike many of the writers of his day, Hawthorne was not interested in social and worldy matters; instead, he burrowed "into the depths of our common nature," as he said. What he found there often saddened and even shocked him. It will do the same to you, as "Young Goodman Brown" shows.

Lit Speak

Goodman and **Goodwoman** (often abbreviated **Goody**) were the Puritan equivalents of Mr. and Mrs.

A Walk on the Wild Side

Story: Young Goodman Brown

Time: 1600s

Place: Salem, Massachusetts

At sunset, young Goodman Brown leaves his wife, Faith, and spends a haunting night in the forest, where he realizes the town's most respected men and women are secretly in league with the devil.

Here's how the story begins:

"Young Goodman Brown came forth at sunset, into the street of Salem village, but put his head back, after crossing the threshold, to exchange a parting kiss with his young wife. And Faith, as the wife was aptly named, thrust her own pretty head into the street, letting the wind play with the pink ribbons of her cap, while she called to Goodman Brown.

'Dearest heart,' whispered she, softly and rather sadly, when her lips were close to his ear, 'pr'y thee, put off your journey until sunrise, and sleep in your own bed to-night. A lone woman is troubled with such dreams and such thoughts, that she's afeard of herself, sometimes. Pray, tarry with me this night, dear husband, of all nights in the year!'

'My love and my Faith,' replied young Goodman Brown, 'of all nights in the year, this one night must I tarry away from thee. My journey, as thou callest it, forth and back again, must needs be done 'twixt now and sunrise. What, my sweet, pretty wife, dost thou doubt me already, and we but three months married!'

'Then God bless you!' said Faith, with the pink ribbons, 'and may you find all well, when you come back.'

'Amen!' cried Goodman Brown. 'Say thy prayers, dear Faith, and go to bed at dusk, and no harm will come to thee.'"

Well, some harm does indeed come to Faith—she's lost forever. That's because "faith" operates on a symbolic and literal level: "Faith" is Goodman Brown's wife and "faith" is Goodman Brown's religious belief:

"'Poor little Faith!' thought he, for his heart smote him. 'What a wretch am I, to leave her on such an errand! She talks of dreams, too. Methought, as she spoke, there was trouble in her face, as if a dream had warned her what work is to be done tonight. But, no, no! 'twould kill her to think it. Well; she's a blessed angel on earth; and after this one night, I'll cling to her skirts and follow her to Heaven.'"

The Write Stuff

Nathaniel Hawthorne and Herman Melville have been labeled "anti-transcendentalists" because they focused on the limitations and potential destructiveness of the human spirit rather than on its possibilities. The characters in their novels and stories all have deep flaws, and these are usually the points on which the story turns.

Shades of Gray

Goodman Brown—Mr. Everyman—returns home with his faith shattered, his belief in goodness gone:

"A stern, a sad, a darkly meditative, a distrustful, if not a desperate man, did he become, from the night of that fearful dream. On the Sabbath-day, when the congregation were singing a holy psalm, he could not listen, because an anthem of sin rushed loudly upon his ear, and drowned all the blessed strain… Often, awaking suddenly at midnight, he shrank from the bosom of Faith, and at morning or eventide, when the family knelt down at prayer, he scowled, and muttered to himself, and gazed sternly at his wife, and turned away."

The story's central ambiguity concerns the events in the forest: Are they real or just a dream? Hawthorne is deliberately ambiguous, filling the story with words such as "seemed," "perhaps," and "appeared." "Young Goodman Brown" can be read several ways. Here are the three most common interpretations:

➤ An indictment of Puritan hypocrisy

➤ A study of sexual awareness and guilt

➤ A reenactment of Adam and Eve's temptation by the devil

This ambiguity conveys Hawthorne's theme: There's no clear-cut line between good and evil. Sound familiar? It's the theme of all his works, short stories and novels alike.

Lit Speak

"Young Goodman Brown" is an **allegory**—a story in which the characters, setting, and action represent abstract concepts apart from their literal meaning.

The Least You Need to Know

➤ *The Scarlet Letter,* as with all of Hawthorne's works, is about people who are torn between the tragic evil of human nature and a human sympathy for our natural passions.

➤ Hawthorne cornered the market on sin and guilt, including the consequences of pride, selfishness, and concealed culpability.

➤ Hawthorne did romance as the Colonel does chicken. Remember that a romance is a work of fiction that, in Hawthorne's own words, "claims a certain latitude" with the ordinary course of human experience.

➤ Hawthorne also showed keen psychological insights that paved the way for his friend Herman Melville and the 20th-century Southern novelist William Faulkner, among others.

Chapter 10

Just Don't Call Me Hermie: Herman Melville (1819–1891)

In This Chapter

➤ Herman Melville's (lousy) life

➤ The plot of Melville's *Moby Dick*

➤ The meaning of Melville's *Moby Dick*

➤ The plot of Melville's "Bartleby the Scrivener"

➤ The meaning of Melville's "Bartleby the Scrivener"

"Herman Melville died yesterday at his residence, 104 East Twenty-sixth Street, this city, of heart failure, aged seventy-two. He was the author of Typee, Omoo, Mobie Dick, [Moby Dick] and other sea-faring tales, written in earlier years. He leaves a wife and two daughters, Mrs. M.B. Thomas and Miss Melville."

—*in The* New York Times, *September 29, 1891*

One of America's greatest writers—arguably the greatest—rated a mere three sentences in The *New York Times* when he died.

The *New York Herald's* obituary gave him even less space—and they spelled his name wrong. His last novel, *The Confidence Man*, had been published more than three decades earlier. By his death, all his books were out of print. Melville was virtually forgotten by the time he died.

But 44 years before his death, when his most famous tale, *Typee*, appeared, Herman Melville was the best-known writer in America. Publishers fought over him, and editors

The Write Stuff

In the mood for something a little different? Why not visit Melville's grave the next time you're in the Big Apple? He's buried next to his wife, Elizabeth Shaw, in Woodlawn Cemetery, Bronx, New York.

considered themselves fortunate to secure his books to add to their lists. What happened to send his career into eclipse? How did it get resuscitated? That's what you'll learn in this chapter.

Man Overboard

Herman Melville made his debut August 1, 1819, the third child of Allan Melvill, a prosperous importer of elegant French goods. Both Allan and his wife, the former Maria Gansevoort, came from money and often made the New York scene. Long on charm but short on sense, Allan plundered his inheritance to stave off bankruptcy, but by 1830 the till was empty.

Creditors stormed the gates two days after Herman's 11 birthday. By then there were 11 little Melvills, meaning lots of shoes to buy. Mentally and physically wrecked, Allan died two years later. Left in financial limbo, the family moved to a small town near Troy, New York. Eager to get a fresh start, Maria doctored the family name, adding an *e* at the end. With the stroke of a pen, the *Mevills* became the *Melvilles*.

Herman's education can most charitably be described as "uneven," since he wasn't keen on studying. His mother noted in a letter at the time…that her darling "does not appear so fond of his Books as to injure his Health." Not wanting to throw good money after bad, his mother yanked him from school when he was just 12 years old. Herman then worked at a variety of menial jobs to help feed the family kitty.

When he was 18, Herman tried his hand at teaching, but between his rambunctious students and demanding mother, Herman decided it was time for a change. He signed on at the *St. Lawrence,* a British merchant ship. Herman managed to stretch his initial voyage into five years, but the boat finally docked. Herman headed west, but the family's mail still got through.

In 1841, in his early 20s, Herman handed over responsibility for his mother to his brother and set sail for the Pacific aboard a whaling ship.

Club Med, Circa 1800

A whaler's life isn't all guns and roses, however, so Melville and a shipmate jumped ship at the Marquesas Islands. After a brief stay with a cheerful group of natives who turned out to be a cheerful group of cannibals, Melville escaped on an Australian whaler, hopping off at Tahiti. From there, it was a simple hitch to Hawaii and then home. In 1844, Melville sat down to write about his exotic adventures.

The Man Who Had Lived Among the Cannibals

Typee and *Omoo,* Melville's novels of cannibal banquets and nubile slave girls, delighted readers and reviewers alike. The *Brooklyn Eagle's* literary critic, none other than the star of Chapter 12, Walt Whitman, called *Omoo* "thorough entertainment." But Melville yearned to write about more serious themes and ideas.

A few years later, Melville married Elizabeth Shaw and settled in New York City. Flush with success and love, he wrote *Mardi,* a complex allegorical novel that turned off his fans. Instead of celebrating, they clamored for Melville to bring back the hula girls. Melville consented, producing *Redburn* and *White Jacket.* With his bank balance back in the black, Melville bought a 160-acre Massachusetts farm. Despairing that he was doomed to be remembered as "the man who had lived among the cannibals," Melville wrote *Moby Dick.* This was a great career move in the long run—but not in the short term.

All Washed Up

Reviews were poor, and *Moby Dick* didn't sell. The novel was panned by every critic except Melville's friend Nathaniel Hawthorne, who courageously said that he liked it. Demand for the book was virtually nil, and it was not reprinted for 60 years.

Lit Wit

Melville dedicated *Moby Dick* to his friend Nathaniel Hawthorne, who wrote the sole glowing review.

Hurt by the criticism, Melville attacked the hand that fed him—his loyal reading public—in his next novel, *Pierre.* The following review was typical of the scorn heaped upon the novel:

> *"Mr. Melville has to thank himself only if his horrors and his heroics are flung aside by the general reader, as so much trash belonging to the worst school of Bedlam literature—since he seems not so much unable to learn as disdainful of learning the craft of an artist."*

> —Henry F. Chorley, in the *London Athenaeum,* October 25, 1851

One reviewer got right to the point: "Herman Melville [is] Crazy!" he shrieked. His reputation in decline, Melville suffered a breakdown. After recovering he wrote several other novels, but his career was over as far as the reading public was concerned.

His health and will shattered, Melville never again ventured into the literary market-place. To keep his family solvent, he took a job as a New York City customs inspector for a daily pay of $4. He detested the job but worked there for two decades until an inheritance enabled him to retire. Melville died in 1891 in obscurity.

Not So Fast

The story of Melville's literary resurrection is one of the strangest in American literature. It began in England shortly before his death and was strong enough to give Melville hope that his work would indeed have a permanent place on the Great Books Shelf.

The revival gathered steam in 1919, on the centennial of his birth. After a laudatory biography was published in 1921, Melville started moving up the ranks. He was seen as a symbol of artistic integrity—a true talent rejected and destroyed by the petty minds of his time. The new myth was itself a distortion, of course, but it was strong enough to move Melville up the literary ranks.

From the 1940s to 1950s, Melville Mania reigned in the academic world as his novel, stories, and poems were celebrated. Although Melville had burned many of his letters, and his surviving child, Frances, was so bitter against her father that she refused to speak about him, the Melville machine continued to churn out biographies, critical studies, and articles. He became a pop-culture icon as well: Seafood restaurants, comic books, and cartoons bore the mark of his fearsome white whale. Today, Melville's reputation is firmly secure.

A Whale of a Tale: *Moby Dick*

Upon completing his masterpiece, *Moby Dick,* Herman Melville wrote to his friend Nathaniel Hawthorne, "I have just written a very wicked book."

When Melville began writing it in May of 1850, *Moby Dick* seemed destined to be another relatively simple adventure narrative in the manner of *Typee* or *Redburn*, "a romance of adventure, founded upon certain wild legends of the Southern Sperm Whale Fisheries, and illustrated by the author's own personal experience, of two years and more, as a harpooner," Melville told his publisher. That August, his publisher noted that the story was "a romantic, fanciful and literal and most enjoyable presentment of the Whale Fishery—something quite new."

Melville had promised his publisher that the book would be ready the following autumn, and he dreadfully needed the money. Nevertheless, he spent an entire year rewriting the novel. Clearly, along the way, *Moby Dick* morphed from a straightforward adventure story into something quiet different—and better.

Now let's meet the crew:

> ➤ *Captain Ahab:* Crazed, one-legged hero-villain whose defiant quest for revenge on the whale drives the book.

The Write Stuff

Mocha Dick, the "White Whale of the Pacific," was a real white sperm whale that had become infamous among whalers for its violent attacks on ships and their crews. The whale was often sighted in the vicinity of the island of Mocha—hence its first name. *Dick* was merely a generic name like *Tom, Dick,* or *Harry.* No one is sure how *Mocha* became *Moby,* however. Melville himself remained mum on the issue.

➤ *Ishmael:* The narrator—compassionate, intelligent, and not hard on the eyes.

➤ *Starbuck:* The mate who fights the destiny Ahab has carved out for him.

➤ *Stubb:* Joe Average Sailor—no brain surgeon, but handy in a pinch.

➤ *Flask:* A materialistic blockhead.

➤ *Queequeg:* A huge cannibal, handy with a harpoon.

➤ *Pip:* A small black man driven mad by whales in particular and life in general.

➤ *Fedellah:* The harpooner who represents pure evil. (He also needed a good orthodontist.)

Writer's Block

Unlike iguana, frog, and other exotic meats the servers try to foist on you at trendy restaurants, whale tastes like beef (not chicken).

Cruising for a Bruising

The narrator, identified only as *Ishmael,* believes that the sea is a fine mistress and sets about to learn more of her mysteries. The novel's opening is very famous:

"Call me Ishmael. Some years ago—never mind how long precisely—having little or no money in my purse, and nothing particular to interest me on shore, I thought I would sail about a little and see the watery part of the world. It is a way I have of driving off the spleen, and regulating the circulation. Whenever I find myself growing grim about the mouth; whenever it is a damp, drizzly November in my soul; whenever I find myself involuntarily pausing before coffin warehouses, and bringing up the rear of every funeral I meet; and especially whenever my hypos get such an upper hand of me, that it requires a strong moral principle to prevent me from deliberately stepping into the street, and methodically knocking people's hats off—then, I account it high time to get to sea as soon as I can. This is my substitute for pistol and ball."

Unfortunately, his first night in New Bedford, Ishmael ends up rooming with a South Seas cannibal named Queequeg. The next day, Ishmael and Queequeg sign on the *Pequod.* They hear strange rumors about their captain, Ahab, who is confined to his cabin by some vague illness.

The *Pequod* sails, but it's not until they hit the South Seas that Ishmael catches a glimpse of Ahab, his white peg leg anchored in a hole in the deck. Ahab summons the crew to the quarter deck and explains their mission: to hunt down the great white whale Moby Dick, who chomped off his leg during his last voyage. Ahab gives the crew a pep talk:

The Write Stuff

In the book of Genesis, Ishmael is the outcast son of Abraham, the patriarch of the Jews. By using the name Ishmael for his narrator, Melville adopts the fictional posture of an outcast son.

"Now, three to three, ye stand. Commend the murderous chalices! Bestow them, ye who are now made parties to this indissoluble league… Drink, ye harpooners! drink and swear, ye men that man the deathful whaleboat's bow—Death to Moby Dick! God hunt us all, if we do not hunt Moby Dick to his death!"

When he hears more of the story of Ahab's pas de deux with the whale, Ishmael finds out that Moby Dick is a whale to be reckoned with:

"His three boats stove around him, and oars and men both whirling in the eddies; one captain, seizing the line-knife from his broken prow, had dashed at the whale, as an Arkansas duelist at his foe, blindly seeking with a six inch blade to reach the fathom-deep life of the whale. That captain was Ahab. And then it was, that suddenly sweeping his sickle-shaped lower jaw beneath him, Moby Dick had reaped away Ahab's leg, as a mower a blade of grass in the field… Small reason was there to doubt, then, that ever since that almost fatal encounter, Ahab had cherished a wild vindictiveness against the whale, all the more fell for that in his frantic morbidness he at last came to identify with him, not only all his bodily woes, but all his intellectual and spiritual exasperations. The White Whale swam before him as the monomaniac incarnation of all those malicious agencies which some deep men feel eating in them, till they are left living on with half a heart and half a lung."

Just When You Thought It Was Safe to Go Back into the Water

As they hunt whales, the *Pequod* meets with other ships. Each time, Ahab asks the same question: "Hast seen the White Whale?" Just when it appears that the whale might be beached in Bermuda, the *Pequod* meets the *Samuel Enderby*, whose captain has lost his arm to ol' Whitey. After a fierce typhoon, the *Pequod* meets the *Rachel*, which has just done battle with Moby. Tension mounts. Ahab finally sights Moby—and the battle begins:

"…the White Whale churning himself into furious speed, almost in an instant as it were, rushing among the boats with open jaws, and a lashing tail, offered appalling battle on every side; and heedless of the irons darted at him from every boat, seemed only intent on annihilating each separate plank of which those boats were made. But skillfully maneuvered, incessantly wheeling like trained chargers in the field; the boats for a while eluded him; though, at times, but by a plank's breadth; while all the time, Ahab's unearthly slogan tore every other cry but his to shreds."

➤ *Round 1: Moby Dick.* The leviathan bites Ahab's rowboat in half.

➤ *Round 2: Moby Dick.* Mr. Big Fish smashes two more boats, and Fedallah is felled.

➤ *Round 3: A tie.* Ahab gets a harpoon off, but the whale crushes the *Pequod*. Ahab launches another harpoon at His Whaleness, but the rope catches Ahab around the neck and drags him into the soup. The *Pequod* goes down, creating a vortex that pulls down everyone but Ishmael, who is rescued by the *Rachel*.

Swimming with the Fishes

In its questing, complex examination of right and wrong, (what Melville calls "Providence, Foreknowledge, Will, and Fate"), the novel dares to question not only the nature of humanity, but the nature of God as well. Ahab, the central figure, is a madman and the model of the Romantic rebel, hurling his defiance into the teeth of a vast and inscrutable universe.

You can read this novel on several levels:

➤ An allegory of the risks in trying to subjugate nature to the will of humanity.

➤ A rebellion against the evil and chaos in the universe.

➤ A metaphor for Ishmael's search for the Meaning of Life.

Moby Dick, the whale, is read as a symbol of evil, God, or an indifferent universe.

Lit Speak

Moby Dick is considered to be an **epic** story (a long narrative that represents characters in a high position who take part in a series of adventures of significance) because it features a long journey, elevated language, and battles.

Life Before Xerox: Bartleby the Scrivener

In the bantam class, we have "Bartleby the Scrivener." It's equally symbolic but a whole lot shorter than *Moby Dick*. You can knock this baby off in an hour, Scout's honor. It's a great introduction to Melville, too.

Before the days of photocopying machines, all copies were made by hand. The lucky dogs who got these slow-track jobs were called *scriveners*. As the story opens, a successful Wall Street lawyer has hired Bartleby to copy documents for his firm.

"At first Bartleby did an extraordinary quantity of writing. As if long famishing for something to copy, he seemed to gorge himself on my documents. There was no pause for digestion. He ran a day and night line, copying by sun-light and by candle-light. I should have been quite delighted with his application, had he been cheerfully industrious. But he wrote on silently, palely, mechanically."

Lit Speak

A **scrivener** was a person who copied documents by hand.

But two days later, Bartleby refuses to proofread his work, saying, "I would prefer not to." The narrator is speechless:

The Write Stuff

The other characters in this long short story include *Ginger Nut* (the 12-year-old office gofer), *Nippers* (he does his best copying *after* lunch), and *Turkey* (he does his best copying *before* lunch). And you thought the three Martini lunch was a contemporary invention.

"I sat awhile in perfect silence, rallying my stunned faculties. Immediately it occurred to me that my ears had deceived me, or Bartleby had entirely misunderstood my meaning. I repeated my request in the clearest tone I could assume. But in quite as clear a one came the previous reply, 'I would prefer not to.'

'Prefer not to,' echoed I, rising in high excitement, and crossing the room with a stride. 'What do you mean? Are you moon-struck? I want you to help me compare this sheet here—take it,' and I thrust it towards him.

'I would prefer not to,' said he. … This is very strange, thought I. What had one best do? But my business hurried me. I concluded to forget the matter for the present, reserving it for my future leisure."

Good Help Is Hard to Find

Soon after, the narrator finds that Bartleby is living in the office—and he still won't proofread. The narrator fires him, but to his utter astonishment, Bartleby refuses to leave the office. Unable to dislodge Bartleby, the narrator moves his law practice to another building. The new tenants have Bartleby arrested for vagrancy and sent to a prison called "the Tombs."

The narrator visits the Tombs and finds Bartleby staring at the wall, although he is free to roam the prison yard. By his next visit, Bartleby is dead. Later, the narrator learns that Bartleby had been forced out of a job at the Dead Letter Office through a sudden change in administration. The narrator is overwhelmed:

"Dead letters! Does it not sound like dead men? Conceive a man by nature and misfortune prone to a pallid hopelessness, can any business seem more fitted to heighten it than that of continually handling these dead letters and assorting them for the flames? For by the cart-load they are annually burned. Sometimes from out the folded paper the pale clerk takes a ring: the finger it was meant for, perhaps, moulders in the grave; a bank-note sent in swiftest charity: —he whom it would relieve, nor eats nor hungers any more; pardon for those who died despairing; hope for those who died unhoping; good tidings for those who died stifled by unrelieved calamities. On errands of life, these letters speed to death.

Ah Bartleby! Ah humanity!"

The Dead-End Kid

The story can be read as a parable, showing how the world of commerce, symbolized by Wall Street, destroys the human spirit. Imprisoned by physical barriers (the city's various walls) and emotional barriers (a meaningless job), Bartleby represents a tragically wasted life. He's trapped in the Dead Letter Office of Existence.

Early critics saw parallels between Melville's life and Bartleby's, since both were discarded artists walled in by an unappreciative public. The public withdrew its support when Melville attempted to write something more meaningful than a titillating travelogue; the lawyer was equally nonplussed when Bartleby didn't want to be a human Xerox.

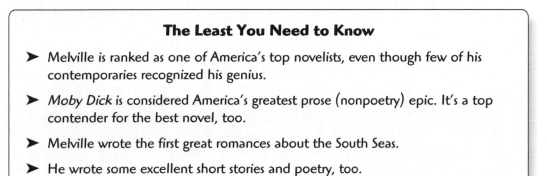

The Least You Need to Know

➤ Melville is ranked as one of America's top novelists, even though few of his contemporaries recognized his genius.

➤ *Moby Dick* is considered America's greatest prose (nonpoetry) epic. It's a top contender for the best novel, too.

➤ Melville wrote the first great romances about the South Seas.

➤ He wrote some excellent short stories and poetry, too.

➤ Nowadays, Melville is the poster child for the misunderstood artist.

Part 3
The War Between the States (1855–1865)

"A house divided against itself cannot stand. I believe this government cannot endure permanently half slave and half free."

—*Abraham Lincoln,* from his Second Inaugural Address

The Civil War (1861–65) between the industrial North and the agricultural, slave-owning South was a watershed in American history. Before the war, idealists championed human rights, especially abolition; after, Americans increasingly idealized progress and the self-made man.

In this section, you'll learn how Harriet Beecher Stowe helped catapult America into the Civil War with her polemic novel, Uncle Tom's Cabin: Life Among the Lowly. *You'll discover the role former slave Frederick Douglass played in helping to awaken Americans to the horror of slavery. Finally, you'll see how two very different poets, social Walt Whitman and solitary Emily Dickinson, revolutionized American poetry.*

Chapter 11

The Little Woman Who Started This Great Big War: Harriet Beecher Stowe (1811–1896)

In This Chapter

➤ Stowe's life and works

➤ The plot of *Uncle Tom's Cabin*

➤ The impact of *Uncle Tom's Cabin*

➤ The message of *Uncle Tom's Cabin*

"A thousand lives seemed to be concentrated in that one moment to Eliza. Her room opened by a side door to the river. She caught her child, and sprang down the steps towards it. …In that dizzy moment her feet to her scarce seemed to touch the ground, and a moment brought her to the water's edge. Right on behind they came and, nerved with strength such as God gives only to the desperate, with one wild cry and flying leap, she vaulted sheer over the turbid current by the shore, on to the raft of ice beyond. It was a desperate leap—impossible to anything but madness and despair…

The huge green fragment of ice on which she alighted pitched and creaked as her weight came on it, but she stayed there not a moment. With wild cries and desperate energy she leaped to another and still another cake;—stumbling—leaping—slipping—springing upwards again! Her shoes are gone—her stockings cut from her feet—while blood marked every step; but she saw nothing, felt nothing, till dimly, as in a dream, she saw the Ohio side, and a man helping her up the bank."

—from Chapter 7, *Uncle Tom's Cabin*

Like the saintly slave Uncle Tom and vicious overseer Simon Legree, Eliza's mad leap to freedom over the ice floes has become part of the American consciousness. All three images come from *Uncle Tom's Cabin,* the first American novel to sell a million copies. In this chapter, you'll learn all about Harriet Beecher Stowe, the woman whom Abraham Lincoln credited with starting the Civil War.

The Beecher Preachers

Harriet Beecher Stowe's father, Lyman Beecher, was a charismatic mover and shaker from the hellfire-and-damnation school of preaching. When not condemning people to hell for regular ol' everyday sinning, Lyman was attacking them for drinking, dancing, and dueling from his pulpit in Lichfield, Connecticut. His sons were expected to follow his footsteps straight to the pulpit; his daughters, to marry into it. All his children were educated for a life of public service, defined by his strict Calvinist values. Lyman recognized the brilliance of his seventh child early on, however. "Hattie is a genius," he said. He also recognized the gender bias of his day. "I would give a hundred dollars if she was a boy," he added.

Lit Speak

Calvinism, a Christian theology created by the French church reformer John Calvin in the 16th century, emphasizes predestination, the sovereignty of God, and the supreme authority of the Bible. Calvinists also believe that thrift and hard work are forms of moral virtue, so business success is evidence of God's grace.

Stowe wrestled with religious doubts at a local Connecticut school until her early teen years, when she fully accepted her father's teachings. When Stowe was 13 years old, her elder sister Catherine started the Hartford Female Seminary. Catherine was as subtle as a poke in the eye with a sharp stick, and Stowe meekly toed the line as both pupil and, later, teacher.

In 1832, the Beecher family was uprooted when Lyman accepted the prestigious position as president of the Lane Theological Seminary in Cincinnati. "It's the Athens of the West," he bragged to his brood, while Stowe claimed, "I never saw a place so capable of being rendered a Paradise."

"Porkopolis," the natives called their city, in a backhanded jab at the slaughterhouses and meatpacking plants. The nickname conveniently overlooked the frequent cholera epidemics—and the slaves right across the river.

What I Did For Love

Catherine opened another school, drafting her obedient sister once again, leaving Harriet little time to learn how to apply lip gloss. Nonetheless, Harriet soon met someone who appreciated her inner beauty, Calvin Stowe, a preacher and widower ten years her senior. By 1836, Harriet and Calvin fell so deeply in love that she was able to overlook his financial incompetence, gluttony, and hypochondria. Calvin soon proved that he was unable to make money, but he sure could make children—they had seven, in all.

Calvin's salary of $600 a year didn't bring home enough bacon to feed the brood, so Harriet took over the breadwinning along with her other responsibilities: childcare, cooking, cleaning, sewing, washing, and ironing. Publishers happily paid $2 a page for Harriet's charming stories of New England life, and Stowe churned them out as fast as her homemade butter. She also wrote poems, travel books, biographical sketches, children's books, adult novels—whatever would turn a buck.

Lit Wit

In 1444, Portugal became the first modern nation to meet its labor needs by importing blacks captured from Africa; Spain and England soon followed, with the New World getting in on the act in 1619. The development of the plantation system in America around 1650 codified the barbarity. In 1800, there were nearly 1 million black slaves in America; by 1860, the figure had quadrupled. Individuals and members of nearly all sects defended slavery on various grounds. Although antislavery views grew steadily, many who supported abolition were unwilling to dispute what many citizens held to be their right to own slaves.

The Traffic in Human Flesh

The horrors of slavery had gnawed at Stowe for years. In Cincinnati, she often came into contact with fugitive slaves because Kentucky, across the Ohio River from Cincinnati, was a slave state. In addition, Stowe's Aunt Mary Hubbard had left her husband, an English plantation owner in Jamaica, because she couldn't tolerate how badly he treated his slaves. Aunt Mary's tales of the cruelty of slavery became part of the Stowe family lore. Stowe's sister Catherine also supported antislavery action. Deeply affected by the passage of the Fugitive Slave Law, she wrote to Harriet, "I wish I could use my pen as you can; I would write something that would make this whole nation feel what an accursed thing slavery is."

Stowe vowed to write something—and in 1852, *Uncle Tom's Cabin* was published. Stowe later claimed that she hadn't written the book: "God wrote it," she said. "I merely wrote his dictation."

Writer's Block

Uncle Tom's Cabin was an abomination to slave owners. One piece of hate mail Stowe received contained the ear of a slave.

The Price of Fame

Uncle Tom's Cabin immediately broke all sales records of the day: It sold 3,000 copies the first day, 10,000 within a week, and 300,000 within a year. Before 1860 alone, there were 30 British editions, 12 German, five French, and 23 other translations. The publisher got rich; the Stowes did not. Stunningly inept with money, Harriet and Calvin managed to let it all run through their fingers.

The novel so inflamed popular opinion—especially in the South, of course—that when Stowe met Abraham Lincoln during the Civil War, he said, "So this is the little lady who made this big war!"

Because she thought that few Northerners would believe her tale if she presented slavery at its cruelest, Stowe had set out to "show the *best side* of the thing, and something *faintly approaching the worst.*" Nonetheless, the novel was so strong that Stowe's own children sobbed when they read the first chapters.

Following the publication of *Uncle Tom's Cabin*, Stowe became a celebrity, speaking against slavery both in America and Europe. To refute critics who argued that *Uncle Tom's Cabin* was not authentic, she wrote *A Key to Uncle Tom's Cabin*, which was published the following year. *A Key* contained documented case histories, newspaper articles, and legal and scholarly treatises. This was followed by a second antislavery novel, *Dred,* in 1856.

The Write Stuff

When one of Stowe's children died, several proslavery critics claimed that God had taken the babe to keep Stowe from growing vain over her success. She replied, "I wrote what I did because as a woman, as a mother, I was oppressed and broken-hearted, with the sorrows and injustice I saw, because as a Christian I felt the dishonor to Christianity—because as a lover of my country I trembled at the coming day of wrath."

Lit Wit

Within a few months of publication of *Uncle Tom's Cabin's*, dramatizations appeared across the country—all without Stowe's knowledge, consent, or cut of the take. At least eight versions were produced before the Civil War, from big-city stages to tent productions in small towns. Since the novel had been written to be read aloud, it played well to the stage. Theatrical productions helped make the characters part of the national consciousness.

Uncle Tom's Cabin: Life Among the Lowly

Uncle Tom's Cabin has a cast of thousands, and since we have neither the space nor time for them all, I'll just introduce the primo players in this epic:

➤ *Uncle Tom:* The Christ figure who gets a bum rap.

➤ *Simon Legree:* The cruelest villain in American literature.

➤ *Eva St. Clare:* An impossibly angelic five-year-old girl. (If a real child of yours ever acted this well, you'd call the *X-Files*!)

➤ *Mr. St. Clare:* A wealthy slave owner who promises Tom his freedom but dies before he can make good on his word.

➤ *Mrs. St. Clare:* Eva's selfish, hypochondriac mother.

➤ *Eliza:* A courageous slave whose fierce love for her family helps them overcome their hardships.

➤ *George Harris:* Eliza's husband. Stalwart and courageous, he heads North and makes it to freedom.

➤ *Harry* ("Jim Crow"): Eliza and George's beautiful five-year-old son.

➤ *Arthur Shelby:* The "good" plantation owner and Uncle Tom's owner.

➤ Topsy: The slave child who functions as a dramatic contrast to Eva's angelic goodness.

➤ *Haley:* The villainous Southern slave trader who chases Eliza across the ice floes.

➤ *Cassy:* A slave on Legree's farm who terrorizes him with her "voodoo."

That Peculiar Institution

The novel opens on the Shelby plantation, a few years before the Civil War. Encumbered with debt, Shelby is forced to sell some of his slaves. Agitated, Mrs. Shelby groans:

> *"This is God's curse on slavery!—a bitter, bitter, most accursed thing!—a curse to the master and a curse to the slave! I was a fool to think I could make anything good out of such a deadly evil. It is a sin to hold a slave under laws like ours,—I always felt it was,—I always thought so when I was a girl,—I thought so still more after I joined the church; but I thought I could gild it over,—I thought, by kindness, and care, and instruction, I could make the condition of mine better than freedom—fool that I was!"*

Lit Speak

Southerners often called slavery the **peculiar institution**.

Haley, the wily slave trader, picks Uncle Tom, Shelby's favorite and most loyal slave, and Harry, a handsome little boy. Eliza, Harry's mother, overhears the conversation, grabs her son, and flees. The scene shows Stowe's ability to craft tear-your-heart-out prose:

"'Hush, Harry,' she said; 'mustn't speak loud, or they will hear us. A wicked man was coming to take little Harry away from his mother, and carry him 'way off in the dark; but mother won't let him—she's going to put on her little boy's cap and coat, and run off with him, so the ugly man can't catch him.'

Saying these words, she had tied and buttoned on the child's simple outfit, and, taking him in her arms, she whispered to him to be very still; and, opening a door in her room which led into the outer verandah, she glided noiselessly out.

It was a sparkling, frosty, star-light night, and the mother wrapped the shawl close round her child, as, perfectly quiet with vague terror, he clung round her neck."

Lit Speak

Technically speaking, *Uncle Tom's Cabin* isn't a novel; it's a **polemic**—a literary argument. As such, it aims to change public opinion rather than entertain. It's propaganda, not pleasure.

Eliza tries to convince Uncle Tom to come with her, but he remains loyal to his "Mas'r." With Haley in hot pursuit, Eliza escapes across the Ohio River by leaping across the ice floes, she and her boy are sheltered by Quakers, and Eliza is reunited with her husband, George, a slave who had escaped from a neighboring plantation. Soon the family is bound for Canada.

Uncle Tom is rewarded for his loyalty by being sold down the river to the ignoble Haley. During the steamboat trip, he is befriended by the angelic Eva St. Clare, a tot who could pass for Shirley Temple on Prozac. Before they reach port, Uncle Tom has saved sweet Eva from drowning.

Lit Wit

Stowe's model for Uncle Tom was a real-life slave named Josiah Henson, born in Maryland in 1789. Henson wrote a widely read autobiographical pamphlet. Henson was far from an "Uncle Tom" in the term's contemporary sense. Like many slaves, he served as the overseer, or manager, of a plantation before he escaped to Canada. Once free, he started a prosperous sawmill; founded a trade school for blacks, whites, and Indians; and helped over 100 slaves escape to Canada. When he traveled to England on business, the Archbishop of Canterbury was so impressed with his speech and learning that he asked what university he had attended. "The University of Adversity," Henson replied.

Eva's father, Mr. St. Clare, buys Tom and makes him the family's head coachman. Tom spends most of his time with Eva, whose charm spreads faster than mono on a college campus. She also touches Topsy's heart. Eva begins to grow more and more frail. Sensing she is going to die, Eva begs her father to free the slaves, as he had long promised. Eva dies, and Sr. Clare is disconsolate. He makes plans to honor his daughter's deathbed wish, but is killed in a brawl before he signs the papers. Mrs. St. Clare recovers from her hypochondria long enough to put another coat of polish on her nails and sell most of the slaves. Uncle Tom is sold to the notorious Simon Legree.

Too Little, Too Late

Tom tries to please his vicious master, but Legree nevertheless flogs him until he passes out. A slave named Cassy takes pity on Tom and comes to his aid. Cassy tries to "haunt" Legree into stopping the abuse, but the beatings continue. Cassy and Emmeline, another slave, try to escape by tricking Legree, who beats Tom to death while trying to get the truth about the runaways. Two days later, George Shelby (Tom Shelby's son) arrives to buy Tom back, but it is too late. It is revealed that Cassy is Eliza's mother, and they are reunited in Canada.

The Write Stuff

If the imagery in *Uncle Tom's Cabin* was any indication, Stowe was haunted by a sense of personal loss over the death of her child that she brilliantly describes as the byproduct of slavery.

The action winds up quickly. The former slaves are reunited with their family.

George Harris and his family travel to Liberia, and Shelby frees his slaves.

The Medium Is the Message

"I have always thought that all men should be free; but if any should be slaves, it should be first those who desire it for themselves, and secondly those who desire it for others. Whenever I hear anyone arguing for slavery, I feel a strong impulse to see it tried on him personally."

—Abraham Lincoln in an address to an Indiana Regiment

Uncle Tom's Cabin suffers from stereotypical characters and a convoluted plot. It's not great literature on the order of Hawthorne's *Scarlet Letter* or Melville's *Moby-Dick*. But that's OK—it wasn't intended to be. *Uncle Tom's Cabin* drives home the evils of slavery. The suffering of Eliza and Uncle Tom touched many people who had been unmoved by the cold rhetoric of the abolitionists. Here's the message:

➤ Slavery is evil—but the evil is in slavery itself and not the South; it's the system, not the slaveholders.

➤ The slavery crisis can only be resolved by Christian love. Uncle Tom is now regarded as a symbol of the cowardly bootlicking slave because he forgives Legree: "Mas'r, if you was sick, or in trouble, or dying, and I could save ye, I'd give ye my heart's blood; and, if taking every drop of blood in this poor old body would save your precious soul, I'd give 'em freely, as the Lord gave his for me."

In the last chapter, Stowe smacks us upside our head with the message. Notice how she urges white Northerners to welcome escaped slaves and treat them with respect:

"On the shores of our free states are emerging the poor, shattered, broken remnants of families,—men and women, escaped, by miraculous providence, from the surges of slavery,—feeble in knowledge, and, in many cases, infirm in moral constitution, from a system which confounds and confuses every principle of Christianity and morality. They come to seek a refuge among you; they come to seek education, knowledge, Christianity.

Writer's Block

Although *Uncle Tom's Cabin* seems racist today in its patronizing attitudes toward African-Americans, remember that in 1852, the novel was radical in its portrayal of slaves' courage and dignity.

What do you owe to these poor, unfortunates, O Christians? Does not every American Christian owe to the African race some effort at reparation for the wrongs that the American nation has brought upon them? Shall the doors of churches and school-houses be shut down upon them? Shall states arise and shake them out? Shall the Church of Christ hear in silence the taunt that is thrown at them, and shrink away from the helpless hand that they stretch out, and shrink away from the courage the cruelty that would chase them from our borders? If it must be so, it will be a mournful spectacle. If it must be so, the country will have reason to tremble, when it remembers that fate of nations is in the hand of the One who is very pitiful, and of tender compassion."

The Mighty Mite

In 1869, the scribe of the Lord once again felt herself summoned to take up her pen in a holy cause, this time in describing the charge that the poet Lord Byron had had an incestuous love for his half sister and in defending his wife, Lady Byron, against charges that she had wronged him. Even though all the principals were safely dead, the issue was anything but—and Stowe soon found herself roundly reviled and even barred from the British Isles for defaming a national hero. The scandal eventually died down, and Stowe embarked on a series of wildly successful lecture tours before quietly succumbing to old age in her 85th year.

The historical significance of Stowe's antislavery writing has tended to draw attention away from her other novels and stories. Her work is as uneven as a San Francisco street. At its worst, it indulges in a romanticized Christian sensibility that was popular in her day, but it's outdated today.

At her best, Stowe was an early and effective realist. Her settings are often accurately described, and her portraits of local social life show a writer in touch with the culture.

Lit Wit

Byron and his half-sister Augusta Leigh had indeed had an affair, which shattered Byron's marriage. Byron and Augusta Leigh had been raised apart, so they were almost strangers when they met as adults. Nonetheless, the affair proved a delicate morsel even to the jaded palate of the dissolute British society and Byron was ostracized by all but a few friends and finally forced in 1816 to leave England forever. By Stowe's time, the affair had been whitewashed, and the British did not enjoy having it brought up again.

The Least You Need to Know

➤ *Uncle Tom's Cabin* was the most influential book of the 19th century. The first book to sell a million copies, it touched readers across the globe.

➤ *Uncle Tom's Cabin* is one of the most effective documents in American literature (note that I don't call it a "novel"—because it's really propaganda) and helped fuel the Civil War.

➤ Stowe was the most famous American woman of her day.

Chapter 12

Rebel with a Cause: Frederick Douglass (1817–1895)

"I appear this evening as a thief and a robber," announced Frederick Douglass at an antislavery meeting in 1842. "I stole this head, these limbs, this body from my master, and ran off with them." With such pathos and outrage, Douglass evoked the suffering of slavery.

Frederick Douglass, an escaped slave, became one of the most effective orators of his day, as an influential newspaper writer, a militant abolitionist, and a famous diplomat. His autobiography, *The Life and Times of Frederick Douglass* (1881) became an instant— and enduring—classic story of courage. In this chapter, you'll learn about one of the true heroes of American life and letters, Frederick Douglass.

Bound and Determined

Frederick Baily was born a slave around 1817 on Holmes Hill Farm, on Maryland's Eastern Shore. Though it was one of the wealthiest plantations in Maryland, Douglass was unimpressed with his birthplace. Later in life, he described it as "a small district of country, thinly populated, and remarkable for nothing I know of more than the worn-out sandy, desert-like appearance of its soil."

Although she was literate, Frederick's mother, Harriet Baily, worked the cornfields surrounding Holmes Hill. Frederick knew little of his father except that he was white. As a child, he heard rumors that his father was the master, Thomas Auld.

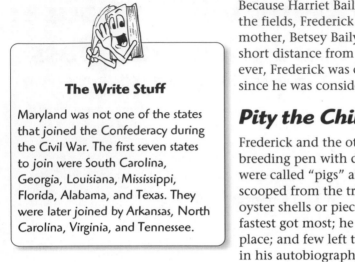

The Write Stuff

Maryland was not one of the states that joined the Confederacy during the Civil War. The first seven states to join were South Carolina, Georgia, Louisiana, Mississippi, Florida, Alabama, and Texas. They were later joined by Arkansas, North Carolina, Virginia, and Tennessee.

Because Harriet Baily was required to work long hours in the fields, Frederick was sent to live with his grandmother, Betsey Baily. Betsey Baily lived in a cabin a short distance from the farm. When he was six, however, Frederick was dispatched to the main plantation, since he was considered old enough to work.

Pity the Children

Frederick and the other small children were put into a breeding pen with dogs and hogs. The slave children were called "pigs" and fed cornmeal mush, which they scooped from the trough with spoons improvised from oyster shells or pieces of old shingles. "He that ate fastest got most; he that was strongest secured the best place; and few left the trough satisfied," Douglass noted in his autobiography.

The children's only clothing consisted of one linen shirt that hung to their knees. They were not given beds or blankets: On cold winter nights they would huddle together in the kitchen of the Anthony house to keep each other warm. As Douglass recalled,

> "I suffered much from hunger, but much more from cold. In hottest summer and coldest winter, I was kept almost naked—no shoes, no stockings, no jacket, no trousers, nothing on but a coarse tow linen shirt, reaching only to my knees. I had no bed. I must have perished with cold, but that, the coldest nights, I used to steal a bag which was used for carrying corn to the mill. I would crawl into this bag, and there sleep on the cold, damp, clay floor, with my head in and feet out. My feet have been so cracked with the frost, that the pen with which I am writing might be laid in the gashes."

Frederick last saw his mother when he was seven years old. He remembered his mother giving a severe scolding to the household cook who disliked Frederick and gave him very little food. A few months after this visit, Harriet Baily died, but Frederick did not learn of this until much later.

In 1826, when he was about nine, Frederick was sent to live with Hugh Auld, his master's brother, who managed a shipbuilding firm in Baltimore, Maryland. Frederick cleaned himself up for the occasion and received his first pair of pants.

Casting Bread upon the Waters

At first, Frederick's only duties were to run errands and care for the Auld's infant son, Tommy. Frederick enjoyed the work and grew to love the child. Sophia Auld was a religious woman and frequently read aloud from the Bible. Frederick asked his mistress to teach him to read, and she readily consented. He soon learned the alphabet and a few simple words. Sophia Auld was very excited about Frederick's progress and told her husband about it. Furious, Hugh ordered Sophia to stop the lessons at once. "If he learns to read, it will forever unfit him to be a slave," Hugh declared.

But Frederick thirsted for knowledge and soon found a way to get the reading lessons his soul craved. In his own words,

> "[I made] friends of all the little white boys whom I met in the street. As many of these as I could, I converted into teachers. With their kindly aid, obtained at different times and in different places, I finally succeeded in learning to read. When I was sent on errands, I always took my book with me, and by doing one part of my errand quickly, I found time to get a lesson before my return. I used also to carry bread with me, enough of which was always in the house, and to which I was always welcome; for I was much better off in this regard than many of the poor white children in our neighborhood. This bread I used to bestow upon the hungry little urchins, who, in return, would give me that more valuable bread of knowledge. I am strongly tempted to give the names of two or three of those little boys, as a testimonial of the gratitude and affection I bear them; but prudence forbids;— not that it would injure me, but it might embarrass them; for it is almost an unpardonable offense to teach slaves to read in this Christian country. It is enough to say of the dear little fellows, that they lived on Philpot Street, very near Durgin and Bailey's shipyard.
>
> I used to talk this matter of slavery over with them. I would sometimes say to them, I wished I could be as free as they would be when they got to be men. 'You will be free as soon as you are twenty-one, but I am a slave for life! Have not I as good a right to be free as you have?' These words used to trouble them; they would express for me the liveliest sympathy, and console me with the hope that something would occur by which I might be free."

Through the daily newspaper, Douglass learned of the abolition movement, which fired his desire to be free.

Lit Wit

Most historians cite 1831 as the beginning of the abolitionist movement in America, when William Lloyd Garrison founded *The Liberator,* which would soon become the leading antislavery newspaper. The movement gained power with the passage of the Fugitive Slave Act in 1850 and seven years later, with the Dred Scott Case, which ruled that blacks were not U.S. citizens. Well-known abolitionists included Stephen C. Foster, Abby Kelley, Charles Lenox Redmond, Wendell Phillips, Angelina and Sarah Grimké, James Russell Lowell, and Frances E.W. Harper.

The Man with the Iron Heart

In 1833, when he was 15, Frederick was shipped back to his former master, Thomas Auld. When he refused to work with "sufficient" speed, he was sent to a notorious "slave breaker" Edward Covey. Describing Covey, Douglass wrote,

"He was a cruel man, hardened by a long life of slave-holding. He would at times seem to take great pleasure in whipping a slave. I have often been awakened at the dawn of day by the most heart-rending shrieks of an own aunt of mine, whom he used to tie up to a joist, and whip upon her naked back till she was literally covered with blood. No words, no tears, no prayers, from his gory victim, seemed to move his iron heart from its bloody purpose. The louder she screamed, the harder he whipped; and where the blood ran fastest, there he whipped longest. He would whip her to make her scream, and whip her to make her hush; and not until overcome by fatigue, would he cease to swing the blood-clotted cowskin."

Douglass was fully aware of the pleasure that Covey derived from inflicting pain:

"Before he commenced whipping Aunt Hester, he took her into the kitchen, and stripped her from neck to waist, leaving her neck, shoulders, and back, entirely naked. He then told her to cross her hands, calling her at the same time a d———d b—h. After crossing her hands, he tied them with a strong rope, and led her to a stool under a large hook in the joist, put in for the purpose. He made her get upon the stool, and tied her hands to the hook. She now stood fair for his infernal purpose. Her arms were stretched up at their full length, so that she stood upon the ends of her toes. He then said to her, 'Now, you d———d b—h, I'll learn you how to disobey my orders!' and after rolling up his sleeves, he commenced to lay on the heavy cowskin, and soon the warm, red blood (amid heart-rending shrieks from her, and horrid oaths from him) came dripping to the floor. I was so terrified and horror-stricken at the sight, that I hid myself in a closet, and dared not venture out till long after the bloody transaction was over. I expected it would be my turn next."

The Write Stuff

In Chapter 29, you'll meet the famous 20th-century African-American writers. The two people who got the ball rolling for future African-American writers were Jupiter Hammond and Phillis Wheatley. Hammond (1711–1790?) did for literature what Jackie Robinson did for baseball: Hammond was the first black writer to smash the color line and make it into print. Wheatley (1753?–1784) was the first black female writer in America. She penned traditional, elegant poems.

Within the week, Frederick received a serious beating for letting an oxen team run wild. During the months to follow, he was continually whipped until he began to feel that he was indeed "broken." On one hot August afternoon, Frederick found the strength to rebel when Covey began tying him to a post in preparation for a whipping. "At that moment—from whence came the spirit I don't know—I resolved to fight," he wrote. "I seized Covey hard by the throat, and as I did so, I rose."

Covey and Frederick fought for almost two hours until Covey finally gave up, telling Frederick that his beating would have been less severe had he not resisted. "The truth was," said Frederick, "that he had not whipped me at all."

Frederick had discovered an important truth: "Men are whipped oftenist who are whipped easiest." He was lucky—a slave could be killed for resisting his master. But Covey had a reputation to protect and did not want it known that he could not control a 16-year-old boy. Frederick decided the time had come to seek his freedom.

Let Freedom Ring

On September 3, 1838, Frederick escaped from slavery. Disguised as a free sailor, he made it to New York and from there used the Underground Railroad to reach Massachusetts. He later wrote, "A new world had opened upon me. Anguish and grief, like darkness and rain, may be depicted, but gladness and joy, like the rainbow, defy the skill of pen or pencil."

> *"I have been frequently asked how I felt when I found myself in a free State. I have never been able to answer the question with any satisfaction to myself. It was a moment of the highest excitement I ever experienced… In writing to a dear friend, immediately after my arrival in New York, I said I felt like one who had escaped a den of hungry lions. This state of mind, however, very soon subsided; and I was again seized with a feeling of loneliness. I was yet liable to be taken back, and subjected to all the tortures of slavery. But the loneliness overcame me. There I was in the midst of thousands, and yet a perfect stranger; without home and without friends, in the midst of thousands of my own brethren—children of a common Father, and yet I dared not to unfold to any of them my sad condition."*

Once in Massachusetts, Frederick joined Anna Murray, a free black woman whom he loved. They had met years ago and maintained their relationship through all their troubles. The couple was married on September 15, 1838. To go along with his new life, Frederick decided to change his surname to make it more difficult for slave catchers to trace him. He named himself after Lord James Douglas, the brave outlawed fictional hero of Sir Walter's Scott's poem "The Lady of the Lake." Thus, Frederick Baily became Frederick Douglass.

Lit Wit

The most radical of the militant abolitionists, William Lloyd Garrison (1805–1879) gained the distinct honor of having a price put on his head for his antislavery stance: In 1831, the state of Georgia anted up $5,000 for Garrison's arrest and conviction. Undaunted, Garrison denounced the Constitution as "a covenant with Death and an agreement with Hell" and burned it publicly. Think of him as the Abby Hoffman of the antislavery set.

A few months later, Douglass became caught up in *The Liberator's* attacks on southern slaveholders. "The paper became my meat and drink," wrote Douglass. "My soul was set all on fire." In 1841, Douglass spoke before the crowd attending the annual meeting of the Massachusetts branch of the American Anti-Slavery Society. William Lloyd Garrison immediately recognized Douglass' potential as a speaker, and hired him to be an agent for the society. Thus a media darling was born. The personal risk for Douglass was staggering—nothing like publicity to make recapture more likely—and even in the North, abolitionists were about as popular as head lice.

True Grit

Introduced as a "a piece of property" or "a graduate from that peculiar institution, with his diploma written on his back," Douglass regaled the public with stirring recollections of his years in slavery. With his flashing eyes, proud carriage, large mass of hair, and eloquent delivery, Douglass was an immediate success on the lecture circuit. "As a speaker, he has few equals," proclaimed the Concord, Massachusetts, newspaper *Herald of Freedom.*

Douglass' early speeches dealt mainly with his own experiences. With dramatic effect, he told of how the slaveowners brutally beat women, children, and the elderly. He told about masters "breeding" their female slaves. Douglass peppered his talks with humor, making his audiences laugh at stories such as his triumphant beating of slave breaker Edward Covey.

In 1845, Douglass set down the story of his life on paper, and a classic was born: *Narrative of the Life of Frederick Douglass, an American Slave, Written by Himself.* Douglass' autobiography became a bestseller. The book is a story of the triumph of dignity, courage, and self-reliance over the evils of the brutal, degrading slave system. It is a sermon on how slavery corrupts the human spirit and robs both master and slave of their freedom. However, Douglass' fame as an author threatened his freedom. Federal laws at the time gave Thomas Auld the right to seize his (the fugitive slave Frederick Baily) property.

Worried about his freedom in America, Douglass traveled to England to spread the word about abolitionism until the heat died down. In 1846, his supporters purchased his freedom from Thomas Auld for $710.96. Soon after, Douglass sailed home, a free man at last. As he wrote to William Lloyd Garrison in January 1846, "I breathe and lo! The chattel becomes a man. I gaze around in vain for one who will question my equal humanity, claim me as a slave, or offer me an insult."

The Write Stuff

Frederick Douglass wrote only one book, his autobiography. It appeared in three versions: Narrative of the Life of Frederick Douglass, an American Slave, Written by Himself (1845); My Bondage and My Freedom (1855); and The Life and Times of Frederick Douglass (1881).

Lit Wit

The abolitionists, temperance leaders, and suffragettes (activists for women's rights group) were a tight bunch. In fact, Frederick Douglass attended the first women's rights convention in 1848 and was a lifelong supporter of the women's movement. As handy with axes as with pens, Susan B. Anthony, Lucretia Mott, and Elizabeth Cady Stanton were women to be reckoned with.

Working Without a Net

On December 3, 1847, Douglass began his second career, when the first issue of his four-page weekly newspaper, the *North Star,* came off the presses. On the masthead appeared the motto, "Right is of no sex—Truth is of no color—God is the Father of us all, and we are all Brethren." Like all worthy causes, the *North Star* hemorrhaged money, and despite a name change, the paper limped along for 17 years before gasping its last breath. Throughout these years, Douglass continued his work with abolitionists John Brown and Sojourner Truth, among others.

Douglass worked tirelessly to ensure that the Civil War would not only preserve the Union, but also free all slaves. He assisted in the recruitment of the first black regiment, the Massachusetts 54th, and his sons Lewis and Charles were among the first to enlist. By the start of the Civil War, Douglass had become the most famous and well-respected black leader in America. He not only made the A-list for White House parties, but was also appointed a U.S. marshal and made Recorder of Deeds for the district.

In 1889, President Benjamin Harrison appointed Douglass the U.S. Minister to Haiti. In keeping with the rest of his achievements, Douglass served with great distinction and dignity. Frederick Douglass died of a heart attack in 1895.

Douglass reminded people that the story of slavery could not be easily forgotten, that it must remain forever etched in our national conscience. After the end of the Civil War, Douglass saw himself as a symbol of former slaves who were not yet fully free, no matter what was written on a piece of paper, and spoke for those who could not. Born at a time when strong voices were desperately needed to cry out for freedom, Frederick Douglass established himself as a powerful speaker for all men and women.

The Write Stuff

With the ratification of the Thirteenth Amendment to the U.S. Constitution in December 1865, slavery was officially abolished in all areas of the United States.

Lit Wit

More than 200,000 blacks enlisted in the Union army, and 38,000 were killed or wounded in Civil War battles. Comprising about 10 percent of the North's troops, the black soldiers made their numbers felt on the battlefields and distinguished themselves in many engagements.

The Least You Need to Know

➤ Frederick Douglass, an escaped slave, became one of the most effective orators of his day, an influential newspaper writer, a militant abolitionist, and a famous diplomat.

➤ His autobiography, *The Life and Times of Frederick Douglass* (1881) became an instant—and enduring—classic story of courage.

➤ The autobiography appeared in three versions: *Narrative of the Life of Frederick Douglass, an American Slave, Written by Himself* (1845); *My Bondage and My Freedom* (1855); and *The Life and Times of Frederick Douglass* (1881).

➤ Frederick Douglass is one of the true heroes of America.

ROSES ARE RED...

Chapter 13

That Barbaric Yawp: Walt Whitman (1819–1892)

In This Chapter

➤ Whitman's life and importance to American literature

➤ "Song of Myself"

➤ "I Sing the Body Electric"

➤ "A Noiseless Patient Spider"

➤ "When Lilacs Last in the Dooryard Bloom'd"

➤ "Out of the Cradle, Endlessly Rocking"

➤ "O Captain! My Captain!"

"I hear America singing, the varied carols I hear,

Those of mechanics, each one singing his as it should be blithe and strong,

The carpenter singing his as he measures his plank or beam,

The mason singing his as he makes ready for work, or leaves off work,

The boatman singing what belongs to him in his boat, the deck hand singing on the steamboat deck,

The shoemaker singing as he sits on his bench, the hatter singing as he stands,

The woodcutter's song, the ploughboy's on his way in the morning, or at noon intermission or at sundown,

The delicious singing of the mother, or of the young
*   wife at work, or of the girl sewing or washing,*

Each singing what belongs to him or her and to none
*   else,*

The day what belongs to the day—at night the party of
*   young fellows, robust, friendly,*

Singing with open mouths their strong melodious songs."

—from "I Hear America Singing"

More than 100 years after his death, Walt Whitman continues to be relevant to the national discourse. Exhibit A: *Leaves of Grass,* Whitman's masterpiece, was one of Bill Clinton's gifts to Monica Lewinsky. If you don't have a copy of the Starr Report handy, don't worry; you'll get to read lots of Whitman's poetry here.

This chapter explains how Walt Whitman created new poetic forms and subjects to fashion a distinctly American idiom. First, you'll learn about Whitman's life and the forces that helped create his unique voice. Then you'll read some of his most famous poems, including excerpts from "Song of Myself" and "I Sing the Body Electric," as well as all of "A Noiseless Patient Spider."

There's the opening and closing of "When Lilacs Last in the Dooryard Bloom'd." Next comes "Out of the Cradle, Endlessly Rocking," a poem that really rocks. Finally, I sum it all up with an excerpt from "O Captain! My Captain!" So let's get to it, already.

Letting It All Hang Out

"I celebrate myself, and sing myself,

And what I assume you shall assume,

For every atom belonging to me as good belongs to you.

I loafe and invite my soul,

I lean and loafe at my ease observing a spear of
*   summer grass.*

My tongue, every atom of my blood, form'd from this
*   soil, this air,*

Born here of parents born here from parents the same,
*   and their parents the same,*

I, now thirty-seven years old in perfect health begin,

Hoping to cease not till death."

—from "Song of Myself"

To sing the song of himself, the song of America, Whitman cut himself loose from conventional themes, traditional literary allusions, and rhyme—all of the accepted poetic customs of the 19th century. This wasn't much of a shock to anyone who had known Walt when he was in knee-pants: It was plain early on that Walter was someone who followed the beat of his own drummer.

"He was a very good, but very strange boy," his mother remarked. One of five children (a sixth died in infancy), Walt categorically refused to do the farm work that was expected of him. "You are stubboner, Walt, than a load of bricks," Walt's brother George once claimed.

Never much interested in school, Whitman left the classroom at age 11 and held a number of McJobs—office boy, gofer, printer's assistant—before turning to teaching.

At 17, Walt was younger than some of the 70 or 80 farmer's sons who were his pupils. Although his students were quite fond of him, Whitman lasted only a year in the classroom. A mellow teacher, he spent most of his time writing and daydreaming.

Writer's Block

Although Whitman is often closely linked to his birthplace, West Hills, Long Island, he lived there only four years before his father moved the family to Brooklyn.

Lit Wit

After all, it wasn't as though Walt was going to miss the food that teachers were usually given by the farmers who boarded them. That's because the standard fare was pickled hog's head with a side of fried turnips.

Walt spent his twenties in the school of hard knocks, roaming around, picking up various odd jobs to keep the wolf from the door. Whitman next became the editor of the *Brooklyn Eagle,* a respected newspaper, but he got canned two years later because of his outspoken opposition to slavery. He was then around 30.

Soul Man

> *"I have said that the soul is not more than the body,*
>
> *And I have said that the body is not more than the soul,*
>
> *And nothing, not God, is greater to one than one's self is,*
>
> *And whoever walks a furlong without sympathy walks to his own funeral drest in his shroud."*

—from "Song of Myself"

In 1855, Whitman published the first version of his masterpiece, *Leaves of Grass*. In the opening manifesto, he declares that the new American poet, referring to himself, will create new forms and subject matter for poetry, rejecting conventional language, rhythm, and rhyme.

Whitman declared that his poems would have…

> ➤ Long lines that capture the rhythms of natural speech

> ➤ Free verse (poetry that doesn't have a regular beat, rhyme, or line length, but instead uses a rhythm that reinforces the meaning and sound of spoken language)

> ➤ Vocabulary drawn from everyday speech—a bards voice to represent all of America

> ➤ A base in reality, not morality

Lit Speak

Free verse isn't poetry on sale at the mall—rather, it's poetry without a regular rhyme and meter. Free verse follows the cadence of ordinary speech. If patents were given on poetry, Whitman would have one on free verse.

The Write Stuff

Ray Bradbury borrowed Whitman's title, "I Sing the Body Electric," for the title of a science fiction short story. Bradbury's story, in turn, was transformed into a classic *Twilight Zone* episode by the same name.

Hoity-toity declarations aside, *Leaves of Grass* made a very small splash with the public. "From a worldly and business point of view," Whitman said in his essay-memoir, *A Backward Glance, Leaves of Grass* was "worse than failure." Ralph Waldo Emerson called the book "the most extraordinary piece of wit and wisdom that America has yet to contribute," while The well-known poet John Greenleaf Whittier threw his copy of the book into the fireplace. Whittier wasn't alone. Another critic dismissed Leaves of Grass with a sneer and the comment, "It's just a barbarbic yawp."

The grand poetry poobahs of the day, including Henry Wadsworth Longfellow, Oliver Wendell Holmes, and James Russell Lowell, weren't impressed. Even Henry David Thoreau was appalled by Whitman's poetry—and we know he wasn't exactly following the party line. People just weren't ready for Whitman's intense, complex, and sexually explicit poems. Take a gander yourself.

I Sing the Body Electric

"I Sing the Body Electric" first appeared in the 1860 edition of *Leaves of Grass*, the third poem in the "Children of Adam" sequence. What do you think Walt's first readers might have thought of this hymn in praise of human sexuality?

"I Sing the Body Electric"

> *1*

"I sing the body electric,

The armies of those I love engirth me and I engirth them,

They will not let me off till I go with them, respond to them,

And discorrupt them, and charge them full with the charge of the soul…

> *2*

This is the female form,

A divine nimbus exhales from it from head to foot,

It attracts with fierce undeniable attraction,

I am drawn by its breath as if I were no more than a helpless vapor, all falls aside but myself and it,

Books, art, religion, time, the visible and solid earth, and what was expected of heaven or fear'd of hell, are now consumed,

Mad filaments, ungovernable shoots play out of it, the response likewise ungovernable,

Hair, bosom, hips, bend of legs, negligent falling hands all diffused, mine too diffused,

Ebb stung by the flow and flow stung by the ebb, love-flesh swelling and deliciously aching,

Limitless limpid jets of love hot and enormous, quivering jelly of love, white-blow and delirious juice,

Bridegroom night of love working surely and softly into the prostrate dawn,

Undulating into the willing and yielding day,

Lost in the cleave of the clasping and sweet-flesh'd day."

Not surprisingly, the poem caused an uproar. Whitman's homoerotic longings were not a great resume-builder. Even Emerson, Whitman's strongest supporter, urged him to cut this poem out of the book. But Whitman refused, believing that sexuality should not be concealed, because it is one of the most vital aspects of life. He even added the "Calamus" poems, which are unmistakably homoerotic. Let's look at the poem closely to see what he's *really* doing here.

Writer's Block

Many years after his homoerotic poems had been published, Whitman was fired from a government post when his supervisors stumbled upon these poems.

➤ Section 1 describes the interconnections among everything the poet loves.

➤ Section 2 describes the entire female body, top to bottom, concluding with a statement of his unity with it all.

The body and soul are united with each other and with the poem: Bodies are "the soul" and "they are my poems," Whitman declared.

Now that I've got your attention, let's look at some of Whitman's less sensual poems. Remember that these poems were just as shocking to Whitman's audience because of their reliance on free verse and nontraditional poetic style and subject matter.

Black-Widow Blues: A Noiseless Patient Spider

"A noiseless patient spider,

I mark'd where on a little promontory it stood isolated,

Mark'd how to explore the vacant vast surrounding,

It launch'd forth filament, filament, filament, out of itself,

Ever unreeling them, ever tirelessly speeding them.

And you O my soul where you stand,

Surrounded, detached, in measureless oceans of space,

Ceaselessly musing, venturing, throwing, seeking the spheres to connect them,

Till the bridge you will need be form'd, till the ductile anchor hold,

Till the gossamer thread you fling catch somewhere, O my soul."

The Write Stuff

In this poem, the spider can be read as a symbol of the pathetic flight of humanity, desperately seeking meaning in life.

The poem opens with a small incident: A spider, alone on a cliff, throws its filaments into space. But here's the difference between me and Whitman: I'd use last week's *TV Guide* to squash that sucker flatter than a Ritz, but Whitman recognized the scene and knew that this was a poetic moment with cosmic meaning.

Sure enough, in the second stanza, the spider's activity becomes a metaphor symbolizing the poet's search for immortality. Whitman sends out his verse as the spider sends out his web, both hoping to connect and so give their lives meaning. But it's not that easy to find meaning in life, as the ending shows.

So what makes this a great poem? It captures the heroic dignity of the human soul, hanging from a slender thread over the abyss of chaos, yet hopeful of finding some meaning in life.

When Lilacs Last in the Dooryard Bloom'd

1

"When lilacs last in the dooryard bloom'd,

And the great star early droop'd in the western sky in the night,

I mourn'd, and yet shall mourn with ever-returning spring.

Ever-returning spring, trinity sure to me you bring,

Lilac blooming perennial and drooping star in the west,

And thought of him I love.

2

O powerful western fallen star!

O shades of night—O moody, tearful night!

O great star disappear'd—O the black murk that hides the star!

O cruel hands that hold me powerless—O helpless soul of me!

O harsh surrounding cloud that will not free my soul."

Aside from That, Mrs. Lincoln, How Did You Like the Play?

Whitman wrote "When Lilacs Last in the Dooryard Bloom'd," his elegy to Abraham Lincoln, a few weeks after Lincoln's assassination on April 14, 1865. The 16 numbered sections of free verse express his grief over Lincoln's death and his attempt to transform the tragedy into an understanding of the cycle of life and death. Here's how the poem is arranged:

➤ Sections 1 and 2 lament the President's death.

➤ Section 3 shifts focus to the lilac bush in the dooryard.

➤ Section 4 brings forth the image of the warbling thrush.

➤ Section 5 describes Lincoln's coffin and society's grief.

➤ Sections 7 to 14 show Whitman merging his grief with society's grief.

➤ Sections 14 and 15 bring in images of death from the Civil War and transform suffering into visions of peace and rest.

The conclusion shows how Whitman has found a way to deal with his grief. That way was through nature:

> *"Lilac and star and bird twined with the chant of my soul,*

> *There in the fragrant pines and the cedars dusk and dim."*

With Malice Toward None, With Charity Toward All

Whitman saw Lincoln as the representative democratic man, the living symbol of his own message to America. "When Lilacs Last in the Dooryard Bloom'd" succeeds in transforming his personal grief into an expression of national mourning. Implicit in this process is Whitman's belief that the meaning of Lincoln's death is so vast that it can be grasped only through poetry. Check out the correspondences:

Symbol	Meaning
Lilacs	Everlasting spring (the poet's love for the president)
Fallen western star	Lincoln himself
Thrush's song	Universalization of the poet's grief

Lit Wit

The American poet James Russell Lowell once described Abraham Lincoln as "the first American." Well over a century later, Lincoln remains a key figure in our national consciousness. Hated as well as loved for his policies, Lincoln patiently endured all setbacks until the Union was saved. The "Great Emancipator" brought about the abolition of slavery and advocated a policy of Reconstruction that provided for the gradual enfranchisement of the freed men and women. It was a disaster for the country that Lincoln did not live to carry out his plans.

Out of the Cradle, Endlessly Rocking

Out of the Cradle, Endlessly Rocking

"Out of the cradle endlessly rocking,

Out of the mocking-bird's throat, the musical shuttle,

Out of the Ninth-month midnight,

Over the sterile sands and the fields beyond, where
    the child leaving his bed wander'd alone,
    bareheaded, barefoot,

Down from the shower'd halo,

Up from the mystic play of shadows twining and
    twisting as if they were alive,

Out from the patches of briers and blackberries,

From the memories of the bird that chanted to me,

From your memories sad brother, from the fitful
    risings and fallings I heard,

From under that yellow half-moon late-risen and
    swollen as if with tears,

From those beginning notes of yearning and love there
    in the mist,

From the thousand responses of my heart never to
    cease,

From the myriad thence-arous'd words,

From the word stronger and more delicious than any,

From such as now they start the scene revisiting,

As a flock, twittering, rising, or overhead passing,

Borne hither, ere all eludes me, hurriedly,

A man, yet by these tears a little boy again,

Throwing myself on the sand, confronting the waves,

I, chanter of pains and joys, uniter of here and
    hereafter,

Taking all hints to use them, but swiftly leaping
    beyond them,

A reminiscence sing."

"Out of the Cradle, Endlessly Rocking" is a poem
about memory, a key concept to the romantics.

The Write Stuff

So what's this fixation on grass
about, anyway? Whitman used grass
as his symbol of life's cycles, the
great cycle of existence. Hence,
Leaves of Grass rather than, say,
Leaves of Paper, Leaves of Pastry, or
Leaves of Potatoes.

Like Wordsworth's "Lines Composed a Few Miles above Tintern Abbey" and Longfellow's "My Lost Youth," Whitman's "Out of the Cradle, Endlessly Rocking" explores how childhood prepared the poet to assume the mantle of Art. The poem opens with a description of Long Island, which Whitman calls by the Native American name "Paumanok," and his childhood there.

The end of the poem focuses on listening to the ocean's song of death. But for Whitman, death is a natural part of the cycle of life, as the poem's strong rhythm and repetition suggest.

Walt got it all together in this poem: The form of the poem echoes its content. Look again at the first three lines: Each opens with the word "out," and the poem rocks with a rhythm the Beatles would envy.

The images also reinforce the cyclical nature of life. The rocking cradle, the singing bird, the youthful poet, and the sea recur throughout, reminding readers both of life's constancy and of its change.

Advertisements for Myself

> *"Creeds and schools in abeyance,*
>
> *Retiring back a while sufficed at what they are, but*
>   *never forgotten,*
>
> *I harbor for good or bad, I permit to speak at every*
>   *hazard,*
>
> *Nature without check with original energy*
>   *I celebrate myself"*

> —from "Song of Myself"

Determined to spread his message, Whitman published his own reviews (under an assumed name, of course) and co-authored his biography, *The Good Gray Poet*. Whitman even managed to become the most photographed poet of his century, perhaps of all time.

O Captain! My Captain!

> *"O Captain! my Captain! our fearful trip is done,*
>
> *The ship has weathered every rack, the prize we sought*
>   *is won,*
>
> *The port is near, the bells I hear, the people all exulting,*
>
> *While follow eyes the steady keel, the vessel grim and*
>   *daring;*
>
> *But O heart! heart! heart!*
>
> *O the bleeding drops of red,*

Where on the deck my Captain lies,

Fallen cold and dead.

O Captain! my Captain! rise up and hear the bells;

Rise up—for you the flag is flung—for you the bugle trills,

For you bouquets and ribboned wreaths—for you the shores a-crowding,

For you they call, the swaying mass, their eager faces turning;

Here Captain! dear father!…"

"O Captain! My Captain!" memorializes Lincoln's passing, the death of a great man and the death of the era he dominated. Unlike Lincoln, Whitman suffered a long decline.

Whitman's final illness began in 1873, when he suffered a stroke and a mental breakdown at his mother's death. Unable to live alone, Walt was taken in by his brother George Washington Whitman, a plain-spoken inspector at a Camden, New Jersey, pipe foundry.

But it was not until the evening of March 26, 1892 that Whitman died. The next day, the famous artist Thomas Eakins made a death mask. The autopsy revealed that Whitman had died of emphysema.

The Least You Need to Know

➤ Whitman created new poetic forms and subjects to fashion a distinctly American type of poetic expression.

➤ He rejected conventional themes, traditional literary references, allusions, and rhyme—all the accepted poetic customs of the 19th century.

➤ He used long lines to capture the rhythms of natural speech, free verse, and vocabulary drawn from everyday speech.

➤ *Free verse* is poetry written without a regular rhyme and meter.

Chapter 14

The Big Mama of American Literature: Emily Dickinson (1830–1886)

...VIOLETS ARE BLUE...

In This Chapter

➤ Dickinson's life

➤ Traditional 18th-century poetry versus Dickinson's poetry

➤ Dickinson's astonishing accomplishments

➤ Select poems

➤ Dickinson's major themes

67

"Success is counted sweetest
By those who ne'er succeed.
To comprehend a nectar
Requires sorest need."

On the surface, Emily Dickinson accomplished very little. An agoraphobic—afraid of open spaces—from age 23 until her death 33 years later at age 56, Dickinson dressed only in white and never left her house—and only rarely her room. And even though she wrote nearly 2,000 poems in her lifetime, she published only seven—and all anonymously.

But below the surface, this odd recluse helped pave the way for modern American poetry. As you learned in the previous chapter, Whitman created the sprawling epic of America. With rich visual imagery and a radically different style, Emily Dickinson plumbed life's philosophical and tragic dimensions in little jewel-like poems.

Without Feathers

"'Hope' is the thing with feathers—

That perches in the soul—

And sings the tune without the words—

And never stops—at all—"

As this poem reveals, Dickinson saw hope as a happy bird perched in our soul. Dickinson certainly needed something to cling to. Although she was born to the upper crust of Amherst, Massachusetts, Dickinson seemed to get nothing but the crumbs. Her grandfather founded Amherst College, and her father was a well-respected lawyer. Emily was born with the dual blessings of family money and social standing, but she lacked the easy social sense that the rest of her kin possessed. This became more evident as she grew up. Stay tuned: it's a great story.

Emily's brother, Austin, was happily married to a social climber. Emily's sister, Lavinia,—while not the sharpest tool in the shed—luckily had the good sense to ignore the instructions that Emily had left in her will to destroy her poems. Instead, Lavinia displayed an admirable fanaticism about having them published.

The Belle of Amherst

1129

"Tell all the truth, but tell it slant—

Success in Circuit lies

Too bright for our infirm Delight

The Truth's superb surprise.

As Lightning to the Children eased

With explanation kind

The Truth must dazzle gradually

Or every man be blind—"

As a child, Emily was a brilliant, determined student. When not grinding away at chemistry, theology, Greek, Latin, ancient history, and other equally frivolous subjects, she enjoyed reading clubs, outdoor jaunts, and social events. At 15, Emily displayed typical adolescent modesty when she wrote, "I am growing very handsome very fast indeed! I expect to be the belle of Amherst when I reach my 17th year. I don't doubt that I shall have perfect crowds of admirers at that age." Although Emily was one heck of a poet, she was no prophet.

After a two-year stint at Mount Holyoke Female Seminary and then a new women's college, Emily's social life began to narrow. For a few more years she enjoyed concerts, lectures, and parties, and in the early 1850s, she even took a trip to Philadelphia and Washington, D.C. It proved to be the longest journey she took in her life: By the end of the decade, the Belle of Amherst became its most famous recluse.

Doing Hard Time

303

"The Soul selects her own Society—

Then—shuts the Door—

To her divine Majority—

Present no more—…"

"I do not go from home," Dickinson wrote in 1853. From age 30 on, Emily withdrew from society; after 1874, she practically never left the family house. She dressed only in white and communicated with people mainly through mysterious notes and fragments of poems. What happened to send Emily Dickinson to her room—for life? Here are the top theories:

➤ A thwarted love affair with the Reverend Charles Wadsworth

➤ A thwarted love affair with her sister-in-law

➤ A deep depression

➤ A deliberate choice to live alone, á la Thoreau

Write Away

441

"This is my letter to the World

That never wrote to Me—

The simple News that Nature told—

With tender Majesty.

Her message is committed

To Hands I cannot see—

For love of Her—Sweet—countrymen—

Judge tenderly—of Me"

With so much time on her hands, Dickinson wrote. And wrote. And wrote. (No writer's block there.) During her 56 years, Dickinson wrote 1,775 completed poems, and piles of fragments. But she published only seven poems during her lifetime, all anonymously, but not for lack of effort. Dickinson could have wallpapered her room with rejection notices.

Lit Wit

Emily was clearly hanging on by her fingernails, but this was nothing unusual for women of her class during her lifetime. Between 1865 and 1920, class differences were especially sharp, and upper-class ladies were considered too delicate for any exertion. Constrained to a life of inaction, many upper-class women succumbed to "nervous disorders." The most well-heeled were subject to Dr. S. Weir Mitchell's famous "rest cure." Isolation, rest, and warm baths were the cornerstones of the treatment. Forbidden to eat spicy foods, these women were fed puddings, milk, and cereal. Nix on visitors, work, and general "mental excitement," too.

Why the cold shoulder from the publishing world? Her poems just didn't match what was out there. Here are the problems:

➤ *Problem #1:* Dickinson's poems didn't look like poems were supposed to look.

➤ *Problem #2:* Her poems didn't rhyme. (Everyone else's did.)

➤ *Problem #3:* Her figures of speech were too striking for her day.

➤ *Problem #4:* Her ideas were too radical.

Dickinson's work had to wait until the 20th century to be appreciated: It wasn't until her complete poems were published in 1955 that she received in-depth attention from the literary critics and the educated reading public. Why the wait? Check out the following chart to better understand how her work was so ahead of her time.

19th-Century Poetic Style	20th-Century Poetic Style
"A Tender Lay"	*Dickinson's Poem 956*
Be gentle to the new laid egg,	What shall I do when the
For eggs are brilliant things;	Summer troubles—
They cannot fly until they're hatched,	What, when the Rose is ripe—
And have a pair of wings.	What when the Eggs fly off in Music From the Maple Keep?

The anonymous poem on the left was a bestseller in 1857; Dickinson's version of the same theme, which appears on the right, was never published during her lifetime. Let's take a more specific look at the problems I've already outlined:

➤ *Problem #1:* Dickinson's poems didn't look like poems were supposed to look. Where are the sentences? Commas, semicolons, and periods? And what's with all the dashes?

➤ *Problem #2:* Her poems didn't rhyme. (Everyone else's did.) In the 19th century, people believed that all poems had to rhyme. Since Dickinson didn't use rhyme, she couldn't be writing poems, could she? (Who knows *what* they were.)

The Write Stuff

Dickinson didn't title her poems. As a result, they are designated by numbers.

➤ *Problem #3:* Her figures of speech were too striking for her day. A ripe rose? "Eggs fly off in Music/from the Maple Keep"?

➤ *Problem #4:* Her ideas were too radical. In the 19th century, poems were supposed to deal with warm-and-fuzzy topics. Dickinson avoided the sticky sentimentality of 19th-century poetry, favoring instead startling images and outlooks. As a result, her poems paved the way for the Imagist movement of the 1920s, and she became one of the movement's patron saints. By then, of course, she was long dead.

Lit Wit

Imagism hawked radical ideas, original images, and hard truths. Shunning rhythm and rhyme, the imagists depended on the power of the image itself to arrest attention and convey emotion. Founded by Amy Lowell in 1912, the imagists' torch was carried by followers Hilda Doolittle (H.D.), Ezra Pound, and William Carlos Williams. Here's a classic imagist poem by Pound:

"In a Station of the Metro"

"The apparition of these faces in the crowd;

Petals on a wet, black bough."

—Ezra Pound, *1913*

Not Waving, But Drowning

435

Much Madness is divinest Sense—

To a discerning Eye—

Much Sense—the starkest Madness—

'Tis the Majority

In this, as All, prevail—

Assent—and you are sane—

Demur—you're straightway dangerous—

And handled with a Chain—"

When Dickinson died, her sister found piles of poems, many bound into neat little booklets. She sought the help of a neighbor, Mabel Loomis Todd, a writer, who arranged with the help of the well-known critic Thomas Wentworth Higginson to have the poems published in 1890. Todd and Higginson cut apart the little booklets and rearranged the poems into the conventional poetic topics of the day:

➤ Love

➤ Nature

➤ Friendship

➤ Death

➤ Immortality

A cult classic in its cut-and-pasted version, the book was reprinted twice in two months and ran into 11 editions within two years. When critics complained that Dickinson was inept, various editors revised her poems to appeal to more conventional tastes: Words were changed, lines revised, and traditional punctuation substituted for dashes. It wasn't until 1955 that the poems were published in their original order (as much as possible) with numbers in place of the titles. The complete philosophical and tragic dimensions of Dickinson's vision became apparent, and her poems were only then fully appreciated. Let's take a look at some of her most famous poems.

Remembrance of Flings Past?

249

"Wild Nights—Wild Nights!

Were I with thee

Wild Nights should be

Our luxury!

Futile—the Winds—

To a Heart in port—

Done with the Compass—

Done with the Chart!

Rowing in Eden—

Ah, the Sea!

Might I but moor—Tonight—

In Thee!"

This passionate yearning for reunion with a lover is a shocker: Could this really be coming from a recluse who rejected Love for Art? The sexual imagery is astonishingly explicit for a woman not known to have ever been out after midnight (and for most of her life, not at any time, for that matter). The speaker fantasizes about an X-rated night when the lovers are reunited. And just to make sure that we don't misread her intentions, Dickinson repeats "Wild Nights" twice and adds an exclamation point. Furthermore, the "port" in stanza 2 and the "moor" in stanza 3 are clearly sexual images.

Beginning with the unusual rhyme scheme a-b-b-b (*nights, thee, be, luxury*), the poem abandons rhyme in the second stanza, only to pick it up again at the end. The varying rhymes, unusual for Dickinson's work, serve to convey the depth of the lover's anguish. The startling comparison of sex to sailing is characteristic of the metaphysical poetry of the 17th century. As you learned in Chapter 2, Puritan Edward Taylor brought this style of poetry to the New World. Dickinson was familiar with all the Puritan poets.

Few poems have captured the power of anticipated love as strongly as this one. The reference to the Garden of Eden in the last stanza suggests that even if love cannot return people to Paradise, it can offer sanctuary to exiles.

The Write Stuff

There are several conventional rhyme schemes. Among the most common is alternating rhyming lines, shown as a-b-a-b. Here's an example from Shakespeare's sonnet 12:

When I do count the clock that tells the time

And see the brave day sunk in hideous night,

When I behold the violet past prime

And sable curls all silvered o'er with white....

Time and *prime* rhyme (the a's); and *night* and *white* rhyme (the b's).

Another common rhyme scheme is pairs of rhyming lines, called *couplets*. Here's an example from A.E. Housman:

Oh who is that young sinner with the handcuffs on his wrists?

And what has he been after that they groan and shake their fists?

And wherefore is he wearing such a conscience-stricken air?

Oh they're taking him to prison for the color of his hair.

Wrists and *fists* rhyme (a's); *air* and *hair* rhyme (b's).

A Snake in the Grass

986

"A narrow Fellow in the Grass
Occasionally rides—
You may have met Him—did you not
His notice sudden is—

The Grass divides as with a Comb—
A spotted shaft is seen—
And then it closes at your feet
And opens further on—

He likes a Boggy Acre
A Floor too cool for Corn—
Yet when a Boy, and Barefoot—
I more than once at Noon

Have passed, I thought, a Whip lash
Upbraided in the Sun
When stooping to secure it
It wrinkled, and was gone—

Several of Nature's People
I know, and they know me—
I feel for them a transport
Of cordiality—

But never met this Fellow
Attended, or alone
Without a tighter breathing
And Zero at the Bone—"

Writer's Block

One of the most hotly debated topics among academics is Dickinson's sex life (which shows you how exciting it is to be a professor). Was Dickinson straight? Gay? Somewhere in-between? Here's my opinion: Regardless of whatever happened behind Dickinson's closed door, the poetry stands on its own.

At first glance, this poem looks like free verse (poetry without a regular rhyme and meter; see Chapter 13 for more information on free verse). But the underlying metrical structure incorporates the traditional pattern of English hymns, alternating lines of eight and six syllables. The tone is deceptively light and simple—first date cool—as we meet that affable fellow, Mr. Snake. The language, however, assaults the reader as much as the encounter with the snake. The inversion in the lines "You may have met Him—did you not/His notice sudden is—" jerks words from their everyday function just as the figurative snake has jerked the speaker from feeling at home in nature.

The metaphors Dickinson uses to describe the snake reflect the speaker's changing feelings about it. Check out this progression:

Tone	Word Choice
civilized	"fellow"
vaguely ominous	"spotted shaft"
hostile	"whip lash"
openly evil	"it"

The snake engenders terror, "tighter breathing/ And Zero at the Bone—". The serpentine lines and repeated *s* sounds at the beginning give way to the long *o* sounds of terror—fell*o*w, al*o*ne, zer*o*, b*o*ne.

The poem describes a journey into the core of nature's darkness, an often used theme in American literature. To Dickinson, nature is more like the hurricane in *Twister*. Nature toys with people, often unraveling their grip on reality. The "Whip lash" shows us that to Dickinson, nature wears hip boots and lots of leather.

The Write Stuff

Dickinson's ability to use language to reflect experience marks her as one of the first modern poets.

Lit Wit

Don't make the mistake of seeing Dickinson as Ms. Doom-and-Gloom. She also had a playful side, as this poem shows:

185

"'Faith' is a fine invention
When Gentlemen can see—
But Microscopes are prudent
In an Emergency."

A Date with Destiny

712

"Because I could not stop for Death—
He kindly stopped for me—
The Carriage held just Ourselves—
And Immortality.

We slowly drove—he knew no haste
And I had put away
My labor and my leisure too,
For His Civility—

We passed the School, where Children strove
At Recess—in the Ring—
We passed in the Fields of Gazing Grain—
We passed the Setting Sun—

Or rather—He passed Us—
The Dews grew quivering and chill—
For only Gossamer, my Gown—
My Tippet—only Tulle—

> *We paused before a House that seemed*
> *A Swelling in the Ground—*
> *The Roof was scarcely visible—*
> *The Cornice—in the Ground—*
>
> *Since then—'tis Centuries—and yet*
> *Feels shorter than the Day*
> *I first surmised the Horses' Heads*
> *Were toward Eternity—"*

A hot date turns out to be a close encounter with that old sneak, Death.

Because the speaker in this poem was too busy to stop and die, Death picks her up in his carriage, bringing along Immortality as a chaperone. Only after Death has the speaker in a nasty embrace does she realize that Death makes a lousy date. (The ghoulish seducer of her poem would be at home in any 19th-century Gothic novel.)

The poem shows that death is always close by, even though we never realize it. As a result, people are caught unprepared when Death comes knocking: The compression of words and ideas in the third stanza demonstrates this. This stanza traces the cycle of life, from childhood (the School) to death (the Setting Sun). Time marches on, even for children—although the pace seems to crawl when they're young.

Seeing the word *passed* in the same stanza shows the irony of time: The occupants of the carriage are not only passing scenes, they are also passing out of life. The disheveled rhyme scheme, alternating iambic tetrameter and trimeter lines, underscores our unpreparedness for death.

Lit Speak

An **iamb** is a pair of syllables, one unstressed syllable followed by a stressed syllable. For example: *I taste.* Iambic tetrameter has four iambs. Here's an example of iambic tetrameter:

I taste/a liq/uour nev/er brewed.

Note: Stress the *a* in taste, *i* in liquor, first *e* in never, and first *e* in brewed. Place an unaccented sign over the first *l, a, o* in liquor, and second *e* in never.

Lit Wit

Death is Emily Dickinson's favorite theme. No doubt this was partly because 33 of her friends and family died between 1851 and 1854 alone.

Speaking of Death...

465

"I heard a Fly buzz—when I died—
The Stillness in the Room
Was like the Stillness in the Air—
Between the Heaves of Storm—

The Eyes around—has wrung them dry—
And Breaths were gathering firm
For that last Onset—when the King
Be witnessed—in the Room—

I willed my Keepsakes—Signed away
What portion of me be
Assignable—and then it was
There interposed a Fly—

With Blue—uncertain stumbling Buzz—
Between the light—and me—
And then the Windows failed—and then—
I could not see—"

Another of Dickinson's uplifting poems, this one describes the events leading up to the speaker's death. The first stanza describes the quiet room; the second, the bedside deathwatch. The little visitor who strafes the third stanza is a symbol for Beelzebub, Lord of the Flies, and King of the Devils. For a believer, the symbol is horrifying, because it suggests that the soul dies with the body.

Like her contemporaries Emerson, Melville, Hawthorne, and Thoreau, Dickinson was deeply concerned with conventional Christianity and death. In this poem, she creates the moment of death to find an instant of clarity, but instead of choirs of angels, she gives us a fly.

What does the fly represent? Death? Hell? Nothingness? The fly points the way, but the living cannot interpret its buzz... and the voice stops.

Although Emily Dickinson published so little during her life, she nonetheless was very conscious of her art and the possibility of fame. Writing to the influential literary critic Thomas Wentworth Higginson, Dickinson commented, "If fame belongs to me, I could not escape her—if she did not, the longest day would pass me on the chase." It took time, but eventually Emily Dickinson became acknowledged as one of the greatest American poets.

The Least You Need to Know

➤ Along with Walt Whitman, Emily Dickinson (1830-1886) is considered one of the founders of Modern American Poetry.

➤ Dickinson's concrete imagery, forceful language, and unique style ushered in poetry as we know it today.

➤ She wrote 1,775 poems but published only seven of them during her lifetime.

Part 4

Realism and the Frontier (1865-1915)

"'But I reckon I got to light out for the territory ahead of the rest, because Aunt Sally says she's going to adopt me and sivilize me, and I can't stand it. I been there before.'"

—*Mark Twain, from* Adventures of Huckleberry Finn

From 1860 to 1914, the United States was transformed from a small, young, agricultural ex-colony into a huge, modern, industrial nation. A debtor nation in 1860, by 1914, America had become the world's wealthiest country. Our population had more than doubled, rising from 31 million in 1860 to 76 million in 1900.

As industrialization grew, so did alienation. Characteristic American novels of the period, including Stephen Crane's Maggie: A Girl of the Streets, *Jack London's* Martin Eden, *and Theodore Dreiser's* An American Tragedy, *depict the damage that economic forces and alienation wreak on the weak or vulnerable. Survivors, like Twain's Huck Finn, London's Humphrey Vanderveyden, and Dreiser's Sister Carrie, endure through luck, pluck, and strength.*

Chapter 15

Samuel Clemens: A.K.A. Mark Twain (1835–1910)

In This Chapter

➤ Twain's humor

➤ Twain's life and times

➤ Twain's "The Celebrated Jumping Frog of Calaveras County"

➤ Vernacular and tall tales

➤ Twain's *The Adventures of Huckleberry Finn*

➤ Twain's artistry

"All modern literature comes from one book by Mark Twain called Huckleberry Finn.*"*

—Ernest Hemingway, from *The Green Hills of Africa*

Mark Twain (the pen name of Samuel Langhorne Clemens) is considered to be the greatest humorist of 19th-century American literature. But he's more than a funnyman. Twain first came to fame with stories that captured the "local color" of the West. Twain established himself as one of the best writers in the history of American literature by transmuting his childhood experiences into the classic American novels *The Adventures of Tom Sawyer* (1876) and *The Adventures of Huckleberry Finn* (1885). The influence of this later novel was so great that Ernest Hemingway, not noted for his generosity toward other writers, gave it his stamp of approval.

This chapter opens with a treat—a generous sampling of Twain's humor. Next comes a survey of Twain's life and times, paying special attention to his most famous works, including "The Celebrated Jumping Frog of Calaveras County" and *The Adventures of Huckleberry Finn.*

Lit Wit

Twain's major books include the following works:

Innocents Abroad (1869)
Roughing It (1872)
The Gilded Age (1873)
The Adventures of Tom Sawyer (1876)
A Tramp Abroad (1880)
The Prince and the Pauper (1881)
Life on the Mississippi (1883)
The Adventures of Huckleberry Finn (1884)
Mark Twain's Library of Humor (1888)
A Connecticut Yankee in King Arthur's Court (1889)
Pudd'nhead Wilson (1894)
Personal Recollections of Joan of Arc (1895)
Following the Equator (1897)
The Man That Corrupted Hadleyburg (1900)
Extracts from Adam's Diary (1904)
What is Man? (1906)
The Mysterious Stranger (1916)
Letters from the Earth (1939)

Fun and Games

Was Twain funny? Don't take my word for it—read a few classic Twain lines and anecdotes and judge for yourself.

➤ "Always do right. This will gratify some people, and astonish the rest."

➤ "It is better to keep your mouth shut and appear stupid than to open it and remove all doubt."

➤ "By trying, we can easily learn to endure adversity. Another man's, I mean."

➤ "Familiarity breeds contempt—and children."

➤ A Mormon arguing with Twain defied him to cite any Biblical passage expressly forbidding polygamy. "Nothing easier," Twain told him. "No man can serve two masters."

➤ "Before I die," a ruthless businessman told Twain, "I mean to make a pilgrimage to the Holy Land. I will climb Mount Sinai and read the Ten Commandments."

"I have a better idea," Twain suggested. "You could stay home and keep them."

➤ "Quitting smoking is easy," said Twain, who was rarely seen without a cigar perched in his mouth. "I've done it a hundred times."

Now let's take a look at Twain's life and career to see how he developed into America's foremost humorist (not to mention one of our best novelists and the master of "local color" writing.)

Ever the Twain Shall Meet

It's not easy to write a biography about Samuel Clemens because he was so darned blameless. Saint Sam Clemens was a vocal champion of any oppressed minority: He campaigned for black rights, supported workers, and deplored anti-Semitism. Twain also supported Native Americans, which was amazing for his time. And he spoke out in favor of women, too. Twain was devoted to his invalid wife and famously tender to his three daughters. So he smoked stinky cigars and enjoyed a beer or two. That's all I could dig up on him.

Samuel Clemens was born in Florida, Missouri, but the family moved soon after to the one-horse town of Hannibal, Missouri, which would become the setting of many of his most famous novels. Sam's father died when the lad was only 12 years old. Sam apprenticed himself to a printer to help keep the wolf from the family's door.

"There comes a time in every rightly constructed boy's life that he has a raging desire to go somewhere and dig for hidden treasure, " Twain later noted. For Twain, the time came when he was in his late teens. Although he was apprenticed to a printer, Twain's restless nature drove him west to mine for gold. However, he didn't strike gold.

At 21, Twain circled back home and learned to pilot a Mississippi riverboat, which was then a prestigious and lucrative career. When the Civil War halted river trade, Sam tried a series of get-rich-quick schemes that succeeded only in making him poorer faster. Scraping bottom, he turned to his pen. Writing under the pseudonym *Mark Twain* (the riverboat pilot's cry for "All clear!"), Sam began to churn out newspaper features.

The Write Stuff

As many have noted, the short length of Twain's boyhood may have made him value it all the more.

Lit Speak

Samuel Clemens's pen name **Mark Twain** is the phrase Mississippi boatmen used to signify 2 fathoms (3.6 meters) of water, the depth needed for a boat's safe passage.

When he started writing, Twain wasn't planning a career; he was just trying to make a living. That quickly changed, however, when he fell in love with and married Olivia Langdon, the delicate flower of a well-to-do family. For years, critics and scholars claimed that Livy, Our Lady of the Slipcover, changed the swaggering, swearing Sam into a sensitive, henpecked weenie. Whether Livy was responsible or not, marriage made Twain realize that he had to take his writing more seriously if he was to make a living by his pen.

Lit Wit

It was very common in the 19th century for writers to take pen names—and often outrageous ones at that. Twain's mentor, the humorist/local colorist Charles Farrar Browne (1834–1867) wrote under the name Artemus Ward. Other frontier humorists included Petroleum Vesuvius Nasby (David Ross Locke), Orpheus C. Kerr (Robert Henry Newell), and Josh Billings (Henry Wheeler Shaw). The tradition continues in our day, with the humorist/filmmaker Woody Allen (Allen Stewart Koningsberg).

However influential she may have been, Livy never did break Twain of his habit of "keeping himself healthy" with frequent doses of whiskey, wearing flamboyant white suits in defiance of the universal Victorian black broadcloth, and telling off-color stories in a frontier drawl. But a close look reveals that whatever concessions each partner made to the other, Twain and Livy's marriage was remarkably happy for both partners.

Lit Wit

"...and every day of his life he put on a clean shirt and a full suit from head to toe made out of linen so white it hurt your eyes to look at it." So noted Huck Finn, describing the "aristocratic" Colonel Grangerford. It wasn't until 1906 that Twain himself started dressing this way, but it seemed so perfect a costume for him that most readers today invariably picture Twain in white. In Twain's own day, his white suit appealed to reporters as a dramatic example of his unconventionality. Twain first appeared in white at a Congressional hearing on copyrights.

The Celebrated Jumping Frog of Calaveras County

Twain jumped into national prominence when he wrote a tall tale about Jim Smiley and his frog, which was first published in a New York newspaper in November 1865 and quickly reprinted around the country. Although Twain later discounted the story as a "villainous backwoods sketch," it nonetheless prefigures motifs that would remain a part of Twain's writing throughout his career. These motifs include

➤ Vernacular

➤ Exaggeration

➤ Humor

➤ Deadpan narrator

➤ Unexplained appearance of a mysterious stranger

A *tall tale* is a folktale that exaggerates the main events or a character's abilities. Originally an oral tradition that included American folk heroes such as Paul Bunyan and his blue ox Babe, John Henry, and Mike Fink (the Mississippi riverman), the tall tale eventually found its way into the American literary tradition around the middle of the 19th century. The stories likely started as entertainment during the long and lonely nights on the frontier. Through exaggeration and outright lies, each speaker would try to top the last one with outrageously far-fetched yarns. "The Celebrated Jumping Frog of Calaveras County" is based on a tall tale Twain heard in a mining camp. (And here I said he didn't strike gold.)

"The Celebrated Jumping Frog of Calaveras County" has only four characters:

➤ *The Narrator:* Name withheld to protect the innocent

➤ *Simon Wheeler:* A blowhard blatherer

➤ *Jim Smiley:* Candidate for Gamblers Anonymous

➤ *Dan'l Webster:* Kermit of Calaveras County

Lit Speak

Vernacular is the ordinary language of people in a particular region. Twain, like many other writers, used vernacular to create realistic characters and an informal tone.

Lit Speak

A **tall tale** is wildly exaggerated a folktale. Tall tales often contain outrageous events and unbelievable occurrences.

Lit Wit

Twain revised *The Celebrated Jumping Frog of Calaveras County* several times, so a number of different versions are in circulation.

The Situation

The unnamed narrator, a stranger in town, calls on Simon Wheeler to ask about Leonidas W. Smiley, a friend of a friend. The narrator soon learns that he's been set up: Leonidas W. Smiley doesn't exist. Wheeler then backs the narrator into a corner and launches into a tale of a man named Jim Smiley, whose love of gambling is rivaled only by Imelda Marcos's love of shoes. The story of Jim Smiley starts this way:

"There was a feller here once by the name of Jim Smiley, in the winter of '49—or maybe it was the spring of '50—I don't recollect exactly, somehow, though what makes me think it was one or the other is because I remember the big flume wasn't finished when he first came to the camp; but any way, he was the curiosest man about always betting on any thing that turned up you ever see, if he could get any body to bet on the other side; and if he couldn't, he'd change sides. Any way that suited the other man would suit him — any way just so's he got a bet, he was satisfied. But still he was lucky, uncommon lucky; he most always come out winner. He was always ready and laying for a chance; there couldn't be no solitry thing mentioned but that feller'd offer to bet on it, and take any side you please, as I was just telling you. If there was a horse-race, you'd find him flush, or you'd find him busted at the end of it; if there was a dog-fight, he'd bet on it; if there was a cat-fight, he'd bet on it; if there was a chicken-fight, he'd bet on it; why, if there was two birds setting on a fence, he would bet you which one would fly first; or if there was a camp-meeting, he would be there reg'lar, to bet on Parson Walker, which he judged to be the best exhorter

The Write Stuff

Notice how Twain stretches the reader's credulity as the bets get more and more exaggerated.

about here, and so he was, too, and a good man. If he even seen a straddle-bug start to go anywheres, he would bet you how long it would take him to get wherever he was going to, and if you took him up, he would foller that straddle-bug to Mexico but what he would find out where he was bound for and how long he was on the road. Lots of the boys here has seen that Smiley, and can tell you about him. Why, it never made no difference to him—he would bet on any thing—the dangdest feller. Parson Walker's wife laid very sick once, for a good while, and it seemed as if they warn't going to save her; but one morning he come in, and

Smiley asked how she was, and he said she was considerable better—thank the Lord for his inf'nit mercy—and coming on so smart that, with the blessing of Prov'dence, she'd get well yet; and Smiley, before he thought, says, "Well, I'll risk two-and-a-half that she don't, any way."

Smiley is especially proud of his "fifteen-minutes nag," who always makes it to the finish line first, despite her asthmatic wheezing. Smiley delights in conning the spectators into giving the nag a huge head start, even though the nag always makes it in first.

The Setup

In the same way, Smiley's ornery bull pup, named Andrew Jackson after the tenacious president, always manages to win dog fights. The little dog waits until all the bets are on the table. Then it grabs onto an opponent's hind leg...

"...jest by the j'int of his hind leg and freeze to it—not chew, you understand, but only jest grip and hang on till they threw up the sponge, if it was a year. Smiley always come out winner on that pup, till he harnessed a dog once that didn't have no hind legs, because they'd been sawed off by a circular saw, and when the thing had gone along far enough, and the money was all up, and he come to make a snatch for his pet holt, he saw in a minute how he'd been imposed on, and how the other dog had him in the door, so to speak, and he 'peared surprised, and then he looked sorter discouraged-like, and didn't try no more to win the fight, and so he got shucked out bad. He give Smiley a look, as much as to say his heart was broke, and it was his fault, for putting up a dog that hadn't no hind legs for him to take holt of, which was his main dependence in a fight, and then he limped off a piece and laid down and died. It was a good pup, was that Andrew Jackson, and would have made a name for hisself if he'd lived, for the stuff was in him, and he had genius..."

The Sting

Soon after, Smiley "ketched a frog one day, and took him home, and said he cal'klated to edercate him; and so he never done nothing for three months but set in his back yard and learn that frog to jump." Smiley calls the frog "Dan'l Webster" after the silver-tongued orator and diplomat. Dan' the frog becomes a champion jumper and so captures the admiration of the local gamblers. One day the proverbial stranger strolls into town and Smiley sets him up for the sting—or so he thinks. Here's how it goes down:

"Well, Smiley kept the beast in a little lattice box, and he used to fetch him down town sometimes and lay for a bet. One day a feller—a stranger in the camp, he was—come across him with his box, and says: 'What might it be that you've got in the box?'

And Smiley says, sorter indifferent like, 'It might be a parrot, or it might be a canary, may be, but it ain't — it's only just a frog.'

And the feller took it, and looked at it careful, and turned it round this way and that, and says, 'H'm —so 'tis. Well, what's he good for?'

'Well,' Smiley says, easy and careless, 'He's good enough for one thing, I should judge—he can outjump any frog in Calaveras county.'

The feller took the box again, and took another long, particular look, and give it back to Smiley, and says, very deliberate, 'Well, I don't see no p'ints about that frog that's any better'n any other frog.'

'May be you don't,' Smiley says. 'May be you understand frogs, and may be you don't understand 'em; may be you've had experience, and may be you ain't only a amateur, as it were. Anyways, I've got my opinion, and I'll risk forty dollars that he can outjump any frog in Calaveras county.'

And the feller studied a minute, and then says, kinder sad like, 'Well, I'm only a stranger here, and I ain't got no frog; but if I had a frog, I'd bet you.'"

Lit Wit

Mark Twain, William Faulkner, and many other writers are indebted to frontier pre-Civil War humorists such as Johnson Hooper, George Washington Harris, Augustus Longstreet, Thomas Bangs Thorpe, and Joseph Baldwin. Local boasters, also known as "ring-tailed roarers," drew strength from natural hazards that would terrify lesser men. "I'm a regular tornado," one swelled, "tough as hickory and long-winded as a nor'wester. I can strike a blow like a falling tree, and every lick makes a gap in the crowd that lets in an acre of sunshine."

Smiley, no rocket scientist, leaves Dan'l with the stranger while he goes off to the swamp to fetch another amphibious opponent. The stranger thinks to himself for a moment and then "took a teaspoon and filled him full of quail shot pretty near up to his chin and set him on the floor." Smiley returns with a choice frog, and the race begins.

"…the new frog hopped off, but Dan'l give a heave, and hysted up his shoulders—so—like a Frenchman, but it wan't no use—he couldn't budge; he was planted as solid as an anvil, and he couldn't no more stir than if he was anchored out. Smiley was a good deal surprised, and he was disgusted too, but he didn't have no idea what the matter was, of course.

The feller took the money and started away; and when he was going out at the door, he sorter jerked his thumb over his shoulders—this way—at Dan'l, and says again, very deliberate, 'Well, I don't see no p'ints about that frog that's any better'n any other frog.'

Smiley he stood scratching his head and looking down at Dan'l a long time, and at last he says, 'I do wonder what in the nation that frog throw'd off for—I wonder if there ain't something the matter with him—he 'pears to look mighty baggy, somehow.' And he ketched Dan'l by the nap of the neck, and lifted him up and says, 'Why, blame my cats, if he don't weigh five pound!' and turned him upside down, and he belched out a double handful of shot. And then he see how it was, and he was the maddest man—he set the frog down and took out after that feller, but he never ketched him. And...'

Simon Wheeler gets interrupted and the narrator attempts a hasty retreat. But Simon buttonholes the man with a new tale of a "yaller [yellow] one-eyed cow that didn't have no tail, only jest a short stump like a bannanner, and—" but the stranger makes good his escape.

Hop to It

Critics agree that "The Jumping Frog" is likely the best humorous sketch ever produced in America. As with many of the funnymen of the American West, Twain created humor by relating wildly exaggerated stories in a deadpan tone, which emphasizes the humor because it implies that the narrator is unaware of the story's absurdity.

Twain wasn't the first writer to combine high style with low, nor the first to squander genius on a shaggy frog story. The "high style" is shown in the elevated diction of the opening and closing, while the "low style" is shown in Simon Wheeler's use of the vernacular.

What was new, electric, and instantly popular, however, was the quality of the story that resulted when he switched from standard written English to the vernacular.

Early 19th-century American writers tended to be flowery, sentimental, or ostentatious—partially because they were still trying to prove that they could write as elegantly as the English. Twain's style, which was based on realistic, colloquial American speech, gave Americans a new appreciation of their national voice. Every humorist since, including James Thurber, Dorothy Parker, Robert Benchley, S.J. Perelman, and Woody Allen, labors in Twain's shadow.

The Adventures of Huckleberry Finn

"The Celebrated Jumping Frog of Calaveras County" put Twain on the literary map, but *The Innocents Abroad* put some money in his pocket. *Life on the Mississippi* made him even more money. In 1871, a year after marrying Olivia, Twain used the money he earned from the sales of these books to buy the manor to which he wasn't born, a tasteful spread in Connecticut. Forty years of fame and fortune followed.

Life on the Mississippi is Twain's own account of his experiences as a boy and young man living on the Mississippi River. As an adult, he claimed he still retained his childhood wish to become a riverboat pilot. Riverboat trade was enormously important in Twain's day; as a result, the position of riverboat pilot had tremendous prestige. Although Twain never did achieve fame as a riverboat pilot, his love of the Mississippi

River and the boats that traveled its length is evident in much of his writing, especially in the rich detail he drew from the setting. This detail helped give his novels their remarkable clarity and depth.

High points in Twain's career include his masterpieces, *The Adventures of Tom Sawyer* and *The Adventures of Huckleberry Finn,* published in 1885.

Although the novel is widely considered to be one of the greatest American works of art, *Huckleberry Finn* was condemned by many reviewers in Twain's time as coarse and by many commentators in our time as racist. In 1885, the novel was banished from the shelves of the Concord Public Library for its foul language. The novel is still frequently in the media, as schools across the country alternately ban it or restore it to their classrooms.

Here's how the novel begins:

> *"You don't know about me without you have read a book by the name of The Adventures of Tom Sawyer; but that ain't no matter. That book was made by Mr. Mark Twain, and he told the truth, mainly. There was things which he stretched, but mainly he told the truth. That is nothing. I never seen anybody but lied one time or another, without it was Aunt Polly, or the widow, or maybe Mary. Aunt Polly—Tom's Aunt Polly, she is—and Mary, and the Widow Douglas is all told about in that book, which is mostly a true book, with some stretchers, as I said before."*

Lit Speak

Life on the Mississippi is a **memoir**, a record of a person's life and experiences or a description of the events associated with a particular event. Certainly, real live people emerge from Twain's account of his training as a riverboat pilot on the Mississippi River.

The Write Stuff

The Adventures of Huckleberry Finn takes place in the Mississippi Valley, from 1835–1845.

Meet the cast:

➤ *Huckleberry Finn:* The self-reliant, mischievous, thoughtful boy you wish you had been, but wouldn't baby-sit for for all the junk food in the world.

➤ *Tom Sawyer:* The guy who taps the keg, wears the toga, and still manages to ace math.

➤ *Jim:* The black man whose only mistake is being born a Southern slave.

➤ *Pap:* Huck's father—a father in name only. He is a poor drunkard who gives new definition to the words *child abuse.*

➤ *The Widow Douglas and her sister Miss Watson*: the well-meaning women who take Huck in and try to "sivilize" him.

➤ *The Duke and King:* Shady con men.

➤ *The Grangerfords and Shepherdsons:* Two perpetually feuding families who have long forgotten what the fight's about; Twain's version of the Hatfields and McCoys.

➤ *Aunt Polly*: Huck's aunt. She comes in at the very end of the book.

➤ *The Mississippi*: A state of mind as much as a body of water; Old Man River represents freedom and unifies the novel.

Do As I Say, Not As I Do

At the beginning of the novel, we learn that the Widow Douglas and her sister Miss Watson are hell-bent on civilizing Huck, the motherless child of the town drunk.

To that end, they're determined to get Huck to stop swearing and smoking. They also want him to attend school, wear clean clothes, and even sleep in a bed rather than outside in an old barrel. Here's what Huck has to say about civilized life:

"The widow rung a bell for supper, and you had to come to time. When you got to the table you couldn't go right to eating, but you had to wait for the widow to tuck down her head and grumble a little over the victuals, though there warn't really anything the matter with them—that is, nothing only everything was cooked by itself. In a barrel of odds and ends it is different; things get mixed up, and the juice kind of swaps around, and the things go better.

After supper she got out her book and learned me about Moses and the Bulrushers, and I was in a sweat to find out all about him; but by and by she let it out that Moses had been dead a considerable long time; so then I didn't care no more about him, because I don't take no stock in dead people."

Huck is quick to notice the hypocrisy in these well-meaning but sanctimonious old ladies:

"Pretty soon I wanted to smoke, and asked the widow to let me. But she wouldn't. She said it was a mean practice and wasn't clean, and I must try to not do it any more. That is just the way with some people. They get down on a thing when they don't know nothing about it. Here she was a-bothering about Moses, which was no kin to her, and no use to anybody, being gone, you see, yet finding a power of fault with me for doing a thing that had some good in it. And she took snuff, too; of course that was all right, because she done it herself."

Nonetheless, Huck slowly adjusts to civilized life—until he finds footsteps that reveal that Pap, his shiftless father, is back in town to get his greasy hands on the $6,000 robbers' treasure Huck and his friend, Tom Sawyer found in a cave. With a caginess that would make a Swiss banker proud, Huck signs the money over to honest Judge Thatcher.

Furious that he can't grab Huck's money, Pap kidnaps his son and locks him in an isolated cabin. What follows is a scene that would make Wes Craven's blood run cold: Pap beats Huck bloody and tries to starve him into submission. Huck finally escapes the abuse by faking his own death by killing a pig and smearing the cabin with its blood. Huck then goes to nearby abandoned Jackson's Island to hide until the excitement blows over.

Lit Wit

It took Twain eight years to finish the novel that would become a turning point in American literature. Twain worked very hard on his new book, but he didn't think much of it at first. "I like it only tolerably well, as far as I have got," Twain wrote to his friend, novelist and critic William Dean Howells, "and may possibly pigeonhole or burn the manuscript when it is done." For some reason never explained, Twain got stuck in the middle of the writing and set the book aside until 1883. At that point, pressured by financial needs, he once again took up the manuscript and pushed through until it was completed.

Huck and Jim

Three days later, Huck discovers Jim, Miss Watson's black slave, who has run away to Jackson's Island because Miss Watson wants to sell him. Although horrified that Jim would try to escape, Huck swears to keep his secret. Fearing capture, the two raft down the Mississippi, planning to hop a steamboat and travel to Ohio, a free state.

Along the way, Huck and Jim have a series of adventures. The first one occurs when they become embroiled in a fictional version of the Hatfield-McCoy feud as the Grangerfords and Shepherdsons shoot it out over an issue that neither side can remember.

A little farther down the river, Jim and Huck are suckered by the King and Duke, two con men pretending to be royalty. The con men profit from revival meetings and fraudulent theatrical productions. When the two con men set out to defraud the bereaved Wilks family, Huck is struck with remorse and determines to protect the family. When the real heirs arrive, however, Huck's carefully laid plans are ruined and he narrowly escapes. Two two con men plot to capture Jim and turn him in for the reward. With all these goings-on, Jim and Huck miss the turn for Ohio and end up heading deeper into slave territory.

Huck struggles with his conscience about whether to help Jim escape from slavery. He finally writes a letter to Miss Watson, revealing their location, but he cannot make up his mind whether or not to actually send it, as the following scene shows:

"I felt good and all washed clean of sin for the first time I had ever felt so in my life, and I knowed I could pray now. But I didn't do it straight off, but laid the paper down and set there thinking—thinking how good it was all this happened so, and how near I come to being lost and going to hell. And went on thinking. And got to thinking over our trip down the river; and I see Jim before me, all the time, in the day, and in the night-time, sometimes moonlight, sometimes storms, and we a floating along, talking, and singing, and laughing.

But somehow I couldn't seem to strike no places to harden me against him, but only the other kind. I'd see him standing my watch on top of his'n, stead of calling me, so I could go on sleeping; and see him how glad he was when I come back out of the fog; and when I come to him again in the swamp, up there where the feud was; and such-like times…and how good he always was; and at last I struck the time I saved him by telling the men we had small-pox abroad, and he was so grateful, and said I was the best friend old Jim ever had in the world, and the only one he's got now; and then I happened to look around, and see that paper.

It was a close place. I took it up, and held it in my hand. I was a trembling, because I'd got to decide, forever, betwixt two things, and I knowed it. I studied a minute, sort of holding my breath, and then says to myself:

'All right, then, I'll go to hell—and tore it up.'"

This is Huck's crisis of conscience. By pushing Huck the "wrong" way in a tug of war between his conscience and temptation, Twain revealed the hypocrisy of institutionalized religion. Consider the Widow's earlier hypocritical attempts to teach Huck about religion—even though she owns slaves. Huck's decision to free Jim indirectly makes him more "religious" than those around him.

Light Out for the Territory Ahead of the Rest

Huck tracks Jim to the Phelps' farm, where he is being held. The Phelps' farm is the home of Tom Sawyer's Aunt Polly. In a silly and unbelievable twist, Huck is mistaken for Tom and Tom is mistaken for Sid Sawyer, Tom's brother.

Tom concocts an elaborate scheme for Jim's escape, chock full of daring schemes such as chains, letters scratched in blood, and hair's-breath escapes. When the scheme fails and Tom is shot in the leg, Tom finally admits that Jim has been free for some time, thanks to Miss Watson's death and the terms of her will. Tom knew for some time that Miss Watson had died and freed Jim in her will, but this ironic twist is news to Huck—and the reader.

Jim tells Huck that Pap has died. Jim and Huck had discovered Pap's partially decomposed body earlier in the novel, but Jim had carefully shielded Huck from the body and its identity. Fed up with writing, Huck ends his tale this way:

"…there ain't nothing more to write about, and I am rotten glad of it, because if I'd a knowed what a trouble it was to make a book I wouldn't a tackled it, and ain't a-going to no more. But I reckon I got to

Writer's Block

The novel's ending is very controversial. To some readers, the slapstick undermines the novel's serious tone, its depiction of a slave as a human being was still a controversial stance at the time. Other critics and readers, in contrast, prefer the humorous ending, seeing it as a frothy conclusion to a serious work. Perhaps Twain planned the ending deliberately, or maybe he had written himself into a corner. It's your call, reader.

light out for the Territory ahead of the rest, because Aunt Sally she's going to adopt me and sivilize me, and I can't stand it. I been there before."

The ending gives the reader the counter-version of the classic American success myth: The open road leading to the pristine wilderness, away from the morally corrupting influences of "civilization." James Fenimore Cooper's novels, Walt Whitman's hymns to the open road, William Faulkner's "The Bear," and Jack Kerouac's *On the Road* are other literary examples of this theme.

Mark My Words

The federal government once asked a committee of English teachers to prepare a list of books that should be required reading for all students. They could agree unanimously on only one book—*The Adventures of Huckleberry Finn.*

Huck Finn is the book that firmly established American literature. Inevitably, it has inspired countless literary interpretations. Here are a few of the standard ones:

➤ The novel is a story of death, rebirth, and initiation.

➤ The escaped slave Jim is a father figure for Huck; in deciding to save Jim, Huck grows morally beyond the bounds of his slave-owning society.

➤ Jim's adventures initiate Huck into the complexities of human nature and give him moral courage.

➤ Twain uses slavery as the metaphor for all social bondage and accepted injustice and inhumanity.

➤ Freedom exists on the raft and the river, not in the North or the South.

Huckleberry Finn also dramatizes Twain's ideal of the harmonious community: "What you want, above all things, on a raft is for everybody to be satisfied and feel right and kind toward the others." Like Melville's *Pequod,* the raft sinks, and with it that special community. The pure, simple world of the raft is ultimately overwhelmed by progress—the steamboat—but the mythic image of the river remains, as vast and changing as life itself.

Besides the novel's uproarious comedy, there is a tragic view of the Garden of Eden, one of the great visions of the unattainable world of freedom in nature. As you've already seen, the theme got its start with James Fenimore Cooper's Natty Bumppo, our first Wild Man. As you'll find out in Chapter 21, the dream gets picked up by F. Scott Fitzgerald, most memorably in his novel *The Great Gatsby.* In the 1950s, this theme is picked up by J.D. Salinger's Holden Caulfield, a sort of Huck Lite.

The Write Stuff

In *Huckleberry Finn,* Twain attacks the romanticism of the South. The senseless feud between the Grangerfords and the Shepherdsons epitomizes the South's mindless adherence to the myths of its past, its reliance on form over substance.

Mr. Clemens and Mark Twain

"Every one is a moon, and has a dark side which he never shows to anybody."

—Mark Twain

The good times never last. By the 1890s, Twain's life was in a shambles. His health broken, his fortune lost in the Panic of 1893, his daughter dead of meningitis, Twain plunged into a deep depression. "Of all the animals, man is the only one that is cruel. He is the only one that inflicts pain for the pleasure of doing it," Twain said during this time.

Although deeply embittered by the turn his life had taken, Twain nonetheless continued to write and lecture. He was extraordinarily popular on the lecture circuit, a top venue for public entertainment before movies, television, and radio.

Mark Twain.

Twain was born when Halley's comet appeared in 1835 and died—as he had predicted—when it appeared again in 1910. "It will be the greatest disappointment of my life if I don't go out with Halley's Comet," he wrote. "The Almighty has said, no doubt: 'Now here are two unaccountable freaks; they came in together, they must go out together.'"

Lit Wit

Rumor has it that in 1897 an American newspaper mistakenly announced Twain's death. When another paper sent a reporter to check the story, Twain opened the door to his Connecticut home and gave the following statement: "James Ross Clemens, a cousin of mine, was seriously ill two or three weeks ago, but is well now. The reports of my illness grew out of his illness. The reports of my death are greatly exaggerated."

Huck Finn "don't take no stock in dead people," but Clemens' death was treated in all parts of the country as a major event in America's history. Twain's obituary in the April 22, 1910 issue of the *New York Times* noted that...

> *"Samuel L. Clemens was the greatest American humorist of his age nobody will deny. ... We may leave it an open question whether he was not also the greatest American writer of fiction. The creator of Mulberry Sellers and Pudd'nhead Wilson, the inventor of that Southwestern feud in "Huckleberry Finn," which, with all its wildly imaginative details, is still infused with rare pathos, has certainly an undying vitality. ... His death will be mourned, everywhere, and smiles will break through the tears as remembrance of the man's rich gift to his era comes to the mourners' minds. However his work may be judged by impartial and unprejudiced generations his fame is imperishable."*

The Least You Need to Know

➤ Samuel Langhorne Clemens ("Mark Twain") is widely thought to be the greatest American humorist and one of our greatest novelists.

➤ His most famous books include *The Adventures of Huckleberry Finn, Tom Sawyer, Life on the Mississippi, The Prince and the Pauper,* and *A Connecticut Yankee in King Arthur's Court.*

➤ A mythic tale of death, rebirth, freedom, and bondage, *The Adventures of Huckleberry Finn* is one of America's most influential novels.

➤ He used vernacular, exaggeration, and a deadpan narrator to create humor.

I SERVED WITH HIM I TELL YOU!

Chapter 16

Life Is Short and Then You Die: Stephen Crane (1871–1900)

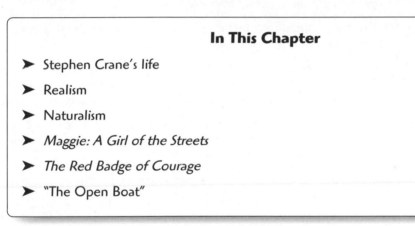

In This Chapter

➤ Stephen Crane's life

➤ Realism

➤ Naturalism

➤ *Maggie: A Girl of the Streets*

➤ *The Red Badge of Courage*

➤ "The Open Boat"

"A man said to the universe:
'Sir, I exist!'
'However,' replied the universe,
'The fact has not created in me
A sense of obligation.'"

—Stephen Crane, "Black Riders and Other Lines"

Crane was a literary Terminator, attacking long-standing traditions with a bold new style and theme. He smashed through patriotism, nationalism, individualism, and organized religion to confront the meaningless of the world.

Stephen Crane died broke in 1900 at the age of 28. Although his life was brief and painful—he died of tuberculosis and malaria—Crane published an amazing amount: five novels, two volumes of poetry, three big story collections, two books of war stories, and countless works of short fiction and reporting. He'd also *done* an amazing amount of things by the time he died.

The frail-looking, chain-smoking, boyishly handsome author-correspondent went to a rebellion in Cuba (well, almost: The boat taking him there sank in a storm), covered a war in Greece, set up a large brick villa for his wife, and cultivated an array of celebrated literary and artistic friends.

In this chapter, you'll learn all about this landmark novelist and short story writer—and the literary movement he spawned, naturalism.

Even Stephen

Stephen Crane was born in Newark, New Jersey, a preacher's kid. Papa Crane was devout and Mama Crane was fertile—Stephen was the fourteenth child. Sickly and frail, Stephen didn't attend school until he was eight. This wasn't a major issue, however, for Stephen far preferred baseball to books.

Encouraged by his parents to pursue a career as a clergyman, Stephen enrolled in a seminary for two years when he was in his late teens.

Religion didn't stick. Then came a brief stint at Claverack College, a military academy in upstate New York, followed by a fly-by at Lafayette College in Pennsylvania. After he failed five of seven classes, Stephen transferred to Syracuse University in New York.

At Syracuse, Crane played baseball and wrote for the school paper. After deciding that "College life is a waste of time," Crane elbowed his way on to the *New York Tribune* as a cub reporter.

Two years later, when he was 22 years old, Crane published his first novel, *Maggie: A Girl of the Streets*. This tale of a good girl who becomes a prostitute because of her environment and heredity was a milestone in the development of literary realism. The book was generally ignored by the public but won the admiration of other realistic writers such as William Dean Howells, the most influential literary critic of the day.

Two years later, in 1895, Crane published his masterpiece, *The Red Badge of Courage*. Set during the Civil War, the novel was praised for its realism. The first modern war novel, *The Red Badge of Courage* depicts the American Civil War from the point of view of a young soldier. An immediate hit, the novel established Crane's professional reputation. He was only 24 years old.

Lit Speak

A **cub reporter** is an apprentice reporter just learning the trade.

Besides writing poems ("The Black Riders and Other Lines," "War Is Kind"), short stories, and novels, Crane made time to sail off to Greece as a war correspondent for William Randolph Hearst's New York *Journal*. This experience inspired his short story "Death and the Child." In 1898, Crane traveled to Cuba to report on the Spanish-American War for the New York *World*, resulting in his classic story "The Open Boat."

Besides ambition, Crane had, in the words of his colleague John Northern Hilliard, "a hankering for the women." At age 20, Crane proposed to a married woman; when Crane was 22, noted Chicago drama critic Amy Leslie moved in with him—the relationship ended after a "misunderstanding" over $800. And though Crane was a loyal customer and friend of the Tenderloin hookers, he set up housekeeping with Cora Taylor, the proprietress of a well-known Jacksonville brothel in 1898.

Regulars at Crane's debt-ridden, ramshackle, but wildly attractive literary household included Ford Maddox Ford, H.G. Wells, Harold Frederic, and Joseph Conrad, who considered the decade-younger Crane to be his literary mentor.

Crane died before he was 30, leaving enough writing to fill 10 fat books.

Writer's Block

Don't confuse Stephen Crane with fellow writer Hart Crane. Hart Crane (1899-1932) saw himself as a seer and prophet like his idol Walt Whitman, but unlike Whitman, Crane was unable to withstand the public's indifference to his work. He could sing but he couldn't swim, as his suicide off the side of a ship in the Gulf of Mexico tragically proved.

The March of Time

Literary theories come and go, but they all have two things in common: They all end in *-ism* and they all attempt to overthrow the theory that came before. Sometimes the vanguard succeeds in fomenting a literary revolution; other times, they build on what came before to make something new. In either event, literature gets a complete overhaul and the way we look at reality changes.

The two groundbreaking literary *-isms* of the 19th century were *realism* and *naturalism*. Let's see how these two literary movements redirected American writers.

The Write Stuff

Crane's poetry has much in common with Emily Dickinson's simple, stripped-down style.

The Mother of -ism: Realism

"I saw a man pursuing the horizon;
Round and round he sped.
I was disturbed at this;
I accosted the man.
'It is futile,' I said,
'You can never—'
'You lie,' he cried,
And ran on."

Lit Speak

Realism was a literary movement that presented the details of ordinary life in art.

—Stephen Crane, "Black Riders and Other Lines"

Realism was a reaction to romanticism. The realists, the 19th century's answer to the 6 p.m. news, told it like it was, focusing on the lives of ordinary people. Rejecting the heroic and adventurous (hallmarks of romanticism), the realists concentrated on pessimistic views of poverty, prostitution, and pain.

The Son of -ism: Naturalism

Lit Speak

Naturalism was a literary movement that traced the effects of heredity and environment on people who were helpless to change their situations. Naturalism is also called **determinism** for its belief in the effects of environment, heredity, and chance on human fate.

"In the desert

I saw a creature, naked, bestial,

who, squatting upon the ground,

Held his heart in his hands,

And ate of it.

I said, 'Is it good, friend?'

'It is bitter bitter,' he answered;

'But I like it

Because it is bitter,

And because it is my heart.'"

—Stephen Crane, from "Black Riders and Other Lines"

Like the realists, the naturalists focused on the lives of ordinary people and attempted to portray life truthfully and accurately. But the naturalists took a darker view of the world. According to the naturalists,

➤ The universe is unpredictable, spontaneous, and discontinuous.

➤ Our fate is determined by our environment, heredity, and chance.

➤ Free will is an illusion.

➤ Life is a cruel joke.

The Write Stuff

What's one advantage of reading a naturalist novel? You never have to read the last page first because you can assume that everyone is going to come to a bad end.

As a result, the naturalists created characters whose lives were shaped by forces they could neither understand nor control.

Naturalism flourished in the early 1900s but exploded again in the 1930s in John Dos Passos' *U.S.A.*, depicting a panoramic view of America—both its positive side and its underbelly—and *Grapes of Wrath*, John Steinbeck's masterpiece about the Okies and the dust bowl. (In 1948, media darling Norman Mailer gave the nod to naturalism when he published *The Naked and the Dead*.)

Lit Wit

The early naturalists include the French writer Gustave Flaubert (1821-1880), famous for his novel *Madame Bovary*, and George Eliot (1819-1880), the female writer celebrated for such novels as *Adam Bede*. Other early naturalists were Hamlin Garland (1860-1940), author *of Son of the Middle Border* and *Main-Travelled Roads*. However, Émile Zola (1840-1902) was undoubtedly the best-known and most influential early Naturalist. Zola's impressive Rougon-Macquart series in 20 volumes dominated the literary scene from 1871 to 1893.

Only the Good Die Young: *Maggie: A Girl of the Streets*

"'Smash 'im, Jimmie, kick deh damn guts out of 'im,' yelled Pete, the lad with the chronic sneer, in tones of delight.

The small combatants pounded and kicked, scratched and tore. They began to weep and their curses struggled in their throats with sobs. The other little boys clasped their hands and wriggled their legs in excitement. They formed a bobbing circle about the pair. A tiny spectator was suddenly agitated.

'Cheese it, Jimmie, cheese it! Here comes yer fader,' he yelled.

The circle of little boys instantly parted. They drew away and waited in ecstatic awe for that which was about to happen. The two little boys fighting in the modes of four thousand years ago, did not hear the warning.

Up the avenue there plodded slowly a man with sullen eyes. He was carrying a dinner pail and smoking an apple-wood pipe.

As he neared the spot where the little boys strove, he regarded them listlessly. But suddenly he roared an oath and advanced upon the rolling fighters.

'Here, you Jim, git up, now, while I belt yer life out, you damned disorderly brat.'

He began to kick into the chaotic mass on the ground. The boy Billie felt a heavy boot strike his head. He made a furious effort and disentangled himself from Jimmie. He tottered away damning.

Jimmie arose painfully from the ground and confronting his father, began to curse him. His parent kicked him. 'Come home, now,' he cried, 'an' stop yer jawin', er I'll lam the everlasting head off yehs.'

They departed. The man paced placidly along with the apple-wood emblem of serenity between his teeth. The boy followed a dozen feet in the rear. He swore luridly, for he felt that it was degradation for one who aimed to be some vague soldier, or a man of blood with a sort of sublime license, to be taken home by a father."

—from Chapter 1, *Maggie: A Girl of the Streets*

In this novel, Maggie and her two brothers grow up on the wrong side of the tracks. The kids' parents have crawled inside the bottle and set up housekeeping, and the children spend a lot of time cowering under the bed as their parents duke it out. One son dies young, while the other, Jimmie, follows in his father's footsteps to become a drunken lout. Miraculously, Maggie remains untouched by the filth around her—until she falls in love with Jimmie's best friend, the flashy barkeep Pete. Two dates with Pete and Maggie's a Fallen Woman.

Writer's Block

Around the turn of the century, sailors were considered disreputable, since long ocean voyages had made them raucous and rude. In addition, they were often disease-ridden. Clearly, this was before the gentrification of the waterfront!

The Write Stuff

Crane's attack on the hypocritical religious values of the late 19th century opened the floodgates for the so-called loss of traditional values, a major 20th-century theme.

Once he gets what he wants, Pete drops Maggie so fast her teeth rattle. Her mother and the neighbors, judging Maggie a disgrace, refuse to offer her shelter. As a result, Maggie finds herself homeless. Jimmie, an expert in seducing other men's sisters, joins the general hypocritical indignation and decides to punch out Pete's lights for Maggie's honor. When Jimmie fails to inflict any real damage, he lays the blame on Maggie. Crane's attack on the hypocritical religious values of the late 19th century opened the floodgates for the so-called loss of traditional values, a major 20th-century theme.

Maggie begs Pete to take her back, but he refuses. Homeless and penniless, Maggie turns to the world's oldest profession, but gigs are slim for the inexperienced, and she sinks lower and lower, finally ending up trying to seduce men on the waterfront.

Shortly thereafter, Jimmie comes home from one of his weeks on the town to find out that Maggie has died. Maggie's mother shrieks and laments that she now forgives her daughter her sins. Since Maggie is dead, she cannot benefit from her mother's beneficence.

A Book of Firsts

The publication of *Maggie* in 1893 heralded a major new talent in American letters. The first novel to deal realistically with life in the slums, *Maggie* has been called "the first truly American novel," "the first naturalistic novel," and "the first novel that divides the English novel from the American novel."

Trapped Like a Rat

"The wayfarer,
Perceiving the pathway to truth,
Was struck with astonishment.
It was thickly grown with weeds.
'Ha,' he said,
'I see that none has passed here
In a long time.'
Later he saw that each weed
Was a singular knife.
'Well,' he mumbled at last,
'Doubtless there are other roads.'"

—Stephen Crane from "Black Riders and Other Lines"

As with this excerpt from "Black Riders and Other Lines," *Maggie: A Girl of the Streets* describes a bitter, bleak world. Both works are naturalistic because they trace how people are controlled by their environment and heredity. Maggie never stands a snowball's chance in heck, which was Crane's intention all along. Signing a copy of a book for a friend, Crane wrote, "For it [the novel] tries to show that environment is a tremendous thing in the world and frequently shapes lives regardless."

Crane's masterpiece, *The Red Badge of Courage*, does for naturalism what Hagaan-Dazs does for ice cream. Here's how:

The Red Badge of Courage

"The cold passed reluctantly from the earth, and the retiring fogs revealed an army stretched out on the hills, resting. As the landscape changed from brown to green, the army awakened, and began to tremble with eagerness at the noise of rumors. It cast its eyes upon the roads, which were growing from long troughs of liquid mud to proper thoroughfares. A river, amber-tinted in the shadow of its banks, purled at the army's feet; and at night, when the stream had become of a sorrowful blackness, one could see across it the red, eyelike gleam of hostile camp-fires set in the low brows of distant hills.

Once a certain tall soldier developed virtues and went resolutely to wash a shirt. He came flying back from a brook waving his garment bannerlike. He was swelled with a tale he had heard from a reliable friend, who had heard it from a truthful cavalryman, who had heard it from his trustworthy brother, one of the orderlies at division headquarters. He adopted the important air of a herald in red and gold.

'We're goin' t' move t'morrah—sure,' he said pompously to a group in the company street. 'We're goin' 'way up the river, cut across, an' come around in behint 'em.'"

—from Chapter 1, *The Red Badge of Courage*

Who's Who

➤ *Henry Fleming:* The main character, a callow youth who finds himself through battle.

➤ *Jim Conklin:* The tall soldier.

➤ *Wilson:* The loud soldier.

➤ *The Tattered Soldier:* The soldier who reflects Henry's early infatuation with the blood and guts of war.

➤ *Mrs. Fleming:* Henry's mother, a simple, uneducated farm woman who has a brief cameo appearance.

You're in the Army Now

As the novel opens, dripping-wet behind the ears farm boy Henry Fleming listens to the tall soldier, Jim Conklin, and the loud soldier, Wilson, argue over the rumor that the troops are about to leave. Henry is just itching to see action because he is utterly convinced that war is glorious.

Lit Wit

The Civil War, which raged from 1861–1865, pitted the United States (The Union) against the Confederacy (the 11 secessionist Southern states). Measured in physical devastation and human lives, the Civil War was the costliest war in America's history. By the war's end, more than 600,000 men had been killed and at least that many more injured. The North lost nearly 20 percent of their soldiers; the South, nearly 25 percent. More than $4 billion worth of property was destroyed. Much of the South was shattered, including Richmond, Charleston, Atlanta, and Vicksburg.

As Jim Conklin predicts, the troops do indeed move, but it is only to make another march. When the fighting finally begins, Henry starts off at ground zero, lost in the haze. Suddenly he finds himself in the middle of the attack, firing his rifle over and over. The skirmish ends as suddenly as it began, and Henry is astonished to see the sun shining over the carnage. In the middle of the mop-up, the enemy springs another attack. Exhausted and unprepared, Henry and the rest of the men beat a hasty retreat.

In an orgy of guilt, Henry then hightails it to the forest:

> *"To the youth it was an onslaught of redoubtable dragons. He became like the man who lost his legs at the approach of the red and green monster. He waited in a sort of a horrified, listening attitude. He seemed to shut his eyes and wait to be gobbled…*
>
> *He yelled then with fright and swung about. For a moment, in the great clamor, he was like a proverbial chicken. He lost the direction of safety. Destruction threatened him from all points.*
>
> *Directly he began to speed toward the rear in great leaps. His rifle and cap were gone. His unbuttoned coat bulged in the wind. The flap of his cartridge box bobbed wildly, and his canteen, by its slender cord, swung out behind. On his face was all the horror of those things which he imagined…*
>
> *He ran like a blind man. Two or three times he fell down. Once he knocked his shoulder so heavily against a tree that he went headlong.*
>
> *Since he had turned his back upon the fight his fears had been wondrously magnified. Death about to thrust him between the shoulder blades was far more dreadful than death about to smite him between the eyes. When he thought of it later, he conceived the impression that it is better to view the appalling than to be merely within hearing. The noises of the battle were like stones; he believed himself liable to be crushed."*

Henry later rejoins his fellow soldiers and realizes that he is the only one without a war wound, a "red badge of courage." Henry approaches a badly injured soldier and is horrified to find that it is Jim Conklin. Despite Henry's encouragement, Jim dies. This causes Henry to temporarily head for the hills once again.

Be All That You Can Be

Henry envies the dead, since they're heroes and he's a coward. As he returns to his regiment, the men break ranks and run frantically in his direction, shouting incoherently. One man hits him with his rifle butt and Henry sees stars. He walks for a long while until he catches up with his regiment. There, he speaks with Wilson, who had been a blowhard before the battle. Feeling superior to the blowhard, Henry manages to forget his cowardice.

Another battle starts, and this time Henry takes it on the chin, and everyone praises him as a hero.

At the next battle, Henry behaves admirably. He gets so heated that he keeps firing even after the Rebel Army has been repelled.

So What Did You Do in the War, Daddy?

Crane never intended *The Red Badge of Courage* to be a history of the Civil War; rather, he was going for a psychological portrayal of fear. As seen through the eyes of Henry Fleming, the novel becomes cosmic in scope because it deals with the really scary issues that jolt us awake at 3:00 a.m.:

➤ Isolation

➤ Lack of identity

➤ Fear of death

➤ Failure

➤ Guilt

Lit Speak

The term **impressionist** is often used to describe Crane's vivid renderings of moments of visual beauty and uncertainty. When described this way, Crane's style is being likened to the painting movement of the same name.

Throughout the course of the novel, Henry finds his identity, learns that courage is unselfish, and is able to judge himself dispassionately. In short, he becomes a Man.

The novel is classified as naturalistic because Henry is propelled by outside actions.

The Red Badge of Courage is considered the first truly modern war novel. Ironically, when Crane wrote the book, he had never seen a war, much less fought in one. Luckily for us all, wars can be tough to find, and the Civil War was six years in the past when Crane was born. But he had done his groundwork; his portrait of war was so vivid that several early reviewers were adamant that only a war-scarred battle veteran could have written the book.

Lit Wit

For you history buffs, the battle of Chancellorsville was one of the battles described in the novel. The generals were Joseph Hooker (Union) and Robert E. Lee and Stonewall Jackson (Confederate). Nearly 30,000 men perished in the encounter, including Stonewall himself, who was mistakenly shot by one of his own men. None of this is mentioned in the novel.

The Open Boat

"The Open Boat," subtitled "A Tale Intended to be After the Fact, Being the Experience of Four Men from the Sunk Steamer Commodore," is based on an actual experience, when Crane's ship sank on the journey to Cuba in 1897. Crane and three other men spent nearly 30 terrifying hours in a 10-foot dinghy before reaching the shore at Daytona, Florida. Here's how the story opens:

"None of them knew the color of the sky. Their eyes were fastened upon the waves that swept toward them. These waves were of the hue of slate, save for the tops, which were of foaming white, and all of the men knew the colors of the sea. The horizon narrowed and widened, and dipped and rose, and at all times its edge was jagged with waves that seemed thrust up in points like rocks.

Many a man ought to have a bath-tub larger than the boat which here rode upon the sea. These waves were most wrongfully and barbarously abrupt and tall, and each froth-top was a problem in small boat navigation."

As dawn breaks, the four men are adrift on a small dinghy off the Florida coast—the narrator, an oiler, a cook, and the captain—begin to realize that they might be doomed. The oiler and correspondent are rowing in an attempt to reach the lifesaving station that the cook claims is located in Mosquito Inlet. As the day passes, spirits sink, but the captain, although badly injured, jollies the other men along. Let's pause to meet the cast and crew of tonight's voyage.

Who's Who

> ➤ *The Correspondent:* Crane himself.
> ➤ *The Oiler (Billy):* The Rocky Balboa of the seafaring set.
> ➤ *The Cook:* Better with an oven than an oar.
> ➤ *The Captain:* A brave old salt.
> ➤ *The Sea:* The villain of the story, a cold and cruel mistress.

The Write Stuff

Notice that with the exception of Billy, Crane doesn't name the men—they are the "correspondent," "cook," "captain, and "oiler." This is meant to show that they are as anonymous as pieces of driftwood, symbols for every one of us. Ironically, the only man with a name, the oiler Billy, perishes, as though having an identity marks a person for death.

Cruise to Nowhere

After a long while, the men spy a lighthouse far on the horizon and fashion a sail from the captain's coat. The beach is deserted, and there is no lifesaving station. The men row on, despite their aching muscles.

Suddenly, they spot a man on the beach. They scream to attract his attention, and an omnibus from one of the large resorts drives onto the sand. Since the people on the beach are part of an outing, not a rescue party, they assume that the men on the boat are bored fishermen and ignore them. The wind shifts, the sun sets, and the men are adrift on the indifferent sea.

That night, the exhausted men sleep as best they can, despite the crashing waves that drench them with icy blasts. The oiler, the strongest of the lot, does most of the rowing. Finally, even he falls asleep, and the correspondent rows on. An enormous shark trolling for a midnight snack keeps him company. As is the tendency of people sitting up late at night in a small boat on the open sea, the correspondent muses on his fate:

"If I am going to be drowned—if I am going to be drowned—if I am going to be drowned, why, in the name of the seven mad gods who rule the sea, was I allowed to come thus far and contemplate sand and trees? Was I brought here merely to have my nose dragged away as I was about to nibble the sacred cheese of life? It is preposterous. If this old ninny-woman, Fate, cannot do better than this, she should be deprived of the management of men's fortunes. She is an old hen who knows not her intention. If she has decided to drown me, why did she not do it in the beginning and save me all this trouble. The whole affair is absurd..."

Finally, the shark moves on, the oiler awakens and takes over, and the correspondent gets to grab some sleep.

When You Should Have Taken the Bus

The next morning, the desperate men realize that they must get the boat to shore very soon—or die. The treacherous surf makes it highly unlikely that they will survive. As they approach shore, the men jump into the raging sea.

"The January water was icy, and he reflected immediately that it was colder than he had expected to find it off the coast of Florida. This appeared to his dazed mind as a fact important enough to be noted at the time. The coldness of the water was sad; it was tragic. This fact was somehow mixed and confused with his opinion of his own situation that it seemed almost a proper reason for tears. The water was cold."

Lit Wit

On January 1, 1897, Crane sailed to Cuba on the *Commodore*, laden with arms and ammunition destined for Cuban revolutionaries. Crane was involved in the Cuban struggle for independence, which peaked a year later in the Spanish–American War, newspaper mogul William Randolph Hearst's 1898 sell-more-newspapers war. Ostensibly, the United States waged the war against Spain to liberate Cuba from Spanish rule; in reality, Americans wanted to protect their rights to Cuban sugar. The actual war was as brief as an Elizabeth Taylor marriage: Hostilities began on April 24, 1898, and the peace treaty was signed on December 10. As a result of this skirmish, the United States became an even greater power to be reckoned with.

The oiler and the correspondent swim for it. The injured captain and cook cling to the capsized boat. Ironically, the only one to perish is the oiler, seemingly the strongest of the lot. "In the shallows, face downward, lay the oiler. His forehead touched sand that was periodically, between each wave, clear of the sea." Go figure.

When night fell, the white waves paced to and fro in the moonlight, and the wind brought the sound of the great sea's voice to the men on shore, and they felt that they could then be interpreters.

Rub-a-Dub-Dub: Four Men in a Tub

"The Open Boat" is more than an English teacher begging you to "write what you know." The story concerns the conflict between humanity and nature. The sea, a symbol of nature, is indifferent to people. Alternately cruel and kind, teasing or menacing, the sea is as heartless as teenage acne.

It's naturalism at its purist: Survival on the sea is a matter of total chance. Humanity's struggles are grimly ironic: The oiler, ironically the strongest of the lot, drowns, but the wounded captain and cowardly cook survive. Crane and the Careful Reader (that's you) realize the accident of their survival, the tenuousness of life.

"The Open Boat" has become the poster child of naturalism because of Crane's use of imagery to portray nature's heartbreaking indifference:

➤ The boat is compared to a "bath-tub."

➤ The waves are "slate walls."

➤ The waves have "snarling" crests.

➤ The correspondent compares himself to a mouse, "nibbling at the sacred cheese of life."

The famous line "none of them knew the color of the sky" emphasizes the single-minded focus on survival, on glimpses of land over the jagged horizon.

Lit Speak

"The Open Boat" is a symbolic story. A **symbol** is anything that stands for or represents something else; **Symbolism** was a 19th-century literary movement whose followers tried to express emotions by using a pattern of symbols.

The Least You Need to Know

➤ Crane attacked patriotism, individualism, and organized religion to confront the meaningless of the world.

➤ He is considered to be one of the first naturalists because of his belief in *determinism:* the effects of environment, heredity, and chance on human fate.

➤ Crane is most famous for writing *The Red Badge of Courage,* a novel set in the Civil War.

➤ Crane's writing is celebrated for its images and symbolism.

191

Three on a Match: The Naturalists Jack London, Frank Norris, and Theodore Dreiser (1890–1925)

In This Chapter

➤ More about naturalism

➤ Jack London's life

➤ London's *The Call of the Wild*

➤ London's short story "To Build a Fire"

➤ Frank Norris' life

➤ Norris' *McTeague, a Story of San Francisco*

➤ Theodore Dreiser's life

➤ Dreiser's *An American Tragedy*

An unidentified man in Buenos Aires pushed his wife out of an eighth-floor window this week, but his plan to kill her failed when she became entangled in some power cables below. Seeing she was still alive, the man jumped with the intention of landing on top of her. He missed.

Lit Wit

For those of you who don't spend your nights watching old World War I movies, the saying "three on a match" means bad luck. It comes from the fact that three soldiers lighting a cigarette from one match, a common occurrence since matches were in short supply, could alert the enemy of the men's position. Hence, bad luck.

What's the most likely explanation for this mishap? (Check one.)

➤ A *romanticist* would say: Isn't Nature glorious?

➤ A *realist* would say: That's the way the cookie crumbles.

➤ A *naturalist* would say: He was fated to die this way—that it's the inescapable effects of the man's environment and heredity.

(I call it poetic justice.)

In the previous chapter, you read about Stephen Crane, one of the first naturalists. In this chapter, you'll learn about the three American writers who pushed naturalism to its limits: Jack London, Frank Norris, and Theodore Dreiser.

First, you'll review what you learned about naturalism and delve a little deeper into this literary movement. Next, I'll give you the lowdown on Jack London, the He-Man of the naturalist set. This part of the chapter also includes a discussion of London's most famous novel, *The Call of the Wild*, and his best-known short story, "To Light a Fire."

Then we'll cover Frank Norris, whose novel *McTeague* shows you what happens when a dentist reverts to humanity's primeval roots rather than sticking to your average root canal. Next comes Theodore Dreiser, a big man who made big books and big noise. But first, let's look at naturalism.

The Law of the Claw: Naturalism

"Men were naught, life was naught; FORCE only existed—FORCE that brought men into the world; FORCE that made the wheat grow, FORCE that garnered it from the soil to give place to the succeeding crop."

—Frank Norris

Naturalism, also called literary determinism, denies religion as a motivating force in the world and instead perceives the universe as a blind machine. This results in a bleak, realistic depiction of lower-class life.

To the naturalists, people are human insects, squished on the windshield of life by forces they cannot understand, much less control. Life is a wilderness, and people fight tooth and nail for survival. The abuses of the Industrial Revolution, combined with Darwin's theories of natural selection and survival of the fittest, convinced these writers that people are mere playthings in a cold, cruel universe. The naturalists believed that…

➤ An individual's life is determined by environment, heredity, and chance.

➤ Conditions, not people, are at fault for the way things turn out.

➤ As a result of some crisis, the veneer of civilization can be stripped away, leaving us with the animal within.

➤ Survival of the fittest and natural selection govern people as well as nature.

Naturalistic writers took a scientific or objective approach to their material, striving for an accurate representation of life without idealization. Suffice it to say that naturalistic novels are not a great choice when you're in the mood for a little light reading.

It's a Hard-Knock Life

So why are naturalistic novels so grim? It was a grim time, ladies and gentlemen: In 1860, most Americans lived on farms or in small villages, but by 1919, half of the population was concentrated in about 12 cities. This resulted in poor and overcrowded housing, unsanitary conditions, low pay (called *wage slavery*), difficult working conditions, and inadequate restraints on business.

Labor unions grew out of this, and strikes brought the plight of working people to national awareness. Farmers also struggled against the robber barons like J.P. Morgan and John D. Rockefeller.

Their Eastern banks tightly controlled mortgages and credit vital to Western development and agriculture, while railroad companies charged high prices to transport farm products to the cities.

The robber barons ruled with an iron fist. In 1882, for example, John D. Rockefeller established the

The Write Stuff

Like romanticism, naturalism first appeared in Europe in the works of Honoré de Balzac, Gustave Flaubert, Edmond and Jules Goncourt, Émile Zola, and Guy de Maupassant. These writers daringly opened up the seamy underside of society by probing such topics as divorce, sex, adultery, poverty, and crime.

Lit Speak

The ruthlessly powerful and unscrupulous captains of industry of the late 19th century were nicknamed the **robber barons**. "Barons" came from their power; "robber" from their looting of America's natural resources. (Not to mention their corruption of legislators and other unethical practices.)

Writer's Block

Even the federal government was opposed to the labor movement: In 1877, for instance, President Rutherford B. Hayes sent federal troops to crush railroad strikes and riots.

Standard Oil Trust, a group of some 40 oil companies, and used cutthroat methods to suppress competition. In 1892, Andrew Carnegie, the great steel magnate, used hired thugs to break up a strike among his workers. There was no effective legislation on the side of the laborer.

Over 23 million foreigners—German, Scandinavian, and Irish in the early years, and increasingly Central and Southern Europeans thereafter—flowed into the U.S. between 1860 and 1910. Chinese, Japanese, and Filipino contract laborers were imported by Hawaiian plantation owners, railroad companies, and other American business interests on the West Coast. This great influx of non-English–speaking immigrants flooded the labor market, making it easier for the industrialists to keep salaries and working conditions at rock bottom.

Walk the Walk and Talk the Talk

Since naturalism has a pseudoscientific base, the naturalist writers tended to use scientific and philosophical terms to express their beliefs. Here are the key terms you need to know:

➤ **Atavism**: The reappearance in an individual of characteristics of some distant ancestor that have not been present in intervening generations, such as a hand like a hairy paw.

➤ **Darwinism**: People who are best adapted to survive are chosen through the process of natural selection.

➤ **Determinism**: All events follow natural laws.

➤ **Nativism**: The belief that the "true" Americans were those of earlier Anglo-Saxon descent, and that this "race" was under threat from the growing influx of Central European and Asian immigrants.

➤ **Nietzscheism**: Friedrich Nietzsche's belief in the "will to power" as the primary force of society and the individual.

➤ **Racialism**: A false science that argued that different human races possessed distinguishing traits that determined their particular behavior and achievement in society.

➤ **Scientism**: The primacy of science over religious, mythical, or spiritual interpretations of life.

➤ **Social Darwinism**: Applying the evolutionary "survival of the fittest" concept to a world marked by struggle and competition. (It was promulgated by Herbert Spencer, a best-selling sociologist of the late 19th century.)

Pair Off and Square Off: Realists Versus Naturalists

Realists and naturalists: They walk alike and talk alike, but they're not exactly alike. Let's see how realists and naturalists compare:

➤ Naturalists are generally more pessimistic than realists. A realist believes that people can make moral choices, while a naturalist does not.

➤ Naturalists believe that all actions are deter-mined by heredity and/or environment, and that individuals are "trapped" by driving forces such as money, sex, and power. Realists, in contrast, do not believe in deter-minism.

> **Writer's Block**
>
> Naturalists celebrate the hero who is bold enough to challenge nature, even when the odds are against him or her.

The best-known naturalist in his day was Jack London, a hard-living man's man. Let's look at his life and work now.

Jack London (1876–1916)

> *"Mercy did not exist in the primordial life. It was misunderstood for fear, and such misun-derstanding made for death. Kill or be killed, eat or be eaten, was the law."*
>
> —Jack London from *The Call of the Wild*

Jack London was the original rebel without a cause and the highest-paid writer of his day (earning more than $70,000 a year), who nonetheless considered himself a social-ist. London lived hard and died young—he was in his grave by the time he was 40.

Jack was born in San Francisco to Flora Wellman, an unmarried mother with a driving ambition. Unfortunately, Flora's efforts were always misplaced, as she plunged into one disastrous get-rich scheme after another. Her only smart move was marrying quiet, gentle John London, giving her son the name that he would make famous.

Jack left school at 14 to try various jobs, including pirating for oysters in San Francisco Bay, serving on a fish patrol to capture poachers, sailing the Pacific on a sealing ship, joining Kelly's Industrial Army (consisting of unemployed working men—see Appen-dix C, *1893*, for more information), and being a hobo around the country. Along the way, he served a brief jail term in the Erie Penitentiary (near Niagara Falls) for vagrancy.

In the process, London became acquainted with socialism. Known as the "Boy Socialist of Oakland" for his street corner oratory, after he became successful as a writer, Lon-don ran repeatedly (but unsuccessfully) on the Socialist ticket as mayor.

Spending the winter of 1897 in the Yukon provided London with the metaphorical gold for his first stories (albeit not the physical gold he sought). He began publishing his stories in 1899.

Lit Wit

London's autobiographical novel *Martin Eden* (1909) depicts the stresses of the American dream as London experienced them during his meteoric rise from obscure poverty to wealth and fame. Eden, a poor but brainy and hardworking sailor/laborer, is determined to become a writer. Eventually, his writing gets him success, but Eden realizes that the woman he loves cares only for his money and fame. His despair causes him to lose faith in human nature. He also feels alienated from those around him, since he no longer belongs to the working class. He comes to reject the wealthy whom he worked so hard to join. Eden ultimately commits suicide in the South Pacific.

Writer's Block

After London's death, a story made the rounds that he was an alcoholic and a womanizer who committed suicide. True or false? It all depends on your spin on events.

From then on, London was a highly disciplined writer, eventually producing more than 50 volumes of stories, novels, and political essays. His most famous books are *The Call of the Wild*, *White Fang*, and *The Sea Wolf*.

Although *The Call of the Wild* (1903) brought London fame, many of his short stories also deserve to be called classics, as does his critique of capitalism and poverty in *The People of the Abyss* (1903) and his stark discussion of alcoholism in *John Barleycorn* (1913).

London died in 1916 of kidney failure caused by too much time spent with his close friend Demon Rum. By the time of his death, London had been married and divorced twice and become estranged from his children and political comrades.

The Call of the Wild

The Call of the Wild, London's most famous book, opens with a brief poem that introduces the theme: Strip away the thin veneer of civilization, and you find the beast:

"'Old longings nomadic leap,

Chafing at custom's chain;

Again from its brumal sleep

Wakens the ferine strain.'

Buck did not read the newspapers, or he would have known that trouble was brewing, not alone for himself, but for every tidewater dog, strong of muscle and with warm, long hair, from Puget Sound to San Diego. Because men, groping in the Arctic darkness, had found a yellow metal, and because steamship and transportation companies were booming the find, thousands of men were rushing into the Northland. These men wanted dogs, and the dogs they wanted were heavy dogs, with strong muscles by which to toil, and furry coats to protect them from the frost."

—from Chapter I, "Into the Primitive"

The Call of the Wild shows how a tame dog comes to revert to his original primitive state. When bold-spirited Buck is removed from his comfortable California estate and thrust into the rugged terrain of the Klondike, we see the savage lawlessness of man and beast.

Lit Speak

According to London, buried within the individual is a **"ferine strain,"** a bestial instinct that has been subdued by civilization. It's in a **"brumal sleep,"** a winter's hibernation.

Leader of the Pack

Anyone who picks up this novel expecting a sweet animal story is in for a jolt. Told from the point of view of the dog, Buck, *The Call of the Wild* is brutal, vicious, and cold. Here's the rundown:

➤ *Chapter I:* Buck is removed from his civilized environment and forced to fight for survival. He quickly learns the law of the club—he's no match for a man with a club.

➤ *Chapter II:* Buck comes to grasp the law of the fang—in the wilderness, civilization doesn't exist. It's each dog (or man) for himself. Only the fittest and strongest will survive.

➤ *Chapters III–IV:* Buck learns to survive in the fight against nature.

➤ *Chapter V:* Some can't survive in the North because they won't adapt.

➤ *Chapter VI:* Man and dog work together to overcome great difficulties.

➤ *Chapter VII:* Buck has heard the "call of the wild" and answered it. He becomes the leader of the wolf pack.

Writer's Block

The Call of the Wild is not really a *novel;* rather, it's more like seven short stories, each with its own characters, plot, and climax. Buck stars in each chapter, an episode in the story of his return to the primitive state. Though the chapters rely on each other for continuity, each one could be read separately and appreciated for itself.

It's a Dog-Eat-Dog World

The Call of the Wild operates on three levels:

➤ *Narrative:* On the surface, the book tells the story of Buck, the dog who learns to survive by reverting to his wolf roots.

➤ *Biological:* The novel reveals what London himself lived and felt as he climbed out of poverty and obscurity to become wealthy and famous. Symbolically, Buck represents London and his struggle for success.

➤ *Political and philosophical:* The novel exemplifies the naturalist's pet theory of Social Darwinism—only the fittest survive.

To Build a Fire

First published in 1902, London's short story "To Build a Fire" has become a classic. The story starts out this way: Ignoring the advice of a more experienced man, a rookie prospector in the Yukon attempts a long journey on foot during an intense cold spell with only his dog as his companion. Here's what London has to say about the prospector:

> *"The trouble with him was that he was without imagination. He was quick and alert in the things of life, but only in the things, and not in the significances. Fifty degrees below zero meant eighty-odd degrees of frost. Such fact impressed him as being cold and uncomfortable, and that was all. It did not lead him to meditate upon his frailty as a creature of temperature, and upon man's frailty in general, able only to live within certain narrow limits of heat and cold; and from there on it did not lead him to the conjectural field of immortality and man's place in the universe. Fifty degrees below zero stood for a bite of frost that hurt and that must be guarded against by the use of mittens, ear-flaps, warm moccasins, and thick socks. Fifty degrees below zero was to him just precisely fifty degrees below zero. That there should be anything more to it than that was a thought that never entered his head."*

When the man gets wet, he stops to build a fire to restore his circulation. He succeeds at first, but snow falls from a tree onto the fire and extinguishes it. He tries to get another fire going, but he is too numb and clumsy. Panicked, the man starts to run toward the camp where his partners are waiting for him. But he doesn't have the strength to go very far. He eventually collapses in the snow, falls asleep, and dies. The dog remains until the man is dead, then, seeking warmth, heads toward the camp.

Freezing was not so bad as people thought. There were lots worse ways to die…

> *"You were right, old hoss; you were right," the man mumbled to the old-timer of Sulphur Creek.*

> *Then the man drowsed off into what seemed to him the most comfortable and satisfying sleep he had ever known. The dog sat facing him and waiting. The brief day drew to a close in a long, slow twilight. There were no signs of a fire to be made, and, besides, never in the*

dog's experience had it known a man to sit like that in the snow and make no fire. As the twilight drew on, its eager yearning for the fire mastered it, and with a great lifting and shifting of forefeet, it whined softly, then flattened its ears down in anticipation of being chidden by the man. But the man remained silent. Later, the dog whined loudly. And still later it crept close to the man and caught the scent of death. This made the animal bristle and back away. A little longer it delayed, howling under the stars that leaped and danced and shone brightly in the cold sky. Then it turned and trotted up the trail in the direction of the camp it knew, where there were the other food-providers and fire-providers."

Lit Wit

The Yukon, a region in northwest Canada, is a land of great beauty and mineral wealth. Part of the last great wilderness in North America, the Yukon was virtually uninhabited until the Klondike gold strike of 1896. Two years later, at the peak of the gold rush, the population of the Klondike town of Dawson alone was more than 40,000 people. Some $100 million worth of gold was discovered in the region between 1896 and 1904. After the ore was exhausted, the population declined, but mining resumed in the 1960s, and the population has continued to grow steadily.

Frank Norris (1870–1902)

Like Stephen Crane, Benjamin Franklin Norris lived hard and died young. But unlike Crane, Norris' parents had bucks and took an active interest in their son's intellectual and artistic development, even schlepping him to Europe when he was still in high school so he could study painting.

When he was 20, Norris left the Paris art studio where he was studying and enrolled in the University of California at Berkeley to pursue a career as a writer. By the time he left there for a year at Harvard, Norris had already published a long poem called *Yvernelle*. He was 21 years old.

Writer's Block

Even though Crane and Norris were contemporaries and friends (they met during the Spanish-American War), don't make the mistake of confusing them. Crane was a vastly superior stylist, but Norris had a better handle on scope.

War, What Is It Good For?

After a brief jaunt to South Africa to write for the *San Francisco Chronicle,* Norris took a staff position on another weekly newspaper in the Bay area.

Like Crane, Norris was sent to Cuba to report on the Spanish-American War; meanwhile, he was publishing his naturalistic novels at a brisk clip.

By 1900, at the age of 30, Norris' reputation was growing, in large part because he wrote well in many genres: poetry, reportage, adventure-romance, realism, and psychological probing. When he embarked on his next project, the *Epic of the Trilogy of the Wheat*, he intended to provide a panoramic view of America's social, cultural, political, and economic life. Unfortunately, he only finished the first two books, *The Octopus* and *The Pit,* before he died of appendicitis at 32.

"The Literature of Chambermaids"

Norris scorned the pale, bloodless romances of his time, which he dismissed as "literature of chambermaids." The popular romances of the time always erred on the side of caution: there was little depression, despair, or desperation. Instead, reality was cleaned up to make it palatable to sheltered sensibilities.

Norris, in contrast, embraced a red-blooded plunge into reality, where nothing exists but force. Under his hand, American fiction turned from tentative realism to in-your-face naturalism.

Today, Norris' most famous book is *McTeague, a Story of San Francisco,* a fascinating naturalistic tale of moral degeneration under economic pressures. The novel shows how a man's long-suppressed animal instincts can break through his outwardly civilized wrapper—with dramatic and devastating results. And the main character is a dentist, no less.

McTeague, a Story of San Francisco

"Gold can kill ya… gold can spill yer guts all over the barroom floor."

—from *McTeague*

McTeague is the story of an ox-like dentist and his wife, Trina, and their fatal obsession with wealth—or, more specifically, with gold. The dentist, Dr. McTeague, owns a successful practice in San Francisco around the turn of the century. One day, McTeague's best friend, Schouler, arrives at McTeague's office with his girlfriend, Trina, who has broken a tooth. When McTeague sees Trina, it's love at first sight. Schouler leaves, and McTeague administers ether to the beautiful girl. As Trina nods off, Maria, the maid, induces the drugged girl to buy a lottery ticket.

A month later, McTeague and Schouler are alone together in a garden. Distraught with unrequited love, McTeague tells Schouler of his feelings. After some cursory consideration, Schouler agrees to hand over Trina to McTeague. "But remember," he says as he leaves McTeague, "you owe me…"

Lit Wit

Erich von Stroheim's 1924 silent film *Greed* was based on Frank Norris' 1899 novel, *McTeague.*

Schouler's words soon become prophetic; during McTeague and Trina's wedding party, a mysterious man appears and announces that Trina has won $5,000 in the lottery. Schouler is shocked, then outraged; as the other guests depart, Schouler picks a fight with McTeague, claiming that he is owed half the money. When McTeague refuses, Schouler vows revenge and storms out.

Trina is a miser with her money, refusing to spend a penny of the $5,000. Schouler falls in love with the maid Maria, and together they depart for her childhood home in Nevada, where she promises they will find a trove of golden cutlery, plates, and coins. In a parting shot, Schouler sics the health inspector on McTeague. When the inspector discovers that McTeague is unlicensed as a dentist, he shuts down McTeague's practice.

McTeague's fall comes quickly; he cannot find work, and within months, he and Trina are forced to sell his office space and live in the back room, which they rent from the new dentist. Despite their suffering, Trina won't give up a single penny of the $5,000. In a fit of desperate rage, McTeague kills Trina and steals the gold. He flees the city, eventually ending up in Death Valley. There he has his final encounter with Schouler, who has abandoned Maria and adopted the life of a cowboy. The two men have a fistfight in which McTeague gets hold of Schouler's gun and shoots him with it.

The novel converges on societal injustice and individual weakness. Every character is overwhelmed by lust for gold. The effects of this greed are shown from both sides, however, as McTeague encounters a brutal life of poverty after his downfall. Is McTeague a victim of society or a victim of selfish greed?

No Teddy Bear: Theodore Dreiser (1871–1945)

Dreiser made it to the short list for the Nobel Prize for Literature (several times, in fact) but never made the final cut. Okay, so he alienated just about everyone he ever met with his boorish behavior. He was suspicious of most men and desired most women, and questioned everyone's motives but his own. But can't we have a little pity for the guy? After all, his childhood was rotten.

Dreiser was the twelfth of 13 children in an unhappy family. He endured a childhood oppressed by poverty and strife, one step ahead of the bill collector. Only Theodore and his brother Paul ended up making good; the rest of the Dreiser kids ended up drifting into drunkenness, promiscuity, and poverty.

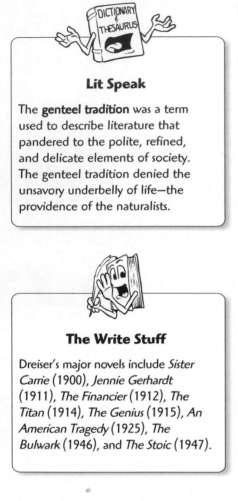

Lit Speak

The **genteel tradition** was a term used to describe literature that pandered to the polite, refined, and delicate elements of society. The genteel tradition denied the unsavory underbelly of life—the providence of the naturalists.

The Write Stuff

Dreiser's major novels include *Sister Carrie* (1900), *Jennie Gerhardt* (1911), *The Financier* (1912), *The Titan* (1914), *The Genius* (1915), *An American Tragedy* (1925), *The Bulwark* (1946), and *The Stoic* (1947).

Essentially on his own from the age of 15, Dreiser's education was erratic, although he did manage one year at Indiana University, thanks to the generosity of one of his elementary school teachers. After his brief college experience, Dreiser got involved in journalism and wrote in Chicago, St. Louis, and Pittsburgh. This launched Dreiser's career as a novelist, dramatist, and poet.

> *"I never can and never want to bring myself to the place where I can ignore the sensitive and seeking individual in his pitiful struggle with nature—with his enormous urges and his pathetic equipment."*
>
> —Theodore Dreiser

Considered by many to be the leader of naturalism in American writing, Dreiser is also remembered for his stinging criticism of the genteel tradition—what literary critic William Dean Howells described as the "smiling aspects of life"—typifying America. In his fiction, Dreiser deals with social problems and with characters who struggle to survive.

He's also remembered for his sprawling, shapeless novels (they make great doorstops) and clichéd writing. But despite indulgent overwriting and stylistic shortcomings, Dreiser's best novels express a brooding insistence on the essential tragedy of life and have lost none of their haunting strength more than half a century later.

Dreiser's most famous novel is *An American Tragedy* (1925), which explores the dangers of the American dream.

An American Tragedy

The novel relates, in fascinating—or numbing, depending upon your perspective—detail, the life of Clyde Griffiths, a boy of weak will and little self-awareness. He grows up dirt poor in a family of wandering evangelists but dreams of wealth and the love of beautiful women. A rich uncle eventually employs him in his factory, and when Clyde's girlfriend Roberta becomes pregnant, she demands that he marry her. Meanwhile, Clyde has fallen in love with a wealthy society girl who represents success, money, and social acceptance. She returns his affection.

Clyde decides to drown Roberta on a boat trip, but at the last minute, he changes his mind. However, Roberta accidentally falls out of the boat. Clyde, a good swimmer, doesn't budge to save her, and she drowns. As Clyde is brought to justice, Dreiser replays his story in reverse, using the vantage points of prosecuting and defense attorneys to analyze the motives that led Clyde to decide to commit murder by letting Roberta die when he could have saved her.

Lit Wit

An American Tragedy is based on the sensational true story of Chester Gillette (**C**lyde **G**riffiths—get it?), who did indeed drown his poor, pregnant girlfriend to clear the way to marry a society babe.

An American Tragedy is a scathing portrait of the American success myth gone sour, but it is also a universal story about the stresses of urbanization, modernization, and alienation. Despite Dreiser's famously awkward style, the novel's precise details build up an overwhelming sense of tragic inevitability.

Lit Wit

Carrie, the title character in Dreiser's *Sister Carrie,* strayed with no consequences, which made the novel a grave insult to late 19th-century conventionality. As an editorial reader for Doubleday, the young novelist Frank Norris helped get the book accepted for publication. In a cheesy attempt to honor the letter of the contract rather than its spirit, Dreiser's publishers issued a minimum number of copies, without advertisement. More than a decade passed before the novel received its proper critical acclaim.

The Least You Need to Know

➤ The naturalists believed that life is determined by environment, heredity, and chance. As a result, we live by the law of the jungle.

➤ Jack London's most famous novel, *The Call of the Wild*, shows how a tame dog is forced to revert to his original primitive state.

➤ London's short story "To Build a Fire" shows how life is marked by "survival of the fittest."

➤ Frank Norris' best novel, *McTeague*, helped transform American fiction from tentative realism to in-your-face naturalism.

➤ Although lambasted for their awkward style and overwriting, Theodore Dreiser's novels express a brooding insistence on the essential tragedy of life.

➤ Dreiser's *An American Tragedy* is a scathing portrait of the American success myth gone sour, as well as a universal story about the stresses of urbanization, modernization, and alienation.

Chapter 18

Color My World: The Local Colorists

The local colorists first drew attention to undiscovered parts of the country.

As America became increasingly homogenized, the so-called "local colorists" used their skill to preserve the customs and culture of their special corners of America. By the end of the century, there were local colorists from Maine to California, from the northern plains to the Louisiana bayous.

In this chapter, you'll learn about the local color movement and its most famous writers, including Bret Harte, Mary Wilkins Freeman, Sarah Orne Jewett, Kate Chopin, Charlotte Perkins Gilman, and Willa Cather.

In Living Color

The regional writers captured the essence of a particular area, its "local color." They did this by accurately describing the distinctive qualities of the people, focusing on their...

➤ Habits

➤ Speech

➤ Customs

➤ Beliefs

Lit Speak

The **local colorists** got their name from the painters of the time, who preserved their environments with paint rather than words.

Now, it's true that many pre–Civil War writers, from Henry David Thoreau and Nathaniel Hawthorne to John Greenleaf Whittier and James Russell Lowell, had created striking portraits of specific American regions. What sets the local colorists apart from these earlier writers is their interest in rendering a given location, as well as their scrupulously factual, realistic writing techniques.

Although only a few of his stories were successful from a commerical or critical standpoint, Bret Harte played an important role in creating a vivid and lasting portrait of the Wild West. I think he deserves to be placed first for effort, don't you?

Bret Harte (1836–1902)

"Mr. Oakhurst's calm, handsome face betrayed small concern for any of these indications. Whether he was conscious of any predisposing cause was another question. 'I reckon they're after somebody,' he reflected, 'likely it's me.' He returned to his pocket the handkerchief with which he had been wiping away the red dust of Poker Flat from his neat boots, and quietly discharged his mind from any further conjecture."

—Bret Harte from "The Outcasts of Poker Flat"

The Write Stuff

Charles Dickens greatly admired Harte's work and adapted many of his local color techniques to his own work.

Where would Gary Cooper, John Wayne, and our other celluloid cowboys be without Bret Harte? Bret Harte helped create our impression of the Old West with such stories as "The Luck of Roaring Camp" and "The Outcasts of Poker Flat," set along the Western mining frontier. As the first writer in the local colorist school to attract widespread attention, for a brief time Harte was perhaps the best-known writer in America, thanks to the tremendous appeal of his romantic version of the gunslinging West.

Harte was also one of the first writers to introduce lowlife characters—cunning gamblers, gaudy prostitutes, and uncouth robbers—into serious literary works. He got away with it by showing in the end that these seeming derelicts really had hearts of gold. (*Gunsmoke, Bat Masterson,* and *Bonanza* were no doubt inspired by Harte's work.)

Born and raised in Albany, New York, Harte headed West when he was 18. Success didn't come easily: Harte worked as a teacher, messenger, clerk, and prospector before he struck the literary mother lode in 1868 with the publication of "The Luck of Roaring Camp." Tragically, he peaked only two years later. Although he continued writing for more than 20 years, Harte's later stories were flat and empty. What's a failed writer to do? Harte turned to politics, serving as a diplomat in Germany and Switzerland.

The Outcasts of Poker Flat

"The Outcasts of Poker Flat" takes place in California during the gold rush, in 1849. When the story opens, a secret committee in Poker Flat has decided to "rid the town of all improper persons." Two women of loose repute, Mother Shipton and the Duchess, the drunken thief Uncle Billy, and the gambler John Oakhurst are escorted to the outskirts of town. The outcasts are soon joined by Tom Simson and his girlfriend, Piney Woods. Tom and his girlfriend have eloped and are on their way to Poker Flat when he meets the outcasts. Tom idolizes the gambler, Oakhurst, and decides to camp with the outcasts in order to help them. They all camp at Sandy Bar in the foothills of the Sierra Nevadas.

The next morning, Oakhurst awakens to find that it has snowed heavily during the night. Uncle Billy has taken off with the horses and mules, so the outcasts are stranded. The blizzard continues. By the third day, rations are running low. On the tenth day, Mother Shipton dies, but not before giving her previous week's rations, untouched, to Piney. In a last-ditch effort to survive, Oakhurst sends Tom to Poker Flat to get food and help.

When the rescue party arrives, they discover that Piney and the Duchess have frozen to death and Oakhurst has shot himself. The story ends:

> *"And pulseless and cold, with a Derringer by his side and a bullet in his heart, though still calm as in life, beneath the snow, lay he who was at once the strongest and yet the weakest of the outcasts of Poker Flat."*

> —from "The Outcasts of Poker Flat"

Oakhurst was the strongest because he sacrificed himself to help others—yet he was also the weakest because he shot himself rather than wait to see if help would arrive.

Paint by Number

Harte has two main techniques for conveying the flavor of the place and times: dialect and description. For example,

➤ *Dialect:* "I reckon now you're used to fine things at Poker Flat." (Catch that "reckon.")

➤ *Description:* "the red dust of Poker Flat." (Notice how he describes the color as well as the texture of the town.)

We also see the Old West's distorted concept of justice: The settlers are all too eager to throw their fellow citizens out of town for not being "respectable" Ironically, the very men and women who judge the settlers are themselves guilty of disrepectful crimes, such as drinking and gambling.

Lit Wit

Although Harte was obsessed with the role of chance and death in human affairs, it's unlikely that even *he* could have foreseen that his stories would be translated into Russian. After the translation, Harte's stories fell into Joseph Stalin's hands. The ruthless dictator unaccountably decided after reading "The Outcasts of Poker Flat" in 1927 to reopen the Siberian gold mines. A decade later, the mines were producing nearly $200 million a year. Few writers can claim such dramatic results from their work.

Mary Wilkins Freeman (1852–1930)

Mary Wilkins Freeman and Sarah Orne Jewett cornered the market on New England's local color. Freeman carved out her niche with stories that hauntingly explore the lives of "mature" New England women who confront their poverty with ferocious independence. Her characters recognize their isolation but struggle to preserve their dignity. Unfortunately for her, Freeman didn't have to do any research.

The details are a little sketchy, but it appears that when Freeman was a young woman, she fell in love with a young man named Hanson Tyler.

At the same time, Freeman's father lost his business, her younger sister died, and her mother took a job as the

The Write Stuff

Then, as now, women made up the major audience for fiction. And during that time, many women wrote popular novels, poems, and humorous pieces. Resenting their generous slice of the literary pie, Nathaniel Hawthorne called his female counterparts "That damned mob of scribbling women."

Tyler's housekeeper. Not surprisingly, Freeman's love affair fizzled. When each of her parents died suddenly within the next three years, 31-year-old Mary found herself alone and destitute.

Mary moved in with a childhood friend and continued the writing career she had just begun.

When she was 49, Mary met Dr. Charles Freeman, a physician. He must have been a patient man, because it took her 10 years to decide to marry him. Unfortunately, she should have waited even longer; only a few years later, he was committed to a sanitarium for alcoholism. The end of their marriage and his life were long and messy.

Freeman published more than 20 volumes of fiction and children's stories; *A Humble Romance and Other Stories* (1887) and *A New England Nun and Other Stories* (1891) are her most famous works.

Sarah Orne Jewett (1849–1909)

Unlike most of the local colorists who looked ahead to the developing Western frontier, Jewett looked back to a time fast disappearing in rural New England.

People who made a living from the rugged New England coast were dealt a serious blow with the Embargo of 1807, which forbade all commerce with foreign nations. The Civil War finished the job by taking away the men who worked on the sea. And if that wasn't bad enough, textile mills and tourists streamed in to change the face of the region.

Jewett's originality, exact observations of her Maine characters and settings, and sensitive style are best seen in her fine story "The White Heron" in *Country of the Pointed Firs* (1896). Although loaded with local color, "The White Heron," like all of Jewett's stories, revolves around character and crucial choices.

Lit Wit

Even though she's most famous today as the author of *Uncle Tom's Cabin,* Harriet Beecher Stowe was a brilliant local colorist, too. Check out *The Pearl of Orr's Island* (1862).

Going to the Birds: "The White Heron"

Sylvia, a child, shares a special bond with the woodland creatures. One night, while taking the cow home, she meets a handsome young ornithologist who is looking for a white heron. He offers Sylvia $10 if she will point out the location of the heron's nest.

The Write Stuff

Jewett enjoyed a 30-year relation-ship with Annie Adams Fields. In the days of euphemisms, their cohabita-tion was called a "Boston marriage." However, there's no evidence to decide her sexual orientation one way or the other.

Writer's Block

Jewett's work has often been criticized as nothing more than "sketches," with very little plot and therefore not worthy of much critical study. Jewett herself realized this about her work, writing to her editor,

"It seems to me I can furnish the theatre, and show you the actors, and the scenery, and the audience, but there never is any play! ...I seem to get very bewildered when I try to make these come in for secondary parts. ...I am certain I could not write one of the usual magazine stories. If the editors will take the sketchy kind and people like to read them, is not it as well to do that and do it successfully as to make hopeless efforts to achieve something in another line which runs much higher?"

Although infatuated with the young man, Sylvia cannot understand how he could destroy animals. She climbs a tall pine tree and locates the heron, but doesn't tell the ornithologist the bird's exact location, for fear that he will kill it. In the story's climax:

> *"The murmur of the pine's green branches is in her ears, she remembers how the white heron came flying through the golden air and how they watched the sea and the morning together, and Sylvia cannot speak; she cannot tell the heron's secret and give its life away."*

The heron symbolizes the beauty of life, its dignity, and the endangered wilderness.

Reality Check

> *"Don't try to write about things: write the things themselves just as they are."*
>
> —Sarah Orne Jewett

Jewett's work features the people she was most familiar with—the inhabitants of Maine, of the everyday world of villages and ordinary people. What makes Jewett's brand of local color writing different from the other New England regional writers? Focus on these elements:

➤ Idiomatic language

➤ Conservative values

➤ Imagery and vivid descriptions of rural New England

Jewett's work was largely forgotten and even scorned after her rather successful lifetime; one critic went so far as to call her "merely a New England old maid."

Down in the Bayou: Kate Chopin (1851–1904)

Kate Chopin was born Katherine O'Flaherty in St. Louis, Missouri. At 19, Kate married Oscar Chopin, a young cotton broker, and moved with him to New Orleans. It was a happy and fruitful union, although it lasted but 12 years. When Oscar died in 1882, Chopin returned with their six children to St. Louis and began writing to keep the kids in shoes.

Chopin was widely accepted as a writer of local color fiction and was generally successful until the publication of her scandalous novel, *The Awakening,* in 1899. While it strongly evokes the region, *The Awakening* is primarily a lyrical, stunning study of a young woman whose deep personal discontents lead to adultery and suicide. Now widely read and honored, *The Awakening* was decidedly ahead of its time.

The novel's sexually aware and shocking protagonist, Edna Pontillier, pushed Chopin into literary oblivion. It wasn't until the 1970s that Chopin's novel was finally accepted.

Strip away the scandal, and Chopin's writing is memorable for its

- ➤ Vivid and economical style
- ➤ Rich local dialect
- ➤ Penetrating views of the culture of south Louisiana

Lit Speak

Chopin, like the great composer, is pronounced *show-pan.*

The Awakening

Praised for its craft and damned for its content, *The Awakening* was a scandalous book for its time. It was condemned all over America and banned in libraries. And boy, did Chopin's self-appointed judges ever play dirty: Community leaders even banned Kate Chopin from membership in a local arts club.

Who's Who in The Awakening

- ➤ *Edna Pontellier:* She rejects the role of domestic goddess.
- ➤ *Leonce Pontellier:* Her clueless Creole husband.
- ➤ *Robert Lebrun*: Edna's male friend.
- ➤ *Madame Adele Ratignolle:* Edna's female friend, the earth mother.
- ➤ *Mademoiselle Reisz:* Her beautiful piano music contributes to Edna's "awakening."
- ➤ *Alcee Arobin:* Edna's suave lover.

Not Free to Be You and Me

Time: Turn of the 20th century

Place: Louisiana

The story concerns Edna Pontellier's doomed attempt to find her own identity through passion. Edna is a young married woman with attractive children and an indulgent and successful husband, but she's not into the mothering gig:

"She was fond of her children in an uneven, impulsive way. She would sometimes gather them passionately to her heart; she would sometimes forget them. The year before they had

spent part of the summer with their grandmother Pontellier in Iberville. Feeling secure regarding their happiness and welfare, she did not miss them except with an occasional intense longing. Their absence was a sort of relief, though she did not admit this, even to herself. It seemed to free her of a responsibility which she had blindly assumed and for which Fate had not fitted her… In short, Mrs. Pontellier was not a mother-woman."

During a summer vacation, Edna "begins to realize her position in the universe as a human being, and to recognize her relations as an individual to the world within and about her." Chopin realizes that it's a dangerous journey:

"But the beginning of things, of a world especially, is necessarily vague, tangled, chaotic, and exceedingly disturbing. How few of us ever emerge from such beginning! How many souls perish in its tumult!"

Edna gives up her family, money, respectability, and eventually her life in search of self-realization. Poetic evocations of the ocean, birds, and music endow this short novel with unusual intensity and complexity. With nothing left to live for, Edna kills herself. The novel ends with her death:

"The voice of the sea is seductive; never ceasing, whispering, clamoring, murmuring, inviting the soul to wander for a spell in abysses of solitude; to lose itself in mazes of inward contemplation.

The voice of the sea speaks to the soul. The touch of the sea is sensuous, enfolding the body in its soft, close embrace.

The foamy wavelets curled up to her white feet, and coiled like serpents about her ankles. She walked out. The water was chill, but she walked on. The water was deep, but she lifted her white body and reached out with a long, sweeping stroke. The touch of the sea is sensuous, enfolding the body in its soft, close embrace…

She thought of Léonce and the children. They were a part of her life. But they need not have thought that they could possess her, body and soul. How Mademoiselle Reisz would have laughed, perhaps sneered, if she knew! 'And you call yourself an artist! What pretensions, Madame! The artist must possess the courageous soul that dares and defies.'"

Chopin died five years after publishing *The Awakening* of a brain hemorrhage after a strenuous day at the St. Louis World's Fair, where she had been a regular visitor.

Among the most distinguished writers of the local colorist school, Chopin's place in American literature was secured by *The Awakening* alone.

Charlotte Perkins Gilman (1860–1935)

When Charlotte was just a baby, her father went out for a pack of cigarettes and never came back. And back then, they rolled their own.

As the poor relations, the family made the rounds of the kinfolk, relying on their charity. Although vowing never to marry, in her early 20s, Charlotte fell for Charles Walter Stetson and decided to tie the knot. They married in 1884, when Charlotte was

24 years old. Their union was rocky from the beginning, eventually ending in a controversial divorce. They separated in 1888, after only four years of marriage.

They had one daughter, Katherine Beecher Stetson. (Yes, Gilman was related to Harriet Beecher Stowe who was her great aunt.)

After the birth of her child, Gilman suffered a severe nervous breakdown. To save her sanity, she moved to California, got a divorce, and left her daughter in care of her ex-husband. These bold actions were unheard of during this time. Of course, she was roundly denounced and called names I can't repeat in this book. Many years later, in 1900, Gilman married her cousin George Houghton Gilman; they remained happily married until his sudden death in 1934.

In 1932, Gilman learned that she had incurable breast cancer. As an advocate for the right to die, Gilman chose chloroform over cancer and took her own life in 1935.

During her life, Gilman published a huge volume of work—much of which is unavailable to the modern reader because it has only recently been rediscovered The feminist presses have reissued some of Gilman's best-known works, but much of her work remains out of print. Gilman is best known for her short novel "The Yellow Wallpaper."

The local color angle? Gilman's concentration on the prevalent attitudes of the time, especially regarding the treatment of women.

In Literature as in Life: The Yellow Wallpaper

Often paired with *The Awakening* is Gilman's terrifying story "The Yellow Wallpaper" (1892). The story describes a woman who suffers a mental breakdown due to the birth of her child. She's given a "rest cure," which drives her completely around the bend. (Bet you can't guess how Gilman did *her* research.)

The woman projects her entrapment onto the yellow wallpaper, in the design of which she sees imprisoned women creeping behind bars:

> *"I didn't realize for a long time what the thing was that showed behind, that dim sub-pattern, but now I am quite sure it is a woman...*
>
> *The front pattern does move—and no wonder! The woman behind shakes it!*
>
> *Sometimes I think there are a great many women behind, and sometimes only one, and she crawls around fast, and her crawling shakes it all over.*
>
> *Then in the very bright spots she keeps still, and in the very shady spots she just takes hold of the bars and shakes them hard.*
>
> *And she is all the time trying to climb through. But nobody could climb through that pattern—it strangles so; I think that is why it has so many heads."*

In her madness, the woman gnaws through the bedstead and rips the wallpaper from the walls. She also creeps smoothly on the floor, her shoulder making a long "smooch" around the wall. At the end of the story, the woman begins to completely identify with the women trapped in the design of the yellow wallpaper. When her husband finds her creeping about the bedroom, she declares:

"'I've got out at last,' said I, 'in spite of you and Jane. And I've pulled off most of the paper, so you can't put me back!'

Now why should that man have fainted? But he did, and right across my path by the wall, so that I had to creep over him every time!"

Some Days It Just Doesn't Pay to Tell It Like It Is

When "The Yellow Wallpaper" was first published in 1892, a Boston physician said the story was enough to drive anyone mad. Another physician said it was the best description of incipient insanity he had ever seen.

In response to her feedback, Gilman penned the essay "Why I Wrote the Yellow Wallpaper" (1913). "For many years I suffered from a severe and continuous nervous breakdown tending to melancholia," she wrote.

After three years of this, she was sent to a noted specialist, S. Weir Mitchell,

Writer's Block

When "The Yellow Wallpaper" first came out in 1892, the critics read it as a description of female insanity and mayhem instead of a critique of society's values. You'd never make that mistake!

"…who applied a 'rest cure.' His advice? 'live as domestic a life as far as possible' with 'but two hours' intellectual life a day,' and 'never to touch pen, brush, or pencil again.'"

Gilman gave the rest cure her best shot. The results? "I came so near the borderline of utter mental ruin that I could see over," she wrote. Desperate to hang on to her sanity, Gilman decided to write her own prescription—work, work, and more work. The result was "The Yellow Wallpaper" and a dash to California sans husband and child.

The story can also be read as a conventional ghost tale, however. To some critics, the narrator is not at all insane; rather, she truly is trapped in a haunted house.

Bet I made you want to read it!

Prairie Tales: Willa Cather (1873–1947)

"I tried to go to sleep, but the jolting made me bite my tongue, and I soon began to ache all over. When the straw settled down, I had a hard bed. Cautiously I slipped from under the buffalo hide, got up on my knees and peered over the side of the wagon. There seemed to be nothing to see; no fences, no creeks or trees, no hills or fields. If there was a road, I could not make it out in the faint starlight. There was nothing but land: not a country at all, but the material out of which countries are made. No, there was nothing but land—slightly undulating, I knew, because often our wheels ground against the brake as we went down

into a hollow and lurched up again on the other side. I had the feeling that the world was left behind, that we had got over the edge of it, and were outside man's jurisdiction. I had never before looked up at the sky when there was not a familiar mountain ridge against it. But this was the complete dome of heaven all there was of it. I did not believe that my dead father and mother were watching me from up there; they would still be looking for me at the sheep-fold down by the creek or along the white road that lead to the mountain pastures. I had left even their spirits behind me. The wagon jolted on, carrying me I knew not wither. I don't think I was homesick. If we never arrived anywhere, it did not matter. Between that earth and that sky I felt erased, blotted out. I did not say my prayers that night: here, I felt, what would be would be."

—Willa Cather, from *My Antonia*

The eldest of seven children, Willa Cather moved to Nebraska when she was very young, a journey her most famous character, Antonia, would later make. During the trip West from her birthplace in Virginia, Cather imagined that, "I had left even their spirits [her grandparents] behind me. The wagon jolted on, carrying me I knew not whither… Between that earth and sky I felt erased, blotted out."

As with many authors, Cather held a variety of jobs, including journalist, teacher, and editor. Her reputation as a writer rests on her novels about Nebraska and the American Southwest, which show her awareness of the tradeoffs required to live the pioneer life—isolation, loneliness, and loss of culture balanced against courage, natural beauty, and independence. Of Cather's 12 novels, *My Antonia* and *Death Comes for the Archbishop* are considered to be the finest.

Here's what to look for when reading Cather:

➤ Admiration for the courage and spirit of immigrant settlers

➤ Intense awareness of pioneers' isolation and loss

➤ Keen awareness of the culture of city life

Willa Cather's landscapes capture a land that had almost been erased by the time she began writing. Her fictional frontiers evoke the beauty of the Nebraska lanscape and the heroism of the people that inhabited it.

In their own, unique ways, each of the local colorists preserved a slice of the American lansdscape for us to savor decades later. Whether describing the rocky Maine shores, the sultry southern bayous, or the desolate midwestern prairies, the local colorists painted vivid word pictures of a vanishing way of life.

The Write Stuff

In her day, Cather was the most celebrated of the writers profiled in this chapter; she won a Pulitzer prize in 1923 for her novel *One of Ours.*

The Least You Need to Know

➤ The regional writers tried to capture the essence of a particular area, or its "local color."

➤ Bret Harte (1836–1902) fashioned our impression of the Old West with such stories as "The Outcasts of Poker Flat."

➤ Mary Wilkins Freeman (1852–1930) carved out her niche with stories that hauntingly explore the lives of isolated, poor, "mature" New England women.

➤ Sarah Orne Jewett (1849–1909) immortalized rural Maine.

➤ Kate Chopin (1851–1904) made her mark with stories of the Louisiana bayou, until she blew the lid off the pot with her story of a woman's sexual coming of age in *The Awakening* (1899).

➤ Charlotte Perkins Gilman (1860–1935) recorded her postpartum nervous breakdown in "The Yellow Wallpaper," exposing women's lot around the turn of the century.

➤ Willa Cather (1873–1947) probed life on the Nebraska prairie, winning a Pulitizer Prize for her achievements.

Chapter 19

Lifestyles of the Rich and Famous: Edith Wharton and Henry James

Edith Wharton and Henry James enjoyed a fine standard of living, thanks to their clever choice of parents. Edith Wharton's maiden name was Jones; the family had so much money that the phrase "keeping up with the Joneses" was coined to describe society's frantic efforts to match their tasteful opulence. Henry's family was equally upper crust, and extraordinarily cultured and well-traveled.

Read on to discover what landmark books these two writers produced when they weren't traveling around the world, dining in the finest restaurants, summering in Newport, and generally enjoying La Dolce Vita.

High Society: Edith Wharton (1862–1937)

Edith's parents, George and Lucretia Jones, were descendants of English and Dutch colonists who had made enormous fortunes in shipping, banking, and real estate.

As a result, Edith belonged to the very upper reaches of New York society, the folks who live off the interest, not the principal. Her earliest years were spent touring Europe. The family returned to America when Edith was 10 years old to live near Fifth Avenue in Manhattan.

As was the custom in her social strata, Edith was educated at home by a governess and made her formal debut into society at 17. In 1885, when she was 23, Edith married Edward ("Teddy") Wharton. They seemed to be a perfect match, for he came from a similar social background and was attractive, kindly, and athletic. But as the Scottish writer Robert Burns said, "The best laid plans of mice and men oft go astray." Teddy had none of Edith's artistic or intellectual interests; instead, he liked to drink and carouse. As a result, their marriage was a disaster. After years of pain, they divorced in 1913.

Wharton's writing career was launched in 1897 with the publication of her first book, *The Decoration of Houses,* written with her architect friend, Ogden Codman.

The Write Stuff

Wharton's style of decorating matched her style of writing: Both were elegant, graceful, and honest.

The two tastemakers denounced Victorian decorating practices—rooms heavily curtained and crammed with overstuffed furniture, "lambrequins, jardinières of artificial plants, wobbly velvet-covered tables littered with gewgaws, and festoons of lace on mantelpieces and dressing tables." Instead, they proposed creating rooms based on simple, classical design principles, stressing symmetry, proportion, and balance in the architecture. *The Decoration of Houses* was an immediate success, launching an entirely new style of decorating.

Know Your Place

Although she was destined to become the highest-paid novelist in the country during her lifetime, Wharton didn't find that writing—or publishing—came easily. As a result, she didn't publish her first book of fiction until she was 36 years old and recovering from a nervous breakdown. Why did Wharton have such a hard time being a writer, even though she realized her talent?

The Write Stuff

Wharton was not above modeling her fictional characters on real people—such as Mrs. William Astor, the famous social leader, or Cornelius Vanderbilt, the owner of The Breakers, one of Newport's palatial "cottages."

Wharton had been raised to follow the course laid out by generations of the elite. As a wealthy woman, she was expected to be a passive social ornament. She was not expected or encouraged to have a career, even one as genteel as writing. Of course, her controversial choice of themes didn't make matters any easier.

The Inside View

As a member of the upper crust, Wharton was in an ideal position to view the social ambitions of the newly rich of the Gilded Age. In her fiction, especially in *The House of Mirth* (1905), Wharton described the very rich and their intense materialism. It's not a good idea to bite the hand that feeds you, especially if you're eating caviar and bonbons. As a result, many people in Wharton's social class actively discouraged her literary ambitions. These included friends, relatives, and wealthy, socially-connected publishers.

Lit Speak

The **Gilded Age** was the name given to the post–Civil War period of American expansion in business, foreign affairs, and the arts, because many of the newly rich disguised their ambition with only a thin veneer of respectability.

Birds in Gilded Cages

Wharton viewed Victorian society with ironic detachment. Like her friend Henry James, Wharton was also concerned with the subtle interplay of emotions in a society that censured the free expression of passion. Her grasp of the conflicting values in this artificial environment gives her stories a tragic intensity.

Wharton's characters are often victims of cruel social conventions, trapped in bad relationships or other confining circumstances. The core of her concern is the gulf separating social reality and the inner self. In a Wharton novel, a sensitive character often feels smothered by unfeeling people or social forces.

The Write Stuff

Wharton's own life stands as an example of the obstacles that a woman of her stature, time, and place had to overcome to find self-realization.

As Wharton's Pulitzer prize–winning biographer, R.W.B. Lewis, says of his subject, "Wharton's works are continuing testimony to the female experience under modern historical and social conditions, to the modes of entrapment, betrayal, and exclusion devised for women in the first decades of the American and European twentieth century."

Less Is More

Wharton was also skilled at capturing a moment, including the importance of that which is left unsaid. The following excerpt from Wharton's *The Age of Innocence* illustrates her ability to say volumes through allusion and indirection:

> *"It was not the custom in New York drawing-rooms for a lady to get up and walk away from one gentleman in order to seek the company of another. Etiquette required that she should wait, immovable as an idol, while the men who wished to converse with her succeeded each other at her side. But the Countess was apparently unaware of having broken any rule; she sat at perfect ease in a corner of the sofa beside Archer, and looked at him with the kindest eyes…"*

Top Drawer

In 1907, Wharton settled permanently in Paris, France, in part to distance herself from Teddy, whom she had not yet divorced.

During World War I, she became fiercely dedicated to the Allied cause. She led the Committee to Aid Refugees from northeastern France and Belgium and created hostels and schools for them.

These last years brought great rewards, as Wharton became the grande dame of American letters and was visited by many scholars, artists, intellectuals, and society friends.

In 1921, Wharton became the first woman to win the Pulitzer prize. It was awarded for her novel *The Age of Innocence*.

In her long career, which stretched over 40 years and included the publication of more than 40 books, Wharton portrayed a fascinating segment of the American experience. She was a born storyteller, whose novels are justly celebrated for their vivid settings, satiric wit, ironic style, and moral seriousness.

Wharton's best novels include *The House of Mirth* (1905), *The Custom of the Country* (1913), *Summer* (1917), *The Age of Innocence* (1920), and the beautifully crafted novella *Ethan Frome* (1911). Let's look at this one now.

Lit Wit

Sinclair Lewis (1885–1951) was the first American writer to win the Nobel Prize for Literature (1930). *Arrowsmith* was noted for its achievements in replacing the traditional romantic and complacent conception of American life with a realistic, even bitter view. In *Main Street* (1920), Lewis revealed the emotional frustration and lack of spiritual and intellectual values in American middle-class life. He extended the theme in *Babbitt* (1922), a merciless characterization of small-town businessmen who conform to the social and ethical standards of their environment. Lewis greatly admired Wharton; he dedicated *Babbitt* to her. Lewis' *Arrowsmith* (1925) probes the lack of idealism sometimes found in the medical profession; *Elmer Gantry* (1927) portrays religious hypocrisy.

Ethan Frome

Ethan Frome is a tragic love story of simple people in a bleak New England environment. Many critics judge this book to be Wharton's masterpiece, because its simplicity has a universality that is lacking in her society novels.

The novel, a tragedy of irony, is set in the small New England town of Starkfield, Massachusetts. The community is plagued by harsh winters that seem to suck the life from the inhabitants. The novel centers on Ethan Frome, a crippled farmer who has cornered the market on pain. A newcomer to town, our narrator, is fascinated by Ethan Frome. As the narrator muses,

> *"Even then he was the most striking figure in Starkfield, though he was but the ruin of a man. It was not so much his great height that marked him, for the "natives" were easily singled out by their lank longitude from the stockier foreign breed: it was the careless powerful look he had, in spite of a lameness checking each step like the jerk of a chain. There was something bleak and unapproachable in his face, and he was so stiffened and grizzled that I took him for an old man and was surprised to hear that he was not more than fifty-two."*

The narrator learns that Ethan's life has been a tragic tale of pain and suffering.

After his parents die, Ethan marries Zenobia ("Zeena"), an older woman who quickly becomes a cold, complaining hypochondriac. Ethan finds joy with Zeena's younger cousin Mattie Silver, an orphan who comes to help care for Zeena. When Zeena realizes that Ethan has fallen in love with Mattie, she forces her to leave. Unable to start a new life together and unwilling to be separated, Ethan and Mattie try to commit suicide by sledding into a tree:

> *"As they flew toward the tree Mattie pressed her arms tighter, and her blood seemed to be in his veins. Once or twice the sled swerved a little under them. He slanted his body to keep it headed for the elm, repeating to himself again and again: 'I know we can fetch it'; and little phrases she had spoken ran through his head and danced before him on the air. The big tree loomed bigger and closer, and as they bore down on it he thought: 'It's waiting for us: it seems to know.' But suddenly his wife's face, with twisted monstrous lineaments, thrust itself between him and his goal, and he made an instinctive movement to brush it aside. The sled swerved in response, but he righted it again, kept it straight, and drove down on the black projecting mass. There was a last instant when the air shot past him like millions of fiery wires; and then the elm…"*

Their suicide attempt is a failure: Ethan is crippled; Mattie is paralyzed. Now Ethan is trapped with two wretchedly unhappy women. As a family friend notes,

> *"There was one day, about a week after the accident, when they all thought Mattie couldn't live. Well, I say it's a pity she did. I said it right out to our minister once, and he was shocked at me. Only he wasn't with me that morning when she first came to… And I say, if she'd ha' died, Ethan might ha' lived; and the way they are now, I don't see's there's much difference between the Fromes up at*

The Write Stuff

Ethan Frome is also highly symbolic: "Starkfield" is a *stark field;* Mattie "Silver" stands for something rare and precious.

the farm and the Fromes down in the graveyard; 'cept that down there they're all quiet, and the women have got to hold their tongues."

Wharton's niche is narrow but impressive nonetheless. Her word pictures of society's upper reaches remain unsurpassed; her glimpse into the mystery and misery of the human heart still has the ability to reach our own souls.

Henry James (1843–1916)

Henry James came from the kind of family that would inspire Aaron Spelling: His father was a well-known (if eccentric) theologian and philosopher; his elder brother William was America's first famous psychologist and perhaps our most influential philosopher. Two younger brothers and a sister finished the family tree.

Enormous wealth, foreign travel, jealousy, scandal—the saga of the James family contains all the elements of a television miniseries.

James was first taken abroad as an infant, then returned home for a brief stay in Manhattan. Next it was off to Geneva, Paris, and London during his teens, where he learned several languages and absorbed European culture. The family trekked through every museum, theater, library, and art gallery on the continent.

Henry entered Harvard Law School in 1862. In his spare time, he penned reviews and short stories for magazines. Henry's early publication record isn't astonishing when you consider that he once admitted to having a "ferocious ambition" under his "tranquil exterior." Deciding that he wasn't cut out for the law, James turned to writing full time in 1863.

In 1875, James spent a year in Paris, where he met the French writer Gustave Flaubert and the Russian writer Ivan Sergeevich Turgenev among other literary figures. The next year, James moved to London, where he was so popular that he attended 107 parties during the winter of 1878 to '79 alone.

Lit Wit

Every distinguished American writer of James' time made a journey to Europe, often right after graduating from college. The trip, which usually lasted about two years, was called "The Grand Tour."

During the next decade, James worked as an occasional art reviewer for the *Atlantic Monthly*. He traveled to Canada to write articles for a journal called *Nation*. In 1898, James left America and went to live in England.

The climate and people suited his soul, and Henry decided to become a Brit. He never married, and there is no report of any love interest—of either gender. Despite his wide circle of friends, relatives, and acquaintances, James lived and worked alone.

In addition to many short stories, plays, books of criticism, autobiographies, and travel, Henry James produced about 20 novels, starting with *Roderick Hudson* in 1875. James' most famous novels include *The Europeans, Washington Square, The Portrait of a Lady, The Bostonians, The Princess Casamassima, The Tragic Muse, The Spoils of Poynton, The Awkward Age, The Wings of the Dove, The Ambassadors,* and *The Golden Bowl.*

Writer's Block

James' fiction has been lambasted as bloodless and sexless, long-winded and excessively introspective.

Culture Vulture

Henry James has been criticized as a snob, a deserter of his country, and an "old maid." We *can* debate what labels to pin on James, but we *can't* debate that he was the first American writer to plan a Big Writing Career, one that spanned the oceans: He deliberately set out to be an international artist. He felt that art, especially writing, "makes life, makes interest, makes importance." As a result of his goals, James' fiction and criticism is the most highly conscious, complex, and sophisticated of its era. As a result, it is very difficult to read, since it's marked by long sentences and elevated vocabulary.

Today, Henry James is generally ranked beside Mark Twain as the greatest American novelist of the second half of the 19th century. In James' day, everyone who was anyone talked about his novels—but few people read them because of the complexity of his writing.

The main theme of James' work is the innocence and exuberance of America contrasted with the corruption and wisdom of Europe. In *The Portrait of a Lady,* for example, the characters of Madame Merle and Gilbert Osmond seem tainted from the years they have spent in Europe, compared to Isabel Archer's freshness and innocence.

James' career is so vast and varied that it's commonly divided into three phrases: *international, experimental,* and *major.*

Phase 1: International

James is noted for his international theme—that is, the complex relationships between naive Americans and cosmopolitan Europeans. What his biographer Leon Edel calls James' first, or "international," phase encompassed such works as

➤ *Transatlantic Sketches* (travel pieces, 1875)

➤ *The American* (1877)

➤ *Daisy Miller* (1879)

➤ *The Portrait of a Lady* (1881)

The Write Stuff

Accept no substitutes: Henry James' official biographer is Leon Edel (he's a wonderful writer, too).

In *The American,* for example, Christopher Newman, a naive but intelligent and idealistic self-made American millionaire industrialist, goes to Europe seeking a bride. He picks a sweetie, but her family rejects him because he lacks an aristocratic background. Newman has a chance to revenge himself; in deciding not to, he demonstrates his moral superiority.

The Portrait of a Lady, first published in three volumes in 1881, is considered the masterpiece of the first phase of James' career, with its shrewd appraisal of the American character and its embodiment of the national myth of freedom and equality hedged with historical blindness and pride.

Lit Wit

Many of Henry James' novels have been adapted to film. The highlights include *The Europeans* (1979) and *The Bostonians* (1984), François Truffaut's *La Chambre Verte* (1978, based on two of James' short stories), Peter Bogdanovich's *Daisy Miller* (1974), William Wyler's *The Heiress* (1949), and Jack Clayton's *The Innocents* (1961, the most successful of a number of adaptations of *The Turn of the Screw).*

Phase 2: Experimental

James' second period is called his *experimental* period. He exploited new subject matters—feminism and social reform in *The Bostonians* (1886), and political intrigue *in The Princess Casamassima* (1885). He also attempted to write for the theater, but failed embarrassingly when his play *Guy Domville* (1895) was booed off the stage on the first night. (It was the right reaction, unfortunately.)

Phase 3: Major

In the final part of his career, James returned to international subjects but treated them with increasing sophistication and psychological penetration. The complex and almost mythical *The Wings of the Dove* (1902*), The Ambassadors* (1903; James felt this was his best novel), and *The Golden Bowl* (1904) date from this period of major works.

In Henry James' novels, self-awareness and clear perception of others yield wisdom and self-sacrificing love. As James developed, his novels became more psychological and less concerned with external events. In James' later works, the most important events are all internal—usually portrayed by moments of intense illumination that show characters their previous blindness.

For example, in *The Ambassadors,* the idealistic, aging Lambert Strether uncovers a secret love affair and, in doing so, discovers a new complexity to his inner life. His rigid, upright morality is humanized and enlarged as he discovers a capacity to accept those who have sinned.

Bet You Can't Read Just One

The Turn of the Screw (1898) has been perhaps the most widely read and discussed story by Henry James. This story is both typical of his main phase and different from it. On the one hand, it has a convoluted style and technique; on the other, it's highly readable and so was immediately popular. I've always liked *The Turn of the Screw* because it's a walloping good ghost story, full of terror and suspense. The story involves a governess who sees a ghost. It has a sock-o twist that I won't spoil by revealing. (Here's a hint, though: Either the ghosts are real or they aren't.)

The tale begins 'round the fire:

> *"I can see Douglas there before the fire, to which he had got up to present his back, looking down at his interlocutor with his hands in his pockets. 'Nobody but me, till now, has ever heard. It's quite too horrible.' This, naturally, was declared by several voices to give the thing the utmost price, and our friend, with quiet art, prepared his triumph by turning his eyes over the rest of us and going on: 'It's beyond everything. Nothing at all that I know touches it.'*
>
> *'For sheer terror?' I remember asking.*
>
> *He seemed to say it was not so simple as that; to be really at a loss how to qualify it. He passed his hand over his eyes, made a little wincing grimace. 'For dreadful—dreadfulness!'*
>
> *'Oh, how delicious!' cried one of the women.*
>
> *He took no notice of her; he looked at me, but as if, instead of me, he saw what he spoke of. 'For general uncanny ugliness and horror and pain.'*
>
> *'Well then,' I said, 'just sit right down and begin.'"*

Douglas' sister's governess, dead for more than 20 years, had written down the story before she died and sent it to Douglas.

> *"'I remember the time and the place—the corner of the lawn, the shade of the great beeches and the long, hot summer afternoon. It wasn't a scene for a shudder; but oh—!' He quitted the fire and dropped back into his chair."*

The Turn of the Screw caused an uproar. One admirer called the work "the most hopelessly evil story that we have ever read in any literature, ancient or modern." (*The Independent*, January 5, 1899, p. 73). Suffice it to say that it's worth reading.

Edie and Hank

Edith Wharton and Henry James first met in France in the late 1880s, but they didn't become friends until after 1900. At that time, he was a famous author nearing the end of his brilliant career (but with the masterpieces of his last period yet to come), while she was at the beginning of her fame.

In 1900, Wharton sent James a copy of her story "The Line of Least Resistance;" he praised it, but included some detailed criticism, which she found devastating. In time, however, she learned to accept criticism as advice from one professional to another, and James became a valued literary adviser. Their relationship was complex and close.

Wharton overcame her shyness with James when she discovered that she could talk to him with ease "of the things we both cared about; while he, always so helpful and hospitable to younger writers, at once used his magical faculty of drawing out his interlocutor's inmost self. Perhaps it was our common sense of fun that first brought out our understanding."

Henry James' great theme was the innocence and exuberance of the New World in conflict with the corruption and wisdom of the old. Edith Wharton described upper-class life and the constraints it placed on both men and women. Both Edith Wharton and Henry James polished American literature, adding a sheen of cosmopolitan sophistication.

The Least You Need to Know

➤ Edith Wharton (1862–1937) was a wealthy society matron whose novels show the subtle interplay of emotions in a society that censured free expression.

➤ Wharton's characters are often victims of cruel social conventions, trapped in bad relationships or confining circumstances.

➤ Her writing style is elegant, graceful, and honest.

➤ Henry James (1843–1916) was the first American writer to plan an international career.

➤ James is now ranked with Mark Twain as the greatest American novelist of the second half of the 19th century.

➤ James' first phrase used international themes, his second phase was experimental, and his third phase dealt with sophisticated psychological insights.

Part 5
Modern Literature (1915–1945)

You Can't Go Home Again.

—Thomas Wolfe, title of novel

By World War I, the United States had become a significant world power. Nothing's ever easy, however, including becoming a major player in the economic and political realm. Two world wars and a decade of economic depression tempered America's innocence and optimism.

From 1918 to 1945, American writers explored new literary techniques. Influenced by developments in modern psychology, novelists began using the stream-of-consciousness technique, attempting to re-create the natural flow of a character's thoughts. Poets were equally innovative. e.e. cummings, for example, experimented with typography, capitalization, and syntax to stretch the boundaries of written expression. At the same time, the African-American writers of the Harlem Renaissance burst forth with an extraordinary outpouring of creativity.

F. Scott Fitzgerald celebrated the Roaring Twenties in a series of glittering short stories and one gem of a novel, while Ernest Hemingway took a different view of the times, poignantly expressing the angst of the "Lost Generation." Meanwhile, William Faulker became celebrated for his fables of the South—and of human destiny.

So much of the writing between the wars was bleak and despairing that the buoyant voices of the period tend to be forgotten. Dorothy Parker and James Thurber weighed in with their wry comments on the human condition.

Now let's take a look at what American lit was like during the first half of the 20th century.

Chapter 20

Macho, Macho Man: Ernest Hemingway (1899–1961)

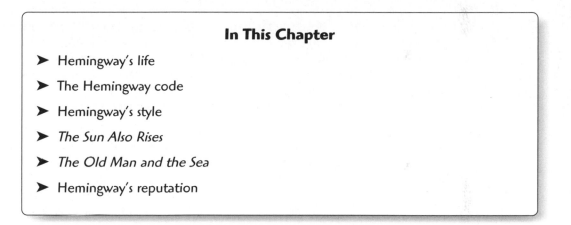

In This Chapter

➤ Hemingway's life

➤ The Hemingway code

➤ Hemingway's style

➤ *The Sun Also Rises*

➤ *The Old Man and the Sea*

➤ Hemingway's reputation

"All good books are alike in that they are truer than if they had really happened and after you are finished reading one you will feel that all that happened to you and afterwards it all belongs to you; the good and the bad, the ecstasy, the remorse and sorrow, the people and the places and how the weather was. If you can get so that you can give that to people, then you are a writer."

—Ernest Hemingway

In his nearly 62 years on earth, Ernest Hemingway forged a literary reputation unsurpassed in the 20th century and created a mythological hero in himself that captivated and confounded not only serious literary critics but also the average reader. In a word, Hemingway was a star.

In this chapter, you'll first learn about Hemingway's life, from his boyhood in the Midwest to his adventures around the world. Then I'll explain the famous Hemingway code of behavior and assess Hemingway's equally famous writing style. Next comes a detailed description and analysis of two of Hemingway's most famous novels, *The Sun Also Rises* and *The Old Man and the Sea*. The chapter concludes with an assessment of Hemingway's literary heritage.

Hunt and Peck

"It's enough for you to do it once for a few men to remember you. But if you do it year after year, then many people remember you and they tell it to their children, and their children and grandchildren remember and, if it concerns books, they can read them. And if it's good enough, it will last as long as there are human beings."

—Ernest Hemingway

All writers worry that their first book will be their last. That first book is enough to get them some small measure of fame—enough "for a few men to remember you," as Hemingway noted. But Ernest Hemingway wrote so much and so well that he won a permanent place in the literary hall of fame.

Ernest Miller Hemingway was born in Oak Park, Illinois, on July 21, 1899, the second of Dr. Clarence and Grace Hemingway's six children. Oak Park was a WASP suburb of Chicago that Hemingway would later call a town of "wide lawns and narrow minds." Not surprisingly, the conservative Midwestern values of strong religion, hard work, physical fitness, and self-determination were paramount in the Hemingway home. Following these guidelines, Ernie was taught, would inevitably lead to success in whatever field he chose.

Lit Speak

WASP stands for "white, Anglo-Saxon Protestant."

From his father, Hemingway learned to hunt and fish; from his mother, he took lessons in basic piano. Nature would be the touchstone of Hemingway's life and work, and though he found himself living in major cities like Chicago, Toronto, and Paris early in his career, once he became successful, he chose to live in isolated places that were close to nature—Key West, Florida; San Francisco de Paula, Cuba; and Ketchum, Idaho. Not accidentally, each of these locations boasted rich hunting and fishing. And the music? What little Hemingway did learn, he used to woo his first wife, Hadley.

Astonishingly, our *Field and Stream* poster boy was mediocre at organized sports. Nonetheless, he tried, playing high school football and joining the swim team. However, he most enjoyed writing for the newspaper. A loner, Hemingway was not especially popular. He ran away from home twice and spent months on the road working at a variety of jobs. From this he learned that life is hard, and that only the tough survive.

Hemingway graduated from high school in the spring of 1917, but instead of going to college the following September, he got a job as a cub reporter for the *Kansas City Star*, thanks to a good word from an uncle who had connections with the paper.

In the short time that Hemingway worked for the *Kansas City Star*, he picked up the writing style that would later become the hallmark of his fiction. The newspaper advocated:

➤ Short sentences

➤ Brief paragraphs

➤ Active verbs

➤ Authenticity

➤ Compression

➤ Clarity

➤ Immediacy

Hemingway later said, "Those were the best rules I ever learned for the business of writing. I've never forgotten them."

The War to End All Wars

"There are some things which cannot be learned quickly, and time, which is all we have, must be paid heavily for their acquiring. They are the very simplest things, and because it takes a man's life to know them the little new that each man gets from life is very costly and the only heritage he has to leave."

—Ernest Hemingway

When Hemingway turned 18, he tried to enlist in World War I, but was deferred because of poor vision. He got a chance to see action after all, though, by signing up to be a Red Cross ambulance driver.

Lit Wit

The citation that accompanied Hemingway's medal read, "Gravely wounded by numerous pieces of shrapnel from an enemy shell, with an admirable spirit of brotherhood, before taking care of himself, he rendered generous assistance to the Italian soldiers more seriously wounded by the same explosion and did not allow himself to be carried elsewhere until after they had been evacuated."

Hemingway plunged right into the war: The day he arrived in Milan, Italy, a munitions factory exploded and he had to carry mutilated bodies and body parts to a makeshift morgue. On July 8, 1918, Hemingway was seriously wounded when a mortar shell exploded too close for comfort. He later said, "There was one of those big noises you sometimes hear at the front. I died then. I felt my soul or something coming right out of my body, like you'd pull a silk handkerchief out of a pocket by one corner. It flew all around and then came back and went in again and I wasn't dead any more."

What happened next is still unclear. One of his fellow ambulance drivers wrote that even though Hemingway had more than 200 pieces of shrapnel lodged in his legs, he still managed to carry another wounded soldier back to the first-aid station. To add injury to injury, along the way his legs were sprayed by machine guns. Other sources claim the wounded soldier/carrying never happened. In any event, Hemingway was awarded the Italian Silver Medal for Valor.

Hemingway later mined his war experience in his acclaimed novel *A Farewell to Arms*— focusing on his injuries, subsequent recovery at a hospital in Milan, and his romantic relationship with his nurse Agnes von Kurowsky.

Home Not-So-Sweet Home

"You and me, we've made a separate peace."

—Ernest Hemingway, *In Our Time*

When Hemingway returned home from Italy in January 1919, he found Oak Park dull compared to the drama of war. He was not yet 20 years old, but the war had matured him beyond his years. His parents pressured him to find work or go to college, but Hemingway couldn't work up the energy to do either. He had received about $1,000 in insurance payments for his war wounds, which enabled him to avoid work for nearly a year. To pass the time, he shared his war-time experiences with the locals and meandered around town in his Red Cross uniform.

Again, Hemingway turned life into art: The result was the short story "Soldier's Home," which conveys his frustration and shame upon returning home to people who still clung to a romantic notion of war. They were unable to understand how the war had changed him and others like him.

By the fall of 1920, Hemingway had moved to Chicago and was writing for the *Toronto Star Weekly*. Within a year, Hemingway was married to Hadley Richardson.

The couple decamped to Paris only a month after the wedding, when Hemingway took a job with the *Toronto Daily Star* as its European correspondent.

From the City of Lights to the City of Lit

"This is to tell you about a young man named Ernest Hemingway, who lives in Paris, (an American) writes for the transatlantic Review + has a brilliant future... He's the real thing."

—F. Scott Fitzgerald to his editor Maxwell Perkins, 1924

In the 1920s, Paris was the literary hot spot. Ezra Pound, James Joyce, Gertrude Stein, Sylvia Beach, Max Eastman, Lincoln Steffens, Wyndaham Lewis, and Ford Maddox Ford worked the streets of Paris as they reworked American literature. It's no surprise, then, that Hemingway would head to Paris.

Lit Wit

Sherwood Anderson (1876–1941) sprang to fame in 1919 with the publication of his collection of short stories called *Winesburg, Ohio*. The stories describe the inarticulate, desperate struggle of isolated people to assert their individuality in the face of cruel indifference and outright hostility. Noted for his poetic realism and psychological insight, Anderson's other books include the autobiographies *Tar, a Midwest Childhood* (1926) and *Sherwood Anderson's Memoirs* (1942). By all accounts, Anderson was exceedingly generous to struggling writers. Hemingway repaid Anderson's charity in 1925 by viciously parodying him in his novel *Torrents of Spring*. Who said no good deed goes unpunished?

With a letter of introduction from fellow Midwestern writer Sherwood Anderson, Hemingway met some of Paris' prominent writers and artists and forged quick friendships with them during his first few years there. The painters Joan Miró and Pablo Picasso were also part of his crowd. These friendships would be instrumental in Hemingway's development as a writer. Not only did they introduce Hemingway to publishers, but they also honed his style—and provided him with material to fashion into art. Hemingway became a Prime Time Player among the litterati glitterati.

Learning the Trade

When he wasn't schmoozing, Hemingway did some serious and impressive reporting, covering the Geneva Conference, Greco-Turkish War, Luasanne Conference, and the post-war convention in the Ruhr Valley in early 1923. By his early twenties, Hemingway had interviewed such world-famous figures as Lloyd George, Georges Clemenceau, and Benito Mussolini.

Along with the political articles, Hemingway wrote lifestyle pieces as well, covering fishing, bullfighting, European social life, skiing, bobsledding, and more. Just as Hemingway was beginning to make a name for himself as a reporter and a novice fiction writer, Hadley became pregnant with their first child. Seeking better medical care, they moved to Toronto, where Hemingway wrote for the *Toronto Daily Star*. John Hadley Nicanor Hemingway was born in October; by January, the family was back in Paris.

A Shooting Star

From 1925 to 1929 Hemingway produced some of the most important works of 20th-century fiction:

➤ *1925:* The short-story collection *In Our Time*

➤ *1926:* The novel *The Sun Also Rises*

➤ *1927:* The short-story collection *Men Without Women*

➤ *1929:* The novel *A Farewell to Arms,* arguably the finest novel to emerge from World War I

Hemingway experienced a meteoric rise to success. In four short years, he went from obscurity to fame and was suddenly ranked as one of the most important novelists of his generation.

Trade-In Time

As Hemingway's professional career soared, he decided it was time for a change in his personal life. He divorced Hadley in 1927 and married Pauline Pfeiffer, a fashion reporter he had met in Paris. Hadley got custody of their child.

In 1928, Pauline and Ernest temporarily settled in Kansas City, Missouri, where their son Patrick Hemingway was born.

After Patrick's birth, Hemingway moved to Key West, Florida, where he lived for nearly 10 years. Money wasn't a problem: *A Farewell to Arms* sold 80,000 copies in four months, making Hemingway financially secure.

Then, tragedy struck: Hemingway's father, struggling with diabetes and heart problems, put a bullet through his head. Despite his grief, Hemingway kept writing, resulting in the instant classic, *A Farewell to Arms* (1929).

Lit Wit

Hemingway was not known for being a nice guy. As fellow writer Anthony Burgess *(A Clockwork Orange)* described Hemingway in the late 1920s, "The uncharitable might say that Hemingway was a bully and a liar that was now in flower; the more uncharitable that all this was nothing compared to what was to come; the least uncharitable that he was one hell of a fine writer and entitled to his tantrums."

Lions and Tigers and Bulls, Oh My!

Hemingway's work on *Death in the Afternoon,* a powerful look at bullfighting, gave him the excuse to visit Spain and knock down a few bulls. After Ernest finished *Death in the Afternoon* and Pauline gave birth to another boy, the family set off for west Africa.

Three brilliant short stories resulted from the African jaunt: "The Green Hills of Africa," "The Snows of Kilamanjaro," and "The Short and Happy Life of Francis Macomber." In "Kilamanjaro," Hemingway used F. Scott Fitzgerald's decline to depict the guilt of a talented yet unfulfilled artist as he faced death.

A bout with dysentery sent the Hemingway back home to Key West.

Lit Wit

Hemingway and Marlene Dietrich had their famous meeting on the ship *Ile de France.* Dietrich had decided to join a dinner party in the ship's dining room, but when she saw that she would be the thirteenth person at the table, she refused to sit down. Hemingway, who was dining nearby, offered to join the dinner party, making the group a safe 14. This was the beginning of a long and complex relationship. Ernest affectionately called Dietrich "The Kraut," while Dietrich was one of the few who was permitted to call him "Ernest" instead of "Papa."

War Can Be Fun

The Spanish Civil War became official in July 1936, and Hemingway traveled to Spain to report on the conflict for mass-market magazines.

At the same time, he completed *To Have and Have Not,* which he published in 1937. In 1940, after the end of the Spanish Civil War, Hemingway divorced Pauline and published *For Whom the Bell Tolls.*

When World War II erupted, Hemingway again leaped into the fray. After editing his book *Men at War* in 1942, he served as a war correspondent for various magazines, accompanying American troops as they pushed the German forces back across Europe. Hemingway took to the war with enthusiasm; known as "Papa" by respectful troops and a celebrity everywhere, he helped "liberate" the Ritz Hotel in Paris, actually posting a guard at the entrance with a notice: "Papa took good hotel. Plenty stuff in cellar."

"Papa" Hemingway in his prime.

Divorced now from his third wife, Martha in 1945, Hemingway next married Mary Welsh, a *Time* magazine correspondent. In 1950, Hemingway published the novel *Across the River and Into the Trees*, to great critical disapproval.

Lit Wit

Getting confused over Hemingway's marriages, divorces, and remarriages? Here's the rundown!

Wife	Term of Office	Children
Hadley Richardson	1921–1927	John Hadley Nicanor
Pauline Pfeiffer	1927–1940	Patrick, Gregory
Martha Gellhorn	1940–1945	
Mary Welsh	1946–1961 (his death)	

Death in the Afternoon

"Dying was nothing and he had no picture of it nor fear of it in his mind. But living was a field of grain blowing in the wind on the side of a hill. Living was a hawk in the sky. Living was an earthen jar of water in the dust of the threshing with the grain flailed out and chaff blowing. Living was a horse between your legs and a carbine under one leg and a hill and a valley and a stream with trees along it and the far side of the valley and the hills beyond."

—from *For Whom The Bell Tolls*

As the young Hemingway had been a legendary adventurer, the old Hemingway took up the role of Grand Old Man, the battle-scarred veteran, the aging but still indomitable combatant. "The Champ" (as he liked to call himself) was better known as Papa, Citizen of the World.

Still rough-edged and manfully poetic, Hemingway was also mellowed by experience, a connoisseur of life, bullfighters, women, fishing, and war.

But by the 1950s, the critics decided that Hemingway had burned himself out. Challenged, he wrote *The Old Man and the Sea* (1952). It earned him the Pulitzer Prize, and in 1954, the biggest fish in the literary pond, the Nobel Prize.

The end of Hemingway's life was long and brutal. Diabetes claimed Hemingway's eyes and kidneys. At the same time, he became paranoid and delusional. Hemingway's condition worsened, and in 1960, he was committed to the Mayo Clinic and given electroshock therapy. Released in 1961, he initially seemed better. But on April 23, he attempted to commit suicide. On July 2, he succeeded. Ernest Hemingway died as his father had, from a self-inflicted shotgun blast to the head.

Less Is More

"I always try to write on the principle of the iceberg. There is seven-eighths of it underwater for every part that shows. Anything you know you can eliminate and it only strengthens your iceberg. It is the part that doesn't show. If a writer omits something because he does not know it then there is a hole in the story."

—Interview with George Plimpton, 1958

Hemingway's deceptively simple, intensely compressed writing style has influenced countless writers the world over. His writing is...

➤ Concise   ➤ Objective

➤ Direct   ➤ Precise

➤ Spare   ➤ Rhythmic

Hemingway used simple sentences and direct words to help readers look beyond the surface to the reality underneath the words.

Lit Wit

Hemingway was not shy about criticizing other writers who didn't embrace his deceptively simple style. Speaking about Faulkner's lush language, for example, Hemingway said, "Poor Faulkner. Does he really think big emotions come from big words? He thinks I don't know the ten-dollar words. I know them all right. But there are older and simpler and better words, and those are the ones I use."

Hemingway's Code

"You are all a lost generation."

—Gertrude Stein

Remember that Europe had been blown apart in World War I. After being exposed to the horrors of war, people were searching for meaning.

Not just those who had seen action but also those who had kept the home fires burning were filled with despair—making them a "lost" generation. It seemed that all hope was gone; even God and religion offered little sanctuary. From this despair, Hemingway fashioned his famous code of behavior.

Lit Speak

Writers like Hemingway turned away from the style, form, and content of 19th-century romantic literature to experiment with new themes and techniques, such as fragmentation, stream of consciousness, and imagery. And so a new literary movement, **modernism**, was born.

Hemingway bases his work on these philosophical premises:

➤ Accept that there are no guidelines, no rules, for life.

➤ Face reality: See things exactly as they are, no matter how difficult, rather than as you might wish them to be. (Especially the Long Good-bye, Death.)

➤ Contain your despair and self-pity by sheer will power. Give into despair only in private or in the company of another member of the breed, someone who thinks the way you do.

➤ Don't make trouble for others.

➤ Impose some meaning on a meaningless universe by achieving form through ritual.

➤ Don't judge others; instead, view the unenlightened with "irony and pity."

According to Hemingway's code, a man must establish his own values by facing life courageously and acting honestly in terms of this reality. As a result, the Hemingway hero's main attribute is courage. He doesn't dodge reality through religion or lies. Further, he avoids self-pity because it is dishonest. Following this code enables the Hemingway hero to maintain his essential manhood and dignity, despite the brutal reality he confronts.

The Code first appeared in Hemingway's brutally affecting novel *The Sun Also Rises,* which introduced the world to the lost generation. Set in Paris and Spain, the novel is a story of unrequited love against a backdrop of bars and bullfighting. Let's take a look at it now.

Writer's Block

The Hemingway hero and the Code are macho, like refusing to ask for directions when you're lost.

The Sun Also Rises

"'You're an expatriate. You've lost touch with the soil. You get precious, Fake European standards have ruined you. You drink yourself to death. You become obsessed by sex. You spend all your time talking, not working. You are an expatriate, see? You hang around cafes.'"

—from *The Sun Also Rises*

Set in the 1920s, the novel deals with a group of aimless expatriates in France and Spain. They are members of the cynical and disillusioned post–World War I Lost Generation, many of whom suffer psychological and physical wounds as a result of the war.

Two of the novel's main characters, Lady Brett Ashley and Jake Barnes, typify the moral and spiritual dissolution of this generation. Lady Brett drifts through a series of affairs despite her love for Jake, who has been rendered impotent by a war wound. Friendship, stoicism, and natural grace under pressure are offered as the values that matter in an otherwise amoral and senseless world.

The novel's central expression of heroism lies in the bullfights, which to Hemingway epitomize the hero's deliberate confrontation with death under the protection of ritual. Here's where we get into the idea of the *aficionado,* one who is passionate about a specific thing, such as bullfights, books, or ballet. This passion forms a bond among its adherents.

Lit Speak

To Hemingway, an **aficionado** is someone who is passionate about bullfights. By extension, the aficionado understands and follows the Hemingway Code of behavior.

Who's Who in **The Sun Also Rises**

World War I veteran Jake Barnes, now living and working in Paris as a newsman, is the novel's main character. He's the Hemingway hero, a man's man who lives by the Code. Due to a terrible but vague war wound, Jake is impotent. As you can surmise, this puts a crimp in his relationship with his love, Lady Brett Ashley.

Meet the gang:

➤ *Jake Barnes:* So he's got a problem with his plumbing, but he's still a real man.

➤ *Lady Brett Ashley:* So she does the right thing in the end, but the lady is a tramp.

➤ *Robert Cohn:* The whiny antihero. He's a well-to-do American writer who lives in Paris and has published his first novel.

➤ *Bill Gorton:* Another embodiment of the Hemingway hero.

➤ *Mike Campbell:* Brett's fiancé, a Scotsman.

➤ *Count Mippipopolous:* A rich Greek who enjoys partying with Brett and the gang.

➤ *Frances Clyne:* Robert Cohn's mistress, an American woman.

➤ *Pedro Romero:* A bullfighter, one of the elect.

The Write Stuff

The characters whom Hemingway portrays in the novel are based on actual people he knew in the Left-Bank cafes, while the character of Pedro Romero is a projection of Niño de la Palma, a famous matador of the time. Check out Harold Loeb's *The Way It Was* for a complete rundown on the identities of the characters in real life. (Loeb was the model for Cohn.)

As Jake notes, "It is only a bullfighter who lives life to the hilt, bringing to his work all his courage, intelligence, discipline, and art."

The plot is very loose, revolving around the characters' pain. All the characters in *The Sun Also Rises* are suffering because of the war, directly or indirectly: Jake has been wounded, Brett lost her lover, and Cohn has not realized the importance of the conflict on his own generation. Those who have been immediately involved with the war go through the most anguish and rely on each other for support. Those who have been less involved are separated from the former by their lack of experience. Cohn is still the idealistic and romantic young man that Jake Barnes might have been had he not gone to war.

The Sun Also Sets

"'Oh, Jake,' Brett said, 'we could have had such a damned good time together.'

Ahead was a mounted policeman in khaki directing traffic. He raised his baton. The car slowed suddenly, pressing Brett directly against me.

'Yes,' I said. 'Isn't it pretty to think so?'"

—from *The Sun Also Rises*

The novel's famous closing lines reveal that the hero struggles constantly to confront the truth and to live by it, and to derive from his struggle a measure of value by which he can live still more honestly.

Nevertheless, the book is a tragedy because even the greatest courage does not enable the characters to rise above their circumstances. They only know how to suck it in and live in it. (That's the best a Hemingway hero can do in the face of reality.)

The title of the novel reinforces the tragedy of the story. A quote from the Old Testament, it suggests that life moves in cycles, and that we are all caught within these forces. The constant activity of the earth is repetitious, and nothing we can do will break the movement of these forces. The novel has little plot and even less action; by the end, Jake, Brett, and the rest of the characters are at exactly the same place they were at the beginning. Don't we feel depressed?

The Write Stuff

Hemingway said that *The Sun Also Rises* was not "a hollow or bitter satire, but a damn tragedy with the earth abiding forever as the hero."

Lit Wit

In his assessment of the novel, critic Oscar Cargill wrote, "*The Sun Also Rises* has no peer among American books that have attempted to take account of the cost of the War upon the morals of the War generation and... no better polemics against war than this, which was meant for no polemic at all."

The One That Got Away: *The Old Man and the Sea*

"I am glad we do not have to try to kill the stars. Imagine if each day a man must try to kill the moon, he thought. The moon runs away. But imagine if a man each day should have to try to kill the sun? We are born lucky, he thought."

—from *The Old Man and the Sea*

The Old Man and the Sea describes an old Cuban fisherman named Santiago who finally catches a magnificent fish after 84 days without a catch. After three days of battling the fish, he finally manages to reel it in and lash it to his boat, only to have sharks eat it as he returns to the harbor. The other fishermen marvel at the size of the skeleton; Santiago is spent but triumphant.

Lit Wit

In a subplot of *The Old Man and the Sea,* Santiago sees in Joe DiMaggio, the great baseball player, much of his own pride, will, and endurance. Like Santiago himself, DiMaggio is no longer the great champion he was; the baseball hero suffers because of a bone spur on his heel. DiMaggio, however, continues to play the game, using his skill, his heart, and his endurance to replace his early strength. Santiago continues to fish for the same reasons.

The Write Stuff

No, you're not the first to see a parallel between *The Old Man and the Sea* and Herman Melville's *Moby Dick.* Both pit man against nature in an epic battle. *The Old Man and the Sea,* however, is a whole lot easier to read.

Lit Speak

An **allegory** is a story with two or more levels of meaning: a literal level and one or more symbolic levels. The events, setting, and characters in an allegory are symbols for ideas or qualities. Hawthorne's "The Minister's Black Veil" is another well-known American allegory.

Like Jake in *The Sun Also Rises,* Santiago the fisherman embodies the Hemingway Code. Despite his age and poverty, Santiago is a *man* in the fullest sense of the word. Although his strength is gone, his endurance and will remain; faced with defeat, he does not quit.

The novel combines the simplicity of a fable, the significance of a parable, and the drama of an epic. On one level, you can read the novel as a fable of the unconquerable spirit of man, a creature capable of snatching spiritual victories from material disaster and defeat.

On another level, you can read the novel as an allegory of the last days of Christ:

➤ Christ and Santiago are both moral teachers. The fish is a symbol of Christ, so that Christ, fish, and fisherman are equated.

➤ Santiago's period of bad luck parallel Christ's 40 days in the wilderness.

➤ Santiago struggles with the fish for three days, as Christ suffered three days on the cross.

➤ Santiago's hands are torn as Christ's were pierced by nails, his back is lashed by the line as Christ's was lashed before being taken to Calvary, and Santiago gets a piercing headache, as Christ was subjected to pain by the crown of thorns.

➤ Santiago kills the fish at noon on the third day, as Christ rose from the tomb on the third day after the crucifixion.

➤ Santiago carries his mast, as Christ carried His cross.

➤ Santiago falls upon his bed in the attitude of Christ on the cross.

The Fickle Finger of Fame

In the 1930s and 1940s, Hemingway was the King of the Literary Hill. Writers all over the world were imitating his writing style, struggling to pare their sentences to a lean precision.

By the 1950s, however, the writing world turned, leaving Hemingway at the bottom. People grew weary of his public posturing. The stoic had become the braggart; the celebrator of a separate peace had become a porky parody of his younger self. The new generation of writers questioned what they saw as his obsession with violence, his scorn of intellect, his denial of his feelings.

Today, Hemingway's writing is honored, but his reputation is still unsteady. He continues to be widely read, but not many writers see him as a model. The Hemingway who 40 years ago seemed so immediate now seems dated. However, the Hemingway mill keeps grinding out criticism, analysis, and studies. The amount of criticism that has been published is far, far more than Hemingway ever wrote. It's a veritable industry.

Writer's Block

The Old Man and the Sea, which appeared in 1952, was seen by some readers as an attack on the critical "sharks" who had attacked Hemingway's previous novels.

The Least You Need to Know

➤ In his day, Hemingway was a larger-than-life hero, a big game hunter, sport fisherman, and headliner the world over. (He appeared on more magazine covers than Cindy Crawford.)

➤ The Hemingway Code advocated "grace under pressure." In the face of a meaningless world, a hero must establish his own values by facing life courageously and by acting honestly in terms of this reality.

➤ Hemingway's simple, spare, and concise style has influenced generations of writers.

➤ Hemingway's major works include *The Sun Also Rises, A Farewell to Arms, For Whom the Bell Tolls,* and *The Old Man and the Sea.*

➤ Hemingway won a Pulitzer Prize and the Nobel Prize for Literature; he also ushered in a new style of writing and looking at the world.

Chapter 21

Party Hearty: F. Scott Fitzgerald (1896–1940)

In This Chapter

➤ Fitzgerald's life

➤ Fitzgerald's success—and excess

➤ Fitzgerald's literary reputation

➤ The Jazz Age

➤ Fitzgerald's masterpiece, *The Great Gatsby*

"If personality is an unbroken series of successful gestures, then there was something gorgeous about him, some heightened sensitivity to the promises of life, as if he were related to one of those intricate machines that register earthquakes ten thousand miles away."

—from *The Great Gatsby*

In this passage, the novel's narrator, Nick Carraway, describes Jay Gatsby—but the description applies just as well to Gatsby's creator, F. Scott Fitzgerald. There *was* something "gorgeous" about Fitzgerald, something that catapulted him for a brief time to the top of the literary heap. Fitzgerald became the voice of the twenties, the symbol of everything that was terrific—and tragic—about the gaudy, glorious Roaring Twenties.

In this chapter, you'll first learn all about Fitzgerald's life, which is crucial to understanding his writing. Then we'll take a look at Fitzgerald's masterpiece, *The Great Gatsby*. By the end of the chapter, you'll understand how and why Fitzgerald came to be the emblem of an era.

Great Scott!

Named after his distant cousin Francis Scott Key, the man who wrote "The Star Spangled Banner," Francis Scott Key Fitzgerald made his debut in 1896 in St. Paul, Minnesota. His mother had come from money, but his father never really got it together financially. As a result, the family moved often, never staying in any one place for more than three years.

The Fitzgeralds had all the traditions of old money... except the money. This didn't stop his mother from enrolling Scott in a private school, but he always felt like he was on the fringes looking in. Nonetheless, Scott gained some measure of fame among his peers at school for his detective stories, encouraging him to pursue writing more enthusiastically than academics.

In 1913, Fitzgerald enrolled in Princeton University. An indifferent student, he dabbled in campus theater productions and began his first novel, *This Side of Paradise* (then called *The Romantic Egotist*). He also wrote stories for the campus humor magazine and published stories in the campus literary magazine. Scott's college friends included Edmund Wilson and John Peale Bishop, both of whom would become distinguished critics and novelists.

Lit Wit

Edmund Wilson (1895–1972) is likely *the* foremost literary critic of the 20th century. Although he wrote novels, short stories, poetry, and nonfiction, his true influence lay in social and literary criticism. Wilson's first major work, *Axel's Castle* (1931), examined the symbolist influence on T.S. Eliot, Ezra Pound, James Joyce, and others. *The Wound and the Bow* (1941) explores the relationship between the emotional lives of writers and their work. *To the Finland Station* (1940) describes the theoretical foundation of the Russian Revolution; *Patriotic Gore: Studies in the Literature of the Civil War* (1962) is ranked as one of his finest critical studies. This fearsome bearer of cultural standards was nicknamed "Bunny."

By 1916, Fitzgerald was on academic probation at Princeton and it seemed unlikely that he would graduate. He took his only out—a temporary withdrawal. He did return to Princeton briefly in the fall, but left again before graduating to join the Army. Convinced that he would die in World War I, he rapidly completed *The Romantic Egotist* and submitted it to Scribner and Sons. The letter of rejection praised the novel's originality and asked that it be resubmitted when revised.

The glamour of WWI in Europe beckoned, but the Army wasn't listening; Fitzgerald was sent to Alabama. It was the most significant move of his life since this was where he met his wife, Zelda.

Belle of the Ball

> *"Then wear the gold hat, if that will move her;*
>
> *If you can bounce high, bounce for her too,*
>
> *Till she cry 'Lover, gold-hatted, high-bouncing lover,*
>
> *I must have you!'"*

—Thomas Parke D'Invilliers

This inscription that opens *The Great Gatsby* perfectly describes Fitzgerald's courtship of his lady love, 18-year-old Zelda Sayre. A celebrated southern belle and the youngest daughter of an Alabama Supreme Court judge, Zelda was renowned for her beauty. She and Fitzgerald soon became engaged, but she was unwilling to proceed with the marriage until he had enough money to support her in the way to which she was accustomed.

The romance intensified Fitzgerald's hopes for the success of his novel, and he resubmitted *The Romantic Egoist* to Scribner's who rejected it a second time. The war ended just before Fitzgerald was scheduled to go overseas. After his discharge in 1919, he went to New York City to seek his fortune. (Remember, no money = no marriage.) In the meantime, Zelda was reluctant to gamble that Fitzgerald would indeed succeed, and unwilling to live on his small salary until such time. Zelda broke off their engagement. The belle of the ball had bigger fish on the line.

A **flapper** was the 1920s slang term for an unconventional young woman—one who bobbed her hair (cut it short), danced such dances as the Charleston, necked in cars, and wore short skirts and makeup.

Once in New York, Fitzgerald didn't set the world on fire—far from it. For eight months, he slaved for $90 a month writing advertising copy. He then decided to return to St. Paul, lock himself in his room, and revise his novel yet again. The work paid off, for in September of 1919 Scribner's agreed to publish the novel. Fitzgerald's life would never be the same.

Paradise Won

This Side of Paradise sold 3,000 copies in three days, catapulting Fitzgerald to instant fame. The hero, Amory Blaine, a young Princeton undergraduate like Fitzgerald, was considered a composite of all the sad young men of the postwar flapper era, and the novel became a social document of its time. The result for Fitzgerald was that magazines began buying his short stories as fast as he could write them and that Zelda finally agreed to be his wife. It was a fairy tale come true. Fitzgerald was the golden boy of American literature.

Lit Wit

The Fitzgeralds ran through an astonishing amount of money in an astonishingly short period of time. In 1929 his peak story fee of $4,000 from *The Saturday Evening Post* had the purchasing power of $40,000 in 1999 dollars. That doesn't go very far, though, when you're buying everything that isn't nailed down and giving $100 tips.

The Saturday Evening Post in particular served as a showcase for his short stories, most of which revolved around a new breed of American woman—the young, free-thinking, independent "flapper" of the Roaring Twenties. The flapper appeared in such Fitzgerald short stories as "The Offshore Pirate" and "Bernice Bobs Her Hair." Fitzgerald's more ambitious stories, such as "May Day" and "The Diamond as Big as the Ritz," were published in another magazine, *The Smart Set,* which had a far smaller circulation but was much more prestigious.

The Beautiful and the Damned

Soon after, Scribner's published a collection of Fitzgerald's stories in a volume called *Flappers and Philosophers*, and the couple moved into a luxury New York apartment. They were the center of a glittering crowd; gin flowed like water and money flowed like gin. Between parties, Fitzgerald made time to write his second novel, *The Beautiful and the Damned.* Their only child, a daughter they named Frances Scott ("Scottie"), was born in 1922.

The Write Stuff

T.S. Eliot praised *The Great Gatsby* as "the first step American fiction has taken since Henry James."

The Beautiful and the Damned sold well, but not as well as Fitzgerald had hoped. Their lifestyle was lavish and money grew tight, despite a second collection of short stories, *The Jazz Age.*

Expecting to hit the jackpot with his play *The Vegetable,* the Fitzgeralds moved to Great Neck, Long Island, in order to be near Broadway.

But the political satire—subtitled *From President to Postman*—failed at its tryout in November 1923, so Fitzgerald had to write his way out of debt with his short stories. The distractions of Great Neck and New York prevented Fitzgerald from making progress on his third novel, and his drinking increased. Fitzgerald was an undeniable alcoholic, Zelda was often smashed, too, and their fights were legendary.

The following spring, Zelda and Scott moved to Paris, where they partied, and partied, and partied some more. Despite his drinking, Fitzgerald completed his masterpiece, *The Great Gatsby*. The novel marked a striking advance in Fitzgerald's technique, using a complex structure and a controlled narrative point of view. Nonetheless, it did not sell well and the Fitzgeralds were bitterly disappointed.

F. Scott Fitzgerald as a young man (1920s).

Paradise Lost

For the next nine years, the Fitzgeralds wandered aimlessly throughout Europe, drinking and carousing. Zelda's mental health, never strong, started to crack. Fitzgerald was soused most of the time. Despite his numerous problems, Fitzgerald managed to complete another novel, *Tender Is the Night*, a thinly disguised account of Scott and Zelda's life, in 1933. Set in France during the 1920s, *Tender Is the Night* examines the deterioration of Dick Diver, a brilliant American psychiatrist, during the course of his marriage to a wealthy mental patient. This novel sold poorly.

The Crack-Up

"In a real dark night of the soul it is always three o'clock in the morning."

—Fitzgerald, "The Crack-Up"

So Fitzgerald described his own "crack-up" in an essay that he wrote in 1936. He was hopelessly in debt, unable to write, nearly estranged from his wife and daughter, and incapacitated by excessive drinking and poor physical health.

In the summer of 1937, Fitzgerald went to Hollywood, lured by a six-month Metro-Goldwyn-Mayer contract that paid $1,000 a week. He received his only screen credit for adapting *Three Comrades* (1938). Based on this success, his contract was renewed for a year at $1,250 a week. This was a great deal of money during the late Depression years when a new car cost about $500, but Fitzgerald was still unable to pay off all his debts.

Fitzgerald managed to avoid clichés in his fiction, but he became one when he went to Hollywood. Like most of the great writers who responded to the allure of Hollywood, Fitzgerald hated it. He became the cliché of a fine writer reduced to a drunken, disillusioned hack. Her mental health shattered, Zelda entered an asylum.

> **Writer's Block**
>
> Read the book instead of watching the movie, because the filmed versions of Fitzgerald's novels are clunkers. The 1949 *The Great Gatsby* is close to unwatchable. Despite great performances by Mia Farrow and Sam Waterston, the 1974 version isn't much better. Hopefully, the final straw was the wretched 1976 film *The Last Tycoon,* which critic Pauline Kael said was so bloodless that it's "like a vampire movie after the vampires have left."

> **The Write Stuff**
>
> *Beloved Infidel* is Graham's tell-all book, giving her version of her time with Fitzgerald.

Love Among the Ruins

In California, Fitzgerald fell in love with movie columnist Sheilah Graham. Their relationship endured, despite his marriage and his alcoholic benders. After MGM dropped his option at the end of 1938, Fitzgerald worked as a freelance script writer and wrote short stories for *Esquire*. He had completed about half of his last novel, *The Love of the Last Tycoon,* when he died of a heart attack in Graham's apartment in 1940. Zelda Fitzgerald perished in a fire in Highland Hospital in 1948.

Snatching Victory from the Jaws of Defeat

"I talk with the authority of failure," F. Scott Fitzgerald once wrote in his notebooks, soon after his famous break with Ernest Hemingway, "…Ernest with the authority of success. We could never sit across the same table again."

At the time of his death, Fitzgerald was considered to be an extravagant drunk who epitomized the excesses of the Jazz Age. Few of the pundits predicted that Fitzgerald would be accorded a secure place among the ranks of the greatest American authors.

Fitzgerald's reputation as an alcoholic party boy sparked the myth that he was an irresponsible writer, yet just the opposite was true. A painstaking reviser whose fiction went through layers of drafts, Fitzgerald created clear, lyrical prose marked by vivid images.

The Fitzgerald revival was sparked only a year after his death, when writer Stephen Vincent Benét reviewed *The Last Tycoon* in the *Saturday Review of Literature*. Benét wrote, "You can take off your hats now, gentlemen, and I think perhaps you had better. This is not a legend, this is a reputation—and seen in perspective, it may well be one of the most secure reputations of our time."

Edmund Wilson set off a flood of Fitzgerald criticism in 1945 when he edited and published "The Crack-Up." *The Great Gatsby* was reissued with a flattering introduction. Soon, full-length Fitzgerald studies, critical anthologies, and articles flooded the market.

When the dust settled, F. Scott Fitzgerald made it to the front row. He's now ranked as one of the major prose writers of the 20th century. His fiction became the symbol of the frenetic energy of the era. No other writer captured so well the spirit of the Jazz Age, the moral decay of a generation.

The Write Stuff

When critics objected to Fitzgerald's concern with love and success, his response was: "But, my God! It was my material, and it was all I had to deal with." By then, nothing he could do would please the critics.

Writer's Block

During her stay for a mental breakdown at Johns Hopkins hospital in 1932, Zelda wrote her only novel, *Save Me the Waltz.* The autobiographical work generated considerable bitterness between the Fitzgeralds, for he regarded it as preempting the material that he was using in his novel in progress. What little was left of the marriage crumbled.

The Jazz Age: "The Greatest, Gaudiest Spree in History"

"It was an age of miracles, it was an age of art, it was an age of excess, and it was an age of satire."

—F. Scott Fitzgerald

The 1920s were perhaps the most astonishing period in American history, for the decade was marked by vast contrasts: certainty and insecurity, stability and confusion, content and discontent, and conformity and rebellion in a time of relative peace and prosperity.

In the 1920s, America was in the midst of the greatest period of prosperity the country had ever known. Economists have pointed out that only a small amount of money was required to be considered well-off in the 1920s because prices and taxes were low. It's estimated that a person earning $6,000 or more a year was in a select income group, approximately the upper five percent of the population. In reality, this era proved to be a brief boom indeed, a precarious period of prosperity lasting a scant five years.

Lit Wit

The political scene of the 1920s was marked by conservatism, inertia, apathy, and social indifference. The domestic social reforms and social legislation initiated by President Theodore Roosevelt and continued by President Woodrow Wilson before World War I were abandoned. In an overwhelming victory in 1920, the country elected Warren G. Harding president. When Harding died three years later, Calvin Coolidge succeeded him to serve a full term, beginning in 1924. Herbert Hoover took the reigns in 1928. All three presidents held the confidence of the business sector, and all represented the views of "normalcy" in a Republican era.

Lit Speak

The term **Lost Generation** refers to the disillusioned survivors of World War I, bitter and disaffected by the "war to end all wars" and what they perceived as the failure of religion and family to provide a bulwark against destruction.

Pop culture was carefree, marked by an enormous rise in movie attendance. The leading figures of the silent screen were the comedians Charlie Chaplin and Harold Lloyd; "America's Sweetheart," Mary Pickford; swash-buckling leading man Douglas Fairbanks; and the "Great Lover" Rudolph Valentino. Director Cecil B. de Mille's films were an orgy of spectacular scenery and included casts of thousands.

In the midst of the spree, a small but influential group of writers expressed their disillusionment with the decades of the '20s. In Chapter 20, you read about the "lost generation," named by writer Gertrude Stein. Fitzgerald recognized the despair beneath the surface merriment when he described American society as "the beautiful and the damned." His writing captures both the merriment and the emptiness of the 1920s.

The Jazz Age came to a screeching halt on October 29, 1929, when the stock market crashed. The world plunged into the dark years of the Great Depression.

Lit Wit

The stock market crash, also known as Black Tuesday, was caused by overspeculation. Investors, taking risks in hopes of profits, bought stocks on margin with money they did not have. On Black Tuesday, more than 16 million shares of stock were traded. With an overabundance of sellers and few buyers, the prices of stocks dropped far below the prices paid for them, and investors lost billions in paper profits within a matter of hours. Banks and businesses had also invested in the stock market, and with the falling prices, the value of their investments plunged, causing them to fold.

The Great Gatsby

"Gatsby believed in the green light, the orgiastic future that year by year recedes before us. It eluded us then, but that's no matter—tomorrow we will run faster, stretch out our arms farther… And one fine morning—.

So we beat on, boats against the current, borne back ceaselessly into the past."

—from *The Great Gatsby*

The Great Gatsby is a lyrical picture of American values, a uniquely romantic materialism in which people try to convince themselves that desire can define reality, that gesture can define action, and that sentiment can define emotion.

One critic called the heart of the novel "the extraordinary gift for hope and romantic readiness," symbolized by Jay Gatsby as he builds his "enchanted palace" for Daisy Buchanan. Daisy, in turn, represents what narrator Nick Carraway calls "a vast, vulgar, meretricious beauty." But before we get ahead of ourselves, let's meet everyone.

Who's Who in The Great Gatsby

➤ *Nick Carraway:* The novel's narrator and moral compass.

➤ *Tom Buchanan:* Daisy's husband, a rich and brutal man.

➤ *Daisy Buchanan:* Her "voice is full of money," but her heart is empty. She represents the embodiment of Gatsby's dreams of perfection, but she is careless and selfish.

➤ *Jordan Baker:* A beautiful woman who cheats in golf and in life.

➤ *Jay Gatsby:* A racketeer and a romantic idealist, the former James Gatz remakes himself to win his dream of ideal love with Daisy. He's crooked but admirable.

➤ *George Wilson:* The owner of a garage in the "valley of ashes," he kills Gatsby and himself when he mistakenly assumes that his wife is Gatsby's mistress.

➤ *Myrtle Wilson:* George Wilson's wife; Tom Buchanan's coarse mistress.

➤ *Catherine:* Myrtle's sister, "a slender, worldly girl of about thirty."

➤ *Mr. and Mrs. McKee:* A photographer and his wife, they live in an apartment below the one Tom keeps for Myrtle.

➤ *"Owl-Eyes":* A middle-aged man who attends Gatsby's parties and his funeral.

➤ *Meyer Wolfsheim:* Gatsby's business partner, a gambler and racketeer; the man reputed to have fixed the 1919 White Sox scandal.

➤ *Ewing Klipspringer:* The piano-playing boarder at Gatsby's house.

➤ *Dan Cody:* The "pioneer debauchee" who gave Gatsby his "education."

Lit Speak

The Wasteland refers to T.S. Eliot's 1922 poem of the same name, the first masterpiece of modernism. The poem describes the emptiness of modern life and established Eliot as an international literary force.

The Write Stuff

"West Egg" is a thinly disguised portrait of Little Neck, New York; "East Egg" is Great Neck, where the Fitzgerald's lived in the 1920s.

Ain't We Got Fun?

The novel opens with the voice of the narrator, Nick Carraway, the son of well-to-do people from America's Midwest. Nick represents America's traditional moral codes: He wants the world "to stand at moral attention forever." He is attracted by the beauty, the wealth, and the sophistication of "the Wasteland," which is represented by New York City, but comes to understand the essential emptiness, the gaudy display of "nothingness," that characterizes the Wasteland itself. The novel is Nick's perspective because he understands the carelessness and corruption at the heart of the world of the rich.

In the spring of 1922, Nick moves to the town of West Egg on Long Island's North Shore, overlooking the twin village of East Egg where Nick's cousin Daisy lives. East Egg is far more fashionable, a nouveau riche bastion of huge mansions and ostentatious parties. Nick's next-door neighbor, Jay Gatsby, has a colossal mansion. Across the bay, Nick can see the mansion of his second cousin, Daisy Buchanan, and her husband Tom, whom Nick had known casually in college. Nick visits Daisy and Tom and meets their friend, Jordan Baker, an attractive and wealthy young woman. During dinner, Jordan tells Nick that Tom has a mistress.

Returning home, Nick catches his first glimpse of the mysterious Gatsby, stretching his arms out toward the green light across Long Island Sound. Nick muses, "Involuntarily I glanced seaward—and distinguished nothing except a single green light, minute and faraway, that might have been the end of a dock."

Let the Good Times Roll

Chapter 2 opens with a description of the valley of ashes that lies between West Egg and New York City, overshadowed by a huge billboard of Dr. T.J. Eckleburg.

Nick is astonished when Tom invites him to meet his mistress, Myrtle Wilson. They drive to her home, an apartment above her husband George's garage. Myrtle then takes the train to Manhattan and meets Tom and Nick in the station. Tom buys her a puppy and they all go to the apartment Tom keeps for Myrtle. She invites friends and relatives over, and the party soon becomes brutal after some of the guests have had too much to drink. When Myrtle shouts out Daisy's name, Tom smashes her face and breaks her nose. The party breaks up and Nick returns home.

The following evening, Gatsby holds a huge party in his mansion. Armies of caterers, florists, and musicians prepare for the onslaught of guests. Amid the madness, Nick runs into Jordan, and together they listen to wild rumors about their host. Is he a killer? Was he a German spy during the war? Did he attend Oxford University in England? As the party winds down, the gaiety dissolves, replaced by physical violence. Couples turn on each other, and one drunken guest has a minor car accident. Nick thinks about his usual dull work routine, broken only by dates with Jordan. Although he is attracted to her cool beauty, he realizes from all her actions that she is incurably dishonest, in contrast to his deep sense of honesty and strict moral code.

The Write Stuff

The billboard face of Doctor T.J. Eckleburg, a fictional optician, is often interpreted as a symbol of America's wasteland, an obvious allusion to T.S. Eliot's 1922 poem "The Wasteland."

Soon after, Gatsby drives to Nick's house and shows off his luxurious car. To Nick's astonishment, Gatsby tells Nick about his past, tracing his adventures since he left his wealthy Midwestern home to his education at Oxford, adventures in the world's capitals, and brilliant war record. Nick is unconvinced until Gatsby shows him his war medals and a picture of himself at Oxford. Later that afternoon, Jordan tells Nick that Daisy had been in love with a young soldier named Jay Gatsby. When Gatsby went off to war, Daisy unwillingly married Tom. Jordan reveals that Gatsby still loves Daisy and moved to East Egg so he could win her away from her husband. Gatsby holds huge parties in hopes that Daisy might attend one. Although she never does, Nick arranges a meeting between them. Soon after, Gatsby and Daisy meet for secret assignations at Nick's house, picking up the romance where they left off years earlier.

Lit Wit

Fitzgerald described his short story "Winter Dreams" as "a sort of first draft of the Gatsby idea." Why not check it out?

When You Wish Upon a Star

In Chapter 6, readers learn the truth about Gatsby's background. Born James Gatz to shiftless and unsuccessful farmers, he learned about the good life as a steward on millionaire Dan Cody's yacht.

Now Gatsby wants Daisy to repudiate her love for Tom and declare her love for him. Gatsby is astonished when Nick tells him that no one can repeat the past. He explains that Daisy represents the incarnation of all his dreams and recalls their first kiss:

> *"He knew that when he kissed this girl, and forever wed his unutterable visions to her perishable breath, his mind would never romp again like the mind of God. So he waited, listening for a moment longer to the tuning-fork that had been struck upon a star. Then he kissed her. At his lips' touch she blossomed for him like a flower and the incarnation was complete."*

Daisy, Daisy, Give Me Your Answer, Do

After Daisy goes off with Gatsby, Tom takes Nick to Wilson's gas station. Wilson realizes that Myrtle has been unfaithful. By accident, everyone meets at the Plaza Hotel, and Tom forces Gatsby to reveal his plans.

The Write Stuff

Gatsby's romanticism, his faith in material success, is so intense that he believes he can re-create reality the way he wants it. He cannot have Daisy in part because it's not Daisy he wants; rather, it's his representation of her.

The scene shifts to the Wilson's garage. Michaelis, who runs the coffee shop next to Wilson's garage, sees Myrtle run across the road and get killed by a yellow car. A few minutes later, Tom arrives on the scene and tells Wilson the car belongs to Gatsby. Later that night, Gatsby reveals to Nick that Daisy was driving. Daisy later makes up with Tom, and they are united by their "vast carelessness." Nick realizes that Daisy will never leave Tom.

Nick and Gatsby discuss the situation, and Gatsby decides to go for a swim. Nick leaves for work, calling after him, "They're a rotten crowd. You're worth the whole damn bunch of them put together." That afternoon, Nick breaks off his relationship with Jordan.

When he returns home that night, he finds that Wilson has shot and killed Gatsby, whom he blames for Myrtle's death. Wilson shoots himself, and the devastation is complete.

Nick notes that none of the people who so eagerly came to Gatsby's parties show up at the funeral. Daisy and Tom leave the country. A few months later, Nick meets Tom in New York City. Nick is still furious about the way Tom set up Gatsby's murder. Soon after, Nick leaves the East and returns to the Midwest.

A Great Novel

Fitzgerald's brilliant editor, Maxwell Perkins, recognized the book's genius after he read the manuscript:

"The presentation of Tom, his place, Daisy and Jordan, and the unfolding of their characters is unequaled so far as I know. The description of the valley of ashes adjacent to the lovely country, the conversation and the action in Myrtle's apartment, the marvelous catalogue of those who came to Gatsby's house—these are such things as make a man famous. …You once told me you were not a natural writer—my God! You have plainly mastered the craft, of course, but you needed far more than craftsmanship for this."

The critical reviews, however, were mixed. *The World* headlined its assessment: "F. Scott Fitzgerald's Latest a Dud," but the influential critic Gilbert Seldes recognized Fitzgerald's achievement: "*The Great Gatsby* is a brilliant work," he wrote, "and it is also a sound one; it is carefully written, and vivid; it has structure, and it has life." The novel was not a commercial success, however. It took time, as it often does, for the now classic to be recognized. Today, Fitzgerald's original publisher, Scribner's, publishes seven different editions of the novel.

At his best, Fitzgerald analyzed the personal and moral corruption in a society based on the social and moral prerogatives of wealth. His most memorable characters give their all for a romantic ideal, no matter what the cost…Just as Fitzgerald himself did.

The Least You Need to Know

➤ Fitzgerald's work and life illustrate American culture in the 1920s.

➤ *The Great Gatsby* is one of the masterpieces of American literature.

➤ *The Great Gatsby* is not only a brilliant comment on the 1920s but also an ironic and tragic treatment of the American success myth.

➤ Fitzgerald produced a fair amount of hack work, but when he was good, he was *very* good.

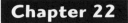

Chapter 22

Mint Juleps, Moonlight, and Madness: William Faulkner (1897–1962)

"The aim of every artist is to arrest motion, which is life, by artificial means and hold it fixed so that a hundred years later, when a stranger looks at it, it moves again since it is life. Since man is mortal, the only immortality possible for him is to leave something behind him that is immortal since it will always move. This is the artist's way of scribbling 'Kilroy was here' on the wall of the final and irrevocable oblivion through which he must someday pass."

—William Faulkner

Regarded as the most innovative writer of his time, William Faulkner was honored with the Nobel Prize in Literature for his mastery of a wide variety of forms and techniques, especially his experiments with multiple points of view. His novels range from potboilers to masterpieces, all written in a famously complex and difficult style. They're not easy to read, but they *are* ripping good reads. Stay tuned to discover what set William Faulkner off from the pack.

Southern Comfort

Born in New Albany, Mississippi, and raised in nearby Oxford, William Faulkner had generations of Southern blood flowing in his veins. In appearance and outlook, Faulkner was indelibly linked to his locale. Few other writers are as closely tied to the land as Faulkner was.

His formal schooling can most charitably be described as "spotty"—he never got around to finishing high school—but he read widely and deeply. In 1918 he tried to join the Army, but he was turned down because he wasn't tall enough. Eager to see action in the waning days of World War I, Faulkner enlisted in the British Royal Flying Corps and was sent to Canada for training. The war ended before he got into battle, however, but the outcome was happy: Thanks to the largess of Uncle Sam, Faulkner was able to enter the University of Mississippi for several semesters of study. He left school in 1920, at the age of 23.

A writer since adolescence, Faulkner decided it was time to pay attention to his muse and get published. To that end, he moved to New York City, the center of the publishing industry. The muse may have been talking, but the publishers weren't listening. Discouraged after six months spent gathering rejection slips, Faulkner returned home and took a job as a postmaster. (This wasn't exactly what he meant when he decided that he wanted to be a man of letters.)

Lit Wit

Faulkner was known for his drinking, but his brother claimed "Bill never did do as much drinking as he got credit for. He never tried to hide it but he did do most of it at home... But people talk and their stories grow and that's the way it was about Bill's drinking."

Break Out

The postmaster job was a disaster from the get-go. After the quick and inevitable parting, Faulkner decided to put his money where his heart was. He started with a name change. He had been born "Falkner." As with 19th-century writer Nathaniel Hawthorne, Faulkner declared his literary independence by adding a letter to his name. So William *Faulkner* was born, and, thus, he pledged himself to being a writer.

Faulkner began writing in earnest. His first book, the collection of poems *The Marble Faun,* sold about 50 copies.

Fellow writer Sherwood Anderson gave Faulkner the break he needed. In 1926 Faulkner published *Soldier's Pay* with Anderson's help; three years later, he gained critical acclaim with *The Sound and the Fury*. The novel is still considered his masterpiece.

Flush with success, Faulkner married and settled into his Southern country-squire existence. He bought a ramshackle colonial mansion, Rowan Oak, and poured money into restoring its former grandeur.

The Write Stuff

Until late in his career (1946, to be exact) Faulkner was generally regarded by many critics as an eccentric southern writer whose work had little literary value.

Take a Meeting

With the publication of *Sanctuary* in 1931, Faulkner gained a small measure of popular as well as critical acclaim. The American Gothic tale of terror, sex, and perversion convinced Hollywood that Faulkner's novels might make racy movies, so he was called out to the Coast to help adapt the novel for the screen under the title *The Story of Temple Drake*. After completing that assignment, Faulkner worked on several other Hollywood literary properties, his own as well as other writers'.

By 1939, Faulkner had produced 10 novels, two volumes of poetry, and two collections of short stories. That same year, he was elected to the National Institute of Arts and Letters. Still, the bills piled up. Critics loved his writing, but the public had really only bought just one of his works—*Sanctuary*. For the most part, only literary types bought his books. So needing the money, Faulkner went back to hacking screenplays in Hollywood.

Lit Wit

Eventually, Faulkner copped all the major American literary prizes: election to the American Academy of Arts and Letters (1948), the Nobel Prize for Literature (1950), the National Book Award, and the Pulitzer Prize for Literature (both in 1955).

My World, and Welcome to It

In all, 19 of Faulkner's novels centered around the fictional Yoknapatawpha County. (Yes, you read that correctly, *19* novels.)

So what was the allure of Yoknapatawpha County? It was the fictional rendering of his birthplace, his home—in the South. Faulkner focused on Southern memory, Southern reality, and Southern myth. His real home, Oxford, Mississippi, became Yoknapatawpha County, and the Faulkners became the fictional Sartorises.

Yoknapatawpha County is complete down to the smallest detail. Here are some facts about it, culled from various Faulkner novels:

➤ Yoknapatawpha County is 2,400 square miles.

➤ Bounded by the Talahatchie and Yoknapatawpha rivers, it consists of farmlands and pine hills.

➤ According to Faulkner's census, the county has 15,611 inhabitants—6,298 white and 9,313 black.

➤ It is a county scarred by poverty.

➤ There are no distinct social classes, but rather a rise of clans reflecting family pride and reverence for ancestors.

➤ Its main towns are Jefferson and Mattson.

The Write Stuff

Of all Faulkner's novels, only *Soldier's Pay, Mosquitoes, Pylon,* and *A Fable* take place outside Yoknapatawpha County.

Faulkner's tragic story of the decay of the genteel society of the post-Civil War South begins in his novel *Sartoris.* The Sartoris and Compson families represent the refined but decadent Old South. As the novels progress and time passes, the Old South is superseded by pragmatic, worldly, and unscrupulous forces. These brutal new forces are embodied in the Snopes family.

Nearly all of Faulkner's heroes carry the guilt of slavery. In Faulkner's novels, this guilt is taken one step further. Any white person who admits that blacks and whites are equal is defying the codes and concepts of the Old South and alienates himself from his family, his society, and his heritage.

The novels are pessimistic, although Faulkner was an optimist, as he revealed in his Nobel acceptance speech:

"I decline to accept the end of man. It is easy enough to say that man is immortal simply because he will endure: that when the last ding-dong of doom has clanged and faded from the last worthless rock hanging tideless in the last red and dying evening, that even then there will still be one more sound: that of his puny inexhaustible voice, still talking. I refuse to accept this. I believe that man will not merely endure: he will prevail. He is immortal, not because he alone among creatures has an inexhaustible voice, but because he has a soul, a spirit capable of compassion and sacrifice and endurance."

Pushing the Envelope: Faulkner's Style

Faulkner experimented with different narrative techniques throughout his writing career. Of course, he wasn't the only writer stretching the boundaries of literature: France's Marcel Proust, Ireland's James Joyce, and England's Virginia Woolf were all exploring new ways of writing. Unlike the others, however, Faulkner was experimenting on every front (and he scored with most of them).

Faulkner's experimental techniques included

➤ Stream of consciousness

➤ Interior monologues

➤ Discontinuous time, fragmenting chronological order

➤ Multiple narrators

➤ Allusions, often to mythology and the Bible

➤ Southern dialects

➤ Complex sentence structure

➤ Elements of the Gothic romance (necrophilia, macabre events, ghosts, and so on)

➤ Allegory (characters represent allegorical figures, such as Death)

Writer's Block

Faulkner's style requires close attention and isn't to everyone's taste. A critic once referred to Faulkner's sentences as "uncommutable life sentences."

Shrink Lit: Faulkner's Top Ten

Space forbids an in-depth survey of Faulkner's entire collection of novels, so let's sample 10 of the biggies: *Sartoris*; *As I Lay Dying*; *Sanctuary*; *Light in August*; *Absalom, Absalom!*; *The Unvanquished*; *The Wild Palms*; *The Hamlet*; *Go Down, Moses*; and *Intruder in the Dust.*

➤ *Sartoris* (1929) As mentioned earlier, *Sartoris* is important because it introduced the key themes Faulkner would develop over his lifetime. The novel concerns the relationship of the present with the past (with the author rooting for the past).

➤ *As I Lay Dying* (1930) Faulkner's fifth novel, *As I Lay Dying*, shows a brief reconciliation between the past and the present, sparked by the approaching death of a cherished family member. It is the shortest of Faulkner's novels.

➤ *Sanctuary* (1931) An intentionally shocking novel, *Sanctuary* concerns a man, a corncob, and a girl. Faulkner himself said it was "a cheap idea, deliberately conceived to make money." The novel did indeed bring in the bucks, got Faulkner invited to Hollywood, and even brought the critics to their feet to boot.

➤ *Light in August* (1932) This novel concerns loneliness brought about by hatred, alienation, and social divisiveness. The novel tells three characters' stories: The pregnant and serene Lena Grove, the Christian symbol/martyr Joe Christmas, and the powerless but well-meaning Reverend Hightower.

➤ *Absalom, Absalom!* (1936) A Gothic romance, the novel deals with incest and miscegenation (cohabitation or mingling between races). The amoral and willful 19th-century plantation owner Thomas Sutpen represents the entire Southern experience.

➤ *The Unvanquished* (1938) *The Unvanquished* takes place during the Civil War. Bayard (later Colonel) Sartoris is the main character.

➤ *The Wild Palms* (1939) This novel has two plots, which alternate from chapter to chapter. The first plot describes Harry and Charlotte, "who sacrificed everything for love, and then lost that." He described the second plot, the so-called "Old Man" plot (as in "Old Man River"), as the tale of a man "who got his love and spent the rest of the book fleeing from it, even to the extent of voluntarily going back to jail where he would be safe."

➤ *The Hamlet* (1940) An outrageous story, a series of exaggerated episodes in the life of the verminlike Snopes family, who spread their corruption throughout Yoknapatawpha. *The Town* (1957) and *The Mansion* (1959) are the other two books in the trilogy.

➤ *Go Down, Moses* (1942) The novel's main themes are the relationship between whites and blacks and the need to respect the land.

➤ *Intruder in the Dust* (1948) Centering on race relations, the novel starts with a black man, Lucas Beauchamp, who is jailed for a crime he did not commit, who will nonetheless be executed due to racial bias. A mystery story, the novel was adapted for the big screen in 1949, with some success.

The Sound and the Fury

None of Faulkner's novels has generated as much critical response as *The Sound and the Fury*. When we get beneath the mass of articles, here's what everyone can agree on:

➤ The novel is a tragedy, the decline of the Compson family.

➤ The style is stream of consciousness, an attempt to reproduce the way our minds actually think.

➤ The primary themes are honor and sin.

➤ It's a masterpiece.

Lit Wit

The Sound and the Fury's title is a reference to Shakespeare's *Macbeth*. When he hears that his wife has died, Macbeth says,

"To-morrow, and to-morrow, and to-morrow,
Creeps in this petty pace from day to day,
To the last syllable of recorded time;
And all our yesterdays have lighted fools
The way to dusty death. Out, out brief candle!
Life's but a walking shadow, a poor player,
That struts and frets his hour on the stage,
And then is heard no more. It is a tale
Told by an idiot, full of sound and fury,
Signifying nothing."

The Sound and the Fury tells the same story through four different viewpoints: that of the three Compson brothers—Benjy, Quentin, and Jason—and their black servant Dilsey. Here's how it sorts out.

Section 1: April 7, 1928

The first section is told from the point of view of Benjy Compson, a mentally retarded, 33-year-old man. Even though Benjy's thoughts are recorded in short sentences with simple words, reading this section is extraordinarily difficult because Benjy has no concept of time or place. As a result, random stimuli from the present—a word, a smell, a taste—propel him to the past, instantly and without warning.

Benjy's earliest memory dates from 1898, when he was three years old. The children have not been told that their grandmother, "Damuddy," has died. Benjy's sister Caddy is the only Compson child brave enough to climb the pear tree and look through the window at the wake while her brothers stand below, gazing up at her muddy underpants (called "drawers" in the novel), which were soiled earlier when they were playing in a creek adjoining the Compson estate.

The Write Stuff

Fortunately, Faulkner changes the typeface from Roman to italic every time Benjy shifts from the present to the past. Watch the type to understand the shifts in time.

The Write Stuff

To better rearrange events in chronological time, zero in on Benjy's caretakers. Three black servants take care of Benjy at different times: Versh when Benjy is a small child, T.P. when Benjy is approximately 15 years old, and Luster in the present, when Benjy is 33.

Most of Benjy's other memories also focus on Caddy, probably because she was the only sibling who loved him. He recalls when Caddy first used perfume, when she lost her virginity, and when she got married. Benjy also remembers when his name was changed from Maury to Benjamin, his brother Quentin's suicide, and the sequence of events that lead to his being castrated.

Section 2: June 2, 1910

The second section tells the same story from Quentin Compson's point of view on the day he commits suicide. A student at Harvard University, he is wandering around Boston preparing to take his life. Although his thoughts are obviously more intelligent than Benjy's, they are no less easy to follow, since he is deranged.

When the section begins, Quentin is obsessed with time, to the point of breaking his watch in a useless attempt to escape it. On a deeper level, Quentin cannot accept his sister Caddy's sexual activity and resulting pregnancy. In an attempt to restore "honor" to Caddy and to the Compson family, he has physically confronted Dalton Ames, likely the man who impregnated Caddy. But Ames overpowered him. Quentin is unable to shed the traditional Southern conception of Southern womanhood, virginity, and honor.

Section 3: April 6, 1928

This section is seen through the eyes of the third Compson brother, Jason, and takes place on Good Friday. The voice is very different from the two that came before: Unlike his brothers, Jason is neither retarded nor suicidal. Rather, he's hopping mad.

Writer's Block

Just to add to the novel's complexity, there are two characters named Quentin: Jason's and Caddy's brother Quentin, who commits suicide at Harvard, and Caddy's daughter, Quentin. (It's a nice gender-free name.)

The opening sentence establishes his anger: "Once a bitch always a bitch, what I say." Jason is cruel, and his portion of the novel reveals just how low the Compson family has sunk—from Quentin's obsessions over heritage, honor, and sin to Jason's viciousness, whining, and conniving.

Here, the focus is on Caddy's daughter, Quentin, sent to live with the Compsons after Caddy's divorce. She's in her late teens and, like her mother, hot to trot. Much of this section of the novel depicts Jason's efforts to find Quentin when she cuts school to be with a circus worker. Some of the fragments presented in sections 1 and 2 fall into place here. For example, we learn that Quentin drowned himself (his suicide wasn't spelled out in his section), that Benjy was castrated, and that

Caddy's marriage disintegrated. Throughout, we become aware of Jason's greed. We learn, for instance, that Jason pockets all the money that Caddy sends to her daughter.

Section 4: April 8, 1928

Everything comes together in the final section. Told from the omniscient viewpoint, it is often called "Dilsey's section," because she is the main player. The entire section takes place in the present, on Easter Sunday. There are two main plot lines: Jason's chasing Quentin to recover the $7,000 she has stolen from him (it's the money Caddy had sent for her) and Dilsey's attendance at an Easter church service. At the service, Reverend Shegog's sermon makes Dilsey realize that the Compsons are doomed. As she says after the service, "I've seed de first en de last... I seed de beginnin, en now I sees de endin."

At the end of the novel, the two plot lines come together. Benjy's caretaker, Luster, is driving Benjy to the graveyard, and he and Jason arrive at the town square at the same time. Luster has passed a statue on what Benjy perceives to be the "wrong" side, which causes Benjy to start crying. Jason hits Luster and tells him to take Benjy home. The novel ends with these lines:

> *"[Benjy's] broken flower drooped over Ben's fist and his eyes were empty and blue and serene again as cornice and façade flowed smoothly once more from left to right, post and tree, window and doorway and signboard each in its ordered place."*

Lit Wit

According to Faulkner, the idea for *The Sound and the Fury* began with a vision of a little girl's muddy drawers as she climbed a tree to look at death while her brothers, lacking her courage, waited below:

"I tried first to tell it with one brother, and that wasn't enough. That was Section One. I tried it with another brother, and that wasn't enough. That was Section Two. I tried the third brother, because Caddy was still to me too beautiful and too moving to reduce her to telling what was going on, that it would be more passionate to see her through somebody else's eyes, I thought. And that failed and I tried myself—the fourth section—to tell what happened, and I still failed."

In 1945, Faulkner added a fifth viewpoint to the same events: "I should have done this when I wrote the book," Faulkner remarked. "Then the whole thing would have fallen into pattern like a jigsaw puzzle when the magician's wand touched it."

When the votes were counted, William Faulkner won "most innovative American novelist" of his time. His novels experiment with narrative chronology, explore multiple points of view, and delve deeply into the human psyche. Although Faulkner's techniques vary, his works are linked through a common setting, the fictional world of Yoknapatawpha County, Mississippi.

The Least You Need to Know

➤ William Faulkner is widely considered to be the most original writer of his time.

➤ His primary subject was his heritage—Southern memory, Southern reality, and Southern myth. His home, Oxford, Mississippi, became the fictional Yoknapatawpha County; the Faulkners became the fictional Sartorises.

➤ The Sartoris and Compson families represent the genteel Old South. The Snopes represent the pragmatic, worldly, and unscrupulous forces of the modern South.

➤ Faulkner experimented with different narrative techniques, including stream of consciousness, interior monologues, discontinuous time, fragmented chronological order, multiple narrators, complex allusions, dialects, elements of the Gothic romance, and allegory.

➤ *The Sound and the Fury,* Faulkner's masterpiece, tells the same story through four viewpoints: Benjy Compson, Quentin Compson, Jason Compson, and their black servant Dilsey.

Chapter 23

Three Big Deals: Ezra Pound, T.S. Eliot, and John Steinbeck

In This Chapter

➤ Ezra Pound's childhood and college years

➤ Pound's efforts to remake literature

➤ Treason, *The Pisan Cantos*, and insanity

➤ T.S. Eliot's life

➤ Eliot's "The Love Song of J. Alfred Prufrock"

➤ Eliot's "The Waste-Land"

➤ John's Steinbeck's life

➤ Steinbeck's sympathy for the underdog

➤ Steinbeck's masterpiece, *The Grapes of Wrath*

Snap Quiz:

Who are the two most famous poets of the twentieth century?

➤ Choice #1: Ben and Jerry

➤ Choice #2: Romeo and Juliet

➤ Choice #3: Orville and Wilbur Wright

➤ Choice #4: Ezra Pound and T.S. Eliot

No fair—you cheated by looking at the title of this chapter. But even if you did, it *is* true that Ezra Pound and Thomas Stearns Eliot did more than any other 20th-century writers to remake Western literature. Novelist John Steinbeck took a different approach, using his fiction to help the underdog and draw attention to critical social problems. Read on to find out how these three writers—two of them Nobel Prize winners—changed the face of the poetry and prose we prize today.

Pound Cake

"No man understands a deep book until he has seen and lived at least part of its contents."

—Ezra Pound

If there was little in Pound's childhood to suggest that he'd later be tied for "Poet of the Century" with his best friend T.S. Eliot, there was even less to suggest that he'd become one of the most notorious traitors of the era as well.

Born in Idaho and raised in Pennsylvania, Pound had a conventional upper middle-class childhood. His father worked for the United States Mint, and Pound loved to accompany his old man to work to watch the gold being melted down. At 12, Pound enrolled in a military college around the block from his home. While the other boys played with bats and balls, Pound kicked around rhythm and rhyme, so it's not astonishing that by the age of 12 he'd already written his first poem. It's also not astonishing that he had few, if any, friends.

How Not to Win Friends and Influence People

Pound was a good student and so enrolled in the University of Pennsylvania only three years later. He decided the time had come to seize center stage, a relatively easy task with his flaming red hair and eccentric personality. (His gold-topped cane and pugnacious approach helped, too.) Not surprisingly, he was known without affection as a "sort of screwball," but he did form a close friendship with the medical student/modernist poet William Carlos Williams.

Writer's Block

Never go hand to hand with a poet: Ezra Pound, an enthusiastic fencer, almost poked out one of William Carlos Williams' eyes with a walking stick. And they were just joking around.

Although Williams liked his new friend, he told his mother the truth about Pound: "not one person in a thousand likes him and a great many people detest him [because] he was full of conceits and affectation."

Pound's mother decided that her sonny boy was hanging around with the wrong sort (what else could explain his odd behavior?) so she yanked him out of U Penn and slapped him into bucolic Hamilton College in upstate New York.

Nothing changed: He was every bit as strange and shunned in New York as he'd been in Pennsylvania.

When Pound wasn't busy rubbing people the wrong way, he was studying foreign languages, especially

Chinese. He graduated from Hamilton in 1905 and returned to the University of Pennsylvania to earn a master's degree in English Literature and Romance Poetry the following year. After a year in Spain, funded by a fellowship, Pound secured a position as an instructor in French and Spanish at Wabash College, a small Presbyterian school in western Indiana.

I've Looked at Love from Both Sides Now

It was an odd match indeed: Wabash forbade smoking and published in the town newspaper the names of students who missed chapel. Keep in mind that Pound was nothing if not flashy—this is someone who a few years later would have a statue made that depicted him as a phallus. It's not surprising, then, that he was very uncomfortable with the school and drove everyone nuts by pushing the envelope. Pound spiked his tea, dressed in odd costumes, and smoked like a chimney. "I do not teach," he announced to his students, "I awake."

To make sure they got the point, Pound had an affair with a woman who was a male impersonator. When the man-woman was discovered in Pound's bedroom, both parties were kicked out into the snow. Soon after, Pound left for London, nursing what would become a lifelong hatred of universities. In his spin on the situation, he was the brilliant international scholar rejected by the Philistine Americans. (History has not recorded the fate of the male impersonator.)

Lit Wit

Ezra Pound mastered jujitsu and once threw Robert Frost over his shoulder in a restaurant.

Make It New!

Pound quickly plunged into London's spirited literary life. While he remade the Western literary tradition, Pound supported himself by teaching, reviewing books, and working for William Butler Yeats, the brilliant Irish poet. In 1914, Pound married Dorothy Shakespeare. Ceaselessly active, he inspired poets and writers on both sides of the pond with his rallying cry, "Make It New!"

Lit Speak

Imagism was a literary movement that flourished from 1912 to 1917. Led by Ezra Pound and Amy Lowell, the imagists used free verse to craft concentrated word pictures.

Imagism

"People find ideas a bore because they do not distinguish between live ones and stuffed ones on a shelf."

—Ezra Pound

Pound first advanced a type of poetry he called *imagism,* an attempt to present an object directly rather than through ornate diction and complex verse forms. Imagism was characterized by…

➤ Ordinary language

➤ Free verse

➤ Concentrated word pictures

➤ Very specific words and phrases

The Write Stuff

Although the formal Imagist movement lasted about as long as a moth on a porch light, it nonetheless had a wide-ranging impact on 20th-century poetry. We see it in the poetry of Wallace Stevens, William Carlos Williams, and Robert Frost, for example.

Imagist poems were often fragments, precise and pointed. Here's one of Pound's best-known imagist poems, "In a Station of the Metro:"

"The apparition of these faces in the crowd;

Petals on a wet, black bough."

No, I didn't forget the rest of the poem. That's all, folks!

Cantos

Despite his recommendations to others, Pound's own poems during this period tended to follow traditional verse forms, including dramatic monologues. He often assumed a *persona,* or mask, to distance himself from his material. For example, here's the opening of his dramatic monologue, "Hugh Selwyn Mauberley":

For three years, out of key with his time,

He strove to resuscitate the dead art

Of poetry; to maintain "the sublime"

In the old sense. Wrong from the start—

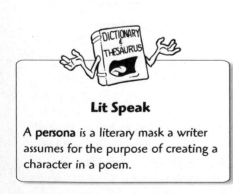

Lit Speak

A **persona** is a literary mask a writer assumes for the purpose of creating a character in a poem.

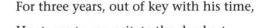

In 1915, Pound started work on his *Cantos,* a series of long and complex poems. Since they are lengthy, highly personal, and filled with fragments from his readings in foreign literature, reading the *Cantos* is not unlike climbing Mt. Everest. However, *Cantos* has had a profound effect on modern poetry.

In form, theme, and content, Pound's model for the *Cantos* was Whitman's *Leaves of Grass*. Ironically, Pound often claimed that *Leaves of Grass* embodied everything that was wrong with poetry.

His most loyal allies included fellow writers H.D. (Hilda Dolittle), T.S. Eliot, James Joyce, Robert Frost, Ernest Hemingway, and Marianne Moore. During his London years, Pound also produced two of his most famous poems, "Hugh Selwyn Mauberly: Life and Contacts" and "Mauberly" (1920). These poems described what Pound saw as the demise of Western civilization after World War I and the resulting sense of emptiness and despair.

Pound of Flesh

"The concept of genius as akin to madness has been carefully fostered by the inferiority complex of the public."

—Ezra Pound

In 1920, Pound left London, moved to Paris, and finally settled in Italy five years later. Left to his own devices, Pound became increasingly extreme in his views—one could even say deranged. He decided that the most successful civilizations had powerful leaders, a stable hierarchy, and an agricultural base. Who fit this bill? None other than the Italian fascist dictator Benito Mussolini. Pound embraced Il Duce with such fervor that when World War II erupted, he offered his services to the regime. From January 1941 until the end of the war in 1945, Pound delivered scores of radio broadcasts denouncing American society in general, Jews, and President Franklin Roosevelt in particular.

When the war ended, Pound was arrested by the American government for treason. Held in an open-air cage in a prison camp near Pisa, Italy, Pound lost his grip on reality, but nonetheless continued to write poetry—some of it judged among his best works, strangely.

While in London, Pound built friendships that would prove invaluable when he later went over to the dark side and became one of the most famous traitors of the 20th century.

In 1945 Pound was brought back to America for his trial, but his death sentence was suspended because he was judged insane. The insanity ruling was largely due to the intervention and support of literary colleagues who respected Pound in spite of his unacceptable politics. Confined for the next 13 years at St. Elizabeth's Mental Hopsital in Washington, D.C., Pound published more of his epic lifework, *Cantos*, which he had begun in 1924.

Lit Wit

In 1948, reviewer Robert Fitzgerald wrote that Pound had sounded "a personal desolation" and had achieved "a kind of repentance that is enormously moving" in his *Pisan Cantos.* No matter how you read them or excuse them, the *Cantos* cast a long shadow over the poetry of the next 20 years because of their experimental form. Poets of the subsequent generation had to grapple with Pound's influence. Strengthening Pound's influence was the conviction that *The Pisan Cantos* were confessions from a contrite fascist by the healing force of nature. The poems' seemingly unconstrained words gave them a certain authenticity, an immediacy that was hailed as the model of poetic modernism.

In 1948, the Library of Congress awarded Pound the Bollingen Prize for poetry, an award that sparked a tremendous outcry. Remember, Pound was being honored for poems that lamented the passing of fascist and Nazi collaborators. Allen Tate summed up the pro-Pound side when he argued that even if Pound had been convicted of treason, he had in his revitalization of language performed an "indispensable duty to society." Others claimed Pound was an anti-Semite whose loathsome views were so abhorrent that no amount of poetry could compensate for the hatred he had fanned. The uproar was so great that the U.S. government forbade the Library from ever awarding the prestigious prize again.

In 1958 Pound was released from St. Elizabeth's and returned to Italy, where he died 14 years later.

For those 14 years, Pound refused to communicate at all. He would not even open his mouth to utter a sound. His polemic against American society was finally silenced. Pound's friend T.S. Eliot was cut from different cloth, fortunately.

T.S. Eliot (1888–1965)

"We know too much, and are convinced of too little. Our literature is a substitute for religion, and so is our religion."

—T.S. Eliot

T(homas). S(tearns). Eliot is a far less controversial public figure and writer than Pound, but no less important to the development of 20th-century literature. Born in St. Louis, Missouri, to a distinguished New England family, Eliot was educated at Smith Academy (of Washington University) and Milton Academy. When he was 18, Eliot enrolled in Harvard University.

An unbeatable combination of hard work and brilliance enabled Eliot to complete his B.A. in three years; the fourth was devoted to earning his M.A. Although shy and quiet, Eliot was an acknowledged genius and leader. He was accepted in both of Harvard's prestigious literary clubs (the *Stylus* and the *Signet)* and even ascended to the editorship of Harvard's literary magazine. Always fussy and precise, Eliot was considered to be a dandy by his classmates, but was nonetheless admired for his wit and precise diction.

In 1910 Eliot took off for Paris, where he studied at the Sorbonne. He then returned to Harvard for a Ph.D. in philosophy. After completing his dissertation, Eliot traveled to Germany, stopping off at England's Oxford University for a year.

The outbreak of World War I prevented Eliot from returning to Harvard for the oral defense required for a doctorate, and so he began to drift into a career as a writer and publisher rather than his planned path as a university professor.

In 1915, Eliot married Vivienne Haigh-Wood and settled in London, earning his living at first by teaching a variety of subjects at Highgate School and later by working as a clerk at Lloyds Bank (from 1917 to 1925). Eliot didn't multitask well, however, and his writing suffered. It was Ezra Pound who set him back on the right track by encouraging him to pursue his writing more earnestly.

Lit Wit

Eliot's book of feline poems, *Old Possum's Book of Practical Cats,* formed the basis of the Broadway hit "Cats."

The Love Song of J. Alfred Prufrock

Pound served as Eliot's mentor and critic, the sounding board he needed as he developed his landmark poems. With Pound's help, "The Love Song of J. Alfred Prufrock" and "Preludes" were completed and published in late 1915, launching Eliot's career. His first book of poetry, *Prufrock and Other Observations*, appeared shortly thereafter, in 1917.

"Prufrock" is a long dramatic monologue about a fastidious middle-aged man who is unable to overcome his emotional timidity to find love and meaning in life. Prufrock's frustrations reflect the dilemmas of modern society, especially middle-class culture. Prufrock's sense of fragmentation and alienation is a hallmark of early 20th-century poetry.

The Write Stuff

As an influential literary critic, Eliot described his aesthetics in the famous essay "Tradition and the Individual Talent." He conceived a poem as an object, an organic thing in itself, demanding a fusion and concentration of intellect, feeling, and experience. He suggests that, through cultural memory, a poet unconsciously continues the tradition of his culture.

Lit Speak

A **dramatic monologue** involves a speaker who addresses an unseen audience. The monologue usually takes place at a crucial moment in the speaker's life.

Writer's Block

Never assume that the speaker in a poem is actually the writer. For example, Prufrock is not Eliot.

The poem opens with these famous lines:

> *"Let us go then, you and I,*
>
> *When the evening is spread out against the sky*
>
> *Like a patient etherized upon a table…"*

The poem concerns Prufrock's visit to a woman, his inability to declare his love for her, and his later recollection of the experience. After the fact, he rationalizes that the woman would have rejected his proposal by saying, "That is not it at all,/That is not what I meant, at all." Unable to force the moment to its climax, Prufrock asks, "Do I dare?" "And should I then presume?" He resigns himself to being a minor player, an "attendant lord," doomed to flutter on the fringes of life.

Painfully aware of the sterility of his life, Prufrock is tormented by…

➤ His inability to love and communicate

➤ The suffocating environment of closed rooms and narrow streets (symbols for his life)

➤ His inability to break out of his isolation

➤ His acute self-consciousness

All Dressed Up and No Where to Go

> *"Do I dare*
>
> *Disturb the universe?*
>
> *In a minute there is time for decisions and revisions which a minute will reverse."*
>
> —from "The Love Song of J. Alfred Prufrock"

The title is ironic, for Prufrock is timid and spiritually numb, a man unable to love, and so the "love song" is sung by no one—least of all him. The "you and I" of the first line can be interpreted as two parts of Prufrock's personality, one part urging him to participate in experience, the other part holding him back. Images of movement are juxtaposed with images of paralysis, reflecting Prufrock's internal conflict.

The Waste-Land

In 1922 Eliot published "The Waste-Land," the most famous poem of the first half of the 20th century. It was a big bang, ladies and gentlemen. The poet William Carlos Williams described the effect of "The Waste-Land" as that of an atom bomb being detonated. Before the poem was published, Pound did a brilliant editing job, deleting a great deal of extraneous material and Eliot acknowledged his debt to him by dedicating the poem to him.

"The Waste-Land" sums up the American and European postwar sense of tragedy and despair. The poem is about spiritual dryness, about the kind of existence in which no regenerating belief gives significance and value to our daily activities. Sex brings no fruitfulness, and death heralds no resurrection.

Why the title "waste land?" On a literal level, the battlefields of World War I were a muddy waste-land planted with corpses. On a figurative level, the war had left Europe and America a spiritual and emotional desert. Many people lost their faith in religion after the war because they couldn't reconcile the idea of a benevolent god with wholesale slaughter. Nothing in history had prepared the world for the sight of so much death. Eliot believed that modern society lacked a vital sense of community and a spiritual center. The wasteland of the poem is modern American and European culture, which had strayed too far from its Christian roots.

Lit Speak

"The Love Song of J. Alfred Prufrock" is chock-filled with **allusions**—literary references. In this case, there are allusions to the biblical Lazarus, the prophet John the Baptist, the dancer Salome, a character damned in Dante's *Inferno,* and Hamlet. They all serve to reinforce Prufrock's frustration and futility.

Lit Wit

Eliot suffered a nervous breakdown as he was working on "The Waste-Land:" he completed the poem in a sanitarium.

Part I: Burial of the Dead

Here's how the poem begins:

> "*April is the cruellest month, breeding*
>
> *Lilacs out of the dead land, mixing*
>
> *Memory and desire, stirring*
>
> *Dull roots with spring rain.*"

In the first part of the poem, a countess looks back on her youth before World War I. She remembers a romantic, beautiful time. This memory is undercut by the present drought, when "the dead tree gives no shelter." The poem then flashes back to a love scene, perhaps the countesses', and then moves to a fortune-teller who reads tarot cards and warns of death. The section ends with an image of London crowds moving along the streets like dead people.

The Write Stuff

"The Waste-Land," as with all of Eliot's poetry, is a tough poem to understand because of its numerous allusions, snippets of foreign languages, metaphysical conceits, and absence of obvious narrative structure. If you decide to read the poem, study Eliot's footnotes closely.

Part II: A Game of Chess

> "*The Chair she sat in, like a burnished throne,*
>
> *Glowed on the marble, where the glass*
>
> *Held up by standards wrought by fruited vines…*"

A variation on the theme established in "Burial of the Dead," the second part of the poem gives the opposing voices of the wealthy and the poor, the sane and the mad. Eliot brings in ancient fertility imagery and Christian symbolism to suggest that all of humankind is desolate.

Writer's Block

In his poetry, Eliot comes off as stiff as a corpse. Don't be fooled—he also had a lighter side. An incurable practical joker, Eliot was never in better form than when he worked as an editor at the London firm of Faber and Faber. Among his favorite pranks were to seat visiting authors in chairs with whoopee cushions and to offer them exploding cigars.

Part III: The Fire Sermon

> "*The river's tent is broken; the last fingers of leaf*
>
> *Clutch and sink into the wet bank.*"

This part of the poem combines lines from an old marriage song celebrating London's famous Thames River with a modern description of the filthy, trash-filled Thames. Then the ancient prophet Tiresias recounts a seedy and passionless love affair, suggesting that sex is meaningless in the postwar world. This is followed by contrasting images of Queen Elizabeth I boating on the Thames with her lover, the Earl of Leicester.

Part IV: Death by Water

"Phlebas the Phoenician, a fortnight dead,

Forgot the cry of gulls, and the deep swell

And the profit and loss."

This section completes the fortune-teller's prophecy from Part I. A short section, it again suggests that death must come before rebirth.

Part V: What the Thunder Said

"After the torchlight red on sweaty faces

After the frosty silence in the gardens

After the agony in stony places..."

The last part of the poem opens with images of a journey over barren and rocky ground. The thunder is sterile, since it is not accompanied by rain. There are chaotic images of rot and of a crumbling city, leading to the rain.

The poem ends with three terms from Hindu lore:

➤ *Datta* (to give alms)

➤ *Dayadhvam* (to have compassion)

➤ *Damyata* (to practice self-control)

Then comes a heap of allusions, a flood of meanings and suggestions. The poem ends with the word *shanti* (peace).

Big Man on Campus

The speaker for a generation, Eliot created poetry that is complex, packed with obscure allusions, and based on the rhythms of natural speech. One critic noted that Eliot combined "trivial and tawdry pictures with traditional poetic subject matter, linking the banalities of conversation to rich rhetoric and interrupting the present with flashbacks of the past."

Eliot became a British citizen in 1926 and shortly thereafter converted to the Episcopalian faith. His growing faith was reflected in his work; increasingly, Eliot saw religion as the antidote for the type of spiritual emptiness he described in "The Love Song of J. Alfred Prufrock" and "The Waste-Land."

In addition to poems, Eliot also wrote plays, such as *Murder in the Cathedral* (1935) and *The Cocktail Party* (1950). In recognition of his enormous contribution to modern literature, Eliot was awarded the Nobel Prize for Literature in 1948.

Eliot's fellow Nobel laureate, novelist and short story writer John Steinbeck, approached the problems of the first half of the 20th century in a very different way.

A man of the people, he rolled up his sleeves and dug right in. The result was an astonishing outpouring of fantastic writing—and a spotlight trained on important social issues.

John Steinbeck (1902-1968)

When asked why he became a writer, Steinbeck answered:

"Like everyone, I want to be good and strong and virtuous and wise and loved. I think that writing may be simply a method or technique for communicating with other individuals... "

Steinbeck certainly knew how to communicate in writing, which made him one of the most popular novelists in America during the 1930s and 1940s. But when it comes to a writer's critical reputation, popularity can be the kiss of death. This is certainly the case with Steinbeck: the fact that his novels have sold enormously and continuously has marked him as a "popular" writer, and therefore unworthy of "serious" attention.

Fortunately, not everyone agreed, and Steinbeck was awarded the Nobel Prize for Literature in 1962. It was a sweet vindication for a writer who never curried popular favor and refused to play the tortured artiste. Rather, Steinbeck always insisted that a writer's primary job is to get his work read. As he said in his Nobel Prize Acceptance Speech:

"The ancient commission of the writer has not changed. He is charged with exposing our many grievous faults and failures, with dredging up to the light our dark and dangerous dreams for the purpose of improvement."

California Dreamin'

John Steinbeck was born in Salinas, California, on February 27, 1902, a descendant of old settlers. His father was a county official; his mother, a teacher. John loved the landscape, which became the setting for many of his novels.

An athlete rather than a scholar, John nonetheless read deeply and widely. He entered Stanford University in 1920 and even though he stayed for five years, he managed to earn very few credits, much less a degree. He did, however, write for the University's literary magazine and work a variety of jobs on the side, including laboring on road-gangs and assisting in the laboratory of a sugar-beet factory.

After a brief stint in the Big Apple (where he helped build Madison Square Garden), Steinbeck headed home and started work on a novel. *Cup of Gold* appeared in 1929. His timing was terrible: The stock market had crashed and books were the last thing on people's minds. Under the circumstances, it is hardly surprising that few reviewers took the book seriously.

Bad luck continued to dog Steinbeck's literary career for a time. After several attempts to get another novel going, he completed *Pastures of Heaven* in 1932, but it also failed to fly off the shelves.

Meanwhile, Steinbeck married Carol Henning, and the couple settled in Pacific Grove. The couple lived on $25 a month contributed by John's father. In 1933, John published the dark, brooding novel *To a God Unknown,* another flop. The success of several short stories, however, including "The Red Pony" in 1933, and the selection of "The Murder" for the O. Henry Prize in 1934, turned the tide in Steinbeck's favor.

Lit Wit

The Grapes of Wrath, published in 1939, created a literary explosion both in the United States and abroad. In the U.S. alone, more than half a million copies of the book were sold, and *The Grapes of Wrath* became an historical as much as a literary event. Translations were published throughout the world; honors were heaped on the rather rattled author. These included the Pulitzer Prize, the National Book Award, the American Bookseller's Award, and membership in the National Institute of Arts and Letters.

Fame and Fortune

Tortilla Flat (1934), an affectionately told story of Mexican-Americans, was the breakthrough. Steinbeck was suddenly famous. Two years later, *In Dubious Battle,* an account of a farm workers' strike, added to his fame. *Of Mice and Men* (1937) showed that Steinbeck's success was not a fluke. This novella, which portrays two drifters whose dream of owning their own farm ends in tragedy, became a best-seller and has been made into many movie versions and a Broadway play.

Two years later, Steinbeck published his finest novel, *The Grapes of Wrath* (1939), the deeply moving story of the "Okies," the Oklahoma farmers dispossessed of their land and forced to become immigrant farmers in California. The novel describes the family's (and the land's) exploitation by a ruthless system of agricultural economics. *The Grapes of Wrath* established Steinbeck as one of the most highly regarded and popular writers of the time. The boy from the West had made the big town take notice—without compromising his artistic and political independence.

Lit Speak

In the 1930s, **Okie** was a derogatory term for migrant farmers from Oklahoma. To the Okies themselves, however, the term meant pride, courage, and determination to accept hardship without showing weakness.

Steinbeck went on to write several other successful works, including *Cannery Row* (1945), *The Pearl* (1947), and *East of Eden* (1951). Nonetheless, by the 1960s, it appeared that Steinbeck had passed the high-water mark of his career. He had become a man more written about than one actually writing. Once again, however, Steinbeck challenged the odds—and won. *Winter of Our Discontent*, 1961, is one of Steinbeck's most powerful books. The novel was a smash hit, and the writer dismissed as an artistic "has-been" received the ultimate pat on the back, the Nobel Prize.

Steinbeck assessed his character this way in his autobiography, *Travels with Charlie:*

"I have always lived violently, drunk hugely, eaten too much or not at all, slept round the clock or missed two nights of sleeping, worked too hard and too long in glory, or slobbed for a time in utter laziness. I've lifted, pulled, chopped, climbed, made love with joy and taken my hangovers as a consequence, not as a punishment. I did not want to surrender fierceness for a small gain in yardage. My wife married a man; I saw no reason why she should inherit a baby. I knew that ten or twelve thousand miles driving a truck, alone and unattended, over every kind of road, would be hard work, but to me it represented the antidote for the poison of the professional sick man. And in my own life I am not willing to trade quality for quantity. If this projected journey should prove too much, then it was time to go anyway. I see too many men delay their exits with a sickly, slow reluctance to leave the stage. It's bad theater as well as bad living.

Lit Wit

Steinbeck wrote a number of movie scripts, including *Forgotten Village* (1941) and *Viva Zapata!* (1952). In addition, many of his novels became movies. The filmed version of *East of Eden*, for example, was notable mainly because it served as a vehicle for that surly hunk James Dean, whose own Cain–rebel image seemed ideally suited to the role of Caleb.

The Grapes of Wrath

"...us people will go on livin' when all them people is gone...We're the people that live. They ain't gonna wipe us out. Why we're the people—we go on."

—from *The Grapes of Wrath*

Steinbeck's primary themes came from the poverty, desperation, and social injustice that he witnessed during the Great Depression of the 1930s, a time when many people suffered under conditions beyond their control. He did all his own research, too.

In 1936, Steinbeck drove to Oklahoma to join the migrant workers and accompany them to California. At one point he was so disturbed by their dire poverty that he wanted to accept a Hollywood contract of $1000 a week for six weeks so he could give two dollars apiece to 3,000 migrant workers. His agent flew to the coast to talk him out of it.

Another time, he refused to go into the field with a photographer and observe the migrants for an article for *Life* magazine, saying, "I'm sorry but I simply can't make money on these people—the suffering is too great for me to cash in on it."

The Grapes of Wrath reflected the Okies' suffering and so much more. As critic Peter Lisca describes it, "*The Grapes of Wrath* was a phenomenon on the scale of a national event." Now, let's look at Steinbeck's masterpiece itself.

Writer's Block

In addition to the bouquets, *The Grapes of Wrath* came in for its share of brickbats. Oklahoma Congressman Lyle Boren called the novel "the black, infernal creation of a twisted, distorted mind." *The Grapes of Wrath* was virtually banned in Oklahoma, while the outrage and indignation of many Californians echoed across the continent.

Who's Who in The Grapes of Wrath

Tom Joad is the novel's central character. Kind, strong, and sensitive, he's not someone you'd throw out of bed for eating crackers. So what if he killed a man in a fight? He did his time—and goes on to help his people. Here's the rest of the cast:

➤ *Pa:* the Dustbowl reduces him to a deer in the headlights. His farm gone, he cannot cope.

➤ *Ma:* the ideal mother figure, strong, loyal, and loving. She's the glue that holds the family together.

➤ *Grampa:* lecherous, loud, cantankerous, the old man seems to have a lot of fight in him. He dies of a sudden stroke on the first night on the road. Most would say that he died of a broken heart at having had to leave his land.

➤ *Granma:* just as cussed as her mate, Granma pines away after his death. What can you expect from a woman who shot away half his heinie to make sure he didn't stray?

➤ *Uncle John*: Pa Joad's older brother, Uncle John is an eccentric loner.

➤ *Noah:* the oldest of the Joad children, dropped on his head once too often.

➤ *Rosasharn* (Rose of Sharon): Tom Joad's younger sister. Married to Connie, she is pregnant and dreams of a better life in California.

➤ *Connie*: Rose of Sharon's no-good husband, who deserts the family once they reach California.

➤ *Al:* Tom's 16-year-old brother likes ladies and machines—and he's good at both.

➤ *Ruthie and Winfield*: the youngest Joad children.

➤ *Jim Casy*: the introspective former preacher is the Christ-figure prophet and suffers a martyr's death. Notice that he shares the same initials as Jesus Christ.

Lit Speak

Hoovervilles were the shantytowns that sprang up all over America to house those displaced by the Great Depression. Their name was a derisive slap at President Hoover, who failed to deal with the Depression.

➤ *Muley Graves*: the Joads' neighbor in Oklahoma, he symbolizes the Okies' ruined lives.

➤ *Sairy And Ivy Wilson*: the couple from Kansas link their fortunes with the Joads' on the first night out. The Joads are forced to abandon them, knowing that Sairy's death is imminent and Mr. Wilson's survival alone uncertain.

➤ *Floyd Knowles*: commentator on the conditions of the migrants.

➤ *The Wainwrights:* A family the Joads meet in the last of the Hoovervilles.

➤ Jessie Bullitt, Annie Littlefield, and Ella Summers: natural leaders.

California, Here I Come

As the novel opens, Tom Joad is hitchhiking home after being paroled from the state prison, having served four years of a seven year sentence. Dropped off near the family's farm, Tom meets Jim Casy, an itinerant preacher. Casy has decided that since all things are holy, he will drop his vocation and live with the people. When they arrive at Tom's place, they are baffled to find that everyone is gone, and that all the farms seem deserted. Muley Graves tells Tom that the Joads are at Uncle John's.

The next day, Tom and Jim walk to Uncle John's, where the family is preparing to go to California to find work. Foreclosures have forced all the farmers off the land; the Dust Bowl has decimated the region. After selling all their belongings, the family has only eighteen dollars. Casy and Tom join them and they all set off. The first night, Grampa dies of a stroke. The Joads get a quilt from another group of displaced farmers, the Wilsons, and bury Grampa. The two families join up and travel together. Just before they reach California, Mrs. Wilson becomes so sick she cannot go on. The Joads give them money and food and press on.

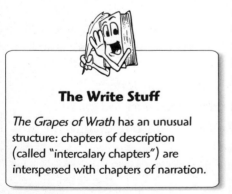

The Write Stuff

The Grapes of Wrath has an unusual structure: chapters of description (called "intercalary chapters") are interspersed with chapters of narration.

Granma dies, but Mrs. Joad convinces a guard that the old woman is only sleeping so they can pass through the desert. They bury her as a pauper because they cannot afford a funeral.

Flat broke, the Joads stop at a filthy migrant worker camp but the men are unable to find work. When a friend of Tom's asks what a contractor is paying for some labor, he is arrested as a "red," a communist. A fight breaks out and the sheriff tells the people that the camp is going to be burned. The Joads flee to a government camp where they find law and order—but still no work. Again they must move on.

They arrive at a peach orchard and despite the demonstrations, immediately set about picking fruit so they will have something to eat. Tom finds Jim Casy, leader of the strike, who tells him that the strikers are trying to correct wage inequalities. When strikebreakers kill Casy, Tom kills one of the men but has his nose broken. The Joads leave and find a place where they can pick cotton. Tom hides in a nearby woods.

Nobel Laureate John Steinbeck championed the underdog, leaving little time for haircuts.

One of the Joad children reveals that Tom has killed a man. Tom decides to carry on Casy's work. He takes a small amount of money from Ma and leaves. When the cotton picking ends, the rains set in. Rose of Sharon goes into labor and her baby is stillborn. The water continues to rise and the family seeks shelter for two days in a boxcar.

When the rain abates, the family escapes to a barn, where they find a man dying of starvation. The Joads have neither money nor food. Rose of Sharon feeds the dying man from her breast.

The Grapes of Wrath is a plea for California land owners to be more tolerant of those who are less fortunate. The Joads' journey West is also a journey from one family's personal concern to a larger concern for all of humanity. And it's a great read, ladies and gentlemen.

Lit Wit

The Great Depression of the 1930s and a drought in the Great Plains forced the Okies to leave their homes and head for California, where they heard that pickers were needed to work in the fields and orchards of the San Joaquin Valley. When the Okies arrived in the Golden State, however, they discovered that few jobs were available and many Californians didn't want the poor and uneducated Okies around. Many of the Okies lived in farm-labor camps, rife with sickness and starvation. Some of the Okie children were dying of starvation while farmers refused to give them surplus crops to eat. Steinbeck called this "a crime that goes beyond denunciation."

The Least You Need to Know

➤ Pound and Eliot were the two most influential poets and critics of their era. They dictated the tone, direction, and subject matter for a generation of poets.

➤ Pound established the Imagist school of poetry, befriended leading American and European writers, committed treason, and spent a decade in a mental hospital.

➤ Eliot's poem "The Love Song of J. Alfred Prufrock" asks *"What is our place in the universe? How can any one love and communicate with anyone else?"*

➤ Eliot's 1922 poem "The Waste-Land," the most important poem of the first half of 20th century, deals with the failure of Western civilization, illustrated by World War I.

➤ John Steinbeck's novels and short stories reflect his belief in the need for social justice and his hope that people can learn from the suffering of others.

➤ Steinbeck's novel *The Grapes of Wrath* combined naturalism and symbolism to express outrage and compassion for the plight of the farmers displaced by the Depression and Dustbowl.

Chapter 24

A Pack of Poets (1900–1960)

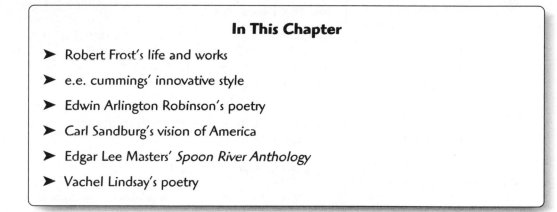

In This Chapter

➤ Robert Frost's life and works

➤ e.e. cummings' innovative style

➤ Edwin Arlington Robinson's poetry

➤ Carl Sandburg's vision of America

➤ Edgar Lee Masters' *Spoon River Anthology*

➤ Vachel Lindsay's poetry

T.S. Eliot and Ezra Pound may have dominated the highbrow literary landscape, but from 1914 until his death in 1963, Robert Frost was probably America's best-known and best-loved poet. It was proof of Frost's special place in American literature and life that President Kennedy invited him to read a poem, "The Gift Outright," at his inauguration in 1961.

In addition to Frost, e.e. cummings, Edwin Arlington Robinson, Carl Sandburg, Edgar Lee Masters, and Vachel Lindsay were well-known and influential American poets of the time. In this chapter, you'll learn all about these writers and their place in American letters.

Robert Frost (1874–1963)

"I'm always saying something that's just the edge of something more."

—Robert Frost

Lit Speak

A **sonnet** is a 14-line lyric poem. Sonnets have many variations but are usually written in iambic pentameter, a line of poetry with five iambic feet, each containing one unstressed syllable followed by one stressed syllable.

Blank verse is unrhymed iambic pentameter. Blank verse captures the natural rhythm of speech.

The Write Stuff

In a dig at his arch rival, Carl Sandburg, (who used free verse), Frost claimed that he would as soon play tennis without a net as write free verse.

With an armful of Pulitzer Prizes (four, to be exact), Robert Frost ranks as a top 20th-century poet. His ambition as a poet was to write "a few poems it will be hard to get rid of," and he unquestionably succeeded. His achievement was a result of his use of…

➤ Traditional verse forms, especially the sonnet, rhyming couplets, and blank verse

➤ The plain speech of rural New Englanders.

In his poems, Frost comes across as a wise country person living close to nature. But don't be fooled: The voice of his poetry was a brilliant artistic creation, a "persona" or mask very similar to what Ezra Pound created. In his poetry, Frost comes across as calm and kind—the person Frost would like to be but knew all too well that he was not.

As a nature poet, Frost belongs to the romantic tradition of the transcendental poet Ralph Waldo Emerson. Like his poetic predecessor, Frost embodies the cliche, "Still waters run deep."

Under the guise of a folksy tone, Frost probes an irrational and indifferent universe with its mysteries of darkness and irrationality.

Frosty the Poet

"Every poem is a voyage of discovery. I go in to see if I can get out, like you go to the North Pole. Once you've said the first line, the rest of it's got to be."

—Robert Frost

America's most famous New England poet was actually born in San Francisco, California, in 1874 where he lived until he was 11 years old. In 1885, his father died, and the family resettled in Lawrence, Massachusetts. Frost attended public high school and copped highest honors, sharing the valedictorian spot with his future wife, Elinor White.

After graduation, Frost enrolled in Dartmouth College, but he remained there for less than a year. Returning to Massachusetts, he tried his hand at a variety of jobs, including teacher, mill hand, and reporter. Frost sold his first poem, "My Butterfly: An Elegy," when he was 20 years old. Flush with success, he married Elinor and spent two years at Harvard as a special student. Over the next 10 years, Frost wrote a big pile of poems. Since only a few were accepted for publication, Frost supported his growing family by running a dairy farm in Derry, New Hampshire, and teaching on the side. He hated the farm, but he had four kids and a wife to support.

In 1912 Frost decided that he had had enough of Green Acres, so he sold the farm and took his wife and four children to England to try to make it as a writer.

It was a good career move, for the following year, he published his first book of verse, *A Boy's Will*; the next year, *North of Boston* hit the shelves. The reviews were good, and Frost's reputation was established on both sides of the Atlantic. The family returned to America three years later.

Lit Wit

Reviewing *A Boy's Will*, Ezra Pound praised it as showing "VURRY Amur'k'n talent."

Poetry has never been a big bucks career, even for the headliners. Although Frost's poetry enjoyed critical success, he did not see much financial gain. He supplemented his income again with teaching. He delivered lectures at Amherst, the University of Michigan, Yale, Harvard, and Dartmouth. One of his students recalled that Frost...

"was a short, stocky man, but I felt at once that here was a man with an immense spread. He was the center of the audience, and no one could mistake his strength and confidence. As he shouldered his way along, he seemed purposefully intent...his hair was very white and thin, his face square and strong, and there was a continual half-smile around the lips. From the start he seemed at home with his audience."

The Write Stuff

Lawrance Thompson is Robert Frost's "official" biographer. (Some writers have 'em, some don't.)

Sound of Sense

In July 1913, Robert Frost explained his theory of poetry while giving himself a pat on the back:

"...To be perfectly frank with you I am one of the most notable craftsmen of my time. That will transpire presently. I am possibly the only person going who works on any but a worn out theory...of versification... I alone of English writers have consciously set myself to make music out of what I may call the sound of sense."

Some of Frost's most well-known poems include

➤ "Death of the Hired Man"

➤ "Birches"

➤ "Stopping by Woods on a Snowy Evening"

➤ "The Road Not Taken"

➤ "Mending Wall"

Let's take a look at the last two poems on the list now.

The Road Not Taken

"Two roads diverged in a yellow wood,

And sorry I could not travel both

And be one traveller..."

"A poem should say one thing and mean something else," Frost said, referring to his "sound of sense" theory. This excerpt from "The Road Not Taken," one of his most famous poems, illustrates his point. The "road" is usually interpreted as more than a garden-variety macadam highway; most critics interpret the road as a symbol of the different paths we take in life.

Writer's Block

Frost always poked fun at the critics' efforts to find Big Themes in his work. Was he serious or disingenuous? No one knows.

Frost claimed that the "The Road Not Taken" is about Edward Thomas, his English poet-friend killed early in World War I. He said that the poem "has something to do with the question of being understood and not being understood."

What's the "real" interpretation? It's up to you, gentle reader, which is what makes good literature so much of a pleasure to read and interpret.

Stopping by Woods on a Snowy Evening

"The woods are lovely, dark and deep,

But I have promises to keep,

And miles to go before I sleep.

And miles to go before I sleep."

Frost knew "Stopping by Woods on a Snowy Evening" had often been read as a meditation on death, but "I never intended that," he said. Nonetheless, he did have the feeling that it was "loaded with ulteriority." He claimed to have written the poem one night back in the 1920s, when he was a "little excited from getting over-tired—they call it autointoxicated."

While reading this poem at a writers' conference in 1958, Frost said: "Some people have said it's a suicide poem. That's going some. But it can be seen as a death poem. And I can see how you could say: 'Life is lovely, dark and deep.' See. 'But I have promises to keep. I have heaven to go to, you know.' Like that. You could do that. That analogy's in it.'"

No matter how you ultimately interpret this poem and his others, Frost guides his readers into an examination of themselves through the work. "My utmost ambition," Frost claimed, "is to lodge a few poems where they will be hard to get rid of." He succeeded. We all have shards of Frost's poem embedded in our subconscious. During his 1960 political campaign, for example, John Kennedy ended his speeches by saying, "But I have miles to go before I sleep." Everyone in the audience knew the line.

Lit Wit

During the more than two decades of struggle to become a recognized poet, Frost experienced great despair and even contemplated suicide. One of his sons did commit suicide, and a daughter had a nervous breakdown. Many readers notice the despair under the surface of Frost's verse.

e(dward). e(stlin). cummings (1894–1962)

"To be nobody-but-myself—in a world which is doing its best, night and day, to make you everybody else—means to fight the hardest battle which any human being can fight, and never stop fighting."

—e.e. cummings

e.e. cummings cornered the poetry market on innovation. In his nearly 1,000 poems, cummings created a new, highly idiosyncratic means of poetic expression. His poetry is known for its eccentric style, its unusual typography and spellings, and deliberate misuse of grammatical structure. He experimented with the "rhythm of the phrase" discovered by Walt Whitman and called the "variable foot" by poet William Carlos Williams. All told, cummings played around with…

Writer's Block

The commonly held belief that cummings had his name legally changed to lower-case letters is erroneous.

➤ Form

➤ Punctuation

➤ Spelling

➤ Typography (type style)

➤ Grammar

➤ Imagery

➤ Rhythm

➤ Syntax

cummings even adjusted his name to reflect his poetic experiments: Sometimes he signed it in conventional upper- and lowercase, as in "E.E. Cummings." Most often, however, he signed his name in all lowercase letters, as in "e.e. cummings."

Thematically, however, cummings is a traditional poet, especially in his love poems and his celebrations of families, parents, children, and values.

cummings' primary theme is solidly conventional: In nearly all of his poems, he extols individualism in a world of conformity like his predecessor Walt Whitman.

The Write Stuff

cummings used capital letters to emphasize words or phrases, not necessarily where readers expect them to appear.

somewhere I have never travelled, gladly beyond

"somewhere I have never travelled, gladly beyond

any experience, your eyes have their silence...

(i do not know what it is about you that closes

and opens; only something in me understands

the voice of your eyes is deeper than all roses)..."

—e.e. cummings

Edward Estlin Cummings was born in Cambridge, Massachusetts in 1894.

Some kids cut their eyeteeth on a baseball bat; for cummings, it was poetry and art. Fortunately, his parents encouraged their beloved son and supported his interests in poetry and art. After earning his B.A. in English in 1915 and his M.A. in Classics in 1916, both from Harvard, cummings moved to Greenwich Village in New York City, where he stayed until World War I.

Like Hemingway, cummings saw a great deal of action as an ambulance driver during World War I. His outspoken antiwar stance earned him some jail time in a French prison camp, an experience recounted in his novel *The Enormous Room*. It is ranked as one of the best American works to come out of the war experience. Written as a journal of his prison stay, it's heightened by an experimental prose style and a hatred of a bureaucracy that treats civilians cruelly.

Lit Wit

Speaking about his poetic innovations, cummings wrote: "It's no use trying to pretend most people and ourselves are alike. Most people have less in common with ourselves than the square root of minus one. You and I are human beings; most people are snobs..." (Introduction to *Collected Poems*)

After the war, cummings devoted himself entirely to poetry, publishing 12 volumes of poems, including a posthumous volume. A painter as well as a writer, he was not the least interested in wealth and celebrity. By carefully budgeting a stipend from his parents and the money he won from prizes, cummings was able to devote himself full-time to his art.

The Write Stuff

cummings' love poems are sometimes sexually explicit, but almost always marked by a gusto and humor that is lacking in the work of other modernist poets. (The other modernists were a grim lot, but not cummings.)

since feeling is first

"since feeling is first

who pays any attention

to the syntax of things..."

—e.e. cummings

A marrying sort, cummings had three wives—not at the same time, of course. His first marriage to Elaine Orr (who left her husband for him) lasted only six months. His second marriage, to Ann Barton, was stormy and passionate, but also failed to make it to the finish line. He found true love the third time around, however, and his union with the actress/model Marion Morehouse lasted for the remaining 30 years of his life.

Later in his career, cummings was often criticized for not pressing his work toward further evolution. Nevertheless, he attained great popularity, especially among young readers, for the simplicity of his language, his playful mode, and his attention to subjects like war and sex. At the time of his death in 1962, cummings was the second most widely read poet in the United States, after Robert Frost.

Lit Wit

William Carlos Williams (1883–1963) considered himself to be the most underrated poet of his generation, and his assessment isn't too far off. A dedicated pediatrician with a thriving practice in New Jersey, Williams nonetheless carved out the time to write rhythmic poems that he said described "no ideas but in things." Unlike his close friends Ezra Pound and T.S. Eliot, Williams was not interested in the decline of Western civilization. Rather, he concentrated on concrete detail and let his readers find the ideas on their own. He won the National Book Award in 1950, the Bollingen Prize in 1953, and the Pulitzer Prize in 1962.

Here's to You, Mr. Robinson: Edwin Arlington Robinson (1869–1935)

"And so we worked, and waited for the light,

And went without the meat, and cursed the bread;

And Richard Cory, one calm summer night,

Went home and put a bullet through his head."

—E.A. Robinson, "Richard Cory"

The Write Stuff

"Richard Cory" takes its place alongside Dreiser's *An American Tragedy* and Fitzgerald's *The Great Gatsby* as a powerful warning against the overblown success myth that had come to plague Americans in the era of the millionaire.

So ends Robinson's often-anthologized poem "Richard Cory." Like its title character, Robinson led a life of "quiet desperation."

Although he was a New Englander like Robert Frost and a chronicler of small-town life like Sherwood Anderson, Robinson was different from his contemporaries because he felt that he was born in the wrong time period. More at home in the past than the present, Robinson yearned for the glorious, heroic past of myth. As a result, he always felt estranged from his fellow poets, preferring to write about the past. As a result, he created poems dealing with historic myths and characters.

Known primarily for short, ironic character studies of ordinary individuals, Robinson used traditional rhyme and rhythms. Despair runs through his poetry, such as

➤ "Luke Havergal," about a forsaken lover (1896)

➤ "Richard Cory," a somber portrait of a wealthy man who commits suicide (1896)

➤ "Minniver Cheevy," a portrait of a romantic dreamer (1910)

Lit Wit

The 1970s folk singing duo Simon and Garfunkel recorded their own version of Robinson's "Richard Cory." The haunting melody captures the hidden, tragic life of the title character, who seemed to have so much, but felt he had so little.

Robinson may have felt cut off from the crowd, but his achievements were recognized by the literary establishment: He won three Pulitzer Prizes. The first was for *Collected Poems* (1922); the second for *The Man Who Died Twice* (1925); the third for *Tristram* (1927).

The Chicago Poets: Carl Sandburg, Edgar Lee Masters, and Vachel Lindsay

By the turn of the century, Chicago had become a great city, home of innovative architecture and cosmopolitan art collections. Chicago was also the home of Harriet Monroe's *Poetry,* the most important literary magazine of the day.

Carl Sandburg, Edgar Lee Masters, and Vachel Lindsay are part of the *Midwestern* or *Chicago* school that arose before World War I to challenge the East Coast literary establishment, made popular by Frost and Cummings. The "Chicago School" was a watershed in American letters, for it demonstrated that America's interior had come of age.

These three poets have more in common than locale:

➤ Their verses often concern ordinary, everyday people.

➤ Their realist poems and dramatic emphasis attracted a large audience.

Let's see what makes these poets so special, starting with the most famous one, Carl Sandburg.

Carl Sandburg (1878–1967)

"Hog Butcher for the World,

Tool Maker, Stacker of Wheat,

Player with Railroads and the

Nation's Freight Handler;..."

—Carl Sandburg, "Chicago"

A friend of Sandburg's once said, "Trying to write briefly about Carl Sandburg is like trying to picture the Grand Canyon in one black-and-white snapshot." Poet, historian, biographer, novelist, musician, essayist—Sandburg, son of a railroad blacksmith, was all of this and more. A journalist by profession, he wrote a massive biography of Abraham Lincoln that is one of the classic literary works of the 20th century.

Carl Sandburg, one of America's bardic poets.

To many readers, Sandburg was a latter-day Walt Whitman, writing expansive, evocative urban and patriotic poems and simple, childlike rhymes and ballads. Like Whitman, Sandburg's poems...

➤ Describe everyday Americans

➤ Have a positive tone

➤ Use simple words

➤ Are easy to understand

➤ Are written in free verse

Sandburg traveled around the country reciting and recording his poetry in a lilting, mellifluous voice that was a cross between speaking and music. His poetry expresses the hearty, earthy nature of America.

Notwithstanding his national fame, Sandburg was a quiet and unassuming man. What he wanted from life, he once said, was "to be out of jail...to eat regular...to get what I write printed,...a little love at home and a little nice affection hither and yon over the American landscape,...(and) to sing every day."

Edgar Lee Masters (1868–1950)

"Life is too strong for you—

It takes life to love Life."

—Edgar Lee Masters, "Lucinda Matlock"

Edgar Lee Masters was famous for creating the bold *Spoon River Anthology* (1915), a group of poems presented as epitaphs that sum up the lives of individual villagers as if in their own words. *Spoon River* presents a panorama of a country village through the headstones in its cemetery: 250 people speak from beyond the grave, revealing their deepest secrets. Because they are dead and so have nothing to fear from the living, the speakers are honest about their lives, including the resentment, hatred, and despair they felt during their time on earth.

The poems in *Spoon River Anthology* are characterized by...

➤ An "unpoetic" colloquial style

➤ Frank descriptions of sex

➤ A very critical view of small-town life

➤ A description of the inner lives of ordinary people

The Write Stuff

Many of the characters in *Spoon River Anthology* are the related members of about 20 families who speak of their failures and dreams in free-verse monologues, poems written without a standard meter or rhyme.

Lit Speak

Epitaphs are words that are inscribed on gravestones.

Few collections of poetry had the impact of *Spoon River Anthology*. The poems outraged the public and critics alike, so it flew off the shelves. The book went through 19 printings of the first edition alone, a record for poetry at that time. *Spoon River Anthology* remains an important collection of poems for what it reveals about the inner lives of modern Americans.

None of Masters' other collections of poetry were as good (or as popular) as *Spoon River Anthology*, but he nonetheless enjoyed a distinguished career as a well-known novelist and biographer, with more than 50 books to his credit.

Lit Wit

In the 1920s, Edna St. Vincent Millay (1892–1950) became a symbol of the "modern" woman, freed from Victorian standards of the proper role of women. Her love of poetry in particular, with its frank endorsement of sex without guilt, fanned her reputation. But she was much more than a cause célèbre: A skilled writer, Millay produced a vast range of work, everything from traditional English sonnets to political speeches. Some of her work resembles that of the Chicago poets in theme and style. Along with Elinor Wylie and Louise Bogan, Millay carved out a niche that set her apart from the sentimental "female" poetry of the past and the hard-edged modernism of Pound, Eliot, and others.

Writer's Block

Racist by today's standards, Lindsay's famous poem "The Congo" (1914) celebrates the history of Africans by mingling jazz, poetry, music, and chanting.

Vachel Lindsay (1879–1931)

Vachel Lindsay celebrated small-town Midwestern populism and created strong, rhythmic poetry designed to be read aloud. His work bridges folk poetry and modernist poems. An extremely popular public reader in his day, Lindsay's readings prefigure "Beat" poetry readings of the post—World War II era that were accompanied by jazz.

To popularize poetry, Lindsay developed what he called a "higher vaudeville," using music and strong rhythm. At the same time, he immortalized such figures on the American landscape as Abraham Lincoln ("Abraham Lincoln Walks at Midnight") and John Chapman ("Johnny Appleseed"), often blending facts with myth.

The Least You Need to Know

➤ Robert Frost was probably America's best-known and best-loved poet of his time.

➤ Frost's poems used traditional verse forms and the plain speech of rural New Englanders to probe life's irrationality.

➤ e.e. cummings created a new, highly idiosyncratic poetry, marked by unusual typography and spelling.

➤ E.A. Robinson wrote ironic poems about ordinary people.

➤ Carl Sandburg's poetry expresses America's hearty, earthy nature.

➤ In his *Spoon River Anthology,* Edgar Lee Masters used an "unpoetic" colloquial style to provide a frank description of sex and the drawbacks of small-town life.

➤ Vachel Lindsay celebrated small-town Midwestern populism and created strong, rhythmic poetry.

Chapter 25

The Harlem Renaissance (1915–1929)

"At every subway station I kept watching for the sign: 135TH STREET. When I saw it, I held my breath…I went up the steps and into the bright September sunlight. Harlem! I looked around. Negroes everywhere!… I took a deep breath and felt happy again."

—Langston Hughes, from *The Big Sea*

The artistic African-Americans was one of the most striking literary developments of the first part of the 20th century. In the writings of Richard Wright, Langston Hughes, Countée Cullen, Zora Neale Hurston, Jean Toomer, Claude McKay, and others, the roots of modern black American writing took hold, in the forms of novels, poetry, autobiographies, and protest literature.

In this chapter, you'll learn all about these remarkable African-American writers. Let's start with some background on the brilliant outpouring of African-American art and culture known as the "Harlem Renaissance."

The Place to Be

Upon arriving in Harlem in the early 1920s, jazz great Duke Ellington exclaimed, "The world's most glamorous atmosphere! Why, it is just like the Arabian nights!" Harlem in the 1920s was a place where life began at night. More than 100 night spots lined the 10 blocks of New York City along 125th and 135th streets between Lennox and Seventh avenues known as Harlem.

There were at least 40 nightclubs; about 20 cafes, speakeasies, cellars, lounges, bars, and grills; 10 theaters; and eight ballrooms where jazz bands played and people danced the night away. Pianists and composers like Duke Ellington and Fats Waller; blues singers like Ethel Waters and Bessie Smith; and entertainers such as Josephine Baker, Florence Mills, and Bill Robinson ("Mr. Bojangles") kept crowds enthralled. What had caused this great cultural explosion?

Lit Wit

The most famous Harlem nightspots in the 1920s were the Apollo Theater and the Savoy Ballroom; the latter establishment took up an entire city block between 140th and 141st streets. The Savoy boasted marble staircases, crystal chandeliers, and a polished wood dance floor.

During the late 1800s and early 1900s many African-Americans from the south moved north, looking for employment in the industrial cities of the northeast. In 1915, about 50,000 African-Americans lived in Harlem; less than 15 years later, the population had swelled to 150,000 people. As the population increased, the New York City community of Harlem developed into a cultural mecca for American blacks. The cultural blowout included literature, music, and art. It became known as the "Harlem Renaissance."

As with many cultural movements of the time, the Harlem Renaissance ended with the Great Depression: The money to support the arts simply dried up.

While the individual works of literature produced by the writers of the Harlem Renaissance were as different as the men and women who created them, most of the writing deals with the same topic: The relationship between race and literature. Some of the poets, for example, viewed their writing as a way to express what it meant to be black in America while others, in contrast, used their talent to explore more "traditional" poetic subjects, such as nature, childhood, and love.

Lit Wit

Harlem occupies much of the northern part of Manhattan. The area was established in 1658 by the Dutch governor Peter Stuyvesant. In 1776, during the American Revolution, the Battle of Harlem Heights was fought there. The community grew as a suburb of New York City from 1830 to about 1880 and was a fashionable residential area. From about 1900 to World War I, it developed as the center of black culture. By the end of World War II, however, housing conditions had deteriorated; today, Harlem contains vestiges of its famous past alongside extensive slums as well as newer housing developments and blocks of renovated brownstones. The main business district, on 125th Street, runs east to west across the area.

Although the specific literary concerns and techniques varied from writer to writer, these writers shared a common purpose: to prove that African-Americans could produce great literature. Simultaneously, they expressed the mood of the African-American community of the time—often, their resentment concerning the overall treatment of African-Americans. Richard Wright's legacy has been the most enduring—and problematic.

Richard Wright (1908–1960)

"The day Native Son appeared, American culture was changed forever. No matter how much qualifying the book might later need, it made impossible a repetition of old lies."

—critic Irving Howe

Richard Wright has the distinction of being the first African-American author whose work appeared on the national bestseller lists. *Native Son* was an instant success and sold a quarter of a million copies in its first month of publication in 1940. Together with his autobiography, *Black Boy*, *Native Son* established Wright as a writer of power and intensity. *Native Son* is a brutal portrait of a poor black man spurred on to murder by the oppression and hatred of the white world.

Behind the Eight Ball

Wright was born on a Mississippi farm in 1908; soon after, the family moved to Memphis. His father left when Richard was six, plunging the family into poverty. In desperation, Richard's mother placed him and his brother in an orphanage. It proved to be a wretched place, and Richard ran away.

Wright was then shuttled among various relatives, which he found just about as intolerable as the orphanage especially since his relatives tried to make him accept religion as a panacea for prejudice.

The world of work gave Wright a first-hand taste of racism, but he hid his anger as best he could in order to buy the food, clothes, and books he needed. He accomplished this through a series of short-term, menial jobs.

Lit Speak

The **WPA Writers' Project** was a government-sponsored program to help support authors during the Depression.

Writer's Block

For years, Wright claimed that the FBI had kept him under surveillance and compiled a file on him. Even Wright's closest friends concluded that he was paranoid. After Wright's death, it was revealed that he had been right—the FBI had indeed been monitoring his life.

Despite his horrific childhood, Wright managed not only to stay in school but also to publish a story called "The Voodoo of Hell's Half-Acre" in a local black newspaper. Praise was as hard to come by as food, however, for his friends and family thought his writing was sinful and a waste of time.

By the age of 17, Wright had moved 25 times. The maltreatment he experienced along the way convinced him that the hidden anger of African-Americans was justified. Wright felt that only by expressing this anger could African-Americans move on.

Better Red than Dead?

He moved north toward Memphis, and eventually went to Chicago. There, he held a series of odd jobs until he joined the WPA Writers' Project as director of the Federal Negro Theater. He began to study Marxist theory and contribute articles to the Communist Party journals. By 1935, he had established himself as a fiction writer. Two years later, in 1937, he moved to New York, where he wrote for the New York Writers' Project and the became the Harlem editor for the Communist publication, *Daily Worker*.

Parlez-Vous Equality?

After publishing *Native Son* in 1940, Wright produced *Black Boy*, an autobiographical work (1945). His novels greatly influenced writers Ralph Ellison and James Baldwin, profiled in Chapter 29.

America's "native son" Richard Wright eventually sought refuge in France.

Wright left the Communist Party in 1944. Three years later, he settled in France, where he was warmly received—the French ranked him among the great white writers of the period: Hemingway, Fitzgerald, and Faulkner.

During the last 10 years of his life, Wright continued to publish from his home in France. His novels from this period include *The Outsider, Savage Holiday, Black Power, The Color Curtain, White Man, Listen!,* and his last novel, *The Long Dream.* He died of a heart attack in 1960 at the age of 52.

Native Son

Set in Chicago in the 1930s, Wright's explosive novel *Native Son* is just as meaningful today as it was when it was written, both in its unsparing description of poverty and feelings of helplessness experienced by people in inner-cities and what it means to be black in America.

The novel is divided into three sections, called *books*," in which the reader traces the main character's (Bigger's) inexorable slide into tragedy.

Book One: Fear

Twenty-year-old Bigger Thomas, an African-American, lives in a Chicago southside tenement

The Write Stuff

Native Son is often compared to Theodore Dreiser's *An American Tragedy,* since both novels are naturalistic descriptions of young men who never had a snowball's chance in heck of surviving, much less succeeding.

with his mother, sister, and younger brother. He accepts a job with the wealthy white Dalton family as a chauffeur. One night, Bigger has to carry the Daltons' beautiful daughter Mary into her bedroom because she is too drunk to walk on her own.

Hearing Mary's muttering, Mrs. Dalton, who is blind, enters her daughter's bedroom. Bigger panics. If he is found alone with a white woman in her bedroom, he will surely be charged with rape. In a panic, Bigger tries to stifle Mary's drunken mutterings with a pillow and accidentally pushes the pillow too firmly against her face, and Mary suffocates. He burns her body in the furnace but first has to cut her head off to fit her body in the furnace. After her body is reduced to ash, he flees home.

Book Two: Flight

Deciding to capitalize on the crime, Bigger concocts a scheme for extorting money from the Daltons by sending a fake ransom note. His plan falls apart when bones and an earring are found in the furnace ashes. Deciding to run from the scene, Bigger knows he can neither leave his black girlfriend Bessie behind nor take her with him. He kills her and throws her body down an air shaft in a vacant building. Bigger evades capture for a full day by hiding in empty southside apartments but is finally forced down from the top of a watertank by a stream from a fire hose. He is dragged by his feet to the snowy street below.

Lit Wit

Right after *Native Son* appeared, Wright published an article entitled "How Bigger Was Born" in the *Saturday Review*. In the article, Wright described five "Biggers" he had known in the South, beginning with: a child who bullied his playmates and continuing with older black youths who resorted to violence in their revolt against Southern Jim Crow laws. Each of the five died young. When Wright moved to Chicago, he encountered other "Biggers." Later, Wright realized that there were white "Biggers" also, young men irremediably conditioned toward crime.

Book Three: Fate

At the inquest three days after Bigger's capture, the court rules that he be held on a murder charge. Taken to the Dalton home, Bigger refuses to reenact his crime, and when he sees a flaming cross, he tears off the wooden cross he is wearing.

Although Bigger's Communist lawyer Max enters a plea of not guilty at Bigger's arraignment, he later changes the plea to guilty. As a Communist, Max feels that society is to blame for Bigger's crime, not Bigger himself.

During the dramatic three-day trial, Max attempts to convince the court that Bigger's crime is part of the nation's guilt, but Prosecuting Attorney Buckley's vehement denunciations prevail, and Bigger is sentenced to die. Before his execution, Bigger comes to an understanding of other people and of himself that enables him to face death with dignity and courage.

Writer's Block

Don't make the mistake of feeling sorry for Bigger; he steals, he lies, he schemes to extort money, and he murders.

Even though Bigger's humanity and his potential for good are evident, Wright didn't intend for readers to sentimentalize him.

Crime and Punishment

"I didn't want to kill!… But what I killed for, I am!… What I killed for must've been good!… It must have been good!… I didn't know I was really alive in this world until I felt things hard enough to kill for 'em."

—Bigger Thomas from *Native Son*

Native Son describes a society that commits a crime against one of its own. The novel explores the themes of inequality, racial conflict, and as this quote shows, violence as a personal necessity—clearly the most controversial of Wright's themes. In addition, the story shows Wright's belief at the time that Communism was Black American's best hope for equality.

Richard Wright may be the most famous and controversial writer from this era, but many other African-Americans helped create America's rich heritage of black literature. Let's explore some of the other notable contributors to the Harlem Renaissance, starting with Langston Hughes.

Langston Hughes (1902–1967)

"Well, son, I'll tell you:

Life for me ain't been no crystal stair."

—Langston Hughes, from "Mother to Son"

In his day, Langston Hughes was the most successful black writer in America. Nicknamed "the bard of Harlem," Hughes is most famous for his poetry, although he also wrote drama, novels, songs, articles, autobiographical pieces, and movie scripts. Unlike Richard Wright, Jean Toomer, and Countée Cullen, Hughes wanted to capture the dominant oral traditions of black culture in written form.

Lit Wit

"Among the many talented black writers connected with the Harlem Renaissance," wrote critic David Kalstone, "Langston Hughes was the most popular, the most versatile, and the most durable."

Born in Missouri and raised in the Midwest, Hughes attended high school in Cleveland, where he wrote for the school literary magazine. When he was 19 years old, Hughes moved to New York City to attend Columbia University, but a year later he decided to travel to Europe and Africa as a merchant seaman. When Hughes returned to the United States, he met the poet Vachel Lindsay, who helped him publish his first book of poetry, *The Weary Blues* (1926). The book was a hit, and Hughes was on his way.

Hughes published several collections of poetry, including *The Dream Keeper* (1932), *Fields of Wonder* (1947), and *Montage of a Dream Deferred* (1951). In his poetry, Hughes experimented with a variety of forms and techniques and often tried to re-create the rhythms of jazz. He also wrote poems of protest against racism.

Hughes' poetry inspired many other black writers. By eloquently chronicling the heritage of black people and expressing their pride and determination, Hughes provided all Americans with a look at the rich culture of his people.

Countée Cullen (1903–1946)

"The ills I sorrow at

Not me alone

Like an arrow.

Pierce to the marrow,

Through the fact

And past the bone."

—Countée Cullen, from "Any Human to Another"

Countée Cullen's origin is shrouded in mystery; the exact date of his birth and his parentage are both unknown. Fortunately, his childhood was secure and happy. As the adopted son of a Methodist minister and his wife, Cullen was much loved. He attended rigorous DeWitt Clinton High School in New York and completed his undergraduate work at New York University. He earned his M.A. from Harvard.

His first collection of poetry, *Color,* was published in 1925, followed by *Copper Sun* and *The Ballad of the Brown Girl* two years later. Cullen's youth (he was only 22 when *Color* was published), skill as a poet, and themes evoked comparisons to the 19th-century English poet John Keats, and so Cullen was called the "black Keats." He was celebrated as a genius.

During his later years, Cullen published two children's books, *The Lost Zoo* (1940) and *My Lives and How I Lost Them* (1942).

Unlike many of the other black poets of the period, Cullen worked within traditional poetic forms rather than experimenting with jazz rhythms. Nonetheless, his poems brought black themes to the attention of white readers.

Zora Neale Hurston (1891–1960)

"…I am not tragically colored. There is no great sorrow damned up in my soul, nor lurking behind my eyes. I do not mind at all… No, I do not weep at the world—I am too busy sharpening my oyster knife."

—Zora Neale Hurston, "How It Feels to Be Colored Me"

Zora Neale Hurston arrived in New York City in 1925 and came to represent the best of the Harlem Renaissance. By her death in 1960, she had published more books than any other black American writer; nonetheless, she died alone and penniless.

When Hurston was 11 years old, her mother died and the child was shuttled from relative to relative. Hurston was so eager to learn that even though she never finished high school, she was able to study at Howard University. She decided to move to New York after her first short story "Drenched in Light" was published in an Afro-American magazine.

Vivacious and spirited, Hurston got a job as a personal secretary to the white novelist Fanny Hurst. In her spare time, she enrolled in Barnard College. There, Hurston developed an interest in African-American folk literature and became a popular performance artist and storyteller.

In 1927 Hurston graduated from Barnard College and was awarded a fellowship to study the black oral traditions. Her subsequent publications were controversial among her fellow black writers because they were not political. She refused to follow a political agenda; rather, she argued that she should be free to write about what she wanted, regardless of appearance or perception.

In the 1930s, Hurston produced her finest writing, even though the public's interest in black literature had waned. These works include *Jonah's Gourd Vine* (1934), *Mules and Men* (1935), *Their Eyes Were Watching God* (1937), and *Dust Tracks on a Road* (1942). Her most popular book earned less than $1,000, but still she persevered. Finally, overworked to the breaking point, Hurston moved back to Florida. She worked as a maid to support herself. Rediscovered by the women's movement in the 1970s, Hurston is now considered one of the key black writers of the 20th century.

Jean Toomer (1894–1967)

> *"The sky, lazily disdaining to pursue*
>
> *The setting sun, too indolent to hold*
>
> *A lengthening tournament for flashing gold,*
>
> *Passively darkens for night's barbecue,…"*

—Jean Toomer, from *Cane*

Like other Harlem Renaissance writers, Jean Toomer had a deep interest in the cultural roots of the African-American experience. In his poetry, Toomer expressed his belief that maintaining a sense of pride in the black heritage was vital to the freedom of black people.

Born in Washington, D.C., Toomer attended a number of different colleges but never earned a degree. After teaching high school for several years in Georgia, he created a series of sketches, poems, and a one-act play that he published under the title *Cane* (1923).

Cane elevated Toomer to a preeminent position among his fellow black writers.

Unlike Langston Hughes and Zora Neale Hurston, Toomer wanted to be consciously literary; *Cane* does not use the voices of black people of that era. Toomer was praised not only for his sensitive portrayals of black life, but also for writing "without surrender or compromise of the artist's vision," as one admirer said.

Cane fell into obscurity, and Toomer followed suit. Recently, however, *Cane* has regained attention and is now regarded as one of the most influential and important works to emerge from the Harlem Renaissance.

Claude McKay (1890–1948)

> *"My eyes grew dim, and I could no more gaze;*
>
> *A wave of longing through my body swept,*
>
> *And, hungry for the old, familiar ways*
>
> *I turned aside and bowed my head and wept."*

—Claude McKay, from "The Tropics in New York"

Although Claude McKay was born in Jamaica and lived in many countries during his life, he considered Harlem his spiritual home. The son of poor farmers, McKay moved from the village of Sunny Ville to Kingston, the capital of Jamaica, when he was 14 years old and began writing poetry while still a teenager.

When his poetry collection *Songs of Jamaica* won a major award in 1912, he was able to emigrate to America. Much of McKay's poetry evokes the rich heritage of his native

Jamaica. McKay's American reputation was secured with the publication of *Harlem Shadows* in 1922. This collection of passionate and vibrant poems is the first great literary achievement of the Harlem Renaissance. That year, McKay moved to Russia, where he was celebrated by the Bolshevik leaders and the Russian masses as a leftist poet. Around 1925, McKay left Russia for France, where he wrote his first novel, *Home to Harlem* (1928) and gathered material for his second, *Banjo* (1929). This was followed by two short story collections about Harlem life, *Gingertown* (1932) and *Banana Bottom* (1933).

The last 14 years of McKay's life were a let down. Back in America, he found both his health and creativity declining. His last book was *Harlem: A Negro Metropolis* (1940).

Additional Voices

➤ ***W.E.B. Du Bois* (1868–1963)** Born in New England and educated at Harvard University and the University of Berlin, Du Bois demonstrated in his landmark book, *The Souls of Black Folk* (1903), that segregation would inevitably lead to inequality, particularly in education. Du Bois, a founder of the National Association for the Advancement of Colored People (NAACP), also wrote sensitive appreciations of the African-American traditions and culture; his work helped black intellectuals rediscover their rich folk literature and music.

➤ **James Weldon Johnson (1871–1938)** Johnson explored the complex issue of race in his fictional *The Autobiography of an Ex-Colored Man* (1912), about a mixed-race man who "passes" (s considered) white. The book effectively conveys Black America's concern with issues of identity in America. Johnson himself was of mixed white and black ancestry. He also wrote the National Negro Anthem "Lift Every Voice and Sing."

➤ **Charles Waddell Chesnutt (1858–1932)** The author of two collections of stories, *The Conjure Woman* (1899) and *The Wife of His Youth* (1899); several novels, including *The Marrow of Tradition* (1901); and a biography of Frederick Douglass, Chesnutt was ahead of his time. His stories deal with racial themes but avoid predictable endings and generalized sentiment; his characters are distinct individuals with complex attitudes about many things, including race. Chesnutt often shows the strength of the black community and affirms ethical values and racial solidarity.

➤ **Booker T. Washington (1856–1915)** An educator and the most prominent black leader of his day, Washington grew up as a slave in Franklin County, Virginia. Born to a white slave-holding father and a slave mother, he became famous for his efforts to improve the lives of African-Americans through education. His policy of integration with whites—an attempt to involve the recently freed black American in the mainstream of American society—was outlined in his famous Atlanta Exposition Address (1895). Check out his autobiography, *Up From Slavery* (1901), for more information about this remarkable man.

The Least You Need to Know

➤ The Harlem Renaissance was a black cultural movement that emerged in Harlem, New York, during the 1920s. Literature, music, and art flourished.

➤ Richard Wright's *Native Son* is a brutal portrait of a poor black man spurred on to murder by the oppression and hatred of the white world.

➤ In his day, Langston Hughes was the most successful black writer in America. He wrote poetry, drama, novels, songs, articles, autobiographical pieces, and movie scripts.

➤ Countée Cullen was called the "black Keats" for his youth, skill as a poet, and use of traditional forms.

➤ Rediscovered by the women's movement in the 1970s, Zora Neale Hurston is considered one of the key black writers of the 20th century.

➤ Jean Toomer's *Cane* is now regarded as one of the most influential, important works of the era.

➤ Claude McKay's poetry evokes the rich heritage of his native Jamaica.

➤ W.E.B. Du Bois, James Weldon Johnson, Charles Waddell Chesnutt, and Booker T. Washington were other important black writers of the time.

Chapter 26

Cult Figures (1945–Present)

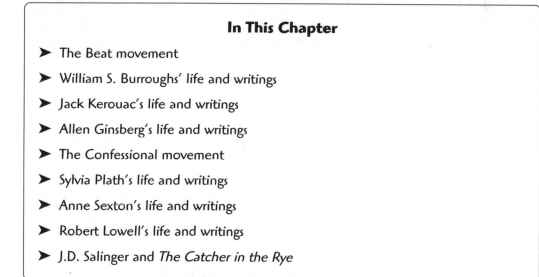

In This Chapter

➤ The Beat movement

➤ William S. Burroughs' life and writings

➤ Jack Kerouac's life and writings

➤ Allen Ginsberg's life and writings

➤ The Confessional movement

➤ Sylvia Plath's life and writings

➤ Anne Sexton's life and writings

➤ Robert Lowell's life and writings

➤ J.D. Salinger and *The Catcher in the Rye*

Political life in the 1950s may have been calm and conforming, but the literary front was exploding with wildly different visions. The "beat" writers—William S. Burroughs, Jack Keroauc, and Allen Ginsberg—explored the need for spontaneity in living and writing. The "confessional" poets—Sylvia Plath, Anne Sexton, and Robert Lowell—used the anguish of their own lives to explore America's hidden despair. J.D. Salinger's *The Catcher in the Rye* became the symbol for a generation of disaffected youth.

So settle back, ladies and gentlemen, and discover how some of our favorite writers expressed their vision of American life in mid-century.

The Beat Goes On

The recent deaths of Allen Ginsberg and William S. Burroughs ended one of the most intriguing literary movements in American history: the beats. Burroughs was the beats' father figure and literary innovator, Ginsberg its publicist and poet laureate. Though the beat movement is largely over, it will always be remembered for changing the way Americans view modern life.

Beat It

The Beat movement started in New York City in 1944, when William Burroughs, Jack Kerouac, Allen Ginsberg, and Lucien Carr began their quest for a "New Vision" in literature. It flourished through fellow beatniks such as Neal Cassady, who arrived in New York in 1946 to become Kerouac's friend and Ginsberg's lover.

According to a *Time* magazine article of the period, the beats were easy to spot because "they spoke their own argot, mostly picked up from the Negro Jazz musicians and juvenile street gangs: "bread" for *money* and "dig" for *admiration*. They experimented with marijuana, which they called "pot." Both sexes huddled up in flats they called "pads," furnished with no more than a guitar, hot plate, bare mattress and a few records and books."

The beats were careful to point out that they weren't nearly as dangerous as the public thought. As Kerouac remarked, "We love everything—Billy Graham, the Top Ten, Rock and Roll, Zen, apple pie, Eisenhower—we dig it all."

Running on Empty

Under these surface differences, however, the beats were curiously like the other great literary architects of the 20th century, such as the Modernists spearheaded by Ezra Pound and T.S. Eliot. As with these writers, the beats were struggling with the quality of contemporary life. Their writing reflected the emptiness of a world devoid of spontaneity and creative possibility, which has "driven the best minds mad," in Ginsberg's words. The beat writers attempted to convey pure emotion through words in order to break through what they saw as the sterility of the times.

Writer's Block

Life in the 50s was calm and comforting as long as you didn't run afoul of "Tailgunner Joe," Senator Joseph McCarthy (1908–1957). who led a campaign against Communist subversion in the early 1950s. McCarthy first attracted national attention in February 1950 by charging that the Department of State had been infiltrated by Communists. Although his accusation was never substantiated, during the next three years he accused various high-ranking officials, entertainers, and writers of subversive activities. Before his downfall in April of 1954, McCarthy shattered hundreds of lives.

Lit Speak

In 1957, after Kerouac's *On the Road* became a bestseller, Herb Caen of the *San Francisco Chronicle* coined the term **beatnik** to refer to the unorthodox writers who hung around the bars and coffee houses of San Francisco's North Beach.

The beats catapulted to nationwide attention in the 1950s, when they joined forces with the poets of the so-called "San Francisco Renaissance": Kenneth Rexroth, Robert Duncan, Jack Spicer, Lew Welch, and others. It was a San Francisco poet, Lawrence Ferlinghetti, who published and popularized the beat writers via his City Lights Books and City Lights Bookstore.

Lit Wit

To conservatives, the beats were "a pack of unleashed poets, pushers, and panhandlers, musicians, male hustlers, and a few marginal esthetes seeking new marginal directions" (Herbert Gold, *The Nation*). The beat generation, wrote another critic, "became the spokesmen for people rejected by the mainstream, whether drug addicts, homosexuals, the emotionally dispossessed, or the mentally ill."

Since William S. Burroughs is usually considered the patriarch of the Beat movement, let's look at his life and work first.

William S. Burroughs (1914–1997)

William Burroughs was the beat generation's most innovative writer. Born into serious money—his grandfather invented the Burroughs adding machine—Burroughs' personal life can be summarized by the titles of two of his novels, *Junky* and *Queer*. Much of his life was marked by drama: Burroughs was arrested on drug charges in 1949 and fled to Mexico with his wife, Joan. In 1951, Burroughs caused a bigger sensation when he accidentally killed Joan in a drunken game of William Tell.

Burroughs spent much of the 1950s and 1960s in Europe and North Africa, where he wrote a series of controversial books. The most famous of these, *Naked Lunch* (1959) was tried for obscenity in Boston.

Lit Speak

The "game" of **William Tell** was named after the legendary Swiss patriot of the 1300s. According to legend, the despotic Austrian governor Gessler ordered William Tell to shoot an arrow through an apple set on his son's head. Tell accomplished the feat, but stated that if he killed his son, he would have killed Gessler himself. Tell was then imprisoned, escaped, and sparked an uprising. Don't try this at home, kids.

Jack Kerouac (1922–1969)

Kerouac came from Lowell, Massachusetts, a down-and-out former mill town. Kerouac's father took up gambling when his business failed. Jack was then in high school.

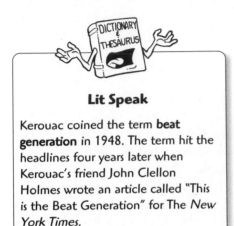

Lit Speak

Kerouac coined the term **beat generation** in 1948. The term hit the headlines four years later when Kerouac's friend John Clellon Holmes wrote an article called "This is the Beat Generation" for The *New York Times*.

Jack tried to save the family by winning a football scholarship to college and entering the insurance business. He would then make enough money to support them.

He did indeed win a scholarship to Columbia University in New York. His parents followed him there, settling in Ozone Park, Queens.

But life didn't go as planned for Kerouac in the Big Apple. Kerouac's football coach refused to put him in the games, and his father sank rapidly into alcoholism. In desperation, Kerouac dropped out of Columbia and joined the Merchant Marines. When he wasn't sailing, Kerouac was hanging around New York with the wild crowd he had come to know while at Columbia: Allen Ginsberg, Lucien Carr, William S. Burroughs, and Neal Cassady.

Soon after he finished his stint in the service, Kerouac published his first novel, a conventional book called *The Town and the City* in 1950. It earned him some recognition as a writer but no real money. Kerouac found his niche when he decided to write about the cross-country trips he and Neal Cassady had taken. In 1950, he presented the resulting manuscript to his editor on a single long roll of unbroken paper, but the editor wasn't impressed. It took seven years for his most famous novel, *On the Road*, to be published. The novel changed Kerouac's life for good.

Dissatisfied with traditional fiction, Kerouc used *On the Road* to develop a new, spontaneous, nonstop, and unedited method of writing that shocked more polished and conventional writers. The novel, written in three weeks, drew public attention to the widespread subterreanean culture of beat poets, folksingers, hipsters, mystics, and eccentrics.

After *On the Road*, Kerouac published *The Dharma Bums* (1958), *The Subterranean* (1958), Doctor Sax (1959), *Lonesome Traveler* (1960) and *Desolation Angels* (1965). All Kerouac's books are autobiographical.

Always a drinker, Kerouac found the loss of privacy difficult to handle and began to drink heavily. Kerouac lived out his final years with his mother in St. Petersburg, Florida. *Visions of Cody* was published posthumously, in 1972. It was originally part of *On the Road*.

Lit Wit

Despite the "beatnik" stereotype, Kerouac was a political conservative. He supported the Vietnam War and was friendly with William F. Buckley.

Allen Ginsberg (1926–1997)

*"I saw the best minds of my generation destroyed by
   madness, starving hysterical naked,*

*dragged themselves through the Negro streets at dawn
   looking for an angry fix,…"*

—Allen Ginsberg, "Howl"

A shy child growing up in Paterson, New Jersey, Allen Ginsberg's home life was dominated by his mother's mental illness. He discovered the poetry of Walt Whitman (the original beatnick) in high school, but despite his interest in poetry, Ginsberg followed the advice of his father, and began planning a career as a labor lawyer. Allen's father, Louis, was a poet of some note, so we can assume he knew first-hand the problems that poets face.

During his first year at Columbia University in 1948, Ginsberg fell in with a crowd of wild and crazy men and quickly was suspended from Columbia for various offenses. He began consorting with junkies and thieves in the Times Square area of New York City (mostly friends of Burroughs), experimenting with drugs, and cruising gay bars in Greenwich Village. He was convinced that he and his friends were working toward some kind of as-yet-undefined poetic breakthrough.

"Howl"

When his friend William Burroughs was arrested in 1951 for the murder of his wife, Ginsberg immersed himself in psychoanalytic treatment and took a job as a marketing researcher. This phase didn't last long, and Ginsberg headed west to plunge into the San Francisco poetry scene. He was the first beat writer to become well-known when he delivered a dramatic reading of his new poem, "Howl," at the now-legendary Six Gallery poetry reading in October 1955. This great poem was conveniently publicized by a bungled obscenity charge that made Allen a worldwide symbol of sexual depravity. "Howl" was a visible expression of beat defiance, just as Kerouac's *On the Road*, published two years later, would be the great expression of beat yearnings for creative freedom.

Unfortunately for Ginsberg, the San Francisco poets' enthusiastic reception for "Howl" was not shared by the population at large. To most of the public, "Howl" was simply a dirty poem. Ferlinghetti, owner of the City Lights Bookstore in San Francisco, and the bookstore manager were both arrested for selling an obscene book.

Ginsberg published "Howl" with several other important collections of poems, such as "Empty Mirror" and "Kaddish and Other Poems" (1963). He mellowed considerably, likely the result of discovering Buddhism and falling in love with Peter Orlovsky, who would remain his constant companion for 30 years. Perhaps most importantly, he exorcised some internal demons by writing "Kaddish," a brilliant poem about his mother's insanity and death.

Lit Wit

Ginsberg got around. He can be seen standing in the background of Bob Dylan's 1965 "Subterranean Homesick Blues" video and played a major part in Dylan's 1977 film *Renaldo and Clara.* He was a key figure at the Chicago Democratic Convention antiwar protests in 1968. In the early 1980s, Ginsberg joined the punk rock movement, appearing on the Clash's "Combat Rock" album and performing with them onstage.

Writer's Block

The "beat generation" was not a media hype concept like today's "generation X." Generation X is just a convenient label for millions of people whose only similarity is age; the beats, in contrast, were a small group of grown-ups based in New York City and San Francisco who were involved in writing and publishing.

Ginsberg carried on an active social schedule until his death in April 1997. He never moved away from his humble apartment on New York City's lower east side.

Not everyone was a Ginsberg fan—far from it. The influential intellectual scholar, writer, and critic Norman Podhoretz, for example, started out as a friend, but ended up branding Ginsberg a fraud, a writer who passed off little talent with a lot of bombast. Podhoretz attacked Ginsberg's ethic: insanity is sanity, drugs are sacramental, homosexuality is holy, normality is horror.

Nonetheless, Ginsberg's reputation remains undiminished after his death. If anything, his followers are more devoted than ever. I can understand the admiration people feel for Ginsberg, for we had him speak twice at the Visiting Writers Program at the State University at Farmingdale, and found him provocative yet sweet.

The Family

Store ad: "We treat you like family."

That bad, huh? The columnist Murray Kempton coined the term *the Family* to describe the New York intellectuals who buzzed around the highbrow literary magazines *Commentary* and *Partisan Review* in the 1940s and 1950s. The Family included the following intellectuals:

➤ Hannah Arendt

➤ Lillian Hellman

➤ Irving Howe

➤ Dwight Macdonald

➤ Mary McCarthy

➤ Norman Podhoretz

➤ Philip Rahv

➤ Harold Rosenberg

➤ Lionel Trilling

➤ Diana Trilling

This was the other side of the coin, the "highbrow" cult, which today survives as the "New York Review of Books." In their intellectual world of criticism and scholarship, these writers made a quiet splash in the literary pool—but an equally important one. That's because they influenced the books taught in colleges and the critical slants taken toward them. As a result, these writers and critics helped establish many of the books we today esteem as classics.

More Than I Needed to Know

There's nothing new about letting it all hang out; the so-called *confessional* poets were sharing their feelings long before depression became obligatory cocktail party chatter. Sylvia Plath, Anne Sexton, and Robert Lowell were "confessional poets," so called because their poetry dealt with deeply personal, emotional, and psychological matters. Confessional poetry moved away from the earlier notion that poetry was to be universal rather than personal. The confessional poets described the experience of suffering, often in the context of the family, and through this suffering, suggested the cost of the national practices and ideologies of the 1950s on the individual.

The Write Stuff

Mere expression of personal feeling does not in itself constitute Confessional poetry. Rather, skillful handling of language and distance from personality (achieved through a persona or mask) are also crucial factors.

The result is a body of work of universal significance, an expression of a psychological condition that is public as well as private. Robert Lowell was the teacher of the group, but Sylvia Plath has become the patron saint, so let's start with her.

Sylvia Plath (1932–1963)

"...Every woman adores a Fascist,

The boot in the face, the brute

Brute heart of a brute like you."

—Sylvia Plath, "Daddy"

In "Daddy," perhaps Plath's best-known poem, she examines the father/daughter relationship. Criticized as a "racking personal confession" as well as for its use of "ready-made" public images of terror, "Daddy" has also reaped much praise. Critic George Steiner, for example, said the poem succeeds in translating private suffering into universal truths. Most positive responses to the poem, though, note the careful interplay between the poem's content and form as possibly Plath's highest poetic achievement. It is this interplay that effectively conveys the ambiguity of the emotion behind the poem, the love/hate relationship between the speaker and her father.

Daddy Dearest

"Daddy" opens in rejection: "You do not do, you do not do"—suggesting an anti-marriage vow. The speaker is declaring that after 30 years, she wants to free herself of the awful influence of her dead father. He has become a burden, "marbleheavy" in his death; like the bastard child of a Nazi soldier ("In the German tongue, in the Polish town"), she has sought her father unsuccessfully and suffered for it. Then, "stuck in a barb wire snare," she suddenly becomes not the child of a Nazi, but his victim. On her way "to Dachau, Auschwitz, Belsin," she imagines herself, in her persecuted state, a Jew.

The father/Nazi image is extended to her lover, as she marries a model of her father, "A man in black with a Meinkampf look/And a love of the rack and screw." The irony, though, is that while she says "I'm finally through" with Daddy, she also says "I do, I do" to his replacement, reversing the renunciation of the opening line. While she has finally laid her blood-sucking, vampire father to rest, she has married his replica and deliberately continued her own persecution. The speaker becomes both victim and victimizer, finding pleasure in her own pain, torn between life and death.

What drove Plath to create a poem this powerful, this sad? On the surface, there was little in her life to suggest the harrowing images found in her verse.

The Perfect Child

Sensitive, intelligent, compelled toward perfection in everything she attempted, on the surface Plath was the model daughter—popular, brilliant, and accomplished. By the time she entered Smith College on a scholarship in 1950, Plath had already compiled an impressive list of publications. While at Smith, she wrote more than 400 poems.

Plath's surface perfection was an illusion, however, for she was actually mentally ill. During the summer following her junior year at Smith, Plath barely escaped death after swallowing sleeping pills. She later described this experience in an autobiographical novel, *The Bell Jar*, published in 1963. After electroshock and psychotherapy, Plath graduated from Smith and won a Fulbright scholarship to study at Cambridge, England.

In 1956, she married the English poet Ted Hughes, and in 1960, when she was 28, her first book, *The Colossus,* was published in England. She and Hughes settled for a while in the English countryside, but less than two years after the birth of their first child, the marriage collapsed. It was 1958, but by then, Sylvia had given birth to a second child.

The poems Plath wrote during the winter of 1962 to '63 became more powerful: Death now takes on a physical allure and psychic pain that is almost tactile. On February 11, 1963, Plath killed herself. It was a grisly death. She set two mugs of milk by her children's beds, barricaded herself in the kitchen, stuffed cloth under the door, and stuck her head into the oven. Two years later, *Ariel,* a collection of some of her last poems, was published; this was followed by *Crossing the Water* and *Winter Trees* in 1971, and in 1981, *The Collected Poems* appeared, edited by Ted Hughes.

Plath's life and death have evoked astonishing fire among her devoted fans. Ted Hughes is often painted as a heinous villain who controlled access to her work and stifled her life. Check out any of the many Web sites on the Internet for a peek at the passion Plath evokes even today, decades after her suicide.

Anne Sexton (1920–1974)

Born in Newton, Massachusetts, Anne Harvey attended Garland Junior College for a year before her marriage in 1948 to Alfred M. Sexton II. They lived in New York and Massachusetts for some years and in Baltimore and San Francisco while Alfred served in the navy during the Korean War. Sexton worked at various times as a fashion model and as a librarian. In 1960, Sexton published her first book of poetry, *To Bedlam and Part Way Back."* Her second book of poems, *All My Pretty Ones,* appeared in 1962 and continued her uncompromising self-exploration. (Or self-obsession, depending on how you look at it.)

Live or Die (1966) won a Pulitzer Prize and was followed by several other volumes of poetry.

The Write Stuff

Sexton emphasized that she did not understand *confession* literally: She admitted to confessing things that never happened. Sexton stated that "As I once said to someone, if I did all the things I confess to, there would be no time to write a poem... I mean I'll often assume the first person and someone else's story."

Sexton's ongoing mental illness led to repeated hospitalizations in psychiatric institutions.

And if that wasn't enough to have on one plate, Sexton was also addicted to alcohol and sleeping pills. Sexton took her own life with on overdose of medication on October 4, 1974, in Weston, Massachusetts, at the age of 54.

Robert Lowell (1917–1977)

Poet Elizabeth Bishop wrote to Robert Lowell:

"In general, I deplore the confessional — however, …when you wrote Life Studies perhaps it was a necessary movement, and it helped make poetry more real, fresh, and immediate."

Writer's Block

Elizabeth Bishop was fed up to *here* with confessional poetry: "But now—ye gods—anything goes, and I am so sick of poems about the students' mothers & fathers and sex lives and so on."

The Write Stuff

Lowell admitted that he tinkered with the "truth," even inventing the occasions for poems, yet would still attempt to convince the reader that "he was getting the real Robert Lowell." He explained that "this is true of any kind of autobiographical writing and historical writing—you want the reader to say, This is true."

Robert Lowell hailed from a distinguished literary family: his great-grand uncle James Russell Lowell had been a poet and America's ambassador to England; his cousin Amy Lowell was also a well-known poet. (So what if she smoked big fat cigars before it became fashionable?)

Rebel Robert left Harvard in 1937 before completing his degree in order to study at Kenyon College with John Crowe Ransom, the poet and critic. Lowell further alienated himself from his family when he converted to Roman Catholicism in 1940 and refused to be drafted into the army in World War II. As a result, he served a year in jail; the judge scolded him for scarring his family's grand heritage. Lowell's first book of poems, *Lord Weary's Castle* (1946) was a stunning indictment of his elegant Protestant Boston background.

"A car radio bleats,

'Love, O careless Love…' I hear

my ill-spirited sob in each blood cell,

as if my hand were at its throat…

I myself am hell;

nobody's here—"

—Lowell, from "Skunk Hour"

In Life Studies (1959), Lowell changed his style dramatically to become a confessional poet. *For The Union Dead,* published five years later, continued in the same self-revelatory vein. More books followed, as Lowell divided his time between New York and teaching at Harvard. By his death, Lowell had completed 10 books of poetry and had become a revered elder statesman. At the Vietnam War protest in 1967, Norman Mailer said that Lowell "gave off at times the unwilling haunted saintliness of a man who was repaying the moral debts of ten generations of ancestors."

J.D. Salinger (b. 1919)

The son of a prosperous meat importer, Jerome David Salinger was born in New York City. His life resembled that of his fictional creation Holden Caufield: He enjoyed the benefits of an upper middle-class family life, including an education at private schools.

After graduating from high school, Salinger briefly attended New York University, Ursinus College, and Columbia University. In 1940, he published his first short story. Drafted in 1942, Salinger served as a sergeant in the counterintelligence corps. He participated in the D-Day invasion and the Battle of the Bulge and was hospitalized in Nuremberg for psychiatric reasons. Honorably discharged from the Army in 1946, Salinger returned to New York City.

Lit Wit

During World War II, Salinger met Ernest Hemingway in Paris. At their second meeting, he and Hemingway got into an argument over the merits of the German Luger versus the U.S. .45 caliber, and Hemingway blew the head off a chicken to make a point about the value of his gun. Put away the weapons, boys.

Once in New York, Salinger continued writing and publishing stories in *Collier's, Esquire,* and the *New Yorker.* His stories were well received by the critics but attracted little popular attention. But everything changed in 1951, with the publication of *The Catcher in the Rye.*

Kvetcher in the Rye

The Catcher in the Rye was a smash success. A Book-of-the-Month Club selection, it gave Salinger a huge audience. The popularity disturbed Salinger so much, however, that he ordered his portrait removed from subsequent printings of the book. He remarked later to a friend that "I feel tremendously relieved that the season for success for *The Catcher in the Rye* is nearly over. I enjoyed a small part of it, but most of it I found hectic and professionally and personally demoralizing."

Reviews of the novel were mixed, from out-and-out approval to questions about Salinger's attitudes, his use of the colloquial style, the focus on an adolescent boy, and the amount of s-e-x. As a result, *The Catcher in the Rye* is in the odd position of being just as often required reading as it is banned in high schools and colleges.

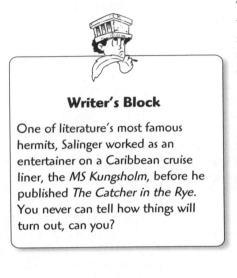

The novel's main character, Holden Caulfield, captured the mood of a generation of high school and college students. Holden has became a symbol for misunderstood youth. (John Lennon's assassin was clutching a copy of *The Catcher in the Rye* when he fired the fatal shots.) The public attention that followed the success of the book led Salinger to move from New York to the remote hills of Cornish, New Hampshire.

Hide-and-Seek

So reclusive that he makes Big Foot look like a party animal, Salinger now refuses all professional interviews (he did speak to a high school student a few years ago, however). He claims that he is still writing, although he has not published anything since 1953. Salinger-spotting has become a minor sport, like balancing spoons on your nose.

Writer's Block

One of literature's most famous hermits, Salinger worked as an entertainer on a Caribbean cruise liner, the *MS Kungsholm*, before he published *The Catcher in the Rye*. You never can tell how things will turn out, can you?

The Catcher in the Rye

Recovering from a mental breakdown in a California rest home (a fancy name for a mental institution), Holden Caufield, a 17-year-old high school junior, narrates his decline the previous December following his expulsion from Pencey Prep, an exclusive boy's prep school in Pennsylvania. Four days before the Christmas break, Holden is expelled because he has failed four out of five classes, passing only English.

Holden visits his former history teacher, Mr. Spencer, to say good-bye and then returns to his dorm and talks to Robert Ackley, the slovenly student who rooms next door. Holden's handsome roommate, Ward Stradlater, asks Holden to write a composition for him, borrows Holden's jacket, and dresses for a date with Jane Gallagher, Holden's old friend. Holden has dinner with friends and fights with Stradlater over Jane. In the middle of the night, Holden leaves Pencey and takes a train to New York City where he plans to stay until Wednesday, when he is expected home. By that time, the headmaster's letter will have arrived home with the news of his expulsion.

Once in New York, Holden takes a cab to the Edmont Hotel and calls an acquaintance named Faith Cavendish who refuses to meet him. He goes to the Lavender Room, the hotel nightclub, and dances with three women. Lonely and restless, he takes a cab to Ernie's, a Greenwich Village nightclub. Although the club is one of his brother B.D.'s favorite spots, Holden is put off by the insincere people he meets there.

Holden then walks the 41 blocks back to the Edmont Hotel, where Maurice, the elevator operator, offers to send him a prostitute for $5. Holden agrees, but when Sunny the prostitute arrives, he pretends to be recovering from surgery. Maurice then shakes Holden down for ten dollars.

The next day, Sunday, Holden invites his friend Sally Hayes to go to a Broadway show. He tries to explain his disillusionment with phonies, but Sally, herself a phony, doesn't understand. They quarrel. Holden meets Carl Luce, a friend from another school, but that meeting goes badly as well. After wandering around Central Park, Holden goes home where he awakens his 10-year-old sister, Phoebe, who is overjoyed to see him. He then visits a former English teacher, Mr. Antolini. Convinced that Antolini is making homosexual advances, Holden flees his apartment.

Holden decides to go West. He tells Phoebe of his plans, and she begs to come with him. He refuses but takes her to the zoo and park, where he watches her ride the carousel. Confused and unsure about whether to return to school the following September, Holden has a nervous breakdown. He ends his narrative from the mental institution.

The Catcher in the Rye won critical acclaim and thousands of devoted followers for its poignant description of a teenager trying to find his way in the world. Given Salinger's tremendous cult following, it's surprising to realize that his entire body of published works consists of this one novel and 13 short stories.

The Least You Need to Know

➤ The beat writers—William S. Burroughs, Jack Kerouac, and Allen Ginsberg—countered the hidden despair of the 1950s with wildly exuberant language and behavior.

➤ William S. Burroughs' best-known books are *Queer, Junky,* and *Naked Lunch.*

➤ Jack Kerouac's book *On the Road* captured the beats' ebullient spirit.

➤ Allen Ginsberg's poem "Howl" became the beat anthem.

➤ The "confessional" poets—Sylvia Plath, Anne Sexton, and Robert Lowell—used the anguish of their own lives to explore America's hidden despair.

➤ Sylvia Plath is the most famous confessional poet, as much for her suffering and suicide as for her poetry.

➤ Anne Sexton won a Pulitzer Prize in 1966 for *Live or Die;* she committed suicide less than a decade later.

➤ Robert Lowell produced 10 volumes of brilliant, anguished poetry.

➤ J.D. Salinger's *The Catcher in the Rye* became the symbol for a generation of disaffected youth.

Chapter 27

Horror and Humor (1930–1960)

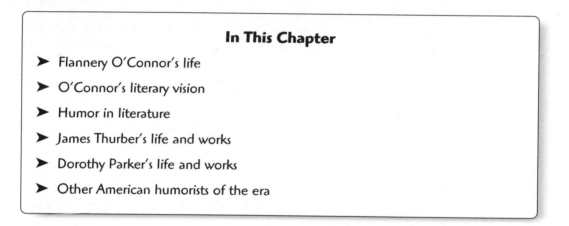

In This Chapter

➤ Flannery O'Connor's life

➤ O'Connor's literary vision

➤ Humor in literature

➤ James Thurber's life and works

➤ Dorothy Parker's life and works

➤ Other American humorists of the era

Three buddies die in a car crash and go to heaven for the orientation. They're all asked, "When you're in your casket being mourned, what would you like to hear your friends and family say about you?

The first guy says, "I'd like to hear them say that I was a great doctor and a great family man."

The second guy says, "I'd like to hear that I was a wonderful teacher who made a big difference in America's future leaders."

The last guy replied, "I'd like to hear them say—Look, *he's moving!*"

Humor and horror—they go together like love and marriage. Many of America's finest horror writers create stories with a touch of macabre humor that serves to intensify the chills and thrills. Our humorists find their own type of terror in courtship, the battle of the sexes, and everyday life. Their writing is funny, but let's not overlook the subtle undercurrent of apprehension.

In this chapter, you'll first meet Flannery O'Connor, one of the most intriguing writers of the second half of the 20th century. Labeled "Southern Gothic" for her obsession with death and dark humor, O'Connor's gallows humor reflected her vision of the world. The writings of New York wit Dorothy Parker have their own mordant humor, grimly ironic but more cosmopolitan than O'Connor's work. James Thurber created characters whose struggles against the unpleasant realities of life are both amusing and awesome.

Flannery O'Connor (1925–1964)

"To the hard of hearing you shout, and for the almost-blind you draw large and startling figures."

—Flannery O'Connor, *Mystery and Manners*

At first glance, Flannery O'Connor's writing is as subtle as a smack to the side of the head. Her stories are loaded with physical deformities, freak fatalities, and spiritual depravity. In one story, an entire family is violently murdered in the Georgia back-woods; in another, a con man disguised as a Bible salesman steals a woman's artificial leg—but not before displaying his collection of other faux body parts. For O'Connor, evil usually triumphs over good.

O'Connor admitted that her fiction could be called grotesque, though she cautioned that "anything that comes out of the South is going to be called grotesque by the northern reader, unless it *is* grotesque, in which case it is going to be called realistic." More than three decades after her death, readers are still shocked by O'Connor's grotesque images.

Peacocks and Pain

"…Highly unladylike…a brutal irony, a slam-bang humor, and a style of writing as balefully direct as a death sentence."

—*Time* magazine on Flannery O'Connor

The Write Stuff

You'll notice that peacocks frequently show up in O'Connor's work as part of her religious symbolism. They represent Christ.

Born in Savannah, Georgia, to devout Catholic parents, Mary Flannery O'Connor attended St. Vincent's grammar school and Sacred Heart parochial school. When Flannery was 13 years old, her father took a job as an appraiser for the Federal Housing Administration. The family first moved to northeast Atlanta, and then to Milledgeville, where, three years later, O'Connor's father died from complications arising from lupus, a chronic autoimmune disease.

O'Connor attended Georgia State College for Women (now Georgia College) and the State University of Iowa, receiving her Master of Fine Arts from the latter in 1947.

When she was 27, O'Connor published her first novel, *Wise Blood,* the story of a violent rivalry among the members of a fictional religious sect in the South.

At the same time, after complaining of a heaviness in her arms, she was diagnosed with lupus. Despite the disease, O'Connor went on to write two novels and 32 short stories, winning awards and acclaim, and going on speaking tours when her health permitted. Nonetheless, O'Connor spent most of her time on the family farm, Andalusia, in Milledgeville, with her mother. There, she raised peacocks. O'Connor died of lupus in 1964, at the age of 39.

Defender of the Faith

"When people have told me that because I am a Catholic, I cannot be an artist, I have to reply, ruefully, that because I am a Catholic I cannot afford to be less than an artist."

—Flannery O'Connor

O'Connor's work reflects her strong Catholic faith. She lived in the Southern Bible Belt and freely admitted that her friends and neighbors had a strong sense of the absolute. In O'Connor's stories, violent and grotesque characters often symbolize moral depravity and are driven to damnation. Their only salvation lies in divine awareness and redemption.

The Write Stuff

O'Connor is usually compared to William Faulkner, Nathanael West, Graham Greene, Eudora Welty, and Carson McCullers.

Lit Wit

In his article "The Power of Flannery O'Connor," critic Frederick Crews noted that "O'Connor's fiction regularly presents us with a grimmer, more godforsaken world than we could have guessed from her collected remarks about it. At the same time, however, that world is suffused with a portentousness whose undeniable source is the author's religion— her belief in a looming metaphysical presence that casts an ironic shadow on nearly everything her characters attempt to do. Her best writing is that in which 'mystery' as she called it, drastically intrudes on the mundane without requiring us to either embrace a dogma or to suspend our belief in naturalistic causation."

Flannery O'Connor was a Christian writer, and her work is message-oriented, yet she is far too brilliant a stylist to tip her hand; her writing stands up on both literary and religious grounds, and succeeds in doing justice to both.

Make Me Laugh, Make Me Cry

Humor in literature refers to the writer's attempts to evoke laughter or amusement. Humorists evoke yuks by pointing out comical, ludicrous, and ridiculous situations. In addition, humor writers may:

➤ Embellish events

➤ Use sarcasm

➤ Use word play

➤ Include irony

➤ Deliberately misuse words

➤ Exaggerate details

In general, humor doesn't age well. Who, after all, remembers Artemus Ward, Petroleum V. Nasby, or the other so-called "Funny Fellows" from the 19th century?

Almost no one outside universities. When it comes to humor, you just have to be there. Well, maybe not.

Mark Twain claimed: "Humor must not professedly teach, and must not professedly preach, but it must do both if it would live forever. By forever, I mean thirty years." Since most of the books written by James Thurber and Dorothy Parker are in print 30 years after the writers died, I think they've met Twain's standard. Let's see why these American humorists have withstood the test of time.

James Thurber (1894–1961)

"Humor is emotional chaos remembered in tranquillity."

—James Thurber

Born in Columbus, Ohio, Thurber lost his left eye when he was six years old during a game of William Tell with his brother. Despite this handicap, he attended Ohio State University from 1913 to 1918. Due to his vision problems, however, he failed gym and biology, and left the university in 1919 without earning a degree. He moved to New York City where he worked for the *Saturday Evening Post*. In 1927, he joined the staff of The *New Yorker* as staff writer and managing editor.

As with Henry James and T.S. Eliot, Thurber expatriated himself to Europe in the 1930s but returned to New York City with few prospects. The *New Yorker* offered to publish his work, a gesture Thurber repaid by contributing to the magazine's success many times over.

The *New Yorker* was an ideal forum for Thurber, and there his work flourished as he published drawings, stories, and bits of autobiography, the work that earned him fame and honor. Thurber was America's most popular humorist in the 1930s and 1940s. All told, he published more than 30 books.

Lit Wit

Many of Thurber's stories and full-length works have made a successful transition to the silver screen.. *She's Working Her Way Through College* (1952) is based on Thurber's *The Male Animal.* His story "The Secret Life of Walter Mitty" was expanded into a full-length motion picture with Danny Kaye as Walter Mitty. *The Battle of the Sexes* (1959) is a British movie based on "The Catbird Seat." *The War Between Men and Women* (1972) stars Barbara Harris and Jack Lemmon. Thurber even made it to the little screen: The TV show *My World and Welcome To It* (1969–1970) starred William Windom as a Thurber alter ego.

Fables for Our Time

"Thurber's genius was to make of our despair a humorous fable."

—John Updike

Fantasy was Thurber's forte. *Fables for Our Time* (1940) and *Further Fables for Our Time* (1956) remain among his most brilliant creations. Thurber knew that we are funny "in the face of the Awful." It is this knowledge that makes Thurber's fables as relevant today as they were a generation ago.

Perhaps as a result of his failed first marriage, Thurber's stories and fables depict wedlock as a series of power struggles between husbands and wives. However, in these early pieces, this conflict is lightened by touches of irony and idealistic optimism. A typical example is the fable "The Shrike and the Chipmunk." A female chipmunk leaves her husband and declares that he will never survive on his own; on the contrary, he carries along nicely until she returns and gets them both killed during a morning walk she insists on taking. The deeper meaning hinted at by this story—that marriage is not a good thing for men—is lightened

The Write Stuff

Thurber wrote both stories and fables. The former are conventional short stories; the latter, in contrast, have a moral.

by the humor in its moral, "Early to rise and early to bed makes a male healthy and wealthy and dead."

In comparison, darker meanings linger just beneath the surface of *Further Fables for Our Time*. The pessimism shown in these parables resulted from Thurber's revulsion toward the ongoing Red Scare of the 1950s; he composed the bulk of his political satire following the rise of Senator Joseph McCarthy. Thurber's "The Peacelike Mongoose," for instance, details the persecutions facing a mongoose who decides that he doesn't want to spend his life killing cobras. His neighbors and family treat him as deeply subversive and banish him from the colony. The fable's moral has a far darker edge than earlier stories, "Ashes to ashes and clay to clay, if the enemy doesn't get you, your own folks may."

The Secret Life of Walter Mitty

> *"The little wheels of invention are set in motion by the damp hand of melancholy."*
>
> —James Thurber

Thurber's most famous story is "The Secret Life of Walter Mitty," first published in the *New Yorker* in 1939. The story describes a middle-aged man, Walter Mitty, who is henpecked by his overbearing wife. Unhappy with his everyday life, Mitty dreams of grand adventure and heroism.

Lit Wit

Critic Charles S. Holmes said that "It is by now a truism to say that James Thurber is the greatest American humorist since Mark Twain. His imagination was tuned to the discords of the twentieth century with preternatural accuracy. In his stories, essays, and drawings we find comic images of our public and private apprehensions: the character of Walter Mitty, as *Time* magazine once said —stands as an archetype of modern man." Malcolm Cowley called Thurber's prose style one of the best in modern literature, and the *Times Literary Supplement* observed that almost alone among living American writers, Thurber was "comprehensible and lovable to the European mind as... to the mind of his countrymen."

"Walter Mitty" epitomizes Thurber's depiction of the characters he called "Perfect Neurotics." Commenting on these characters, Thurber said, "They lead an existence of jumpiness and apprehension. In the house of Life they have the feeling they have never taken off their overcoats."

Thurber is celebrated for his vision of the urban man needing to escape into fantasy because he is befuddled and beset by a world he neither created nor understands. Thurber's best-known portrait of this character is Walter Mitty, a timid, hapless man who nonetheless outsmarts his overbearing wife by retreating into a rich inner life.

Dorothy Parker (1893–1967)

In the 1920s, Dorothy Parker became a symbol of the liberated woman for her wit and independence. Her clever comments were often quoted in New York gossip columns. Here are some of her most famous witticisms:

➤ "I thought the play was frightful but I saw it under particularly unfortunate circumstances. The curtain was up."

➤ On learning that Calvin Coolidge was dead, she remarked, "How could they tell?"

➤ "You can lead a horticulture but you can't make her think."

➤ "Are you Dorothy Parker?" a guest at a party inquired. "Yes, do you mind?" she replied.

➤ In a book review: "This is not a novel to be tossed aside lightly. It should be thrown aside with great force."

➤ "Brevity is the soul of lingerie."

➤ In a 1933 review of the play "The Lake" starring Katherine Hepburn: "Miss Hepburn runs the gamut of emotions from A to B."

➤ Of the play "The House Beautiful": "The House Beautiful is The Play Lousy."

Born in New York City, Dorothy Rothschild was educated at a private high school. Rather than attending a university,

Dorothy took a job with *Vogue*, the fashion magazine, writing captions for photographs. In her free time, she wrote poetry. When she was 24 years old, Dorothy took a job with *Vanity Fair,* a slick, sophisticated magazine. She and Robert Benchley, the magazine's managing editor, hit it off and became close friends. Robert Sherwood, the drama editor, soon joined the group.

The three *Vanity Fair* writers often ate lunch at the Algonquin Hotel. Soon, they were joined by other journalists, including Franklin Pierce Adams, a humor columnist, and Harold Ross, the founder of the *New Yorker*. This group formed the center of about two dozen of New York's most famous writers, dramatists, and actors. The so-called "Algonquin Group" became famous for its collective wit. When they were in town, the Marx Brothers often dropped by for a drink and a joke.

Lit Speak

The **Algonquin Group** was a loosely organized group of New York City writers who met for lunch and witty repartee at the Algonquin Hotel during the 1920s.

In 1917, Dorothy married Edwin Pond Parker II and became Dorothy Parker. The name change lasted far, far longer than the marriage, which ended in 1928. Canned from *Vanity Fair* for her harsh reviews, Parker became a freelance writer. Life was hard, and twice she attempted suicide. Parker's life improved in 1926 when her book of poems, *Enough Rope,* was published and became a bestseller. Although she published two other books of poems during this time, *Sunset Gun* (1928) and *Death and Taxes* (1931), Parker's reputation was built on her short stories.

In 1929, Parker won the important O. Henry short story award for her story "Big Blond."

Lit Speak

People suspected of being or having been Communists were **blacklisted** during the 1950s and closed out of many fields, including acting, writing, and defense jobs.

She published a stunning series of superb stories during the Depression years. Parker's stories were most often observant studies of the contrast between appearance and reality.

In 1933, Parker married the actor Alan Campbell. Together, they wrote some fine screenplays and were well paid for their work. As with many intellectuals during the 1930s, Parker became a socialist sympathizer. The ideological move would come back to haunt her in the McCarthy era of the conservative 1950s, when she and Campbell were blacklisted and unable to get work. Campbell died in 1963 while Parker endured four years of isolation and poverty before her death in New York City in 1967.

Legends of Laughter

Other American humorists also left their mark on the national consciousness. Among the most popular were Robert Benchley, the Marx Brothers, and Will Rogers. Let's take a look at them now.

➤ **Robert Benchley (1889–1945)** Benchley was one of the most prolific and popular writers of his time. Born in Massachusetts and educated at Harvard, Benchley went into journalism and eventually served as editor of *Vanity Fair.* In his later years, he worked as a drama critic for *Life* and the *New Yorker.* His essay collections include *Pluck and Luck* (1925); *20,000 Leagues Under the Sea, or David Copperfield* (1928*); From Bad to Worse, or Comforting the Bison* (1934); and *My Ten Years in a Quandary, Or How They Grew* (1936).

Lit Wit

Robert Benchley's son, Peter Benchley, wrote the blockbuster movie *Jaws*.

➤ **Will Rogers (1879–1935)** Humorist and writer Will Rogers was born in Oologah, Indian territory (now park of Oklahoma). Rogers got his start in vaudeville with a lasso act in New York City. Later, he added a funny running monologue as he threw the rope, which greatly improved the show. Known for his gentle, self-effacing humor, Rogers became an American icon. His homespun "aw-shucks" manner disguised his brilliant barbs and added to his humor and popularity. Tragically, Rogers was killed when an airplane he was piloting crashed in Alaska. His books include *The Cowboy Philosopher on Prohibition* (1919) and *Will Rogers' Political Follies* (1929).

➤ **The Marx Brothers** Chico Marx (Leonard, 1891–1961), Harpo Marx (Arthur, 1893–1954), Groucho Marx (Julius, 1895–1977), and Zeppo Marx (Herbert, 1901–1979) wrote movies whose humor has become legendary. Trained as musicians, the Marx brothers began their careers in vaudeville as the "Six Musical Mascots." Their films include *Animal Crackers* (1930), *Horse Feathers* (1932), and *Duck Soup* (1933). After Zeppo retired in 1935, Harpo, Chico, and Groucho appeared with enormous success in *Night at the Opera* (1935), *A Day at the Races* (1937), and *Room Service* (1938).

Each brother was easily identifiable: Groucho had a huge (and early in his career, fake) mustache and a sharp wit, Chico spoke in an Italian accent and played the piano, and Harpo communicated in mime and played the harp. Zeppo was in on the early antics, but retired in 1935 before the big movies—*A Night at the Opera, A Day at the Races,* and *Room Service.*

After the brothers ended their film career, Groucho moved to the small screen as master of ceremonies in *You Bet Your Life.*

The Least You Need to Know

➤ The Southern Gothic writer Flannery O'Connor created stories that simultaneously shock readers and reflect her strong Catholic faith.

➤ Humorist writers evoke yuks by pointing out comical, ludicrous, and ridiculous situations.

➤ James Thurber was America's most popular humorist in the 1930s and 1940s.

➤ Thurber's most common theme is the battle between the sexes; his most famous story is "The Secret Life of Walter Mitty."

➤ In the 1920s, Dorothy Parker became a symbol of the liberated woman for her wit and independence. She is known for her caustic and clever poems and short stories.

➤ Robert Benchley, Will Rogers, and the Marx Brothers were other well-known American humorists of the time.

Part 6
Contemporary Literature (1946–Present)

"'I didn't want to harm the man. I thought he was a very nice gentleman. Soft-spoken. I thought so right up to the moment I cut his throat.'"

—Truman Capote, In Cold Blood

Contemporary American literature has been characterized by a tremendous variety of forms, techniques, and outlooks. Some writers embrace fantasy, myth, and innovative style, while others return to more traditional means of expression.

In this section, you'll read about a rich range of literature. There will be stories of optimism, despair, cynicism, violence, abnormality, anger, absurdity, and mysticism, along with revivals of religion, folklore, and myth.

Such variety has produced a degree of confusion among literary scholars, but everyone agrees that American literature is far from stagnant. Rather, it's as vital as the teeming diversity of the current American life it reflects.

Chapter 28

Jewish-American Literature

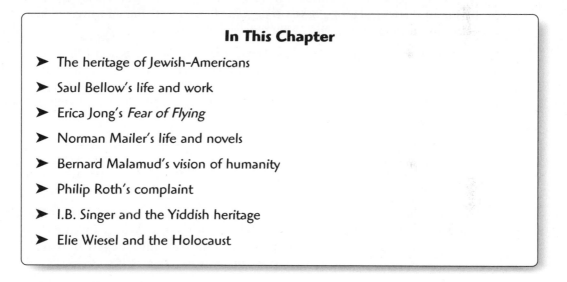

In This Chapter

➤ The heritage of Jewish-Americans

➤ Saul Bellow's life and work

➤ Erica Jong's *Fear of Flying*

➤ Norman Mailer's life and novels

➤ Bernard Malamud's vision of humanity

➤ Philip Roth's complaint

➤ I.B. Singer and the Yiddish heritage

➤ Elie Wiesel and the Holocaust

The Jewish-American culture has given us a group of great writers. This chapter high-lights some of the most talented 20th-century Jewish-American writers, the men and women most closely identified with their cultural heritage. These writers include Saul Bellow, Erica Jong, Norman Mailer, Bernard Malamud, Philip Roth, I.B. Singer, and Elie Wiesel. Each presents a unique vision of what it means to be American, Jewish, and a writer, yet are all united by their common culture.

Lit Wit

Other well-known Yiddish writers include I.J. Singer (Isaac's brother), Sholem Asch, Shalom Aleichem, Isaac Loeb Peretz, I.M. Weissenberg, Avrom Reisen, H.D. Nomberg, David Bergelson, Mani Leyb, Moyshe-Leib Halpern, and Joseph Opatoshu.

Gentleman's Agreement

Jewish culture is one of the foundations of Western civilization, but as the "outsiders" to Christianity, Jews in Europe have been characterized as the alien—mysterious, fearsome, and unrelenting in their adherence to the faith.

When the promise of freedom in America beckoned in the 1800s and 1900s, Jews heeded her siren call. Optimistic and ambitious for each new generation, Jewish immigrants saw their children merge with American life. While traditionalists mourned the loss of Jewish identity, modernists thought assimilation offered the best chance of survival.

But even though the overt restrictions of Europe were removed, America had its own form of discrimination against Jewish people. In terms of literature, the dominance of the WASPs in the 1930s-1950s shut out many Jewish writers (of course, this was true of all "ethnic" writers—Asian, Hispanic, Native American, and African-American).

For quite a while, some Jewish writers maintained a separate culture in Yiddish newspapers and theaters. However, the events surrounding World War II and the Holocaust aroused world attention and interest in "Jewish" literature and the Jewish writer. Ironically, alienation became a passport to the mainstream culture.

The 1950s and 1960s saw a shift in concerns for Jewish-Americans. Though anti-Semitism was still an inescapable fact of life, the post–World War II era saw many Jews finding a measure of acceptance within the non-Jewish world. This was also reflected in the rise in popularity of Jewish writers. Saul Bellow, for example, synthesized the conflicts of modern life in ordinary Jewish people, while Bernard Malamud explored how Jewish folk wisdom operated in the contemporary world. Since then Jewish self-consciousness manifested itself in the poetry of Stanley Kunitz, Delmore Schwartz, and Karl Shapiro, as well as in the dramas of Arthur Miller.

Jewish-American fiction became important for its treatment of the history of persecution and the process of assimilation. By the 1950s, the Jewish-American hero—victim, survivor, joker, and voice of moral conscience—had come of age.

Saul Bellow (b. 1915)

When Saul Bellow was awarded the Nobel Prize for Literature in 1976, the citation read: "For the human understanding and subtle analysis of contemporary culture that are combined in his work." The Nobel committee was right on the mark.

Born in Lachine, Quebec, Bellow grew up in the Jewish ghetto of Montreal and moved to Chicago when he was nine years old. He attended the University of Chicago, but ultimately earned his degree from Northwestern University. After a tour in the Merchant Marines during World War II, Bellow taught English at New York University and Princeton, and he spent some time in Paris. In 1962, he returned to Chicago, where he settled.

A late starter, Bellow was nearly 30 when his first novel, *The Dangling Man*, appeared. Brief and elegant, the novel takes the form of a journal. Then came *The Victim* (1947), which describes a week in the life of one Asa Leventhal, confronted by a figure from his past. Naturalistic and dark, *The Victim* describes a man brought up against forces far greater than he is.

Saul Bellow.

Bellow's writing then took a humorous turn with *The Adventures of Augie March* (1953) and *Henderson the Rain King* (1959). *Augie March* won the National Book Award for fiction in 1954. Critics hailed its vitality, richness, originality, and powerful affirmation that life is worth living.

To many critics, Bellow's finest novel of this era is *Seize the Day*, the bitter comedy that tells the story of a former actor. In *Mr. Sammler's Planet* (1970), Bellow's fiction once again takes a grim turn, as Sammler, an elderly Jew, sees everywhere the "poverty of soul" but admits he has "a touch of the same disease—the disease of the single self explaining what was what and who was who."

Bellow's more recent novels, such as *Him with His Foot in His Mouth* (1984) and *More Die of Heartbreak* (1987) concentrate on the turmoil of modern life, with a comic turn.

Erica Jong (b. 1942)

Erica Jong was catapulted to international fame in 1973 at the age of 31 with the publication of her ribald first novel, *Fear of Flying.* One of the top 10 best-selling novels of the 1970s, *Fear of Flying* describes Isadora Wing's quest for emotional and sexual fulfillment. Jong's heroine aspires to be "one lusty lady who had juice and joy and love and talent too," qualities she shares with her creator. Jong's wry and witty writing celebrates the treats and tricks that await women who seek emotional and sexual satisfaction in contemporary America.

Jong's writing was groundbreaking because she was one of the first women writers to approach sex in such a modern way (for example, acknowledging the desire to have sex with a stranger). Her feelings were previously seen as feelings only a man would have.

Born Erica Mann in New York City, Jong grew up on Manhattan's upper west side. As an undergraduate at Barnard College, she majored in writing and literature, earning her B.A. in 1963 and her M.A. two years later. Her first collection of poetry, *Fruits & Vegetables,* appeared in 1971, followed two years later by *Half-Lives.* Praised by Louis Untermeyer, a well-respected American writer and editor of poetry anthologies, as "sly but penetrating, witty but passionate, bawdy and beautiful," Jong's poems garnered a handful of awards.

Jong's second novel, *How to Save Your Own Life,* tracked Isadora Wing's further adventures. The third installment of the Isadora Wing trilogy was *Parachutes & Kisses* (1984). Greeted by the Associated Press as "Jong's best book," it portrayed Isadora at 39 after three broken marriages and more than her share of fame. The story left her in love again in Venice.

Throughout her career, Jong has also continued to publish more poetry collections: *At the Edge of the Body* (1979), a group of metaphysical poems; and *Ordinary Miracles* (1983), poems on childbirth. *Fanny, Being the*

The Write Stuff

Novelist Henry Miller, no slouch in the sex department himself, said *Fear of Flying* "opened the door for women to find their own voices and give us great sagas of sex, life, joy and adventure."

Writer's Block

Jong writes about the concerns of well-educated, affluent modern women in general; as such, her writing cannot be specifically labeled "Jewish." (Nonetheless, Jong is identified as a "Jewish" writer for her wit as much as her religion.)

True History of the Adventures of Fanny Hackabout-Jones, Jong's picaresque response to the question "What if Tom Jones had been a woman?" was hailed by the *New York Times* as a "quantum leap, a literary prodigy." It was also a bestseller.

Inventing Memory: A Novel of Mothers and Daughters, was published in 1997. A four-generation saga about a Jewish family in America, *Inventing Memory* is the story of four women who embody life in the 20th century. In her novels, collections of poetry, and articles, Jong continues to celebrate women's strengths and possibilities with energy and passion.

Norman Mailer (b. 1923)

As critic Richard Poirier put it, Norman Mailer "has exhibited a literary ambition that can best be called 'imperialistic.' He has wanted to translate his life into a literary career and then translate that literary career into history."

Like all imperialists, Mailer has stepped on more than a few toes in his quest to conquer and succeed. Mailer successfully developed a form of journalism that conveys actual events with the subjective richness and imaginative complexity of the novel. His bold style and rich use of language often blurred the line between journalism and fiction.

Norman Mailer was born in Long Branch, New Jersey. He graduated from Boys High School in 1939 and then studied at Harvard, earning a degree in aeronautical engineering. Despite his choice of majors, Mailer had already decided to become a great American novelist. He had decided that he was going to be one of America's great writers.

During World War II, Mailer was a sergeant in the Army. He enlisted deliberately—not to fight, necessarily, but rather to get the material he needed for a great war novel. Honorably discharged in 1946, in the next 15 months he wrote *The Naked and the Dead,* drawing on his combat experiences in the Philippines. The novel, published two years later, may not have been the greatest war novel to emerge from the conflict, but it was unquestionably a very, very good one. Those who liked it hailed the book as one of the finest American novels of World War II; those who did not criticized it as obscene and motivated by personal disgust with army life.

After a stint in the late 1940s as a Hollywood screenwriter, Mailer moved to Greenwich Village in New York City. His next big novel, *The Deer Park* (1955), was a thinly disguised account of his marriage to Adele Morales. In 1960, he stabbed Adele at the end of an all-night party in Manhattan. He received a suspended sentence, however,

The Write Stuff

The Naked and the Dead describes a group of American soldiers stationed on a Japanese-held island in the Pacific. Flashbacks illuminate their past and mix with feverish combat scenes.

Norman Mailer.

when Adele refused to press charges. During this period of his life, Mailer experimented with drugs, new fictional forms, marriage, and divorce. Of all his experiments, the writing proved most successful.

In the mid-1950s, Mailer started to gain fame as an antiestablishment essayist. He cofounded the *Village Voice,* one of the earliest underground American newspapers. Mailer's collection of essays, *The Presidential Papers* (1963), established him as one of the most vigorous essayists in America. In the 1960s and 1970s, he won admiration with his books *The Armies of the Night* (1968), *Miami and the Siege of Chicago* (1968) and *Of a Fire on the Moon* (1970).

Writer's Block

In the 1970s, Mailer became a target of feminist attacks and was depicted as the quintessential male chauvinist pig in Kate Millett's *Sexual Politics.*

In 1979, Mailer published a highly successful true-life novel, *The Executioner's Song,* based on the life and death of convicted killer, Gary Gilmore.

An outrageous public figure, Mailer ran for mayor of New York City, married and divorced a few more times (he is currently with his sixth wife), fathered many children, appeared on late-night talk shows, and made various films. Whether he has lived up to his ambitions remains to be seen, but the immense quantity of his work and the high quality of some of it sets him apart from many of his fellow writers.

Bernard Malamud (1914–1986)

"Well, we were here, first-generation Americans, our language was English and a language is a spiritual mansion from which no one can evict us. Malamud in his novels and stories discovered a sort of communicative genius in the impoverished, harsh jargon of immigrant New York. He was a myth maker, a fabulist, a writer of exquisite parables. The English novelist Anthony Burgess said of him that he 'never forgets that he is an American Jew, and he is at his best when posing the situation of a Jew in urban American society.' 'A remarkably consistent writer,' he goes on, 'who has never produced a mediocre novel... He is devoid of either conventional piety or sentimentality... always profoundly convincing.' Let me add on my own behalf that the accent of hard-won and individual emotional truth is always heard in Malamud's words. He is a rich original of the first rank."

—Saul Bellow's eulogy for Malamud, 1986

Malamud was one of a number of post–World War II writers whose works draw heavily on their urban New York, Jewish backgrounds. His stories often dramatize the tension arising out of the clash between Jewish conscience and American energy and materialism: the difficulty of keeping alive the Jewish sense of community in American society. His Jewish characters become symbols of all Americans trying to maintain a link with their cultural heritage while coping with the realities of contemporary life.

Born in Brooklyn, New York, the son of Russian immigrants, Malamud lived above the family's grocery store. Both English and Yiddish were spoken at home, and the Malamud family enjoyed attending shows at the Second Avenue Yiddish Theater.

After attending City College (B.A. 1936) and Columbia University (M.A. 1942), Malamud began publishing his short stories in a number of well-known magazines. In 1952, he published his first novel, *The Natural,* which describes the life of a talented baseball player. This was followed by *The Assistant* (1957), *A New Life* (1961), *Pictures of Fidelman* (1969), *The Tenants* (1971), and *God's Grace* (1982). *The Fixer* (1966) won both a National Book Award and a Pulitzer Prize. Malamud's poignant short stories are also collected in *The Magic Barrel* (1958), winner of the National Book Award in 1959, *Idiots First* (1963), and *Rembrandt's Hat* (1973).

Philip Roth (b. 1933)

"Portnoy's Complaint...A disorder in which strongly-felt ethical and altruistic impulses are perpetually warring with extreme sexual longings, usually of a perverse nature... It is believed by Spielvogel that many of the symptoms can be traced to the bonds obtaining in the mother-child relationship."

—Philip Roth, *Portnoy's Complaint*

For nearly 40 years, Philip Roth has been one of the most successful and controversial writers in American literature. First thrust into the spotlight in 1959 by the success of the novel *Goodbye, Columbus,* Roth later achieved even greater acclaim and celebrity with the hugely popular novel *Portnoy's Complaint* (1969). The novel is shocking, crude, and wildly entertaining. The story concerns Alexander Portnoy's memories of his early childhood miseries. Portnoy's memories include hilarious—and often scatalogical—tales of growing up in New Jersey, listening to radio programs, playing softball, ogling girls, and seeking self-gratification in the most outlandish ways.

Roth's work reflects the changing attitude of Jews living in post–World War II America. His stories exemplify a collective identity in turmoil, where the affluence and prosperity of the time is tempered by the memories of the Holocaust. *Goodbye, Columbus,* for example, describes Jewish-Americans on the verge of being or already having been assimilated into the larger American culture—complete with all the conflicts a change in identity can bring.

Roth differs from the other Jewish-American writers, however, by presenting characters who can at any moment play into or out of traditional stereotypes. He also shows how Jews can be victimized by other Jews, as much as by bigots. His daring subject matter sets him apart from his contemporaries, making him a singular identity in both American and Jewish literature.

Born in Newark, New Jersey, Roth attended public schools, followed by Newark College and Rutgers University. He earned his B.A. from Bucknell University and his M.A. from the University of Chicago. In 1955, Roth enlisted in the Army and worked in the Public Information Office in Washington, D.C. Discharged because of a back injury, he began teaching and working on his Ph.D. at the University of Chicago. At the same time, Roth was publishing his short stories.

After the success of *Goodbye, Columbus,* Roth established a pattern of writing and teaching that continued even after the notoriety and acclaim that greeted *Portnoy's Complaint.* After a foray into outrageousness *(The Breast,* 1971),

Roth returned to the topics of his best work: marriage, divorce, family, and his identity as a Jew. These concerns lie at the center of his best works to date, *Zuckerman Bound* (1985) and *The Counterlife* (1987).

Isaac Bashevis Singer (1904–1991)

"Since Yiddish literature is the most unnecessary of all, we are absolutely free. We have no readers. We can say the deepest things. Nobody will say that he doesn't understand."

—I.B. Singer

Ironically, Singer discovered that his writing, far from being isolated, made him one of the most celebrated American writers of his generation.

Born in 1904, Singer was raised in Bilgoray, Poland, in a grim and cheerless family. Surrounded by a weak father, an angry mother, a resentful older brother, and a sister suffering from undiagnosed epilepsy, Singer retreated into "scribbling" as a way to avoid his stressful family. He was "a loner, a solitary observer of the world, a balcony enthusiast who loved to watch from a safe distance," as he later claimed.

In his late teens, Singer followed his brother, Israel Joshua, to Warsaw, where he was introduced to the intimate and fiercely competitive world of Yiddish writers. There Singer had his first experiences with "liberated" female Jewish writers and artists. Having escaped the claustrophobic confines of his Orthodox upbringing, Singer began the womanizing that would characterize his adult life. The quaint, grandfatherly, pigeon-feeding, vegetarian got around.

Lit Wit

Singer is the only Yiddish writer to have won the Nobel Prize for literature (1978).

The Land of Milk and Honey

Singer followed his brother to America in 1935, abandoning an illegitimate child. He first settled in Brooklyn, and then in Manhattan. Working in his brother's shadow—I.J. Singer wrote two well-received Yiddish novels—Singer strove to establish himself by writing prose and fiction for Yiddish publications. In 1940, he married Alma Haimann Wassermann, a German-born fellow refugee who would remain with him until his death. He could not have found a woman with whom he had less in common.

Writer's Block

Men who knew Singer claimed that he was unscrupulous, ungenerous, and unreliable; women, that he was capricious, captivating, and childlike.

Not until 1950 was his writing translated into English, with his novel *The Family Moskat.* Years of struggle followed, until his novels finally reached a wide audience. Singer's fabulous tales are filled with demons and schlemiels, wild plots, and even wilder resolutions.

Lit Wit

Yiddish is the chief language of the Ashkenazic Jews from eastern and central Europe. One of the Germanic languages, Yiddish is written in Hebrew characters. In the early 20th century, Yiddish was spoken by an estimated 11 million people living mainly in eastern Europe and the U.S. The number of people using Yiddish has declined sharply since then, although it is being taught around the world.

The speed with which Yiddish words and phrases have entered English is dazzling. Leo Rosten, an expert on Yiddish, once commented that a person couldn't spend a day in any major American city without hearing a cluster of words gathered from Yiddish. Here's a brief primer to get you started:

Yiddish Word	Meaning
boyckick	boy
bupkes	nothing
dreck	garbage
klutz	clumsy person
maven	expert
mish–mosh	confusion
noodge	nag
plotz	explode
schlemiel	fool
yenta	gossip

Lit Speak

To **bear witness** is to give first-hand testimony about the Holocaust.

Elie Wiesel (b. 1928)

"We know that every moment is a moment of grace, every hour is an offering; not to share them would be to betray them. Our lives no longer belong to us alone; they belong to all those who need us desperately."

—Elie Wiesel, 1986 Nobel Peace Prize acceptance speech

In 1944, when Elie Wiesel was 15 years old, the Nazis marched into his village in Romania and took him and his family to the concentration camps. Only Wiesel and his two older sisters survived. Wiesel fled to France and began trying to reassemble his life.

At first, Wiesel could not bear to think about the tragedy that had befallen his family, his people, and the world. Finally, he was persuaded to "bear witness" to what he had seen.

The result was *Night* (1958), his experience in the concentration camps as a boy. The book also describes his father's experiences in the death camps. The novel describes a boy torn by guilt and anguish over the annihilation of his people. The theme is the loss of his belief in God.

In 1956, Wiesel came to the United States and became a citizen seven years later. Since the publication of *Night,* Wiesel has been a tireless "witness" to the Holocaust. Awarded the Nobel Peace Prize in 1986, Wiesel pledged to speak out not only for Jewish people but also for oppressed people the world over.

Lit Speak

The **Holocaust** refers to Hitler's systematic destruction of European Jews in World War II. In 1941, the Nazis came up with the "final solution to the Jewish question"— death. A month later, the Jews of Germany were marked with a yellow star and tens of thousands were deported to ghettos in Poland. At the same time, camps equipped with facilities for gassing people were built in Poland. By the war's end, about 6 million Jews perished: 3 million in Nazi concentration camps, 1.4 million in shooting operations, and more than 600,000 in ghettos.

The Least You Need to Know

➤ The 1950s and 1960s saw the rise in popularity of Jewish-American writers.

➤ Nobel laureate Saul Bellow's novels concentrate on the turmoil of modern Jewish life.

➤ Erica Jong produces ribald, exuberant, feminist poems, novels, and essays. Her most famous novel is *Fear of Flying.*

➤ Norman Mailer is famous for his writing, as well as for his marriages, divorces, and media hype.

➤ Bernard Malamud was a myth-maker, a fabulist, and a writer of exquisite parables.

➤ Philip Roth's work reflects the changing attitudes of Jews living in post–World War II America. His most famous book is *Portnoy's Complaint* (1967).

➤ Nobel laureate Isaac Bashevis Singer is known for his wild stories, written originally in Yiddish and filled with demons and fabulous events.

➤ Nobel laureate Elie Wiesel describes the horrors of the Holocaust.

Chapter 29

Contemporary African-American Literature

In This Chapter

➤ Ralph Ellison and *Invisible Man*

➤ Gwendolyn Brooks' poems

➤ James Baldwin's novels

➤ Maya Angelou's life and work

➤ Nobel laureate Toni Morrison's achievements

➤ Alice Walker's writings

➤ Jamaica Kincaid's accomplishments

"We will be ourselves and free, or die in the attempt. Harriet Tubman was not our grand-mother for nothing."

—Alice Walker, *You Can't Keep a Good Woman Down*

The end of World War II plunged America into many unexpected situations—not the least of which was the flood of African-American veterans, full of high hopes and aspirations for full citizenship. America was forced to begin anew its search for answers to questions that had gone unanswered since 1865.

This chapter opens with a brief history of black literature in the second half of the 20th century, focusing on the Black Power movement and civil rights. Then you'll read about America's outstanding black writers of the modern age. The discussion starts with the classic writers Ralph Ellison, Gwendolyn Brooks, and James Baldwin. Then it moves on to the brilliant contributions of Maya Angelou, Toni Morrison, Alice Walker, and Jamaica Kincaid.

I Have A Dream

Martin Luther King Jr. had a dream of equality for all men and women, regardless of their creed and color. The American clergyman and Nobel laureate (1929-1968) was one of the principal leaders of the American civil rights movement and a prominent advocate of nonviolent resistance to racial oppression. By the time Ralph Ellison published his masterpiece *Invisible Man* in 1952, assimilation into the mainstream was no longer a crucial need or demand of African-Americans, thanks in great part to the work of Dr. King.

The black individual's dilemma in America had become a worldwide issue, linked with the world's postwar concern with problems of personal identity and invisibility. James Baldwin's novels and essays, especially *Go Tell It on the Mountain* (1953), probed the psychological and political parameters of the black experience within a predominantly white America. Even as a cultural concept of "blackness" was crystallizing, two events occurred in America that determined race relations in our country for decades to come.

Black Power

The first event took place in 1948 in a maximum-security prison in Massachusetts, when Malcolm X (a former Harlem racketeer known as "Big Red") became a Muslim. By the time Malcolm X was installed as minister of a Black Muslim temple in Harlem six years later, he had become a vocal, abrasive, and charismatic speaker for America's largest black separatist movement. His radical militancy acquired a large following, especially among African-American youths, and stimulated considerable literary activity.

The Civil Rights Movement

The second event occurred at the end of 1955 in Montgomery, Alabama, when a tired seamstress, Mrs. Rosa Parks, refused to give up her seat on a bus to a white man, as demanded by Montgomery's segregationist city ordinance.

Her arrest and the subsequent local bus boycott catapulted a little-known Baptist minister—Dr. Martin Luther King, Jr.—to national prominence. His leadership in the civil rights movement changed the course of history and set off an outburst of literary creativity.

Today, African-Americans are free from slavery's bonds, but racial discrimination still exists. The difference between the present and the past, however, is that now America has hundreds and hundreds of black writers to protest, question, change, and record history. This chapter can only do justice to a handful of these outstanding literary figures, so we'll concentrate on the writers whose works have so far withstood the test of time. Let's start with Ralph Ellison, one of America's key literary figures at mid-century.

Ralph Ellison (1914–1994)

"If the Negro, or any other writer, is going to do what's expected of him, he's lost the battle before he takes the field."

—Ralph Ellison

Ellison was true to his word: He followed his own heart, insisting on being an eclectic writer rather than a speaker for any one cause.

Perhaps most surprising of all, he published only one novel; nonetheless, he is ranked as one of the most influential black American writers of the 20th century. The novel, *Invisible Man* (1952), expounds the theme of black invisibility in an American society that willfully ignores blacks.

The novel tells the story of an unnamed young Southern black man's journey from innocence to experience as he searches, first in the South and then in the North, for his place in the world. Ellison uses rich, varied, and powerful language to portray the black experience in all its vitality and complexity.

The Write Stuff

Invisible Man was one of the first novels to describe modern racial problems in the United States from a black American point of view. It received the National Book Award for fiction in 1953.

Ebony and Ivory

Ellison was born in 1914 in Oklahoma and attended Tuskegee University on a scholarship, where he majored in music. Although Ellison was serious about his music, literature eventually became his life. With Richard Wright's encouragement and assistance, Ellison began to publish reviews and short stories.

Based on the success of *Invisible Man,* Ellison taught in a number of fine colleges. In 1970, he accepted a professorship at New York University, where he remained until his retirement in 1979.

In 1985, Ellison was one of the first recipients of the National Medal of Arts award. At his death, his long-awaited second novel, delayed in part by the destruction of hundreds of pages in a 1967 fire, was left uncompleted. In 1995, *The Collected Essays of Ralph Ellison* was published.

Invisible Man

The novel's opening section, a truly horrifying vision, has become a famous set piece. A timid and agreeable young African-American man arrives at a white social event in a Southern town, where he is to be awarded a scholarship. Together with several other black youths, he is rushed to the front of the ballroom, where a sumptuous blonde tantalizes and frightens them by dancing in the nude. Blindfolded, the scholarship honorees are ordered to stage a battle royal, a free-for-all in which they pummel each other to the drunken shouts of the whites. After the humiliation and terror of these events, the young man delivers a prepared speech of gratitude to his white benefactors.

Lit Wit

In "Man Underground," Saul Bellow's review of *Invisible Man*, Bellow focuses on the opening episode: "This episode, I thought, might well be the high point of an excellent novel. It has turned out to be not the high point but rather one of the many peaks of a book of the very first order, a superb book... it is an immensely moving novel and it has greatness."

Nothing, fortunately, in the rest of the novel is quite so harrowing. The novel's nameless narrator (the Invisible Man) represents many intelligent young African-Americans of his generation. Born and raised in the rural South, he is an outstanding student at a predominantly black college. He dreams of success through humility and hard work, a doctrine preached by the school and the larger Southern culture.

The unnamed hero is expelled for innocently taking a white donor through a black gin mill in the black ghetto.

Bearing what he believes to be a letter of recommendation from the university president, Dr. Bledsoe, the Invisible Man moves to New York. The letter actually warns prospective employers against him.

Once in New York, he gets a job in a factory but soon loses it. Next, the Invisible Man accepts an offer to give speeches for the Harlem Communists and becomes a big wheel in the African-American political world and the darling of a Stalinist bohemia.

Through the radical movement, he eventually learns that throughout his entire life his relations with other people have been shallow and unfulfilling. Neither with blacks nor with whites has he ever been visible or real. Finally, he decides to live underground as a truly invisible man after witnessing a frenzied riot in Harlem.

Lit Speak

A **gin mill** is a slang term for a cheap bar.

The naive young man is "educated" by being slowly disabused of all his ideals. Despite this, he ultimately chooses to reject cynicism and hatred and to embrace a philosophy of hope. Ellison wanted his novel to transcend the rage and hopelessness of the protest novel and assert a world of possibility, however remote.

Ellison's *Invisible Man* was what both made and destroyed him. In one stroke, the novel established its author as America's preeminent African-American writer. But at the same time, it set him up against many African-American intellectuals, who argued for a clearer statement of blacks as victims. No less obsessed with questions of race than his fellow African-American writers, Ellison nonetheless insisted on his vision of America as a place where blacks and whites are inextricably tied together.

As we're going to press, Ellison's posthumous novel *Juneteenth* is scheduled for publication. The thousands of pages of manuscript Ellison left behind at his death have been edited to a still-sprawling novel that deals with the Big Themes of race, religion, and identity. The novel aims to give a voice to the entire American experience. Check it out, reader, to see what Ellison accomplished the second time around.

Writer's Block

Invisible Man reflects the rhetorical richness of the African–American culture through Ellison's use of a wide range of idiomatic styles.

Gwendolyn Brooks (b. 1917)

"Our earth is round, and, among other things

That means that you and I can hold

completely different

Points of view and both be right."

—Gwendolyn Brooks, "Corners on the Curving Sky"

Gwendolyn Brooks was born in Topeka, Kansas, and moved to Chicago when she was a toddler. She published her first poem when she was only 13 years old. In 1936, Brooks graduated from Wilson Junior College and embarked on a brilliant literary career. Her first poetry collection, *A Street in Bronzeville* (1945), reveals her talent for making the ordinary life of her neighbors extraordinary.

The Bean Eaters (1960) contains some of her most insightful verse:

➤ "The Bean Eaters," the title poem, offers a glimpse into the life of a poor but contented elderly black couple.

➤ "We Real Cool" explores the attitudes and fate of poor, inner-city black hoodlums.

These are her two most famous poems. They're brief, but very pithy. Like a rich candy, they linger on the palate. *Selected Poems* (1963) was followed in 1968 by *In the Mecca*, half of which is a long narrative poem about people in the Mecca, a fortress-like apartment building erected on the south side of Chicago in 1891, long since deteriorated into a slum. The second half of the book contains individual poems. Some of the highlights are "Boy Breaking Glass" and "Malcolm X." Later works include *Primer for Blacks* (1980), *Young Poets' Primer* (1981), and *Blacks* (1987), a collection of her published works.

Justly celebrated for her accomplishments, Brooks became the first black female poet to win a Pulitzer Prize (for *Annie Allen*, 1949). In 1968, Brooks was named poet laureate of Illinois. She has received two Guggenheim Fellowships and has served as poetry consultant to the Library of Congress. In 1990, she became a professor of English at Chicago State University.

However, Brooks is generally considered one of the most underappreciated poets of her generation. According to critic James M. Johnson, "No white poet of her quality is so undervalued, so unpardonably unread. She ought to be widely appreciated… as one of our most remarkable poets."

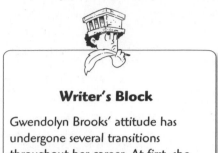

Writer's Block

Gwendolyn Brooks' attitude has undergone several transitions throughout her career. At first, she was a "literary integrationist," as one critic claimed. Shortly thereafter, she adopted a more militant position.

James Baldwin (1924–1987)

"If the concept of God has any validity or any use, it can only be to make us larger, freer, and more loving."

—James Baldwin, "The Fire Next Time"

Baldwin's writings interweave sexual and racial concerns—specifically, what it means to be black and homosexual in America in the second half of the 20th century. This theme is most fully explored in *Another Country* (1962), Baldwin's third novel, but it can also be discerned in his first, *Go Tell It on the Mountain* (1953), and his second, *Giovanni's Room* (1955).

Go Tell It on the Mountain established Baldwin as a leading black commentator on the condition of blacks in America, a position he extended in his fine essays, especially *Notes of a Native Son* (1955). In "Letter from a Region of My Mind," for example, Baldwin advocates love as a means of eliminating racism.

The novels *Tell Me How Long the Train's Been Gone* (1968) and *Just Above My Head* (1979) concern African-American identity. A collection of Baldwin's nonfiction, *The Price of the Ticket,* was published in 1985. If none of his works ranks with Ellison's *Invisible Man* or Wright's *Native Son*, Baldwin's writings nonetheless show great sensitivity to racial and sexual discrimination and a fierce commitment to the American ideal of personal freedom.

The Write Stuff

Critic Joseph Featherstone believes that Baldwin's finest work "… is self-revelatory: the fictional selves who walk the troubled regions of his mind, or the dramatic self he created… The strength lies in his ability to endow his experience, his feelings, with universal significance."

Maya Angelou (b. 1928)

As both a writer and entertainer, Maya Angelou is best known for her portrayals of strong African-American women. Born Marguerite Johnson in St. Louis, Missouri, Angelou spent most of her childhood living with her grandmother in rural Arkansas. She moved to her mother's home in San Francisco after graduating from Lafayette County Training School in 1940. At age 16, Angelou graduated from high school, gave birth to her son Guy, and began working at a series of jobs, including cooking and waiting tables.

In the 1950s, Angelou became a nightclub performer, kicking off a career as a singer, dancer, actor, playwright, magazine editor, civil rights activist, poet, and novelist.

Much of Angelou's writing stresses the themes of courage, perseverance, self-acceptance, and the realization of one's full potential. In her writing, she frequently presents strong female role models. Her most well-known publications include her series of autobiographical books, starting with *I Know Why the Caged Bird Sings* (1970). The series continues with *Gather Together in My Name* (1974), *Singin' and Swingin' and Gettin' Merry Like Christmas* (1976), *The Heart of a Woman* (1981), and *All God's Children Need Traveling Shoes* (1986). In these autobiographies, Angelou describes African-American life in witty, intelligent language rich in rhythm and texture.

Angelou's books of poetry include *Just Give Me a Cool Drink of Water 'fore I Diiie* (1971), *Oh Pray My Wings Are Gonna Fit Me Well* (1975), *And Still I Rise* (1978), *Shaker, Why Don't You Sing?* (1983), *Now Sheba Sings the Song* (1987), *I Shall Not Be Moved* (1990), and *Phenomenal Woman* (1994). A collection of essays, *Even the Stars Look Lonesome*, was published in 1997.

Lit Wit

Angelou read her poem "On the Pulse of Morning" at President Clinton's inauguration in January 1993.

Angelou has received many awards and honorary degrees, including Grammy awards (1994 and 1996) for her recordings of her poetry on the albums *On the Pulse of Morning* (1993) and *Phenomenal Woman* (1995). A self-described six-foot black southwesterner, Angelou currently lives in California. She continues to write, make public appearances, and entertain.

Toni Morrison (b. 1931)

"I really think the range of emotions and perceptions I have had access to as a black person and a female person are greater than those of people who are neither... My world did not shrink because I was a black female writer. It just got bigger."

—Toni Morrison

In 1993, Morrison became the first African-American woman to win the Nobel Prize for literature. Her writing, noted for its poetic language, provocative themes, and powerful story-telling, explores gender and racial conflicts and the many ways that people express their identities.

Morrison was born Chloe Anthony Wofford in Lorain, Ohio, in 1931. She attended Howard University—where she changed her name to "Toni" because "Chloe" was hard to pronounce—and received a master's degree from Cornell University in 1955. Two years later, she returned to Howard University to teach English. There she met Harold Morrison, a Jamaican architect whom she married in 1958. After their divorce six years later, Morrison worked as an editor for a textbook subsidiary of Random House. At the same time, she started writing. Her first novel was *The Bluest Eye* (1970).

Novel Ideas

"[Each of Morrison's novels] is as original as anything that has appeared in our literature in the last 20 years. The contemporaneity that unites them—the troubling persistence of racism in America—is infused with an urgency that only a black writer can have about our society."

—Charles Larson *(Chicago Tribune Book World)*

Some of Morrison's outstanding novels include...

➤ *The Bluest Eye* (1970) Drawing on elements of Morrison's own experience, the novel portrays a dysfunctional black family, the Breedloves, and a healthy, loving black family, the McTeers, modeled after Morrison's own family.

The Write Stuff

Morrison's novels explore the following themes: black cultural identity in contemporary America, tension between individuals and society, moral issues, and the problems of good and evil.

➤ *Sula* (1973) The novel focuses on two black women who have chosen different directions for their lives.

➤ *Song of Solomon* (1977) Here, Morrison follows a black man's quest for identity and his search for his ancestry. This novel won both the National Book Critics' Circle Award and the American Academy and Institute of Arts and Letters Award in 1977.

➤ *Tar Baby* (1981) This novel, set in the Caribbean, has been described as an allegory of colonialism.

➤ *Beloved* (1987) Here, Morrison describes an ex-slave's attempt to deal with her past. This novel won the 1988 Pulitzer Prize and was made into a movie starring Oprah Winfrey in 1998.

➤ *Jazz* (1992) This book concerns a middle-aged couple who migrate from the South to Harlem in the early 1900s.

The Best and the Brightest

Writing in the *Times Literary Supplement,* critic Jennifer Uglow noted that Morrison's novels "explore in particular the process of growing up black, female and poor. Avoiding generalities, Toni Morrison concentrates on the relation between the pressures of the community, patterns established within families... and the developing sense of self."

In 1980, President Jimmy Carter appointed Morrison to the National Council on the Arts. The following year, she won admission to the American Academy and Institute of Arts and Letters.

In addition to writing, Morrison has taught at several universities, including Howard, Yale, Cambridge, Harvard, and Princeton. She has also written a play, *Dreaming Emmett* (1986), and continues to edit for Random House, helping to publish works by authors such as Toni Cade Bambara and Gayle Jones.

Alice Walker (b. 1944)

"They were women then
My mama's generation
Husky of voice—Stout of
Step
With fists as well as
Hands
How they battered down
Doors..."

—Alice Walker, "In Search of Our Mother's Gardens"

Alice Walker's writing most often portrays the lives of poor, oppressed black women in the early 1900s. Born Alice Malsenior Walker in Eatonton, Georgia, she was educated at Spelman and Sarah Lawrence colleges. She wrote most of her first volume of poetry during a single week in 1964; it was published in 1968 as *Once.* Walker's experiences during her senior year at Sarah Lawrence, including undergoing an abortion and making a trip to Africa, provided many of the book's themes, such as love, suicide, civil rights, and Africa.

The Write Stuff

Walker believes that "the grace with which we embrace life, in spite of the pain, the sorrows, is always a measure of what has gone before."

The Color Purple (1982), Walker's best-known work, won the American Book Award and the Pulitzer Prize and was praised for its strong characterizations and the clear, musical quality of its colloquial language. *The Color Purple* was made into a critically acclaimed motion picture in 1985; Walker's book *The Same River Twice: Honoring the Difficult* (1996) contains her notes and reflections on making the film.

Walker's other works include the novels *The Third Life of Grange Copeland* (1970), *Meridian* (1976), *The Temple of My Familiar* (1989), and *Possessing the Secret of Joy* (1992).

Jamaica Kincaid (b. 1949)

"Wash the white clothes on Monday and put them on the stone heap; wash the color clothes on Tuesday and put them on the clothesline to dry; don't walk barehead in the hot sun; cook pumpkin fritters in very hot sweet oil; soak your little cloths right after you take them off…"

—Jamaica Kincaid, "Girl"

Over the course of four books—the novels *Annie John* (1985) and *Lucy* (1990), the short story collection *At the Bottom of the River* (1984), and her nonfiction book about her native Antigua titled *A Small Place* (1988)—Jamaica Kincaid has carved out a unique place in the American literary landscape. Writing in spare, deceptively simple prose, her fiction vividly and often harrowingly describes the difficult coming-of-age of strong-minded girls who, very much like herself, were born into tropical poverty.

Jamaica Kincaid's writing often describes one culture overwhelming another, resulting in deeply conflicted, divided individuals unable to wholly accept the dominant culture. Further, Kincaid's characters sometimes hate their own culture because they cannot help but see it through white eyes.

Writer's Block

Some readers are put off by Kincaid's anger at cultural domination—what she calls her rage: "But nothing can erase my rage… for this wrong can never be made right and only the impossible can make me still: can a way be found to make what happened not have happened?"

Jamaica Kincaid was born in 1949 in St. John's, Antigua, as Elaine Potter Richardson. Her mother's family were landed peasants from Dominica. Her maternal grandmother was a Carib Indian. Kincaid's father was a carpenter and cabinetmaker, her mother a homemaker and political activist.

Kincaid learned to read when she was three years old and then attended several schools on the island. At age 17, Kincaid fulfilled a long-long dream by emigrating to America. There, she first worked as an au pair in upscale Scarsdale, New York, then as a receptionist, and finally, as a magazine writer. Along the way, she earned a high school diploma, attended community college, studied photography at The New School, and attended Franconia College in New Hampshire. In 1973, to celebrate her new life, Elaine Potter Richardson decided to "celebrate her new life" by renaming herself Jamaica Kincaid.

Lit Wit

Kincaid recently had a very public and very messy break with the *New Yorker,* where she had been a staff writer since 1976. Kincaid did not agree with publisher Tina Brown's emphasis on celebrity stories. Ironically, Brown left the magazine shortly after Kincaid.

Kincaid's latest novel, *The Autobiography of My Mother,* charts the wide, troubled arc of 70-year-old Xuela Claudette Richardson's life. Most notably, the book is a striking portrait of Xuela's struggle as a young woman to find her own language and identity in the face of an uncaring father, a country wracked by colonialism, and a mother she never knew.

Kincaid now lives in Bennington, Vermont, with her husband, the composer/actor/writer Allen Shawn, and their two children.

The Least You Need to Know

➤ The rise of black militancy and the civil rights movement in the '50s and '60s changed the course of history and set off an outburst of literary creativity.

➤ Ralph Ellison's *Invisible Man,* a landmark achievement in American literature, expounds the theme that American society willfully ignores blacks.

➤ The first black female poet to win a Pulitzer Prize, Gwendolyn Brooks is best known for her poems "The Bean Eaters" and "We Real Cool."

➤ James Baldwin's writings interweave sexual and racial concerns, especially what it means to be black and homosexual in America in the second half of the 20th century.

➤ The writer and entertainer Maya Angelou is best known for her portrayals of strong African-American women.

➤ The first black woman to win the Nobel Prize for literature, Toni Morrison's novels focus on black cultural identity in contemporary America.

➤ Alice Walker's writing portrays the lives of poor, oppressed black women in the early 1900s.

Chapter 30

Modern Canadian Literature

In This Chapter

➤ Canada's literary history in the colonial and World War I and II years

➤ Stephen Leacock's humorous writings

➤ Alfred Purdy's poetry and working-class roots

➤ Pierre Berton's historical novels

➤ Mavis Gallant's ironic stories and novels

➤ Margaret Laurence's writing

➤ Mordecai Richler's body of work

➤ Alice Munro's fiction

➤ Margaret Atwood's novels, poetry, and criticisms

➤ Michael Ondaatje's career as a novelist and poet

Canada, the world's second-largest country, is known for magnificent scenery, rich natural resources, important manufacturing centers, and some valuable warm-and-fuzzy animals.

But did you also know that Canada has a fascinating literary history? That's what you'll learn about in this chapter.

First we'll survey Canada's literary past, starting with the colonial period, moving on to the early novelists, and pausing at a personal favorite, Lucy Maud Montgomery. Along the way, you'll learn about the humorist Stephen Leacock, too.

As we move on to today's literary lights, I'll explain the importance of Alfred Purdy's poetry, Pierre Berton's historical novels, Mavis Gallant's brilliantly ironic style, and Margaret Laurence's stories of cultural dislocation.

Let's not forget the novelist, journalist, and curmudgeon Mordecai Richler. You'll learn about his best-known novel *The Apprenticeship of Duddy Kravitz,* as well as other significant works. The survey continues with a look at Alice Munro, Margaret Atwood, and Michael Ondaatje. I've arranged the writers chronologically, according to their date of birth, to help you place everyone in historical context.

O Canada!

Explorers' accounts made up the earliest Canadian literature. Samuel Hearne (1745–1792) and Simon Fraser (1776–1862) were among the first to weigh in with their stories of the wild, vast Canadian countryside. Now, no one is going to argue that these books made compelling reading, but Canada did cop an important "first" soon after: the first novel produced in North America—*The History of Emily Montague* (1796). A realistic account of Quebec, it was written by Frances Moore Brooke, the wife of an English Army chaplain.

The first novel based on Canadian history, John Richardson's *Wacousta,* appeared in 1832. Later, he recorded the challenges of pioneer life in both the autobiographical *Backwoods of Canada* (1836) and *Roughing It in the Bush* (1852).

Writer's Block

Recall that Canada has a dual cultural heritage: French and English. Because there are more English-speaking Canadians than French-speaking Canadians, however, until recently there's been far more Canadian literature written in English than in French. This chapter focuses on Canadian literature that's written in English.

The Confederate Poets

The first important Canadian poets made their debut in the 19th century. The so-called "Confederate" school of poetry focused on romantic nature poems. Sir Charles G.D. Roberts (1860–1943), the leader of this group, published the romantic *Orion and Other Poems* (1880) and *Songs of the Common Day* (1893). His poems glorified the New Brunswick countryside. Fellow confederate poet Bliss Carmen was well-known for his romantic love songs and nature poems, collected in *Low Tide on the Grand Pre* (1893) and the five-volume collection *The Pipes of Pan* (1902–1905).

Other important confederate poets included Archibald Lampman and Wilfred Campbell. Lampman (1861–1899) described the Ontario countryside in *New World*

Lit Speak

The 19th-century Canadian nature poets were called the **Confederate** school of poets. They included Sir Charles G.D. Roberts, Bliss Carmen, Archibald Lampman, Wilfred Campbell, Isabella Valancy Crawford, and Pauline Johnson.

Lyrics and Ballads and *Beauty and Life*. In addition, Lampman headed the Department of Indian Affairs. He used his experience to create sensitive and compassionate portraits of Native Americans. Wilfred Campbell (1858?–1918) painted lush word pictures of the Canadian landscape.

Isabella Valancy Crawford (1850–1887) focused on pioneer life; Pauline Johnson (1862–1913), daughter of an Indian chief, wrote about her people.

Lit Wit

Canada stretches 3,426 miles across and extends southward from the North Pole to the U.S. border. Its seacoast includes 36,356 miles of mainland and 115,133 miles of islands, including the Arctic islands almost from Greenland to near the Alaskan border. While generally temperate in climate—public perception notwithstanding—Canada's vastness does include places with freezing winter cold and blistering summer heat. The country's capital is Ottawa; major cities include Toronto, Montreal, Vancouver, Ottawa-Hull, Edmonton, Calgary, Quebec, and Winnepeg.

Early Novelists

William Kirby (1817–1906) and Sir Gilbert Parker (1862–1932), the two most popular Canadian novelists of the late 1800s, penned historical romances about life in Canada. Kirby's *Golden Dog* (1877) and Parker's *The Seats of the Mighty* (1897), both set in Quebec, started the trend of unrealistic historical novels (you know, the kind: bodice-rippers meant to be read on the beach).

Around the 1900s, C.W. Gordon, writing under the name "Ralph Connor" (1860–1937), wrote *Black Rock* (1898) and *The Man from Glengarry* (1901) about Canada's West.

My personal favorites from this period are the *Anne of Green Gables* books written by Lucy Maud Montgomery (1874–1942). These classic novels are set in Montgomery's childhood home of Prince Edward Island.

Writer's Block

Scottish-born Robert Service was the most popular Canadian poet of the early 20th century. His *Songs of a Sourdough* (1907), including the fan favorite "The Shooting of Dan McGrew," grew out of his years in the Yukon. Today, however, Service is regarded as a hack.

Born at Clifton, Prince Edward Island, Montgomery relocated to Ontario in 1911 after her wedding to the Reverend Ewen Macdonald.

Stephen Leacock (1869–1944)

British-born writer Stephen Leacock was arguably the English-speaking world's best-known humorist from 1915 to 1925. He produced wise and witty social criticism in such works as *Sunshine Sketches of a Little Town* (1912), set in Ontario, and *Arcadian Adventures with the Idle Rich* (1914).

Sunshine Sketches of a Little Town humorously describes business, social life, religion, romance, and politics in the typically small Canadian town of Mariposa, whose name has attained mythic significance in the Canadian psyche. *Arcadian Adventures with the Idle Rich* dissects life in an American city with sharper satire, less qualified by Leacock's affection and pathos. Taken together, these books reveal Leacock's nostalgic concern for what is lost with the passing of human communities, as well as his fear for what may come.

Leacock grew up on a farm in Ontario and was educated at Upper Canada College, the University of Toronto, and the University of Chicago, where he studied economics and political science, earning his Ph.D. in 1903. Leacock joined McGill University's Department of Economics and Political Science in 1903, rose quickly to become department head, and remained there until his retirement in 1936.

Lit Wit

In the 1930s and 1940s, poets Francis Reginald Scott and A.J.M. Smith used their verse to explore social issues and literary criticism. Together, they compiled *The Blasted Pine: An Anthology of Satire, Invective, and Disrespectful Verse: Chiefly by Canadians.* This 1957 volume showed that Canadians were not incapable of introspection and self-criticism, as had sometimes been charged.

Between the Wars

During the 1920s, most realistic Canadian writers bit the hand that fed them, condemning Canadian values and institutions. The talented Newfoundland-born poet Edwin John Pratt (1882–1964), for example, expressed his pessimistic world view in his epic work *The Titanic* (1935).

The decade between 1930 and 1940 exploded with poetic talent, especially in Montreal. Publishing in small literary magazines to save printing and paper expenses during the Depression, these poets embraced their country's values and shunned American and British influences. Abraham Moses Klein (1909–1972), for instance, wrote lyrically of Canada's Jewish minorities and their heritage.

In prose, Morley Callaghan explored individuals in conflict within society in such works as *My Beloved* (1934), *They Shall Inherit the Earth* (1935), and *The Loved and Lost* (1961). Hugh MacLennan analyzed the meaning of Canada's past in *Barometer Rising* (1941), *Two Solitudes* (1945), and *The Watch That Ends the Night* (1959).

Since the 1960s, Canadian literature has gained in volume and creativity, reflecting and encouraging a heightened national consciousness. Produced in a time of rebellion and breaks with tradition, the literature has become more experimental in approach and universal in theme.

Among the most interesting of the modern Canadian writers is Alfred Purdy.

Alfred Purdy (b. 1918)

Alfred Wellington Purdy is a member of a group of Canadian poets rooted in working-class culture. Raised in Ontario, Purdy ended his formal education at the high-school level. During the Depression, he worked as a manual laborer in Vancouver.

During World War II, Purdy served in the Royal Canadian Air Force, afterward returning to his work as a laborer. Eventually, he settled in Ameliasburgh, the community celebrated in his poems. By the early 1960s, Purdy was able to support himself by freelance writing, poetry reading, and periods as writer-in-residence at various colleges.

Purdy was at the heart of the 1960s movements that set Canadian poets wandering the country and reading their poems to large audiences. There is no doubt that this experience helped him to develop a poetry style more closely related to oral speech patterns than his 1940s apprentice poems. To date, he has published 25 volumes of poetry.

The Write Stuff

Other Canadian working–class poets in this group include Milton Acorn, Alden Nowlan, and Patrick Lane.

The influence of readings on Purdy's work is one aspect of the close contact between experience and writing. He has been described as a "versifying journalist," and some of his books have in fact been poetic accounts of journeys, such as *North of Summer* (1967), based on a trip to the Arctic, and *Hiroshima Poems* (1972), about a visit to Japan.

Purdy has tried to bring to his poetry a sense of Canada's past, and of the rapid pattern of change.

Pierre Berton (b. 1920)

One of Canada's best-known writers, Pierre Berton is particularly well regarded as a serious popularizer of Canadian history. He wrote for various newspapers and magazines and has been a regular on Canadian television as both host of his own shows and as a guest panelist on others. Berton's first important book was *Klondike* (1958), a narrative of the Klondike Gold Rush of 1898, an event that cast a long shadow under which Berton lived for years, being the son of a gold-seeker and having grown up in Dawson amid the debris of the stampede.

Writer's Block

Saul Bellow can be counted as both Canadian and Jewish. He's discussed in Chapter 28 because he spent nearly all his life in Chicago. As he himself said, "I grew up there and consider myself a Chicagoan, out and out."

After *Klondike* came a series of polemics, *The Comfortable Pew* (1965) and *The Smug Minority* (1968), which attacked the Anglican Church and Canada's big business.

In 1970, Berton returned to history with the publication of *The National Dream* (1970) and *The Last Spike* (1971). The subject was well suited to Berton's strengths: patriotic verve, the marshaling of colorful detail, and above all, a driving narrative.

Berton's other works include *The Dionne Years* (1977), *The Invasion of Canada* (1980), *Flames Across the Border* (1981), and *The Promised Land* (1984), a history of the settling of the Canadian West. *Vimy* (1986), an examination of the World War I battle in which the Canadian Corps took Vimy Ridge in 1917, was hugely successful. In *Starting Out* (1987), Berton picked up the autobiographical thread again with a memoir that ends in 1947.

Lit Wit

Until the mid-20th century, French-Canadian literature focused mainly on religion, Canadian history, and patriotism. Since then, French-Canadian writing has become more involved with the concerns of modern Western society, although the issue of French-Canadian nationalism remains a key issue. Playwright Michel Tremblay, for example, uses the Montreal vernacular in dramas such as *Sainte Carmen of the Main*. Other important Canadians writing in French include Andre Giroux, Robert Elie, and Andre Langevin. The French-Jewish immigrant Monique Bosco described postwar rootlessness in *Un amour maladriot (An Awkward Love*, 1961). Marie Claire Blais was praised for her psychological insight in *Une saison dans la vie d'Emmanuel (A Season in the Life of Emmanuel*, 1965).

Mavis Gallant (b. 1922)

Gallant's brilliant and ironic writing style is highly realistic. She often describes frightened, lonely children and teenagers, writing compassionately of their pain.

Another of her themes is expatriates who have been displaced from their culture through choice or circumstance; lacking a clear sense of direction, these characters are adrift as permanent tourists, eking out miserable lives in run-down European hotels and pensions.

The only child of mismatched parents, Gallant attended 17 different schools, including public schools, convent schools, and boarding schools.

After completing her education in America, she returned to Canada, where she worked briefly in the cutting room of the National Film Board before becoming a feature reporter for the *Montreal Standard* in 1944. Mavis married John Gallant, a musician from Winnipeg, but they soon divorced.

Gallant began writing fiction in Canada, publishing stories in popular magazines from 1944 to 1950. In 1950, determined to write fiction full time, she resettled in Paris, where she still lives. Since 1951, Gallant has published more than 100 stories, most of which first appeared in the *New Yorker,* where she contin-ues to publish. Her short story collections include *The Other Paris* (1956), *My Heart Is Broken* (1964), *The Pegnitz Junction* (1973), *The End of the World and Other Stories* (1974), and *From the Fifteenth District: A Novella and Eight Stories* (1979).

Writer's Block

In *Understanding Media* (1964), University of Toronto professor Marshall McLuhan warned that printed literature is being superseded by electronic means of mass commu-nication. Who knows what form our reading materials will take in the future!

Neglected by the Canadian public for many years, Gallant has finally gained recognition in her homeland. In 1981, she was appointed an Officer of the Order of Canada, and in 1993 she was raised to Companion, the Order's highest level. In unsentimental prose and with trenchant wit, Gallant describes the isolation, detachment, and fear that afflicts rootless North American and European expatriates.

Margaret Laurence (1926–1987)

Margaret Laurence is ranked as one of the top Canadian novelists of the 1960s and 1970s. Laurence's writing is distinguished by penetrating characterizations and fine techniques. Her stories resonate in your mind, echoing long after you've put the book down.

Born in Ontario, Laurence was educated in Winnipeg and married Jack Laurence, a hydraulic engineer, in 1947. Two years later, they moved to England and later to

Somaliland and Ghana, where he worked as a dam builder with the British Overseas Development Service. In 1974, Margaret Laurence returned to live permanently in Ontario.

Although Laurence wrote stories since childhood, her first book, *A Tree for Poverty*, wasn't published until 1954. Africa had a profound influence on Laurence, awakening a realistic appraisal of the problems of emergent nations.

Her African fiction reflects her belief in the dignity and potential of every human being.

Back in Canada, Laurence published her memoirs of the Somaliland years, *The Prophet's Camel Bell* (1963).

The Stone Angel (1964) was a landmark event for Canadian literature and the keystone of Laurence's career. It set the town of Manawaka firmly in Canada's imaginative landscape and pointed the way for the works to follow. The novel describes the ruminations of an old woman, Hagar, as the end of her life nears. Hagar's life was harsh and cruel, marked by tragedy and brutal misunderstandings, yet marked by beauty nonetheless.

A Jest of God (1966) is the story of Rachel Cameron, who, through the ordeal of one summer in Manawaka in the 1960s, finds a fragile but sustaining selfhood. *The Diviners* (1974), a complex and profound novel, was greeted with great praise. Her final literary legacy is the memoir *Dance on the Earth*, which she finished just before she died.

Mordecai Richler (b. 1931)

Canada's most celebrated curmudgeon is proud of his reputation, "because it keeps a lot of people away," he notes. When he's not busy being cranky, Richler is also one of Canada's foremost novelists, a controversial and prolific journalist, and an occasional scriptwriter.

Richler was educated at Sir George Williams College, Montreal. After 20 years abroad, Richler returned to Montreal in 1972. His reputation as a novelist took off with the 1959 publication of *The Apprenticeship of Duddy Kravitz*. A witty portrait of a young Montreal-Jewish entrepreneur, the novel is characterized by the contrast between comedy and pathos; rich dramatic scenes; a lively narrative pace; and a comprehensive depiction of the protagonist as Montréaler, Jew, and individual.

The Incomparable Atuk (1963), a goofy piece on Canadian nationalism, shows Richler's considerable talent for humor. *Cocksure* (1968), a satire on the difficulty of sticking to traditional values in a world gone mad, is equally funny. *St. Urbain's Horseman* (1971) examines the life of a middle-aged man subject to intense, contradictory feelings, who, Richler claimed, is "closer to me than anybody else." *Joshua Then and Now* (1980) explores the past and the effects of time on the individual.

The Write Stuff

Richler's earlier novels, *The Acrobats* (1954), *Son of a Smaller Hero* (1955), and *A Choice of Enemies* (1957), are essentially apprenticeship pieces portraying young, intense characters absorbed with finding proper values in a corrupt world.

Richler has published hundreds of articles in a wide range of publications in Canada, America, and Britain. He published collections of his articles in *Hunting Tigers Under Glass* (1968), *The Street* (1969), *Shovelling Trouble* (1972), *Notes on an Endangered Species* (1974), and *Home Sweet Home: My Canadian Album* (1984). He has also written a handful of movie scripts.

Alice Munro (b. 1931)

The strength of Alice Munro's fiction arises partially from its clear sense of place. Most of her tales are set in Huron County, Ontario, and under her description, the setting comes alive. Munro's early writing concerns the problems teenage girls face coming to terms with family and small-town life. Her more recent work addresses the problems of middle age, of women alone, and of the elderly. Characteristic of Munro's style is the search for some gesture by which an event is illuminated and given personal meaning.

Munro's early years were spent in western Ontario. She met her first husband, James Munro, at the University of Western Ontario, and soon after they moved to Vancouver. The marriage did not last, and in 1972, Munro returned to Ontario, where she married Gerald Fremlin in 1976. She was awarded the Governor General's Award for both *Dance of the Happy Shades* (1968) and *Who Do You Think You Are?* (1978), which was also runner-up for the Booker Prize. Munro is also the recipient of the Canadian Booksellers Association International Book Year Award for *Lives of Girls and Women* (1971), the Canada-Australia Literary Prize (1977), and the Marian Engel Award (1986).

Writer's Block

Some critics claim that Munro's fiction is really autobiography. This charge is often leveled against *Lives of Girls and Women* in particular. In response, Munro has asserted it is "autobiographical in form but not in fact."

Margaret Atwood (b. 1939)

> *"How do you learn to spell?*
>
> *Blood, sky & the sun,*
>
> *your own name first,*
>
> *your first naming, your first name,*
>
> *your first word."*

—Margaret Atwood, "Spelling"

The prolific Canadian novelist, poet, and critic Margaret Atwood is best known for her 1986 novel *The Handmaid's Tale*, which was made into a film in 1990. She has been instrumental in separating Canada's cultural identity from both American and British influences. Atwood accomplishes this by writing poems, novels, and stories that consider the issues that prevent many Canadians, especially women, from achieving their goals and dreams.

Born in Ottawa in 1939, Atwood earned degrees from the University of Toronto and Radcliffe College, and has lived in many places, including Vancouver, Montreal, Edmonton, Boston, England, Scotland, and France. Her frequent travels started when she was a child, when her family trekked through the Quebec bush as her father conducted scientific research.

A full-time writer since 1972, Atwood has also done a spot of teaching here and there. She has won a pile of impressive awards, including the Giller Prize for *Alias Grace* (1996), the Governor General's Award for Fiction for *The Handmaid's Tale* (1986), and the Governor General's Award for Poetry for *The Circle Game* (1966).

Lit Wit

William Patrick Kinsella (b. 1932) is a Canadian cult figure for the novel *Shoeless Joe* (1982), made into the movie *Field of Dreams* in 1989. A professor at the University of Calgary, Kinsella has also written *The Iowa Baseball Confederacy* (1986) and *The Further Adventures of Slugger McBatt* (1988).

Michael Ondaatje (b. 1943)

Poet, novelist, and filmmaker Michael Ondaatje was born in Sri Lanka in 1943 and came to Canada in 1962. He now lives in Toronto and teaches at Glendon College, York University.

His most famous book, *The English Patient,* was published in 1992 and was awarded the prestigious Booker Prize. The celebrated film version, starring Ralph Finnes, was box office gold.

Perhaps the most notable aspect of Ondaatje's writing is his preference for images over standard novelistic cause-and-effect plots. The action is always enhanced by his intense sense of motion and picture. Ondaatje even claims that he is less influenced by books than by other art forms, such as music and painting.

Ondaatje's own family history has been as fantastic as that of the characters he creates. As he relates in his memoir, *Running in the Family,* Ondaatje grew up in Ceylon (now Sri Lanka), the child of a strong-willed mother and a brilliant, eccentric father who, when drunk, held guns on trains and forced the trains to run back and forth at his pleasure. As Ondaatje explores his Dutch-Ceylonese genealogy, he paints a sad, hilarious, memorable picture of lives lived to a surreal tropical hilt: an entire society consumed by compulsive gambling, endless affairs, and bitter feuds.

Besides *Running in the Family,* Ondaatje is the author of three collections of poems: *The Cinnamon Peeler, Secular Love,* and *There's a Trick with a Knife I'm Learning to Do.* He has also written the novels *In the Skin of a Lion, Coming Through Slaughter,* and *The Collected Works of Billy the Kid.*

Lit Wit

William Gibson (b. 1943), science-fiction novelist, coined the term *cyberspace* in his 1982 novel *Neuromancer.* Born in Virginia, Gibson earned a B.A. from the University of British Columbia, Vancouver, and has lived there ever since. *Neuromancer* won the three most prestigious accolades in science fiction: the Hugo, Nebula, and Phillip K. Dick awards. With *Count Zero* and *Mona Lisa Overdrive, Neuromancer* is part of the *Sprawl* series of books. In 1995, Gibson wrote the screenplay for the movie *Johnny Mnemonic.*

The Least You Need to Know

➤ Canadian literature began in the 18th century with explorers' accounts; a Canadian wrote the first North American novel, *The History of Emily Montague* (1796).

➤ The British-born writer Stephen Leacock was arguably the English-speaking world's best-known humorist from 1915 to 1925.

➤ Alfred Purdy, Milton Acorn, Alden Nowlan, and Patrick Lane are well-respected poets rooted in Canada's working-class culture.

➤ One of Canada's best-known writers, Pierre Berton, is a serious popularizer of Canadian history.

➤ Mavis Gallant's brilliant and ironic style is highly realistic.

➤ Margaret Laurence is ranked as one of the top Canadian novelists of the 1960s and 1970s.

➤ Mordecai Richler is one of Canada's foremost novelists and journalists.

➤ Alice Munro, Margaret Atwood, and Michael Ondaatje are all outstanding contemporary Canadian writers.

Chapter 31

Native-American, Latino-American, and Asian-American Literature

---

In This Chapter

➤ Modern Native-American writers

➤ The works of N. Scott Momaday, William Least Heat Moon, Leslie Marmon Silko, and Louise Erdrich

➤ Today's Latino-American writers

➤ The writing of Richard Rodriguez, Denise Chávez, Julia Alvarez, and Sandra Cisneros

➤ Contemporary Asian-American writers

➤ The novels and stories of Maxine Hong Kingston and Amy Tan

We all have our own notions of what it means to be American.

Not so long ago, America was considered to be a "melting pot," as diverse groups shed their heritage to become something new, something we call "American."

But over the years, some people began to question how accurately the term "melting pot" described the American experience. They saw that some groups were more easily assimilated—and more welcome—than others. We began to realize that newcomers don't "melt"; rather, they maintain their native heritage within America, in a "salad bowl," "crazy quilt," or "glorious mosaic."

Native Americans didn't immigrate to this country, of course. Nonetheless, they have struggled to maintain an identity within a culture that had taken over. For example, Native Americans believe everything in the world has its life and purpose, and every event is significant, a belief that clashes with the prevailing mood.

Partly as a result of this new way of looking at American identity, multicultural writing has flourished. Perhaps not since the literary community and reading public discovered Jewish-American writers in the 1950s have we experienced such a concentrated ethnic wave of literature. Along with this has come an enthusiastic reception of writers of varied backgrounds and cultures.

In this chapter, you'll explore how Native-American, Latino-American, and Asian-American writers express their vision of American culture.

Modern Native–American Writers

In an astonishing example of irony, it was not until 1924 that Congress declared that Native-Americans were U.S. citizens. Today, about 2 million Americans identify themselves as Native-Americans.

The five largest tribes and their memberships follow:

Tribe	Membership
1. Cherokee	369,035
2. Navajo	225,298
3. Sioux	107,321
4. Chippewa	105,988
5. Choctaw	86,231

Source: 1999 World Almanac and Book of Facts

Lit Wit

Native people know the word "*Indian*" is a misnomer, but they have made it their own. In the same way, they have accepted "American Indian" and "Native American," even though each tribe has a name in their original language. Most Native–Americans refer to each other by their tribe or nation, instead of using the broader "Native-American" label. Each tribe has a name in its original language.

Native-American writers are as diverse as their tribes, but most share an interest in exploring their heritage, their unique place in American life, and what it means to be a Native-American. Let's see how these concerns are voiced in the writing of N. Scott Momaday.

Natachee Scott Momaday (b. 1934)

"Children trust in language. They are open to the power and beauty of language, and here they differ from their elders, most of whom have come to imagine that they have found words out, and so much of the magic is lost on them."

—N. Scott Momaday, "The Names"

Most of Momaday's poems and stories focus on the power of myth and language to shape reality. His works also reveal the traditional Native-American harmony with the environment.

Writer, poet, and artist Momaday, a member of the Kiowa and Cherokee tribes, was born in Fairview, Kentucky, and educated on Indian reservations.

In 1952, he entered the University of New Mexico. By the time he had completed his education, Momaday had earned a Ph.D. in English from the University of Arizona in Tucson. Until 1981, he was a professor of English at Stanford University. Since then, Momaday has served on the faculty of the University of Arizona.

Momaday's novel *House Made of Dawn* won the Pulitzer Prize for fiction in 1969. He has published a number of other books, including his most well-known work, *The Way to Rainy Mountain,* a compilation of myth and personal memory (1969).

The Write Stuff

Natachee Scott Momaday publishes under the name "N. Scott Momaday."

Lit Wit

A storyteller, novelist, and poet, Joseph Bruchac (b. 1942) boasts Abenaki (a Native American tribe), Slovak, and French ancestry. Bruchac earned his Ph.D. at the Union Graduate School in 1975. He is the author of more than 30 books of poetry and Native American folktales and legends. His books include *Keepers of the Earth: Native American Stories* and *Environmental Activities for Children.* Two of his best-known books of poetry are *Indian Mountain and Other Poems* and *Walking with My Son.*

William Least Heat Moon (b. 1940)

William Trogdon of Columbus, Missouri, tells the story behind his pseudonym in the early pages of his best-known book, *Blue Highways: A Journey into America,* "My father calls himself Heat Moon, my elder brother Little Heat Moon. I, coming last, am therefore Least. It has been a long lesson of a name to learn. To the Sioux, the Moon of Heat is the seventh month, a time also known as the Blue Moon, because, I think, of its dusky midsummer color."

Should the writer then call himself "William Trogdon" or "William Least Heat Moon?" Least Heat Moon noted that his father always advised him to use the name "Trogdon" when doing "Anglo" things, such as conducting business, but to use his Native-American name when doing spiritual activities such as writing. Hence, William Least Heat Moon the writer.

After Least Heat Moon lost his job as a college English teacher and watched his marriage disintegrate, he decided to tour America. Before his journey was over, he would travel more than 10,000 miles in a van he named "Ghost Dancing." His travel log, transformed into the work he called *Blue Highways,* became a bestseller. The memoir was praised especially for its vivid descriptions of America.

Today, Least Heat Moon continues to contribute essays and articles to well-respected periodicals such as *The Atlantic Monthly*. His writing has attracted attention and earned respect.

Leslie Marmon Silko (b. 1948)

"The earth is your mother,
she holds you.
The sky is your father,
he protects you.
Sleep.
sleep.
Rainbow is your sister,
she loves you.
The winds are your brothers."

—Storyteller

As this poem suggests, Leslie Marmon Silko seeks to preserve her Native-American heritage, especially the oral tradition. She is also interested in maintaining the ceremonies of the Laguna Pueblo Native-Americans. "Silko emphasizes the need to return to rituals and oral traditions of the past in order to rediscover the basis for one's cultural heritage," one critic noted. Silko has also used her status as a prominent Native-American writer to draw attention to controversial modern issues, such as women's equality and current immigration policies directed at minorities.

Born in Albuquerque, New Mexico, of Laguna Pueblo, Mexican, and white descent, Silko grew up on the Laguna reservation. After graduating from Native-American school, Silko went on to attend the University of New Mexico. Silko published her first work, the novel *Tony's Story,* in 1969 and her first book of poems, *Laguna Women Poems,* in 1974.

Silko's second major novel, *Storyteller* (1981), uses stories from her Native-American heritage to re-create stories about her own family. In 1981, she was awarded a MacArthur "genius" Fellowship for her accomplishments. *Almanac of the Dead* (1991) has thus far attracted the most attention.

In this book, Silko deals with many issues related to Native-Americans, focusing on the history of conquest. Silko continues to write; *Yellow Woman* came out in 1993. This novel again reveals the haunting power with which Silko blends the real and mythic of the people and places in America's Southwest.

Louise Erdrich (b. 1954)

"So when I went there, I knew the dark fish must rise. Plumes of radiance had soldered on me. No reservation girl had ever prayed so hard."

—Louise Erdrich, "Saint Marie"

Louise Erdrich's fiction and poetry draw on her Chippewa heritage and experiences as a Native-American to examine complex family and sexual relationships among full- and mixed-blood Native-Americans as they struggle with questions of identity in white American culture.

Born in Minnesota to a Chippewa mother and a German-American father, Erdrich is a member of the Turtle Mountain Chippewa Tribe. She was raised in Wahpeton, North Dakota, where her parents worked for the Bureau of Indian Affairs. The family's Native-American roots run deep; her grandfather, Patrick Gourneau, was tribal chairman of the Turtle Mountain Reservation for many years.

Erdrich's parents encouraged her precocious literary talents: Her father paid her a nickel for each short story she wrote, and her mother bound them into little booklets. In addition, Erdrich's mother passed on many family stories that found their way into Louise's writings, especially the novel *Tracks* (1988).

Erdrich earned her B.A. from Dartmouth (where she met her husband-to-be, fellow Native-American and writer Michael Dorris) and her M.A. from John Hopkins University. In 1984, Erdrich's novel *Love Medicine* won the National Book Critics Circle Award for best work of fiction, as well as the *Los Angeles Times* prize for fiction. Her other works

The Write Stuff

Love Medicine (1984) is Erdrich's compelling and tumultuous tale of two Chippewa families, the Kapshaws and the Lamrtines, whose lives are inextricably bound by blood and history. Filled with elements from the Chippewa oral tradition, it is an exhilarating story of love, betrayal, and the search for identity—altogether typical of Erdrich's writing.

include the novel *The Beet Queen* (1986), *Baptism of Desire: Poems* (1989), *The Bingo Palace* (1994), *The Blue Jay's Dance: A Birth Year* (1995), and *Antelope Woman* (1998).

Erdrich's career was flourishing, but her personal life took a dive in the 1990s, when her marriage to Dorris fell apart. Separated from Erdrich and depressed over allegations of sexually abusing at least one of his children, Michael Dorris committed suicide in 1997.

Lit Wit

Born in 1966 on the Spokane Indian Reservation in Wellpinit, Washington State, Sherman Alexie belongs to the Spokane and Coeur d'Alene tribes. Alexie earned his B.A. at the University of Washington in 1991. He has garnered high praise for his poems and short stories that illuminate contemporary Native-American reservation life. Winner of the American Book Award in 1996, Alexie has written *The Business of Fancy Dancing: Stories and Poems* (1992), *First Indian on the Moon* (1993), *The Lone Ranger and Tonto Fistfight in Heaven* (1993), and *Indian Killer* (1996). His 1998 movie, *Smoke Signals,* was also well-received.

Today's Latino-American Writers

Latino-American writers have come a long way since the first writers and poets joined union activist Cesar Chavez in the California fields to protest the unequal treatment of Chicano and other minority workers. In the brief span of a quarter of a century, Latino/Chicano-American literature has blossomed. Written in English, it now holds a place in the literature of the United States. With its historical relationship to Mexico and its grounding in the Southwest, Latino-American writing speaks to the Hispanic world south of Mexico as well. This writing is in many ways a bridge across *la frontera,* joining Anglo-America to Latin America.

Recently, there has been a new wave of young, widely read Latino-American authors, not unlike the earlier flowering of African-American writers that brought us everyone from James Baldwin to Terry McMillan. While all of today's Latino-American writer share a Spanish-language background, they are as different from each other as their fiction.

Richard Rodriguez (b. 1946)

Richard Rodriguez knew only a few words of English when he entered kindergarten in a Catholic school in Sacramento, California.

His autobiography, *Hunger of Memory: The Education of Richard Rodriguez* published in 1982, describes how the nuns taught him English, sparked a love of reading, and set him on the path that would help him earn a B.A. from Stanford University and a graduate degree in English from the University of California at Berkeley.

As both a writer and a teacher, Rodriguez traces the intellectual road that took him from his secure and safe family into the difficult and frightening realm of American life. As he became more assured in English, Rodriguez lost his fluency in Spanish and a closeness to his parents, because they never became comfortable speaking and writing English.

Lit Wit

Rodriguez has been a controversial figure on the American intellectual landscape for his strong stance against bilingual education. While his own experiences would seem to suggest that he would be in favor of teaching children in both their home language and English, Rodriguez nonetheless feels that total immersion in English benefits children far more than a bilingual education.

Denise Chávez (b. 1948)

"In our family, men usually come first. Then God and Country. Country was last. Should be last."

—Denise Chávez, *Face of an Angel*

Although her writing often seems to shift focus from the key issues of Chicano culture to self-reflection, Cháves nonetheless welcomes her Chicano heritage. She is deeply grateful for being bilingual. In fact, she uses so many Spanish words and phrases in her writing that she has come into conflict with her editors. "It's time for readers to pick up a little Spanish," she argues. "It's like a plate of food with salsa, with the Spanish words the salsa. It gives [the writings] flavor."

Denise Chávez was born in Las Cruces, New Mexico, only 40 miles from the Mexican border. The bilingual backdrop of the Southern New Mexico town immersed the Chávez home in two distinct cultures. At Madonna High School in Mesilla, New Mexico, Chávez enrolled in a theater class. There, she discovered drama as a means of self-expression. She was awarded a drama scholarship to New Mexico State University, where she studied with Mark Medoff, author of the play *Children of a Lesser God*. She earned her B.A. in drama, then a Master of Fine Arts in drama in 1974, and an M.F.A. in creative writing a decade later.

The Write Stuff

In *The Last of the Menu Girls,* Chávez draws on her own experiences: Rocio, the protagonist, has an absent father and works in a hospital. Chávez's father was not a part of the household, and Chávez once worked in a hospital.

Chávez began writing plays in the early 1970s, focusing on the social and economic issues of the Chicano culture as well as bilingual speech and Chicano humor. Chávez has also published poetry and short stories. In 1986, a collection of her short stories was published as a novel, *The Last of the Menu Girls.*

Chávez has found much strength and support in a network of fellow Chicano and Chicana writers, including Roberto Anaya and Sandra Cisneros. Chávez is very active in the Chicano community and says that her work is written for the poor and forgotten. Indeed, the characters in her writings are typically everyday people, and through these characters Chávez celebrates the strength and dignity of the working class.

Julia Alvarez (b. 1950)

In her poems and novels, Julia Alvarez explores the gulf between alienation and assimilation within the Latino community. Despite the difficulties of bridging two cultures, Alvarez sees advantages to this unique position when she asserts that: "We travel on that border between two worlds and we can see both points of view," she notes. Alvarez has firsthand experience as a member of two cultures: in 1960, at the age of 10, she arrived in the United States from the Dominican Republic.

Alvarez claims that being in America, where she was surrounded by books and women were encouraged to discover their talents, contributed to her becoming an author. In 1971, Alvarez earned her B.A. from Middlebury College; four years later, she completed her M.A. in creative writing from Syracuse University. Currently, she is a professor at Middlebury College.

Alvarez is a prolific writer. *Homecoming,* a collection of poems, was published in 1984; the novel *How the Garcia Girls Lost Their Accents* was published six years later. *How the Garcia Girls Lost Their Accents* describes the experiences of the four Garcia sisters, who like Alvarez, came to New York City from the Dominican Republic. The 15 interconnected chapters explore the girls' struggle to negotiate their place between the two cultures to which they belong.

In 1994, Alvarez published *In the Time of the Butterflies,* which was named an American Library Association Notable Book and a National Book Critics Circle Award finalist. In this historical novel, Alvarez introduces the American public to the legendary Mirabal sisters, who gave their lives defying the oppressive dictatorship in the Dominican Republic. They were called "las miraposas" (the butterflies).

Alvarez published a second collection of poetry in 1995, *The Other Side: El Otro Lado.* Her most recent work, ¡Yo!, was published in 1997.

Lit Wit

José Garcia Villa's poetry reflects his concern for humanity. Villa searches for "man's selfhood and identity in the mystery of Creation." Born in the Philippines in 1912, Villa came to America when he was a teenager. His first poetry collection, *Have Come, Am Here,* appeared in 1942. Since then, Villa has published other collections of poetry and short stories.

Sandra Cisneros (b. 1954)

"In the movies there is always one with red red lips who is beautiful and cruel. She is the one who drives men crazy and laughs at them all the way. Her power is her own. She will not give it away."

—Sandra Cisneros, *The House on Mango Street*

An acclaimed fiction writer, essayist, poet, and teacher, Cisneros says of her writing, "When I was eleven years old in Chicago, teachers thought if you were poor and Mexican, you didn't have anything to say. Now I think that what I was put on the planet for was to tell these stories. Use what you know to help heal the pain in your community. We've got to tell our own history. I am very conscious that I want to write."

Cisneros' style has been shaped by her experiences: feminism, love, oppression, and religion. These themes recut in her work. In "Ghosts and Voices: Writing From Obsession," she says, "If I were asked what it is I write about, I would have to say I write about those ghosts inside that haunt me, that will not let me sleep, of that which even memory does not like to mention."

After earning her B.A. in English from Loyola University in Chicago and an M.A. in writing from the University of Iowa, Cisneros took a variety of jobs. In 1984, she published *The House on Mango Street.* Her collection of poems, *My Wicked Wicked Ways* published in 1987, is widely read.

The Write Stuff

According to Cynthia Tompkins of Arizona State University, "Today Cisneros is perhaps the most visible Chicana in mainstream literary circles. The vividness of her vignettes and the lyrical quality of her prose attest to her craft."

Contemporary Asian-American Writers

It was not until the 1976 publication of Maxine Hong Kingston's mystical memoir of her San Francisco childhood, *The Woman Warrior: Memoirs of a Girlhood Among Ghosts,* that Asian-American writers broke into mainstream American literature. Even so, more than 10 years passed before another Asian-American writer achieved fame and fortune. *The Joy Luck Club,* Amy Tan's first novel, sold an astonishing 275,000 hard-cover copies upon its 1989 publication.

The success of Tan's book made publishers more willing to gamble on first books by Asian-American writers. Two years later, at least four other Chinese-American writers had brisk-selling books:

➤ Gus Lee's *China Boy* had an initial print run of 75,000, huge for a first-time author.

➤ Publishers duked it out for the right to publish David Wong Louie's *Pang of Love,* a collection of short stories.

➤ Gish Jen's *Typical America* had an equally impressive reception.

Lit Wit

Along with fellow writers Dave Barry and Stephen King, Amy Tan is part of the rock group "The Rock Bottom Remainders." Tan plays the tambourine.

In part, this interest in Asian-American literature can be attributed to the near-doubling of America's Asian-American population, from 3.5 million to 6.9 million in the past 10 years. The fact remains, however, that more Asian-Americans than ever are writing, and their books have a fresh and original voice.

Among the most popular contemporary Asian-American writers are Maxine Hong Kingston and Amy Tan.

Maxine Hong Kingston (b. 1940)

"The Woman Warrior is about being Chinese in the way that [the James Joyce novel] Portrait of the Artist as a Young Man is about being Irish. It is an investigation of soul, not landscape. Its sources are dream and memory, myth and desire. Its crises are the crises of a heart in exile from roots that bind and terrorize it."

—*The New York Times Book Review*

The Woman Warrior: Memoirs of a Girlhood Among Ghosts made Maxine Hong Kingston a literary celebrity at the age of 36. Kingston has since written two other critically hailed books. *China Men,* a sequel to *The Woman Warrior,* was published in 1980 and also received the National Book Critic's Circle Award. In 1989, Kingston published her first novel, *Tripmaster Monkey: His Fake Book.* Kingston's writing is often praised for its harmony and poetry.

Kingston had a difficult childhood. Her parents, both Chinese immigrants, operated a gambling house in Stockton, California, when Maxine was born. Shortly after her birth, the family opened a laundry, where she and her five siblings joined their parents as soon as they were old enough to work the long-and-hard hours. Kingston attended public schools, where she was an excellent student. After graduation, with the help of scholarships, she enrolled in the University of California at Berkeley.

In 1962 Kingston earned her B.A. and married fellow classmate Earl Kingston. Five years later, the Kingstons moved to Hawaii, where Maxine taught school. Kingston's memoirs and novels are a fascinating mix of myth and reality, fable and fact. Let's turn to them now.

> *"When fishing for treasures in the flood, be careful not to pull in girls."*

> *"There's no profit in raising girls. Better to raise geese than girls."*

> —Maxine Hong Kingston, *The Woman Warrior*

➤ ***The Woman Warrior* (1976)** This memoir describes the conflicting cultural messages Kingston received as the daughter of Chinese immigrants growing up in 1950s America. It also explores the pressure she felt as an American trying to emerge from the tragedy of her female ancestors in China's male-dominated society.

➤ ***China Men* (1980)** *China Men* explores the Chinese-American men in Kingston's family. The *New York Times* praised it as "a triumph of the highest order, of imagination, of language, of moral perception."

➤ ***Tripmaster Monkey: His Fake Book* (1989)** Set in San Francisco in the 1960s, the novel describes Wittman Ah Sing, who writes a contemporary epic based on an old Chinese novel. Some reviewers compared Wittman Ah Sing to J.D. Salinger's Holden Caulfield and Mark Twain's Huck Finn. The name Wittman is also an homage to Walt Whitman and the triumphant American individual spirit.

Amy Tan (b. 1952)

"Before I wrote *The Joy Luck Club*," Tan remarked in an interview, "my mother told me, 'I might die soon. And if I die, what will you remember?'"

As *The Joy Luck Club* revealed, Tan remembered quite a bit of her heritage. "All the daughters are fractured bits of me," she noted.

American-born Amy Tan is the only daughter of Chinese immigrants. Her family moved a great deal when she was a child, eventually settling in Santa Clara, California. Tan graduated from high school in Montreux, Switzerland, and earned her master's degree in linguistics from San Jose State University, California.

387

Lit Wit

Amy Tan's Chinese name, "An-mei," means "blessing from America."

After becoming a freelance business writer (a job she found dull), Tan began writing fiction as a hobby. She soon quit the freelance business and wrote *The Joy Luck Club* in four months. It was a smash success, as you have already read. The novel describes the lives of four Asian women who flee China in the 1940s and their four very American-ized daughters. The story focuses on Jing-mei (June) Woo, a 36-year-old woman at loose ends. After her mother's sudden death, June comes to appreciate her heritage and the extraordinary hardships experienced by the Chinese immigrant women of her mother's generation.

Tan's second book, *The Kitchen God's Wife,* published in 1991, tells her mother's story through the fictional Winnie, a Chinese refugee. The book was a huge success even before publication.

In 1992, Tan published a children's book, *The Moon Lady. Publishers Weekly* noted, "The haunting tale that unfolds is worthy of retelling."

The Least You Need to Know

➤ Multicultural writing is flourishing today.

➤ Native-American writers are diverse, but most share an interest in exploring their heritage, their unique place in American life, and what it means to be a Native-American.

➤ N. Scott Momaday, William Least Heat Moon, Leslie Marmon Silko, and Louise Erdrich are outstanding Native-American writers.

➤ While all of today's Latino-American writers share a Spanish-language background, their writing varies greatly.

➤ Richard Rodriguez, Denise Chávez, Julia Alvarez, and Sandra Cisneros are a few celebrated Latino-American writers.

➤ Maxine Hong Kingston's 1976 memoir, *The Woman Warrior,* helped Asian-American writers break into mainstream American literature.

➤ Maxine Hong Kingston and Amy Tan are today's most popular Asian-American writers.

Chapter 32

New Frontiers

In This Chapter

➤ John Cheever, John Updike, and middle-class angst

➤ Truman Capote and the "nonfiction novel"

➤ Mary Gordon's faith and fiction

➤ Stephen King's terrifying vision

➤ Joyce Carol Oates' astonishing versatility

Roe v. Wade, Stonewall, the Middle East, biological weapons. Today's turbulence has contributed to the development of a wide variety of literary movements. Some writers react to turmoil by exploring new literary forms and techniques, creating works that blend fiction and nonfiction or fantasy and realism.

Other writers focus on capturing the essence of modern life, often zeroing in on the complex, contradictory, and commercial nature of existence. Still other writers key into the violence they see exploding around them.

What can we conclude about the nature of contemporary literature? The one thing that unites today's writers is their wide diversity of forms and themes.

This chapter starts with a discussion of John Cheever and John Updike, who chronicle suburban manners and morals in their novels and short stories. Then you'll read about Truman Capote and the "nonfiction novel," one of the most influential developments in contemporary American letters. I'll also explain how Mary Gordon has fashioned the raw material of life into literature. And what would a chapter on today's writers be without a look at Stephen King and Joyce Carol Oates?

John Cheever (1912–1982)

"Our Chekhov of the exurbs," critic John Leonard called John Cheever, alluding to Cheever's interest in the lives of upper-class suburban professionals trapped by circumstances—marriages, jobs, possessions. Imprisoned in their beautiful homes and neighborhoods, Cheever's characters long to break free from their routines, but sometimes they don't realize how deeply they are trapped.

Born in Quincey, Massachusetts, Cheever had the typical unhappy childhood, a seeming requirement for a successful career as a writer. His father lost all his money in the stock market crash of 1929, the same year that Cheever was expelled from private school. With admirable cheek, he wrote a story about the experience and promptly sold it to the *New Republic* in 1930. So his career was born.

The Write Stuff

"[Cheever's] best stories move from a base in a mimetic presentation of surface reality—the *scenery* of apparently successful American middle-class life—to fables of heroism," noted one anonymous reviewer.

During the Depression, Cheever lived in Manhattan and eked out a living doing odd jobs. He enlisted in the armed services in World War II but didn't see action.

Soon after the war, Cheever published his first collection of short stories, *The Way Some People Live*, in 1943. Throughout his career, he continuously wrote stories for the *New Yorker*. In 1978, Cheever published *The Stories of John Cheever,* an anthology of his best tales.

Although Cheever's fame rests largely on his short stories, he also wrote several fine novels, including *The Wapshot Chronicles* (1957, National Book Award winner), *The Wapshot Scandal* (1964), and *Bullet Park* (1969). After a bout with alcohol and drug addiction, Cheever published his last two novels, *Falconer* (1978) and *Oh What a Paradise It Seems* (1982).

Writer's Block

Don't mistake Cheever for an "A-list" writer; at this time, the critics do not consider him a "major" author, although his examination of white, upper middle-class life has left its mark on American literature.

John Updike (b. 1932)

"My subject is the American Protestant small-town middle class," Updike says. "I like middles. It is in middles that extremes clash, where ambiguity restlessly rules…" Updike has cornered the market on stories and novels about middle-class life—and the daily ups and downs of that existence.

Updike was born on March 18, 1932, in Shillington, Pennsylvania. His father was a teacher; his mother, a writer. A gifted artist, Updike graduated from Harvard in 1954 and then spent a year studying art in England.

Upon his return to America, Updike took a job writing for the *New Yorker,* a position he held for several years.

In the 1950s, Updike left the *New Yorker* and moved to Ipswich, Massachusetts, where he continues to write full time. (He is still a regular contributor to the *New Yorker*, however.)

Lit Wit

Since 1978, when he published *The World According to Garp,* John Irving has produced eight long novels, all of them bestsellers, and has become a well-known American author. Irving is famous for his comically convoluted plots, his penchant for violent fates, and his endless epilogues.

Here's Johnny!

Since 1958, when *The Poorhouse Fair,* Updike's first novel, appeared, he has turned out a steady stream of high-quality fiction, including

➤ *Rabbit, Run* (1960)

➤ *Pigeon Feathers* (1963)

➤ *The Centaur* (1964)

➤ *Of the Farm* (1965)

➤ *Couples* (1968)

➤ *Rabbit Redux* (1971)

➤ *Marry Me* (1976)

➤ *Rabbit Is Rich* (1981)

➤ *The Witches of Eastwick* (1984)

➤ *Roger's Version* (1986)

➤ *S* (1988)

➤ *Rabbit at Rest* (1990)

The Write Stuff

Critics have referred to Updike's writing as displaying "charming but limited gifts" and called his art "essentially one of nuance and chiaroscuro." They do acknowledge that Updike has become a "minor cult," however.

Bunny Hop

Updike is perhaps best known for his three Rabbit books: *Rabbit, Run; Rabbit Redux;* and *Rabbit Is Rich.* Each book characterizes an era—the 1950s, the late 1960s, the late 1970s, and the 1990s—through Harry "Rabbit" Angstrom, a stand-in for Updike in some ways.

➤ In *Rabbit, Run,* Harry is having a midlife crisis and longs to escape from his life, especially his wife, child, and community.

➤ *Rabbit Redux* deals with the effect of the Vietnam War and the black revolution on Harry and a small Pennsylvania town.

➤ *Rabbit Is Rich* paints the sad, quiet story of Harry settling into old age. This one got him a Pulitzer Prize.

➤ *Rabbit at Rest* (another Pulitzer Prize winner) follows Harry in the present.

While John Updike describes the angst of middle-class life, Truman Capote, on the other hand, looked at life from a very different angle.

Lit Wit

Some late 20th-century writers are involved with *hypertext,* an online computer "hotel" wherein writers codevelop stories, do takeoffs on each other's work, play jokes on one another, or try to outwit each other in developing story lines. Some users claim that this intertextual mode and ephemeral sensibility will be the only text-oriented form to survive in the 21st century. We'll see!

Truman Capote (1924–1984)

"He wore blue linen shorts that buttoned to his shirt,

his hair was snow white and stuck to his head like dandruff… As he told a tale his blue eyes would lighten and darken; his laugh was sudden and happy; he habitually pulled at a cowlick in the center of his forehead… We came to know him as a pocket Merlin, whose head teemed with eccentric plans, strange longings, and quaint fantasies."

—Harper Lee, describing Truman Capote as a child

A short story writer and novelist best known for his "nonfiction novel" *In Cold Blood,* Capote was the first author to write a nonfiction book that could be read as a novel. A gifted prose stylist, Capote opened up new literary territory. He was also a flamboyant media celebrity, famous for his lavish parties and excesses.

Born Truman Streckfus Persons to a former New Orleans beauty queen, Truman spent his childhood being shuffled among his relatives after his parents' divorce. Since no one wanted to care for him, Truman was raised in an odd sort of household peculiar to the South at that time, dominated by three quarrelsome sisters (his aunts) and their reclusive other brother (his uncle).

The air was heavy with petty resentments, ancient secrets, and 50 years of accumulated slights.

Lit Wit

When he was a child, Truman had only one friend his own age, Harper Lee, the youngest daughter of the family next door. United by a shared anguish at their similar family situations, the children were inseparable. Thirty years later, Harper Lee used Truman as the model for Dill in her novel *To Kill a Mockingbird*.

When Truman was eight years old, his mother married Joseph Garcia Capote who adopted Truman and renamed him Truman Garcia Capote. But Truman's mother was far less fond of her child, chiefly because she was embarrassed by his effeminate ways, and after Truman's birth, she terminated two pregnancies, saying "I will not have another child like Truman." She even took him to various doctors in an attempt to find a drug that would turn him into a "real boy."

Capote graduated from Greenwich High School in Connecticut. An unsuccessful scholar, he found his real calling that same year when he took a part-time job as a copyboy with the *New Yorker*.

By 18 he had not yet reached his adult height of five feet, three inches and had a high, childlike voice. Despite his lowly position on the publishing food chain, Capote quickly attracted attention for his eccentric mannerisms and flamboyant clothing. His career with the *New Yorker* lasted less than a year, however, when he was fired for misrepresenting himself as a staff writer.

Fame, Fortune, and Friends

In 1945, Capote published his first short story, "Miriam." The plot is interwoven with recurring themes of isolation, dread, and psychological breakdowns, typical concerns in Capote's early writing. The story won the O. Henry Award in 1946, leading to a book contract for Capote.

Truman Capote.

In 1948, Capote published the novel *Other Voices, Other Rooms*. An immediate critical and popular success, it topped *The New York Times* bestseller list. At 23 years old, Capote became the darling of the New York literary circuit—and loving it.

Capote's success continued. His next novel, *The Grass Harp* (1951), was a success in print and was later adapted as a play. By this time, Capote was regularly hanging out with John and Jackie Kennedy, Marlon Brando, Arthur Miller, and Liz Taylor. He was allowed into the world of the rich and famous, feted on yachts, in chalets, and in penthouses.

The Nonfiction Novel

In the midst of his mad social whirl, Capote began to develop a new approach to the role that nonfiction could have on his career and on literature. Late in the 1950s, he began to experiment along this line. His first success at experimenting with nonfiction was *Breakfast at Tiffany's* (1958). Within months, Holly Golightly, the novel's main character, had taken her place in America's consciousness. Even harsh critic Norman Mailer wrote that *Breakfast at Tiffany's* was so perfect that he would not change two words of it.

However, Capote's greatest work and success were yet to come. Capote secured his claim to fame in 1965, when the *New Yorker* published his nonfiction novel *In Cold Blood* in its pages.

A gripping account of the mass murder of a Kansas farm family, the Clutters, the book follows two young killers from the murder scene to their eventual execution five and a half years later. Capote's meticulous research—he had even befriended the murderers—resulted in a literary landmark. Capote's "nonfiction novel" received extrordinary acclaim: *The New York Times* declared the novel a masterpiece.

Lit Wit

To celebrate the publication of *In Cold Blood,* Capote gave perhaps the most celebrated party in modern times, a masked "black-and-white ball" at the Plaza Hotel in Manhattan. One guest joked that the guest book read like "an international list for the guillotine." Those attending included publisher Katherine Graham, socialite Barbara Cushing Paley, entertainers Frank Sinatra and Mia Farrow, and various heads of state and royalty.

The last years of Capote's life were painful and difficult. Shunned by his former friends for using their real names and peccadilloes in his book, *Answered Prayers* in 1975, Capote suffered a nervous breakdown, followed by a host of serious physical conditions. Alcoholism and drug addiction added to his difficulties. Capote died in 1984.

Mary Gordon (b. 1948)

"I think I knew about secrets and lies, although I didn't know that I knew it. And I think I didn't expect that human life was about happiness."

—Mary Gordon

Mary Gordon has been pegged as a religious and moral writer, a tag she has tried to shed. Nonetheless, her ethical stance and the rhythms of her prose reveal that the label is more accurate than she might perhaps like.

Mary Catherine Gordon grew up in the working-class world of Valley Stream, New York. Although intellectual ambitions were discouraged in the neighborhood, Gordon's father took Mary to the library regularly and wrote her poems in German, French, Greek, and Latin. Decades later, Gordon would discover that her beloved father created a completely false past for himself, but his intellectual slant nevertheless helped her become a writer.

Not surprisingly, Gordon was shattered when her father died of a heart attack when she was only seven years old. "When my father died," Gordon remembers, "it was like all lights went out… my only real life, I would say, was reading, and I was quite prayerful. I didn't have many human relations." She and her mother moved into her grandmother's home. Both her mother and grandmother were crippled from polio and did not encourage young Mary's artistic ambitions.

After graduating from Barnard College, Gordon attracted the attention of the celebrated British writer Margaret Drabble, who helped launch her career with her novel *Final Payments* in 1978.

The book was a smash hit. At 29, Gordon became an overnight sensation. The critics compared her to Jane Austen, Doris Lessing, and Flannery O'Connor.

Final Payments

The novel opens with the funeral of Joseph Moore, a conservative Catholic who had been a literature professor. His daughter, Isabel, now 30, has lived at home for the past 11 years, nursing him through a series of strokes: "I gave up my life for him; only if you understand my father will you understand that I make that statement not with self-pity but with extreme pride… This strikes everyone in our decade as unusual, barbarous, cruel. To me, it was not only inevitable but natural. The Church exists and has endured for this, not only to preserve itself but to keep certain scenes intact: My father and me living by ourselves in a one-family house in Queens."

Isabel then sets out to develop a new life for herself. Along the way, she questions the nature of devotion and sacrifice and makes choices between the pull of the flesh and the claims of the spirit.

Religious Rite

After the success of *Final Payments*, Gordon published her second novel, *The Company of Women,* in 1981. In this book, Gordon tries to minimize the Catholic overtones of her work. Continuing this trend, her subsequent books have focused less overtly on religion. *Men and Angels* (1985), for example, portrays an art historian who hires a psychotic religious fanatic as a mother's helper. This novel examines the common struggles of domesticity and companionship.

Gordon's next novel, *The Other Side* (1989), is a multigenerational immigrant saga. Gordon also came out with a collection of short stories, *Temporary Shelter* (1987), a volume of essays, *Good Boys and Dead Girls* (1992), and a book of novellas, *The Rest of Life* (1993). In addition to writing, Gordon currently teaches at Barnard College.

Stephen King (b. 1947)

"People want to know why I do this, why I write such gross stuff. I like to tell them that I have the heart of a small boy—and I keep it in a jar on my desk."

—Stephen King

Stephen King's macabre tales have made him America's best-selling author—ever. But his tales are more than mere bloodbaths. At his best, King creates gripping psychological studies that probe the American subconscious. *Dolores Claiborne* (1992), *Rose Madder* (1995), and *Bag of Bones* (1998) in particular show the depth of King's talent.

King Me

When Stephen King was three years old, his father left one day and never came back. Stephen turned to fiction for solace, writing his first short story just a few years later. King's life became less introspective when he joined the football team and a local rock band in high school. He graduated from the University of Maine at Orono in 1970 with a B.A in English and qualified to teach on the high school level.

He and fellow writer Tabitha Spruce married soon after. Since King couldn't find a teaching job, the couple lived on his earnings as a laborer at an industrial laundry along with her student loan and savings, with an occasional boost from a short story sale to magazines.

In September of 1971, King began teaching high school English. In his spare time, he continued to write short stories and novels. In 1974, *Carrie* was published and King embarked on a wildly prolific and lucrative career. So far, he's sold well over 100 million copies of his terrifying tales and has become the richest writer in world history. In 1989, King signed a deal with Viking that netted him $35 million for four books—a new record. In 1997, Simon & Schuster topped that offer.

Lit Wit

Many of King's works have been adapted for film, including *Carrie*, *The Dead Zone*, *The Shining*, *Christine*, *Salem's Lot*, *Firestarter*, *Cujo*, *Dolores Claiborne*, *Pet Sematary* (for which King wrote the screenplay and had a bit part as a minister), and *Misery*. The movie *Stand By Me* was adapted from his novella, *The Body* (from *Different Seasons*). In 1992, *Sleepwalkers* was produced from King's screenplay.

When not writing, the master of the macabre enjoys bowling, poker, and getting together with Dave Barry, Amy Tan, Robert Fulghum, Matt Groening, and Roy Blount, Jr. in a "hard-listening" band (so dubbed by Barry) called the "Rock Bottom Remainders."

Fright Night

Here's a quick reference list for some of Stephen King's most popular books. Check out your local book establishment for even more Stephen King tales of terror.

➤ *Carrie* (1974) A young woman finds that she has telekinetic powers.

➤ *Salem's Lot* (1975) Vampires take over a small town in Maine.

➤ *The Shining* (1977) A possessed hotel tries to destroy a family.

➤ *The Stand* (1978) Most of humanity is wiped out by a plague, and the survivors fight the ultimate battle of good versus evil.

➤ *The Dead Zone* (1979) A man wakes from his coma with physic powers.

➤ *Firestarter* (1980) A young girl tries to deal with her amazing pyrokinetic powers.

➤ *Cujo* (1981) A rabid dog causes terror in a small town in Maine.

➤ *Christine* (1983) A car with a mind of its own seeks vengeance.

➤ *Pet Sematary* (1983) Pets return from the dead to terrorize people in a small town in Maine.

➤ *Misery* (1987) A "number-one fan" saves the life of an author and keeps him a prisoner for her own twisted purposes.

➤ *The Tommyknockers* (1987) A group of people digs up a UFO, with unsettling results.

➤ *Needful Things* (1991) Having its every need fulfilled tears a small Maine town apart.

➤ *Dolores Claiborne* (1992) An old woman comes to terms with her life by confronting her abusive husband and the estrangement from her daughter.

➤ *Rose Madder* (1995) An abused woman tries to start a new life, but her husband has a different idea.

➤ *Bag of Bones* (1998) A writer deals with the loss of his wife in a haunted house.

The Write Stuff

Stephen King has also written a series of thrillers under the name Richard Bachman, including *Rage*, *The Long Walk*, *Roadwork*, *The Running Man*, *Thinner*, and *The Regulators*.

Joyce Carol Oates (b. 1938)

"The worst cynicism: a belief in luck."

—Joyce Carol Oates

Joyce Carol Oates certainly has talent, but she made her own luck. For starters, since there were few books in Lockport, New York, the working-class town where she was raised, Oates made her own books by binding her stories with covers she designed herself. To make the books look better, she learned to type by the age of 12.

Her talent was recognized early: While attending Syracuse University on scholarship, Oates won the coveted *Mademoiselle* magazine fiction contest. After graduating at the head of her class, Oates earned an M.A. in English at the University of Wisconsin, where she met and married Raymond J. Smith.

Between 1968 and 1978, Oates taught at the University of Windsor in Canada. Tremendously productive, Oates published two or three books a year—even while teaching full time.

In 1978, Princeton University lured Oates to New Jersey to teach in their creative writing program. In addition, she and her husband operate a highly respected publishing company and produce a literary magazine, *The Ontario Review*.

Shortly after arriving in Princeton, Oates wrote *Bellefleur*, the first in a series of ambitious Gothic novels that rework traditional literary genres and reimagine large swaths of American history. Published in the early 1980s, these novels mark a departure from the psychological realism of her earlier work. Oates returned powerfully to the realistic mode with ambitious family chronicles *(You Must Remember This, Because It Is Bitter*, and *Because It Is My Heart)*, compelling contemporary novels *(Solstice, Marya: A Life)*, and a series of suspense novels. All these books show her great versatility as a writer.

The Write Stuff

"Where Are You Going, Where Have You Been?" formed the basis for the movie *Smooth Talk*.

The Least You Need to Know

➤ John Cheever wrote stories and novels about suburban angst.

➤ John Updike's primary subject is Protestant small-town middle-class life.

➤ With *In Cold Blood,* Truman Capote created the "nonfiction novel," a nonfiction book that could be read as a novel.

➤ Mary Gordon's Catholic sensibility shines through her novels, short stories, and memoirs.

➤ Stephen King's thrilling psychological horror tales have made him America's best-selling novelist ever.

➤ Joyce Carol Oates is one of America's most productive contemporary writers.

➤ Stephen King's thrilling psychological horror tales have made him America's best-selling novelist ever.

The Authors and Their Most Famous Works

Alvarez, Julia

Homecoming (1984)

How the Garcia Girls Lost Their Accents (1990)

In the Time of the Butterflies (1994)

Homecoming: New and Collected Poems (1996)

The Other Side: El Otro Lado (1996)

¡Yo! (1997)

En El Tiempo De Las Mariposas (1998)

Something to Declare: Essays (1998)

Atwood, Margaret

Poetry

"The Circle Game" (1964)

"The Animals in That Country" (1969)

"The Journals of Susanna Moodie" (1970)

"Procedures for Underground" (1970)

"Power Politics" (1971)

"You Are Happy" (1974)

"Selected Poems" (1976)

"Two-Headed Poems" (1978)

"True Stories" (1981)

"Interlunar" (1984)

Selected Poems II: Poems Selected and New, 1976–1986 (1986)

Selected Poems 1966–1984 (1990)

Margaret Atwood Poems 1965–1975 (1991)

Eating Fire; Selected Poems, 1965–1995 (1998)

Novels

The Edible Woman (1969)

Surfacing (1972)

Lady Oracle (1976)

Life Before Man (1980)

Bodily Harm (1981)

The Handmaid's Tale (1986)

Cat's Eye (1989)

The Robber Bride (1993)

Morning in the Burned House (1995)

Alias Grace (1996)

Baldwin, James

Another Country (1962)

Giovanni's Room (1955)

Notes of a Native Son (1955)

Go Tell It on the Mountain (1953)

Tell Me How Long the Train's Been Gone (1968)

Just Above My Head (1979)

Bellow, Saul

The Dangling Man (1944)

The Victim (1947)

The Adventures of Augie March (1953)

Seize the Day (1956)

Henderson the Rain King (1959)

Herzog (1964)

Mr. Sammler's Planet (1970)

Humboldt's Gift (1975)

The Dean's December (1982)

More Die of Heartbreak (1987)

A Theft (1989)

The Bellarosa Connection (1989)

Something to Remember Me By (1991)

Brooks, Gwendolyn

Poetry—A Street in Bronzeville (1945)

Annie Allen (1949)

Novel—Maud Martha (1953)

Bronzeville Boys and Girls (1956)

The Bean Eaters (1960)

Selected Poems (1963)

In the Mecca (1968)

Riot (1969)

Family Pictures (1970)

Aloneness (1971)

Report From Part One (1972)

The Tiger Who Wore White Gloves, or, What You Are You Are, (1974)

Beckonings (1975)

Primer for Blacks (1980)

To Disembark (1981)

Black Love (1982)

The Near Johannesburg Boy and Other Poems (1987)

Burroughs, William S.

Naked Lunch (1959)

Capote, Truman

Other Voices, Other Rooms (1948)

The Grass Harp (1951)

Breakfast at Tiffany's (1958)

In Cold Blood (1965)

Cather, Willa

O Pioneers! (1913)

The Song of the Lark (1915)

My Antonia (1921)

One of Ours (1922)

A Lost Lady (1923)

The Professor's House (1925)

My Mortal Enemy (1926)

Death Comes for the Archbishop (1927)

Shadows on the Rock (1931)

Lucy Gayheart (1935)

Sapphira and the Slave Girl (1940)

Chávez, Denise

The Last of the Menu Girls (1986)

The Woman Who Knew the Language of Animals (1992)

Face of an Angel (1994)

Novitiates (1973)

The Flying Tortilla Man (1975)

Plague-Time (1985)

Novena Narrative (1987)

Language of Vision (1988)

Women in the State of Grace (1989)

Chopin, Kate

At Fault (1890)

Bayou Folk (1894)

A Night in Acadie (1897)

The Awakening (1899)

Cisneros, Sandra

The House on Mango Street (1983)

My Wicked Wicked Ways (1987)

Woman Hollering Creek and Other Stories (1991)

Loose Woman: Poems (1994)

Clemens, Samuel

Innocents Abroad (1869)

Roughing It (1872)

The Gilded Age (1873)

The Adventures of Tom Sawyer (1876)

A Tramp Abroad (1880)

The Prince and the Pauper (1881)

Life on the Mississippi (1883)

The Adventures of Huckleberry Finn (1884)

Mark Twain's Library of Humor (1888)

A Connecticut Yankee in King Arthur's Court (1889)

Pudd'nhead Wilson (1894)

Personal Recollections of Joan of Arc (1895)

Following the Equator (1897)

The Man That Corrupted Hadleyburg (1900)

Extracts from Adam's Diary (1904)

What is Man? (1906)

The Mysterious Stranger (1916)

Letters from the Earth (1939)

Cooper, James Fenimore

Precaution (1820)

The Spy (1821)

The Pilot (1823)

The Pioneers (1823)

Lionel Lincoln (1825)

The Last of the Mohicans (1826)

The Prairie (1827)

The Red Rover (1827)

The Wept of Wish-ton-Wish (1829)

The Water-Witch (1830)

The Bravo (1831)

The Heidenmauer (1832)

The Headsman (1833)

The Monikins (1835)

Home as Found (1838)

Homeward Bound (1838)

Mercedes of Castile (1840)

The Pathfinder (1840)

The Deerslayer (1841)

The Two Admirals (1842)

The Wing-and-Wing (1842)

Wyandotte (1843)

Afloat and Ashore (1844)

Miles Wallingford (1844)

The Chainbearer (1845)

Satanstoe (1845)

The Redskins (1846)

The Crater (1847)

Jack Tier (1848)

The Oak Openings (1848)

The Sea Lions (1849)

The Ways of the Hour (1850)

Crane, Stephen

The Black Riders (1895)
The Red Badge of Courage (1895)
"The Blue Hotel" (1896)
"The Bride Comes to Yellow Sky" (1896)
"George's Mother" (1896)
"The Little Regiment" (1896)
"The Third Violet" (1897)
"The Open Boat" (1898)
"Active Service" (1899)
The Monster And Other Stories (1899)
War Is Kind (1899)
Whilomville Stories (1900)
Wounds in the Rain (1900)
Men, Women and Boats (1921)
Collected Works, 12 Vol. (1925–26)
Letters (1960)

Cullen, Countée

Colors (1925)
Copper Sun (1927)
The Ballad of the Brown Girl (1927)
One Way to Heaven (1932)
The Last Zoo (1940)
My Lives and How I Lost Them (1942)

cummings, e.e.

The Enormous Room (1922)
Tulips and Chimneys (1923, 1925)
& (1925)
XLI Poems (1925)
Is 5 (1926)
W (1931)
Eimi (1933)
no thanks (1935)
Collected Poems (1938)

50 Poems (1940)
1 x 1 (1944)
XAIPE (1950)
95 Poems (1958)
73 Poems (1963)

Dickinson, Emily

Poems by Emily Dickinson (1890)

Douglass, Frederick

The Life and Times of Frederick Douglass (1882)

Dreiser, Theodore

Sister Carrie (1900)
Jennie Gerhardt (1911)
The Financier (1912)
A Traveler at Forty (1913)
The Titan (1914)
The Genius (1915)
A Hoosier Holiday (1916)
An American Tragedy (1925)
Tragic America (1931)
The Bulwark (1946)
The Stoic (1947)

Eliot, T.S.

Prufrock and Other Observations (1917)
Poems (1920)
The Sacred Wood (1920)
The Waste Land (1922)
Murder in the Cathedral (1935)
Four Quartets (1936–43)
The Family Reunion (1939)
The Cocktail Party (1950)
The Confidential Clerk (1954)
The Elder Statesman (1958)

Ellison, Ralph

Invisible Man (1952)

Emerson, Ralph Waldo

Nature (1836)

Essays, First Series (1841)

Essays, Second Series (1844)

Poems (1847)

Representative Men (1850)

The Conduct of Life (1860)

Journals (10 volumes)

Erdrich, Louise

Imagination (1981)

Jacklight (1984)

Love Medicine (1984)

The Beet Queen (1986)

Tracks (1988)

Baptism of Desire: poems (1989)

The Bingo Palace (1994)

The Blue Jay's Dance: A Birth Year (1995)

Antelope Woman (1998)

Faulkner, William

The Marble Faun (1924)

Soldier's Pay (1926)

Mosquitoes (1927)

Sartoris (1929)

The Sound and the Fury (1929)

As I Lay Dying (1930)

Sanctuary (1931)

These 13 (1931)

Light in August (1932)

Doctor Martino and Other Stories (1934)

Pylon (1935)

Absalom, Absalom! (1936)

The Unvanquished (1938)

The Wild Palms (1939)

The Hamlet (1940)

Go Down, Moses (1942)

Intruder in the Dust (1948)

Knight's Gambit (1949)

Collected Stories of William Faulkner (1950)

Requiem for a Nun (1951)

A Fable (1954)

Big Woods (1955)

The Town (1957)

The Mansion (1959)

The Reivers (1962)

Fitzgerald, F. Scott

This Side of Paradise (1920)

Flappers and Philosophers (1921)

The Beautiful and the Damned (1922)

Tales of the Jazz Age (1922)

The Vegetable, Or from the Postman to President (1923)

The Great Gatsby (1925)

All the Sad Young Men (1926)

Tender Is the Night (1934)

Taps At Reveille (1935)

The Last Tycoon (unfinished) ed. Edmund Wilson (1941)

The Crack-Up ed. by Edmund Wilson (1945)

Freeman, Mary Wilkins

A Humble Romance and Other Stories (1887)

A New England Nun and Other Stories (1891)

Pembroke (1894)

Frost, Robert

A Boy's Will (1913)

North of Boston (1914)

Mountain Interval (1916)

New Hampshire (1923)

West-Running Brook (1928)

A Further Range (1936)

A Witness Tree (1942)

Steeple Bush (1947)

In the Clearing (1962)

Gallant, Mavis

The Other Paris (1956)

My Heart Is Broken (1964)

A Fairly Good Time (1970)

The Pegnitz Junction (1973)

The End of the World and Other Stories (1974)

From the Fifteenth District: A Novella and Eight Stories (1979)

Gilman, Charlotte Perkins

Women and Economics (1898)

The Yellow Wallpaper (1899)

"The Man-Made World" (1911)

His Religion and Hers (1923)

The Living of Charlotte Perkins Gilman (1935)

Ginsberg, Allen

Howl and Other Poems (1956)

Siesta in Xbalba and Return to the States (1956)

Empty Mirror: Early Poems (1961)

Kaddish and Other Poems, 1958–1960 (1961)

The Change (1963)

Reality Sandwiches: 1953–1960 (1963)

A Strange New Cottage in Berkeley (1963)

Kral Majales (King of May) (1965)

Wichita Vortex Sutra (1965)

TV Baby Poems (1967)

Airplane Dreams: Compositions From Journals (1968)

The Heart Is a Clock (1968)

House of Anansi 1968

Message II (1968)

Scrap Leaves Hasty Scribbles, (1968)

For the Soul of the Planet Is Wakening… (1970)

Bixby Canyon Ocean Path Word Breeze (1972)

Open Head (1972)

The Fall of America: Poems of These States, 1965–1971 (1973)

The Gates of Wrath: Rhymed Poems 1948–1952 (1973)

First Blues: Rags, Ballads and Harmonium Songs, 1971–1974 (1974)

Careless Love: Two Rhymes (1978)

Poems All Over the Place: Mostly Seventies (1978)

Gordon, Mary

The Company of Women (1982)

Final Payments (1983)

Men and Angels (1986)

The Other Side (1990)

Rest of Life; Three Novellas (1994)

The Shadow Man (1996)

Harte, Bret

Condensed Novels (1860)

The Luck of Roaring Camp, and Other Sketches (1870)

Ah Sin (1877) (drama)

Hawthorne, Nathaniel

"Young Goodman Brown" (1835)

Twice-Told Tales (1837, 1842)

The Whole History of Grandfather's Chair (1840)

Mosses from an Old Manse (1846, 1854)

The Scarlet Letter (1850)

The House of the Seven Gables (1851)

The Blithedale Romance (1852)

The Life of Franklin Pierce (1852)

The Snow-Image, and Other Twice-Told Tales (1852)

A Wonder-Book for Girls and Boys (1852)

Tanglewood Tales (1853)

The Marble Faun (1860)

"Chiefly About War Matters" (1862)

Hemingway, Ernest

Three Stories & Ten Poems (1923)

In Our Time (1924)

The Sun Also Rises (1926)

The Torrents of Spring (1926)

Men Without Women (1927)

A Farewell to Arms (1929)

Death in the Afternoon (1932)

Winner Take Nothing (1933)

Green Hills of Africa (1935)

To Have and Have Not (1937)

The Fifth Column and the First Forty-Nine Stories (1938)

For Whom the Bell Tolls (1940)

Men at War: The Best War Stories of All Time (1942)

Across the River and Into the Trees (1950)

The Old Man and the Sea (1952)

A Moveable Feast (1964)

By-Line: Ernest Hemingway (1967)

Islands in the Stream (1970)

The Nick Adams Stories (1972)

The Garden of Eden (1986)

The Complete Short Stories of Ernest Hemingway (1987)

Hughes, Langston

The New Negro (1925)

The Weary Blues (1926)

Not Without Laughter (1930)

One-Way Ticket (1949)

Hurston, Zora Neale

Jonah's Gourd Vine (1934)

Mules and Men (1935)

Their Eyes Were Watching God (1937)

Dust Tracks on a Road (1942)

Irving, Washington

A History of New York From the Beginning of the World to the End of the Dutch Dynasty (1809)

The Sketch Book (1820)

Bracebridge Hall (1822)

Tales of a Traveler (1824)

The Alhambra (1832)

James, Henry

Watch and Ward (1871)

Roderick Hudson (1875)

The American (1877)

Daisy Miller (1879)

The Europeans (1879)

Hawthorne (1880)

Washington Square (1881)

The Portrait of a Lady (1881)

The Bostonians (1886)

The Princess Casamassima (1886)
The Aspern Papers (1888)
The Reverberator (1888)
The Tragic Muse (1890)
The Spoils of Poynton (1897)
What Maisie Knew (1897)
In the Cage (1898)
The Turn of the Screw (1898)
The Awkward Age (1899)
The Sacred Fount (1901)
The Wings of the Dove (1902)
The Ambassadors (1903)
The Golden Bowl (1904)
The American Scene (1907)
New York Edition of James's Work (1907–9)
A Small Boy and Others (1913)
Notes of a Son and Brother (1914)

Jewett, Sarah Orne

Deephaven (1877)
The Country of Pointed Firs (1896)

Jong, Erica

Novels

Fear of Flying (1973)
Parachutes & Kisses (1984)
Inventing Memory: A Novel of Mothers and Daughters (1997)

Poetry

Fruits & Vegetables (1971)
Half-Lives (1973)
At the Edge of the Body (1979)

Kerouac, Jack

The Town and the City (1950)
On the Road (1957)
The Dharma Bums (1958)
The Subterraneans (1958)
Doctor Sax (1959)
Maggie Cassidy (1959)
Big Sur (1962)
Visions of Gerard (1963)
Desolation Angels (1965)
Vanity of Duluoz (1968)

King, Stephen

Carrie (1974)
Salem's Lot (1975)
The Shining (1977)
The Stand (1978)
The Dead Zone (1979)
Night Shift (1979)
Firestarter (1980)
Cujo (1981)
Different Seasons (1982)
Christine (1983)
Pet Sematary (1983)
It (1986)
Misery (1987)
The Tommyknockers (1987)
The Dark Half (1989)
Four Past Midnight (1991)
Needful Things (1991)
Dolores Claiborne (1992)
Insomnia (1994)
Rose Madder (1995)
Bag of Bones (1998)
Storm of the Century (1999)
The Girl Who Loved Tom Gordon (1999)

Under the Name "Richard Bachman"

Rage (1977)

The Long Walk (1979)

Roadwork (1981)

The Running Man (1982)

Thinner (1984)

The Regulators (1996)

Kingston, Maxine Hong

The Woman Warrior (1976)

China Men (1980)

Tripmaster Monkey: His Fake Book (1989)

Leacock, Stephen

Literary Lapses (1910)

Nonsense Novels (1911)

Moonbeams from the Larger Lunacy (1915)

Further Foolishness (1916)

Essays and Literary Studies (1916)

Frenzied Fiction (1918)

The Unsolved Riddle of Social Justice (1920)

My Discovery of England (1922)

The Garden of Folly (1924)

Winnowed Wisdom (1926)

Short Circuits (1928)

Lincoln Frees the Slaves (1934)

Humor: Its Theory and Technique (1935)

Humor and Humanity (1937)

My Discovery of the West (1937)

Too Much College (1939)

Our Heritage of Liberty (1942)

Remarkable Uncle (1942)

Happy Stories (1943)

How to Write (1943)

Last Leaves (1945)

The Boy I Left Behind Me (1946)

London, Jack

The Call of the Wild (1903)

The People of the Abyss (1903)

The Sea Wolf (1904)

Martin Eden (1909)

John Barleycorn (1913)

Lowell, Robert

Lord Weary's Castle (1946)

Life Studies (1959)

The Dolphin (1973)

Day by Day (1977)

Selected Poems (1976)

Mailer, Norman

The Naked and the Dead (1948)

The Deer Park (1955)

The White Negro (1957)

Advertisements for Myself (1959)

The Presidential Papers (1963)

An American Dream (1965)

Cannibals and Christians (1966)

The Bullfight (1967)

Why Are We in Vietnam? (1967)

The Armies of the Night (1968)

The Idol and the Octopus (1968)

Miami and the Siege of Chicago (1968)

Running Against the Machine (1969)

Of a Fire on the Moon (1970)

King of the Hill (1971)

The Long Patrol (1971)

The Prisoner of Sex (1971)

Existential Errands (1972)

St. George and the Godfather (1972)

Marilyn (1973)

The Flight (1975)

Genius and Lust (1976)

Some Honorable Men (1976)

The Executioner's Song (1979)

Of Women and Their Elegance (1980)

The Essential Mailer (1982)

Pieces and Pontifications (1982)

Ancient Evenings (1984)

Tough Guys Don't Dance (1984)

Huckleberry Finn (1985)

Harlot's Ghost (1991)

Pablo and Fernande (1994)

Oswald's Tale: An American Mystery (1995)

Portrait of Picasso as a Young Man (1995)

The Gospel According to the Son (1997)

The Time of Our Time (1998)

Malamud, Bernard

The Natural (1952)

The Assistant (1957)

The Magic Barrel (1958)

A New Life (1961)

Idiots First (1963)

The Fixer (1966)

Pictures of Fidelman (1969)

The Tenants (1971)

Rembrandt's Hat (1973)

God's Grace (1982)

McKay, Claude

Poetry

Songs of Jamaica (1912)

Harlem Shadows (1922)

Prose

Home to Harlem (1928)

Banjo (1929)

Gingertown (1932)

Banana Bottom (1933)

Harlem: A Negro Metropolis (1940)

Melville, Herman

Typee (1846)

Omoo (1847)

Mardi (1849)

Redburn (1849)

White Jacket (1850)

Moby-Dick (1851)

Pierre (1852)

Israel Potter (1855)

The Piazza Tales (1856)

The Confidence Man (1857)

Momaday, N. Scott

House Made of Dawn (1968)

The Way to Rainy Mountain (1969)

Montgomery, Lucy Maud

Anne of Green Gables (1908)

Anne of Avonlea (1909)

Kilmeny of the Orchard (1910)

The Story Girl (1911)

Chronicles of Avonlea (1912)

The Golden Road (1913)

Anne's House of Dreams (1917)

Rainbow Valley (1919)

Rilla of Ingleside (1921)

Emily of New Moon (1923)

Emily Climbs (1925)

The Blue Castle (1926)

Emily's Quest (1927)
Magic for Marigold (1929)
A Tangled Web (1931)
Pat of Silver Bush (1933)
Mistress Pat (1935)
Anne of Windy Poplars (1936)
Jane of Lantern Hill (1937)
Anne of Ingleside (1939)

Morrison, Toni

The Bluest Eye (1970)
Sula (1973)
Song of Solomon (1977)
Tar Baby (1981)
Dreaming Emmett (1986)
Beloved (1987)
Jazz (1992)
Paradise (1998)

Munro, Alice

Dance of the Happy Shades (1968)
Lives of Girls and Women (1971)
Who Do You Think You Are? (1978)
Something I've Been Meaning to Tell You (1974)
The Progress of Love (1986)
Friend of My Youth (1990)
Open Secrets (1994)

Norris, Frank

Yvernelle [verse] (1891)
Blix (1899)
McTeague (1899)
A Man's Woman (1900)
The Octopus (1901)
The Pit (1903)
Vandover and the Brute (1914)

O'Connor, Flannery

Wise Blood (1952)
A Good Man Is Hard to Find (1955)
The Violent Bear It Away (1960)
Everything That Rises Must Converge (1965)
Mystery and Manners: Occasional Prose (1969)
The Complete Stories of Flannery O'Connor (1972)
The Habit of Being: The Letters of Flannery O'Connor (1979)
The Presence of Grace, and Other Book Reviews (1983)
Collected Works (1988)

Ondaatje, Michael

Poetry

"The Dainty Monsters" (1967)
"The Man with Seven Toes" (1969)
"Rat Jelly" (1973)
"Elimination Dance" (1978)
"Claude Glass" (1979)
There's a Trick with a Knife I'm Learning to Do: Poems 1963–1978 (1979)
Rat Jelly and Other Poems (1980)
"Tin Roof" (1982)
"Secular Love" (1984)
Two Poems (1986)
The Cinnamon Peeler: Selected Poems (1991)

Prose

The Collected Works of Billy the Kid (1970)
Coming Through Slaughter (1976)
Running in the Family (1982)
In the Skin of a Lion (1987)
The English Patient (1992)

Plath, Sylvia

Colossus (1960)

Ariel (1965)

Crossing the Water (1971)

The Bell Jar (1973) [prose]

Winter Trees (1972)

Poe, Edgar Allan

"Ligeia" (1838)

The Narrative of Arthur Gordon Pym (1838)

"The Fall of the House of Usher" (1839)

"The Murders in the Rue Morgue (1841)

"The Masque of the Red Death" (1842)

"The Gold Bug" (1843)

"The Pit and the Pendulum" (1843)

"The Tell-Tale Heart" (1843)

"The Purloined Letter" (1845)

"The Raven" (1845)

"The Cask of Amontillado" (1846)

"Annabel Lee" (1849)

Pound, Ezra

A Lume Spento and Other Early Poems (1908)

Personae (1909–1926)

The Spirit of Romance (1910)

Cathay (1915)

Lustra (1916)

Hugh Selwyn Mauberly (1920)

Make It New (1934)

Jefferson and/or Mussolini; L'idea statale; fascism as I have seen it (1936)

Selected Poems (1948)

The Cantos of Ezra Pound (1948)

Richler, Mordecai

The Apprenticeship of Duddy Kravitz (1959)

The Incomparable Atuk (1963)

Cocksure (1968)

Hunting Tigers Under Glass (1968)

The Street (1969)

St. Urbain's Horseman (1971)

Shovelling Trouble (1972)

Notes on an Endangered Species (1974)

Joshua Then and Now (1980)

Home Sweet Home: My Canadian Album (1984)

Roth, Philip

Goodbye, Columbus (1959)

Letting Go (1962)

When She Was Good (1967)

Portnoy's Complaint (1969)

Our Gang (1970)

The Breast (1971)

My Life as a Man (1974)

The Professor of Desire (1977)

Zuckerman Bound (1985)

The Counterlife (1987)

Salinger, J.D.

The Catcher in the Rye (1951)

Nine Stories (1953)

Franny and Zooey (1961)

Raise High the Roofbeams, Carpenters and Seymour: An Introduction (1963)

Sexton, Anne

To Bedlam and Part Way Back (1960)

All My Pretty Ones (1962)

Live or Die (1966)

Love Poems (1969)

Transformations (1971)

The Book of Folly (1972)

The Death Notebooks (1974)

The Awful Rowing Toward God (1975)

45 Mercy Street (1976)

Words for Dr. Y.: Uncollected Poems (1978)

The Complete Poems (1981)

Silko, Leslie Marmon

Languna Women Poems (1974)

Ceremony (1977)

Storyteller (1981)

Almanac of the Dead: A Novel (1991)

Yellow Woman (1993)

Yellow Woman and a Beauty of the Spirit Essays (1996)

Steinbeck, John

Cup of Gold (1929)

The Pastures of Heaven (1932)

To a God Unknown (1933)

Tortilla Flat (1935)

In Dubious Battle (1936)

Of Mice and Men (1937)

The Grapes of Wrath (1939)

The Moon is Down (1942)

Cannery Row (1945)

The Pearl (1947)

The Wayward Bus (1947)

Burning Bright (1950)

East of Eden (1952)

The Winter of Our Discontent (1961)

Stowe, Harriet Beecher

The Mayflower: Or, Sketches Of Scenes And Characters Among the Descendants of the Pilgrims (1843)

Uncle Tom's Cabin (1852)

The Key to Uncle Tom's Cabin (1853)

Sunny Memoirs of Foreign Lands (1854)

Dred (1856)

A Tale of Great Dismal Swamp (1856)

The Minister's Wooing (1859)

The Pearl of Orr's Island (1862)

Little Foxes (1866)

The Chimney Corner (1868)

Old Town Folks (1869)

Lady Byron Vindicated (1870)

My Wife and I (1871)

Old Town Fireside Stories (1871)

Sam Lawson's Old Town Fireside Stories (1872)

Palmetto Leaves (1873)

Woman in Sacred History (1873)

We and Our Neighbours (1875)

Captain Kidd's Money and Other Stories (1876)

Poqanuc People (1878)

A Dog's Mission (1881)

The Writings (1896)

Thoreau, Henry David

"Civil Disobedience" (1849)

A Week on the Concord and Merrimack Rivers (1849)

Walden, or, Life in the Woods (1854)

Thurber, James

Is Sex Necessary? or Why You Feel the Way You Do (with E.B. White) (1929)

The Owl in the Attic and Other Perplexities (1931)

My Life and Hard Times (1933)

The Middle-Aged Man on the Flying Trapeze, (1935)

The Last Flower: A Parable in Pictures (1939)

"The Secret Life of Walter Mitty" (1939)

Fables for Our Time, and Famous Poems Illustrated, (1940)

My World—and Welcome to It (1942)

Thurber's Men, Women and Dogs (1943)

The Thurber Carnival (1945)

The White Deer (1945)

The Beast in Me and Other Animals: A Collection of Pieces and Drawings About Human Beings and Less Alarming Creatures (1948)

The 13 Clocks (1950)

The Seal in the Bedroom & Other Predicaments (1950)

The Thurber Album; A New Collection of Pieces About People (1952)

Thurber Country: A New Collection of Pieces About Males and Females, Mainly of Our Own Species (1953)

Thurber's Dogs: A Collection of the Master's Dogs, Written and Drawn, Real and Imaginary, Living and Long Ago (1955)

Further Fables for Our Time (1956)

Alarms and Diversions (1957)

The Wonderful O (1957)

The Years with Ross (1959)

Let Your Mind Alone! and Other More or Less Inspirational Pieces (1960)

Lanterns & Lances (1961)

Credos and Curios (1962)

Toomer, Jean

Cane (1923)

Twain, Mark

See Samuel Clemens

Updike, John

The Poorhouse Fair (1958)

Rabbit, Run (1960)

Pigeon Feathers (1963)

The Centaur (1964)

Of the Farm (1965)

Couples (1968)

Rabbit Redux (1971)

Marry Me (1976)

Rabbit Is Rich (1981)

The Witches of Eastwick (1984)

Roger's Version (1986)

S (1988)

Rabbit at Rest (1990)

Walker, Alice

The Third Life of Grange Copeland (1970)

Meridian (1976)

The Color Purple (1982)

The Temple of My Familiar (1989)

Possessing the Secret of Joy (1992)

The Same River Twice: Honoring the Difficult (1996)

Wharton, Edith

Fiction

The Greater Inclination (1899)

The Touchstone (1900)

Crucial Instances (1901)

The Valley of Decision (1902)

Sanctuary (1903)

The Descent of Man and Other Stories (1904)

The House of Mirth (1905)

The Fruit of the Tree (1907)

Madame de Treymes (1907)

The Hermit and the Wild Woman and Other Stories (1908)

Tales of Men and Ghosts (1910)

Ethan Frome (1911)

The Reef (1912)

The Custom of the Country (1913)

Xingu and Other Stories (1916)

Summer (1917)

The Marne (1918)

The Age of Innocence (1920)

The Glimpses of the Moon (1922)

A Son at the Front (1923)

Old New York (1924)

The Mother's Recompense (1925)

Here and Beyond (1926)

Twelve Poems (1926)

Twilight Sleep (1927)

The Children (1928)

Hudson River Bracketed (1929)

Certain People (1930)

The Gods Arrive (1932)

Human Nature (1933)

The World Over (1936)

Ghosts (1937)

The Buccaneers (1938)

Nonfiction

The Decoration of Houses (1897)

Italian Villas and Their Gardens (1904)

Italian Backgrounds (1905)

A Motor Flight Through France (1908)

Fighting France, from Dunkerque to Belfort (1915)

French Ways and Their Meaning (1919)

In Morocco (1920)

The Writing of Fiction (1925)

A Backward Glance (1934)

Wright, Richard

Uncle Tom's Children: Four Novellas (1938)

Native Son (1940)

Twelve Million Black Voices: A Folk History of the Negro in the United States (1941)

Black Boy: A Record of Childhood and Youth (1945)

The Outsider (1953)

Savage Holiday (1954)

White Man, Listen! (1957)

The Long Dream (1958)

Eight Men (1961)

Lawd Today (1963)

American Hunger (1977)

Additional Reading

Chapter 1: America the Beautiful—and Talented

Aldridge, Alfred O. *Early American Literature: A Comparatist Approach.* Princeton, N.J.: Princeton University Press, 1982.

Caldwell, Patricia. *The Puritan Conversion Narrative: The Beginnings of American Expansion.* N.Y.: Cambridge University Press, 1983.

Cooper, James F., Jr. "Higher Law, Free Consent, Limited Authority: Church Government and Political Culture in Seventeenth-Century Massachusetts." *New England Quarterly* 69.2 (Jun 1996): 201–223.

Covici, Pascal, Jr. *Humor and Revelation in American Literature: The Puritan Connection.* Columbia and London: University of Missouri Press, 1997.

Delbanco, Andrew. *The Puritan Ordeal.* Cambridge: Harvard University Press, 1989.

Gilmore, Michael T. *Early American Literature: A Collection of Critical Essays.* Englewood Cliffs, N.J.: Prentice-Hall, 1980.

Harlan, David. *The Clergy and the Great Awakening in New England.* Ann Arbor: UMI Research Press, 1980.

Nelson, Dana D. *The Word in Black and White: Reading "Race" in American Literature, 1638–1867.* N.Y.: Oxford University Press, 1992.

Promis Ojeda, Jose. *The Identity of Hispanoamerica: An Interpretation of Colonial Literature.* Translated from the Spanish by Alita Kelley and Alec E. Kelley. Tucson: University of Arizona Press, 1991.

Samuels, Shirley. *Romances of the Republic: Women, the Family, and Violence in the Literature of the Early American Nation.* N.Y.: Oxford University Press, 1996.

Spengemann, William C. *A New World of Words: Redefining Early American Literature.* New Haven: Yale University Press, 1994.

Chapter 2: In the Beginning—America's First Writers (1607–1750)

General

Aldridge, Alfred O. *Early American Literature: a Comparatist Approach*. Princeton, N.J.: Princeton University Press, 1982.

Bercovitch, Sacvan. *Typology and Early American Literature*. Amherst: University of Massachusetts Press, 1972.

Caldwell, Patricia. *The Puritan Conversion Narrative: The Beginnings of American Expansion*. N.Y.: Cambridge University Press, 1983.

Covici, Pascal, Jr. *Humor and Revelation in American Literature: The Puritan Connection*. Columbia and London: University of Missouri Press, 1997.

Delbanco, Andrew. *The Puritan Ordeal*. Cambridge: Harvard University Press, 1989.

Gilmore, Michael T. *Early American Literature: A Collection of Critical Essays*. Englewood Cliffs, N.J.: Prentice-Hall, 1980.

Harris, Trudier. *Afro-American Writers Before the Harlem Renaissance*. Dictionary of Literary Biography. Volume Fifty. Detroit: Gale, 1986.

Spengemann, William C. *A New World of Words: Redefining Early American literature*. New Haven: Yale University Press, 1994.

Anne Bradstreet

Piercy, Josephine K. *Anne Bradstreet*. N.Y.: Twayne Publishers, 1965.

Martin, Wendy. *An American Triptych: Anne Bradstreet, Emily Dickinson, Adrienne Rich*. Chapel Hill: University of North Carolina Press, 1984.

Rosenmeier, Rosamond. *Anne Bradstreet Revisited*. Boston: Twayne, 1991.

Stanford, Ann. Anne Bradstreet, *The Worldly Puritan: An Introduction to her Poetry*. N.Y.: B. Franklin, 1975.

White, Elizabeth. Anne Bradstreet, *"The Tenth Muse."* N.Y.: Oxford University Press, 1971.

Chapter 3: Don't Tread on Me—The Revolutionary Period (1750–1800)

Akers, Charles W. *Abigail Adams*. Boston: Little, Brown, 1980.

Gelles, Edith B. *Portia: The World of Abigail Adams*. Bloomington, Ind.: Indiana University Press, 1992.

Levin, Phyllis Lee. *Abigail Adams*. N.Y.: St. Martin's Press, 1987.

Withey, Lynne. *Dearest Friend*. N.Y.: The Free Press, 1981.

Chapter 4: The Big Daddy of American Literature—Washington Irving (1789–1851)

Aderman, Ralph, ed. *Critical Essays on Washington Irving.* Boston: G.K. Hall, 1990.

Bowden, Mary W. *Washington Irving.* Boston: Twayne, 1981.

Fetterly, Judith. "Rip Van Winkle." *The Resisting Reader.* Bloomington: Indiana University Press, 1978.

Myers, Andrew B., ed. *A Century of Commentary on the Works of Washington Irving, 1860–1974.* Tarrytown, N.Y.: Sleepy Hollow Restorations, 1976.

Pearce, Colin D. "Changing Regimes: The Case of Rip Van Winkle." *Clio* 22.2 (Wntr 1993): 115(14).

Plummer, Laura "'Girls Can Take Care of Themselves': Gender and Storytelling in Washington Irving's 'The Legend of Sleepy Hollow.'" *Studies in Short Fiction* 30.2 (Sprg 1993): 175(10).

Roth, Martin. *Comedy and America: The Lost World of Washington Irving.* Port Washington, N.Y.: Kennikat Press, 1976.

Seelye, John. "Root and Branch: Washington Irving and American Humor." *Nineteenth-Century Fiction* 38 (1984): 415–25.

Wagenknecht, Edward. *Washington Irving: Moderation Displayed.* N.Y.: Oxford University Press, 1962.

Young, Philip. "Fallen From Time: The Mythic Rip Van Winkle," *Kenyon Review,* 22 (August 1960): 547–73.

Zlogar, Richard J. "Accessories that Covertly Explain: Irving's Use of Dutch Genre Painting in 'Rip Van Winkle.'" *American Literature* 54 (1982): 44–62.

Chapter 5: Father of the American Novel— James Fenimore Cooper (1789–1851)

McWilliams, John. *The Last of the Mohicans: Civil Savagery and Savage Civility* (Twayne's Masterwork Studies, No 143), Twayne, 1995.

Peck, Daniel. *New Essays on the Last of the Mohicans (The American Novel).* Cambridge University Press, 1992.

Ringe, Donald A. *James Fenimore Cooper* (Twayne's United States Authors), Twayne, 1998.

Romero, Lora and Donald E. Pease. *Home Fronts: Nineteenth-Century Domesticity and Its Critics.* New Americanists, 1997.

Chapter 6: Life on the Ledge—Edgar Allan Poe (1809–1849)

Abel, Darrel. *Ruined Eden of the Present: Hawthorne, Melville, and Poe: Critical Essays in Honor of Darrel Abel. eds. G.R. Thompson and Virgil L. Lokke.* West Lafayette: Purdue University Press, 1981.

Andrews, William L. *Literary Romanticism in America.* Baton Rouge: Louisiana State University Press, 1981.

Baym, Nina. *"The Fall of the House of Usher". Edgar Allan Poe.* The Norton Anthology of American Literature. N.Y.: Norton, 1995.

Bloom, Harold, ed. *Edgar Allan Poe: Modern Critical Views.* New Haven, Conn.: Chelsea House Publishers, 1985.

Buranelli, Vincent. *Edgar Allan Poe: Twayne's United States Authors Series.* Boston: Twayne Publishers, 1977.

Carlson, Eric W. *A Companion to Poe Studies.* Greenwood, 1996.

Knapp, Bettina L. *Edgar Allan Poe.* N.Y.: Fredrick Ungar Publishing, 1984.

Meyers, Jeffrey. *Edgar Allan Poe: His Life and Legacy.* N.Y.: Scribner's, 1992.

Silverman, Kenneth. *Edgar A. Poe: Mournful and Never-Ending Remembrance.* N.Y.: HarperCollins, 1991.

Silverman, Robert. *Edgar Allan Poe: A Long and Mournful Remembrance.* San Francisco, 1991.

Walker, I.M., ed. *Edgar Allan Poe: the Critical Heritage.* N.Y.: Routledge & K. Paul, 1986.

Wilbur, Richard. *The House of Poe.* N.Y.: Chelsea House Publishers, 1985.

Williams, J.S. Michael. *A World of Words: Language and Displacement in the Fiction of Edgar Allan Poe.* Durham: Duke University Press, 1988.

Chapter 7: The Sage of Concord—Ralph Waldo Emerson (1803–1882)

Allen, Gay Wilson. *Waldo Emerson: A Biography.* N.Y.: Viking Press, 1981.

Bickman, Martin. *American Romantic Psychology: Emerson, Poe, Whitman, Dickinson.* Dallas, Tex.: Spring Publications, 1988.

Brantley, Richard E. *Anglo-American Antiphony: The Late Romanticism of Tennyson and Emerson.* Gainesville, Fla.: University Press of Florida, 1994.

Burkholder, Robert E. and Joel Myerson. *Critical Essays on Ralph Waldo Emerson.* Boston: G.K. Hall, 1983.

Cheyfitz, Eric. *The Trans-Parent: Sexual Politics in the Language of Emerson.* Baltimore: Johns Hopkins University Press, 1981.

Ellison, Julie K. *Emerson's Romantic Style.* Princeton: Princeton University Press, 1984.

Hednut, Robert K. *The Aesthetics of Ralph Waldo Emerson: The Materials and Methods of His Poetry*. Lewiston, N.Y.: Mellen, 1996.

Howe, Irving. *The American Newness: Culture and Politics in the Age of Emerson*. Cambridge: Harvard University Press, 1986.

Ihrig, Mary Alice. *Emerson's Transcendental Vocabulary: A Concordance*. N.Y.: Garland, 1982.

Mott, Wesley T. and Robert E. Burkholder, eds. *Emersonian Circles: Essays in Honor of Joel Myerson*. Rochester, N.Y.: University of Rochester Press, 1996.

Neufeldt, Leonard. *The House of Emerson*. Lincoln: University of Nebraska Press, 1982.

O'Keefe, Richard. *Mythic Archetypes in Ralph Waldo Emerson: A Blakean Reading*. Kent, Ohio: Kent State University Press, 1995.

Packer, B.L. *Emerson's Fall: A New Interpretation of the Major Essays*. N.Y.: Continuum, 1982.

Poirier, Richard, Jr., ed. *Ralph Waldo Emerson*. N.Y.: Oxford University Press, 1990.

—. *The Renewal of Literature: Emersonian Reflections*. N.Y.: Random House, 1987.

Porte, Joel, ed. *Emerson, Prospect and Retrospect*. Cambridge: Harvard University Press, 1982.

Richardson, Robert D., Jr. *Emerson: The Mind on Fire*. Berkeley: University of California Press, 1995.

Chapter 8: Nature Boy—Henry David Thoreau (1817–1862)

Carton, Evan. *The Rhetoric of American Romance*. Baltimore: Johns Hopkins University Press, 1985.

Chai, Leon. *The Romantic Foundations of the American Renaissance*. Ithaca: Cornell University Press, 1987.

Golemba, Henry. *Thoreau's Wild Rhetoric*. N.Y.: New York University Press, 1990.

Chapter 9: Nate the Great—Nathaniel Hawthorne (1804–1864)

Brown, Gillian. *Domestic Individualism: Imagining Self in Nineteenth-Century America*. Berkeley: University of California Press, 1990.

Budick, Emily Miller. *Engendering Romance: Women Writers and the Hawthorne Tradition, 1850–1990*. New Haven: Yale University Press, 1994.

—. *Fiction and Historical Consciousness: The American Romance Tradition*. New Haven: Yale University Press, 1989.

Chai, Leon. *The Romantic Foundations of the American Renaissance*. Ithaca: Cornell University Press, 1987.

Coale, Samuel Chase. *In Hawthorne's Shadow: American Romance from Melville to Mailer.* Lexington, Ky.: University Press of Kentucky, 1985.

Deamer, Robert Glen. *The Importance of Place in the American Literature of Hawthorne, Thoreau, Crane, Adams, and Faulkner.* Lewiston, N.Y.: E. Mellen P, 1990.

Decker, George. *The American Historical Romance.* N.Y.: Cambridge University Press, 1987.

Dryden, Edgar A. *The Form of American Romance.* Baltimore: Johns Hopkins University Press, 1988.

Ellis, William. *The Theory of American Romance: An Ideology in American Intellectual History.* Ann Arbor, Mich.: UMI Research P, 1989.

Gelpi, Albert. *A Coherent Splendor: The American Poetic Renaissance.* N.Y.: Cambridge U P, 1987.

Gilmore, Michael T. *American Romanticism and the Marketplace.* Chicago: U Chicago Press, 1985.

Goodman, Russel B. *American Philosophy and the Romantic Tradition.* N.Y.: Cambridge University Press, 1990.

Greenfield, Bruce. *Narrating Discovery: The Romantic Explorer in American Literature, 1790–1855.* N.Y.: Columbia University Press, 1992.

Greenwald, Elissa. *Realism and the Romance.* Ann Arbor, Mich.: University of Michigan Research Press, 1989.

Grey, Robin. *The Complicity of Imagination: The American Renaissance, Contests of Authority, and 17th-Century English Culture.* N.Y.: Cambridge University Press, 1997.

Harris, Susan K. *19th-Century American Women's Novels: Interpretative Strategies.* Cambridge: Cambridge University Press, 1990.

Johnston, Kenneth R., ed. *Romantic Revolutions: Criticism and Theory.* Bloomington: Indiana University Press, 1990.

Kane, Paul. *Poetry of the American Renaissance: A Diverse Anthology.* N.Y.: G. Braziller, 1995.

Levine, Robert S. *Conspiracy and Romance: Studies in Brockden Brown, Cooper, Hawthorne, and Melville.* N.Y.: Cambridge University Press, 1989.

Luedtke, Luther S. *Nathaniel Hawthorne and the Romance of the Orient.* Bloomington, Ind.: Indiana University Press, 1989.

Morse, David. *American Romanticism.* N.Y.: Barnes and Noble, 1987.

Schirmeister, Pamela. *The Consolations of Space: The Place of Romance in Hawthorne, Melville, and James.* Stanford, Calif.: Stanford University Press, 1990.

Stern, Milton. *Contexts for Hawthorne: The Marble Faun and the Political Openness and Closure in American Literature.* Urbana: University Illinois Press, 1991.

Voller, Jack G. *The Supernatural Sublime: The Metaphysics of Terror in Anglo-American Romanticism.* Dekalb: Northern Illinois University Press, 1994.

Wilson, James D. *The Romantic Heroic Ideal.* Baton Rouge: Louisiana State University Press, 1982.

Chapter 10: Just Don't Call Me Hermie—Herman Melville (1819–1891)

Allen, Gay Wilson. *Melville and His World.* N.Y.: The Viking Press, 1971.

Arvin, Newton. *Herman Melville.* N.Y.: William Sloane Associates, 1950.

Budd, Louis J. and Edwin Cady, eds. *Melville: The Best From American Literature.* Durham, N.C.: Duke University Press, 1988, pp. 1–9.

Garner, Stanton. *The Civil War World of Herman Melville.* Lawrence, Kans.: University Press of Kansas, 1993.

Horth, Lynn. "Letters Lost Letters Found: A Progress Report on Melville's Correspondence." In Melville Society Extracts, no. 81 (May 1990), pp. 1–8.

Winslow, Richard E., III, "New Reviews Trace Melville's Reputation." In Melville Society Extracts, no. 89 (June 1992), pp. 7–12.

Chapter 11: The Little Woman Who Started This Great Big War—Harriet Beecher Stowe (1811–1896)

Adams, John R. *Harriet Beecher Stowe; Updated Version.* Boston: Twayne Pub., 1989.

Ammons, Elizabeth and Dorothy Berkson. *Critical Essays on Harriet Beecher Stowe.* Boston: Hall, 1980.

Anderson, Beatrice A. "Uncle Tom: A Hero at Last." *American Transcendental Quarterly* 5.2 (June 1991): 95–108.

Askeland, Lori. "Remodeling the Model Home in Uncle Tom's Cabin and Beloved." *American Literature: A Journal of Literary History, Criticism, and Bibliography* 64.4 (Dec 1992): 785–805.

Boyd, Richard. "Violence and Sacrificial Displacement in Harriet Beecher Stowe's Dred." *Arizona Quarterly: A Journal of American Literature, Culture, and Theory* 50.2 (Summer 1994): 51–72.

Boydston, Jeanne, Mary Kelly and Anne Throne Margolis. *The Limits of Sisterhood: the Beecher Sisters on Women's Rights and Woman's Sphere.* Chapel Hill: University of North Carolina Press, 1988.

Brown, Gillian. *Domestic Individualism: Imagining Self in Nineteenth Century America.* Berkeley: University of California Press, 1990.

Cherniavsky, Eva. "Revivification and Utopian Time: Poe versus Stowe." *The American Face of Edgar Allen Poe.* Eds. Shawn Rosenheim and Stephen Rachman. Baltimore: Johns Hopkins University Press, 1995. 121–38.

Cole, Phyllis. "Stowe, Jacobs, Wilson: White Plots and Black Counterplots." *New Perspectives on Gender, Race, and Class in Society.* Ed. Audrey T. McCluskey. Bloomington: Indiana University Press, 1990: 23–45.

Davidson, Cathy N., ed. *Reading in America: Literature & Social History*. Baltimore: The Johns Hopkins University Press, 1989.

Fritz, Jean. *Harriet Beecher Stowe and the Beecher Preachers*. N.Y.: G.P. Putnam's Sons, 1994.

Gabler-Hover, Janet. *Truth in American Fiction. The Legacy of Rhetorical Idealism*. Athens: University of Georgia Press, 1990.

Goshgarian, G.M. *To Kiss the Chastening Rod: Domestic Fiction and Sexual Ideology in the American Renaissance*. Ithaca: Cornell University Press, 1992.

Greene, Gayle. *Changing the Story, Feminist Fiction and the Tradition*. Bloomington: Indiana University Press, 1991.

Harris, Susan K. *19th-Century American Women's Novels. Interpretive Strategies*. Cambridge: Cambridge University Press, 1990.

Hedrick, Joan D. *Harriet Beecher Stowe: A Life*. N.Y.: Oxford University Press, 1994.

Johnston, Norma. *Harriet: the Life and World of Harriet Beecher Stowe*. N.Y.: Beech Tree, 1996.

Chapter 12: Rebel with a Cause—Frederick Douglass (1817–1895)

Andrews, William, ed.. *Critical Essays on Frederick Douglass*. Boston: G.K. Hall, 1991.

—. *The Oxford Frederick Douglass Reader*. N.Y.: Oxford University Press, 1996.

Bontemps, Arna. *Free at Last; the Life of Frederick Douglass*. N.Y.: Dodd, Mead, 1971.

Martin, Waldo E. *The Mind of Frederick Douglass*. Chapel Hill: University of North Carolina Press, 1984.

McFeely, William S. *Frederick Douglass*. N.Y.: W.W. Norton, 1991.

Chapter 13: That Barbaric Yawp—Walt Whitman (1819–1892)

Aspiz, Harold. *Walt Whitman and the Body Beautiful*. Urbana: University of Illinois Press, 1980.

Bove, Paul A. *Destructive Poetics: Heidegger and Modern American Poetry*. N.Y.: Columbia University Press, 1980.

Callow, Philip. *From Noon to Starry Night: A Life of Walt Whitman*. Chicago: I.R. Dee, 1992.

Clarke, Graham. *Walt Whitman: The Poem As Private History*. St. Martin's Press, 1991.

Erkkila, Betsy. *Whitman the Political Poet*. N.Y.: Oxford University Press, 1989.

Gardner, Thomas. *Discovering Ourselves in Whitman: The Contemporary American Long Poem*. Urbana: University of Illinois Press, 1989.

Hollis, C. Carroll. *Language and Style in Leaves of Grass*. Baton Rouge: Louisiana State University Press, 1983.

Kaplan, Justin. *Walt Whitman, A Life*. N.Y.: Simon and Schuster, 1980.

Knapp, Bettina L. *Walt Whitman*. N.Y.: Continuum, 1993.

Kuebrich, David. *Minor Prophecy: Walt Whitman's New American Religion*. Bloomington: Indiana University Press, 1989.

Loving, Jerome. *Emerson, Whitman, and the American Muse*. Chapel Hill: University of North Carolina Press, 1982.

Miller, James E. *Walt Whitman*. Boston: Twayne Publishers, 1990.

Schmidgall, Gary. *Walt Whitman: A Gay Life*. N.Y.: Dutton, 1997.

Woodress, James L., ed. *Critical essays on Walt Whitman*. Boston: G.K. Hall, 1983.

Zweig, Paul. *Walt Whitman: The Making of the Poet*. N.Y.: Basic Books, 1984.

Web Sites

www.jefferson.village.Virginia.edu/whitman/

www.jefferson.village.Virginia.edu/whitman/reviews/index.html

www.lcweb2.loc.gov/ammem/wwhome.html

www.liglobal.com/walt/waltbio.html

www.vive.com/connect/walt/whitback.htm

www.vive.com/connect/walt/whitnews.htm

Chapter 14: The Big Mama of American Literature—Emily Dickinson (1830–1886)

Bloom, Harold, ed. *Emily Dickinson* (Bloom's Major Poets). N.Y.: Chelsea House, 1999.

Cameron, Sharon. *Choosing Not Choosing: Dickinson's Fascicles*. Chicago: University of Chicago Press, 1993.

Ferlazzo, Paul J. *Emily Dickinson* (Twayne's United States Authors Series). Twaynes, 1984.

Kirkby, Joan. *Emily Dickinson* (Women Writers). Prentice Hall, 1993.

Miller, Cristanne. *Emily Dickinson: A Poet's Grammar*. Harvard University Press, 1989.

Orzeck, Martin, ed. *Dickinson and Audience*. Ann Arbor: University of Michigan Press, 1996.

Stonum, Gary Lee. *The Dickinson Sublime*. Madison, Wis.: University of Wisconsin Press, 1990.

Wolosky, Shira. *Emily Dickinson: A Voice of War*. Yale University Press, 1984.

Chapter 15: Samuel Clemens—A.K.A. Mark Twain (1835–1910)

Bloom, Harold, ed. *Mark Twain.* N.Y.: Chelsea House Press, 1986.

Budd, Louis J., ed. *Critical Essays on Mark Twain, 1867–1910.* Boston: G.K. Hall, 1982.

Camfield, Gregg. *Sentimental Twain: Samuel Clemens in the Maze of Moral Philosophy.* Philadelphia: University of Pennsylvania Press, 1994.

Chadwick-Joshua, Jocelyn. *The Jim Dilemma: Reading Race in Huckleberry Finn.* Jackson: University Press of Mississippi, 1998.

Emerson, Everett H. *The Authentic Mark Twain: A Literary Biography of Samuel L. Clemens.* Philadelphia: University of Pennsylvania Press, 1984.

Fishkin, Shelley F. *Was Huck Black?: Mark Twain and African-American Voices.* N.Y.: Oxford University Press, 1993.

—. *Lighting Out for the Territory: Reflections on Mark Twain and the American Culture.* N.Y.: Oxford University Press, 1997.

—. General Editor. *The Oxford Mark Twain.* 29 Volumes. N.Y.: Oxford University Press, 1997.

Fulton, Joe B. *Mark Twain's Ethical Realism: The Aesthetics of Race, Class, and Gender.* Columbia: University of Missouri Press, 1997.

Gerber, John C. *Mark Twain.* Boston: Twayne Publishers, 1988.

Harris, Susan K. *The Courtship of Olivia Langdon and Mark Twain.* N.Y.: Cambridge University Press, 1997. (Book Review)

Haupt, Clyde V. *Huck Finn on Film: Film and Television Adaptations of Mark Twain's Novels, 1920–1993.* Jefferson, N.C.: McFarland, 1994.

Hill, Hamlin L. *"Samuel Langhorne Clemens (Mark Twain)." Dictionary of Literary Biography: American Realists and Naturalists.* Detroit: Gale Research Company, 1982.

Hoffman, Andrew. *Inventing Mark Twain: The Lives of Samuel Langhorne Clemens.* N.Y.: William Morrow and Company, 1997.

Horn, Jason G. *Mark Twain and William James: Crafting a Free Self.* Columbia: University of Missouri Press, 1996.

Kaplan, Justin. *Mark Twain and His World.* N.Y.: Simon and Schuster, 1974.

Knoper, Randall. *Mark Twain in the Culture of Performance.* Berkeley: University of California Press, 1995.

Leonard, James and others, eds. *Satire or Evasion?: Black Perspectives on Huckleberry Finn.* Durham: Duke University, 1992.

Michelson, Bruce. *Mark Twain on the Loose: A Comic Writer and the American Self.* Amherst: University of Massachusetts, 1995.

Miller, Robert Keith. *Mark Twain.* N.Y.: Frederick Ungar Publishing Company, 1983.

Rasmussen, R. Kent. *Mark Twain A to Z: The Essential Reference to His Life and Writings.* N.Y.: Facts on File, 1995.

Robinson, Forrest G., ed. *The Cambridge Companion to Mark Twain*. N.Y.: Cambridge University Press, 1995.

Skandera-Trombley, Laura E. *Mark Twain in the Company of Women*. Philadelphia: University of Pennsylvania Press, 1994.

Vallin, Marlene B. *Mark Twain: Protagonist for the Popular Culture*. Westport, Conn.: Greenwood Press, 1992.

Wilson, James D. *A Reader's Guide to the Short Stories of Mark Twain*. Boston: G.K. Hall, 1987.

Chapter 16: Life Is Short and Then You Die: Stephen Crane (1871–1900)

Benfey, Christopher E.G. *The Double Life of Stephen Crane*. N.Y.: Knopf, 1992.

Cady, Edwin H. *Stephen Crane*. Boston: Twayne Publishers, 1980.

Davis, Linda H. *Badge of Courage: The Life of Stephen Crane*. N.Y.: Houghton Mifflin, 1998.

—. *The Red Badge of Courage: Redefining the Hero*. Boston: Twayne Publishers, 1988.

Mariani, Giorgio. *Spectacular Narratives: Representations of Class and War in Stephen Crane and the American 1890s*. N.Y.: P. Lang, 1992.

Nagel, James. *Stephen Crane and Literary Impressionism*. University Park: Pennsylvania State University Press, 1980.

Pizer, Donald, ed. *Critical Essays on Stephen Crane's The Red Badge of Courage*. Boston: G.K. Hall, 1990.

Wolford, Chester L. *The Anger of Stephen Crane: Fiction and the Epic Tradition*. Lincoln: University of Nebraska Press, 1983.

—. *Stephen Crane: A Study of the Short Fiction*. Boston: Twayne Publishers, 1989.

Chapter 17: Three on a Match—The Naturalists, Jack London, Frank Norris, and Theodore Dresier (1890-1925)

Jack London

Auerbach, Johnathan. *Male Call: Becoming Jack London*. Durham, N.C.: Duke University Press, 1996.

Cassuto, Leonard and Jeanne Campbell Reesman, eds. *Rereading Jack London*. Stanford, Calif.: Stanford University Press, 1996.

Labor, Earle. *Jack London*. N.Y.: Twayne, 1974.

Martin, Stoddard. *California Writers: Jack London, John Steinbeck, The Tough Guys*. N.Y.: St. Martin's Press, 1983.

Nuernberg, Susan, ed. *The Critical Response to Jack London*. Westwood, Conn.: Greenwood Press, 1995.

Reesman, Jeanne Campbell, ed. *American Literary Realism*. Vol. 24, Winter 1992.

Sherman, Joan. Jack London: *A Reference Guide*. Boston: G.K. Hall, 1977.

Tavernier-Courbin, Jacqueline, ed. *Critical Essays on Jack London*. Boston, Mass.: G.K. Hall, 1983.

—. *The Call of the Wild: A Naturalistic Romance*. N.Y.: Twayne, 1994.

—. *Thalia: Studies in Literary Humor*. Volume XII, 1992.

Watson, Charles N., Jr. *The Novels of Jack London: A Reappraisal*. Madison, Wis.: University of Wisconsin Press, 1983.

Frank Norris

Bevilacqua, Winifred Farrant. "From the Ideal to Its Reverse: Key Sociocultural Concepts in McTeague." *The Centennial Review* 33.1 (1989 Winter) 75–88.

Bower, Stephanie. "Dangerous Liaisons: Prostitution, Disease, and Race in Frank Norris's Fiction." *Modern Fiction Studies* 42.1 (Spring 1996): 31–61.

Campbell, Donna M. "Frank Norris's 'Drama in a Broken Teacup': The Old Grannis-Miss Baker Plot in McTeague." *American Literary Realism* 26.1 (Fall 1993): 40–49.

Caron, James E. "Grotesque Naturalism: The Significance of the Comic in McTeague." *Texas Studies in Literature and Language* 31.2 (1989 Summer) 288–317.

Cassuto, Leonard. "'Keeping Company' with the Old Folks: Unravelling the Edges of McTeague's Deterministic Fabric." *American Literary Realism* 25.2 (1993 Winter) 46–55.

Civello, Paul. "Evolutionary Feminism, Popular Romance, and Frank Norris's 'Man's Woman'." *Studies in American Fiction* 24.1 (Spring 1996): 23–45.

Cook, Don L. "McTeague at Ninety: The Novel and Its Tensions." *Frank Norris Studies 11*. (1991 Spring) 2–5.

Crow, Charles L. "Recent Trends in McTeague Scholarship." *Frank Norris Studies 13* (1992 Spring): 1–5.

Graham, Don, ed. *Critical Essays on Frank Norris*. Boston: G.K. Hall, 1980.

Hochman, Barbara. *The Art of Frank Norris, Storyteller*. Columbia: University of Missouri Press, 1988.

McElrath, Joseph R. *Frank Norris Revisited*. N.Y.: Twayne Publishers, 1992.

Michaels, Walter Benn. *The Gold Standard and the Logic of Naturalism*. Berkeley: University of California Press, 1985.

Theodore Dreiser

Hakutani, Yoshinobu. *Young Dreiser: A Critical Study*. Rutherford, N.J.: Fairleigh Dickinson University Press, 1980.

Hussman, Lawrence E. *Dreiser and His Fiction: A Twentieth-Century Quest*. Philadelphia: University of Pennsylvania Press, 1983.

Pizer, Donald. *Critical Essays on Theodore Dreiser*. Boston: G.K. Hall, 1981.

Pizer, Donald, Frederic E. Rusch and Richard W. Dowell, eds. *Theodore Dreiser: A Primary Bibliography and Reference Guide*. Boston, Mass.: G.K. Hall, 1991.

Chapter 18: Color My World—The Local Colorists

Kate Chopin

Boren, Lynda S. and Sara Davis, eds. *Kate Chopin Reconsidered: Beyond the Bayou*. Baton Rouge: Louisiana State University Press, 1992.

Ewell, Barbara C. *Kate Chopin*. N.Y.: Ungar Pub. Co., 1986.

Martin, Wendy, ed. *New Essays on The Awakening*. N.Y.: Cambridge, 1988.

Seyersted, Per. *Kate Chopin. A Critical Biography*. Baton Rouge: Louisiana State University Press 1969.

Showalter, Elaine. *Sister's Choice: Tradition and Change in American Women's Writing*. Oxford: Oxford University Press, 1991.

Skaggs, Peggy. *Kate Chopin*. Boston: Twayne Publishers, 1985.

Springer, Marlene. *Edith Wharton and Kate Chopin: A Reference Guide*. Boston: G.K. Hall, 1976.

Taylor, Helen. *Gender, Race, and Region in the Writings of Grace King, Ruth McEnery Stuart, and Kate Chopin*. Baton Rouge: Louisiana State University Press, 1989.

Toth, Emily. *Kate Chopin*. N.Y.: Morrow, 1990.

Walker, Nancy, ed. *The Awakening: Kate Chopin*. Boston: Bedford Books of St. Martin's Press, 1993.

Charlotte Perkins Gillman

Golden, Catherine. ed. *The Captive Imagination: A Casebook on "The Yellow Wallpaper."* Feminist Press, 1991.

Hedges, Elaine. *"Afterword," The Yellow Wall-Paper*. Feminist Press, 1973.

Knight, Denise D., ed. *"The Yellow Wall-Paper" and Selected Stories of Charlotte Perkins Gilman*. University of Delaware Press, 1994.

Lane, Ann, ed. *The Charlotte Perkins Gilman Reader*. N.Y.: Pantheon, 1980.

Chapter 19: Lifestyles of the Rich and Famous—Edith Wharton and Henry James

Edith Wharton

Bauer, Dale M. *Edith Wharton's Brave New Politics*. Madison: The University of Wisconsin Press, 1994.

Bendixon, Alfred and Annette Zilversmit, eds. *Edith Wharton: New Critical Essays*. N.Y.: Garland Publishing, Inc. 1992.

Dwight, Eleanor. *Edith Wharton: An Extraordinary Life*. N.Y.: Harry N. Abrams, Inc., 1994.

Springer, Marlene. *Ethan Frome: A Nightmare of Need*. N.Y.: Twayne Publishers, 1993.

Wagner-Martin, Linda. *The Age of Innocence: A Novel of Ironic Nostalgia*. N.Y.: Twayne Publishers, 1996.

—. *The House of Mirth: A Novel of Admonition*. Boston: Twayne Publishers, 1990.

Web Sites

www.history.hanover.edu/20th/wharton.htm (Electronic versions of works)

www.perry.stark.k12.oh.us/library/language/wharton.html

www.wharton.stark.k12.oh.us/library/language/wharton.html (home page)

www.berkshireweb.com/themount/ (Edith Wharton's home and foundation)

Henry James

Berland, Alwyn. *Culture and Conduct in the Novels of Henry James*. N.Y.: Cambridge University Press, 1981.

Bradley, John R., ed. *Henry James and Homo-Erotic Desire*. N.Y.: St. Martin's Press, 1998.

Edel, Leon. *Henry James: A Collection of Critical Essays*. Englewood Cliffs: Prentice-Hall, 1963.

—. *Henry James. Vols. 1–5*. Philadelphia: Lippincott, 1953–1972.

—. *The Untried Years, 1843–1870*. 1953.

—. *The Conquest of London, 1870–1881*. 1962.

—. *The Middle Years, 1882–1895*. 1962.

—. *The Treacherous Years, 1895–1901*. 1969.

—. *The Master, 1901–1916*. 1972.

Gargano, James W. *Critical Essays on Henry James: The Early Novels*. Boston: G.K. Hall, 1987.

Graham, Kenneth. *Indirections of the Novel: James, Conrad, and Forster*. N.Y.: Cambridge University Press, 1988.

Greenwald, Elissa. *Realism and the Romance: Nathaniel Hawthorne, Henry James, and American Fiction*. Ann Arbor: UMI Research Press, 1989.

Hocks, Richard A. *Henry James: A Study of the Short Fiction*. Boston: Twayne Publishers, 1990.

Hutchinson, Stuart. *Henry James, an American, as Modernist*. Totowa, N.J.: Barnes & Noble Books, 1983.

Long, Robert E. *Henry James, the Early Novels*. Boston: Twayne Publishers, 1983.

Macnaughton, William R. *Henry James: The Later Novels*. Boston: Twayne Publishers, 1987.

Wagenknecht, Edward. *The Novels of Henry James*. N.Y.: F. Ungar Pub. Co., 1983.

Chapter 20: Macho, Macho Man—Ernest Hemingway (1899–1961)

Baker, Carlos. *Hemingway, The Writer As Artist*. Princeton: Princeton University Press, 1972.

Beegel, Susan, ed. *Hemingway's Neglected Short Fiction*. Tuscaloosa: University of Alabama Press, 1992.

Burwell, Rose Marie. *Hemingway: The Postwar Years and the Posthumous Novels*. N.Y.: Cambridge University Press, 1996.

Comley, Nancy and Robert Scholes. *Hemingway's Genders: Rereading the Hemingway Text*. New Haven: Yale University Press, 1994.

Eby, Carl P. *Hemingway's Fetishism: Psychoanalysis and the Mirror of Manhood*. Albany, N.Y.: State University of NY Press, 1998.

Fleming, Robert E. *The Face in the Mirror: Hemingway's Writers*. University of Alabama Press, 1994.

Flora, Joseph M. *Ernest Hemingway: A Study of the Short Fiction*. Boston: Twayne, 1989.

Hays, Peter L. *Ernest Hemingway*. N.Y.: Continuum, 1990.

Kert, Bernice. *The Hemingway Women*. N.Y.: Norton, 1985.

Chapter 21: Party Hearty—F. Scott Fitzgerald (1896–1940)

Bruccoli, Matthew, ed. *New Essays on The Great Gatsby*. Cambridge: Cambridge University Press, 1985.

Bruccoli, Matthew J. *Some Sort of Epic Grandeur: The Life of F. Scott Fitzgerald*. N.Y.: Harcourt Brace Jovanovich, 1981.

Bruccoli, Matthew J. and Judith S. Baughman, eds. *F. Scott Fitzgerald on Authorship*. Columbia: University of South Carolina, 1996.

Bryer, Jackson R. *The Short Stories of F. Scott Fitzgerald: New Approaches in Criticism*. Madison, Wis.: University of Wisconsin Press, 1982.

—, ed. *New Essays on F. Scott Fitzgerald's Neglected Stories*. Columbia: University of Missouri Press, 1996.

Donaldson, Scott, ed. *Critical Essays on F. Scott Fitzgerald's* The Great Gatsby. Boston: Hall, 1984.

Graham, Sheilah. *Beloved Infidel: The Education of a Woman*. N.Y.: Holt, 1958.

Kuehl, John R. *F. Scott Fitzgerald: A Study of the Short Fiction*. Boston: Twayne, 1991.

Chapter 22: Mint Juleps, Moonlight, and Madness—William Faulkner (1897–1962)

Brodhead, Richard H. *Faulkner, New Perspectives*. Englewood Cliffs, N.J.: Prentice-Hall, 1983.

Cox, Leland H. *William Faulkner: Biographical and Reference Guide*. Detroit: Gale Research Co., 1982.

Friedman, Alan W. *William Faulkner*. N.Y.: F. Ungar Pub. Co., 1984.

Goldberg, Wendy Fay. *Faulkner's Haunted House: The Figure of the Recluse in 'Light in August' and 'Absolom, Absolom!'* Ann Arbor, Mich.: University of Michigan Press, 1996.

Kinney, Arthur F., ed. *Critical Essays on William Faulkner—the Sartoris Family*. Boston: G.K. Hall, 1985.

Matthews, John T. *The Play of Faulkner's Language*. Ithaca: Cornell University Press, 1982.

Minter, David L. *William Faulkner: His Life and Work*. Baltimore: Johns Hopkins University Press, 1980.

Mortimer, Gail L. *Faulkner's Rhetoric of Loss: A Study in Perception and Meaning*. Austin: University of Texas Press, 1983.

Phillips, Gene. *Fiction, Film AND Faulkner: The Art Of Adaptation*. Knoxville: University of Tennessee Press, 1988.

Pilkington, John. *The Heart of Yoknapatawpha*. Jackson: University Press of Mississippi, 1981.

Rodden, Richard. *Fictions of Labor: William Faulkner and the South's Long Revolution*. Cambridge: Cambridge University Press, 1997.

Singal, Daniel J. *William Faulkner: The Making of a Modernist*. Chapel Hill: University of North Carolina Press, 1997.

Sundquist, Eric J. *Faulkner: The House Divided*. Baltimore: Johns Hopkins University Press, 1983.

Vanderwerken, David L. *Faulkner's Literary Children: Patterns of Development*. N.Y.: Peter Lang, 1997.

Wagner-Martin, Linda. *New Essays on* Go Down, Moses. N.Y.: Cambridge University Press, 1996.

Chapter 23: Three Big Deals—Ezra Pound, T.S. Eliot, and John Steinbeck

Ezra Pound

Ackroyd, Peter. *Ezra Pound and his World*. N.Y.: Scribner, 1980.

Bacigalupo, Massimo. *The Formed Trace: the Later Poetry of Ezra Pound*. N.Y.: Columbia University Press, 1980.

Beach, Christopher. *ABC of Influence: Ezra Pound and the Remaking of American Poetic Tradition*. Berkeley: University of California Press, 1992.

Bell, Ian F.A. *Critic as Scientist: the Modernist Poetics of Ezra Pound*. N.Y.: Methuen, 1981.

Bloom, Harold, ed. *Ezra Pound*. N.Y.: Chelsea, 1987.

Bornstein, George, ed. *Ezra Pound Among the Poets*. Chicago: University of Chicago Press, 1985.

Coyle, Michael and Wendy S. Ezra Flory. *The American Ezra Pound*. New Haven: Yale University Press, 1989.

Froula, Christine. *A Guide to Ezra Pound's Selected Poems*. N.Y.: New Directions, 1983.

Gibson, Mary E. *Epic Reinvented: Ezra Pound and the Victorians*. Ithaca, N.Y.: Cornell University Press, 1995.

Kaye, Jacqueline, ed. *Ezra Pound and America*. N.Y.: St. Martin's, 1992.

Kearns, George. *Guide to Ezra Pound's Selected Cantos*. New Brunswick, N.J.: Rutgers University Press, 1980.

Korn, Marianne, ed. *Ezra Pound and History*. Orono: University of Maine, 1985.

Kuberski, Philip. *A Calculus of Ezra Pound: Vocations of the American Sign*. Gainesville: University Press of Florida, 1992.

Levy, Alan. *Ezra Pound, the Voice of Silence*. Sag Harbor, N.Y.: Permanent Press, 1983.

Robinson, Alan. *Symbol to Vortex: Poetry, Painting, and Ideas, 1885–1914*. N.Y.: St. Martin's Press, 1985.

Schwartz, Sanford. *The Matrix of Modernism: Pound, Eliot, and Early Twentieth Century Thought*. Princeton, N.J.: Princeton University Press, 1985.

Tiffany, Daniel. *Radio Corpse: Imagism and the Cryptaesthetic of Ezra Pound*. Cambridge: Harvard University Press, 1995.

Wilhelm, J.J. *Ezra Pound in London and Paris: 1908–1925*. University Park: Penn State University Press, 1990.

T.S. Eliot

Canary, Robert H. *T.S. Eliot: The Poet and His Critics*. Chicago: American Library Association, 1982.

Frye, Northrop. *T.S. Eliot: An Introduction*. Chicago: University of Chicago Press, 1981.

Gish, Nancy K. *Time in the Poetry of T.S. Eliot: A Study in Structure and Theme*. London: Macmillan, 1981.

Grant, Michael, ed. *T.S. Eliot: The Critical Heritage*. Boston: Routledge & Kegan Paul, 1982.

Roby, Kinley E. *Critical Essays on T.S. Eliot: The Sweeney Motif*. Boston: G.K. Hall, 1985.

Schwartz, Sanford. *The Matrix of Modernism: Pound, Eliot, and Early Twentieth-Century Thought*. Princeton: Princeton University Press, 1985.

Scofield, Martin. *T.S. Eliot: The Poems*. N.Y.: Cambridge University Press, 1988.

Spurr, David. *Conflicts in Consciousness: T.S. Eliot's Poetry and Criticism*. Urbana: University of Illinois Press, 1984.

John Steinbeck

Benson, Jackson J. (ed) *The Short Novels of John Steinbeck: Critical Essays with a Checklist to Steinbeck Criticism*. Durham: Duke University Press, 1990.

Bloom, Harold and William Golding. *John Steinbeck (Modern Critical Views)*. New York: Chelsea House Publishers, 1988.

Bloom, Harold. *John Steinbeck: Comprehensive Research and Study Guide* (Bloom's Major Short Story Writers). New York: Chelsea House Publishers, 1999.

Davis, Robert Con. *The Grapes of Wrath: A Collection of Critical Essays*. Englewood Cliffs, NJ: Prentice-Hall, 1982.

Ditsky, John. *John Steinbeck: Life, Work, and Criticism*. Fredericton, N.B., Canada: York Press, 1985.

Ditsky, John, ed. *Critical Essays on Steinbeck's The Grapes of Wrath*. Boston: G. K. Hall, 1989.

French, Warren, ed. *A Companion to The Grapes of Wrath*. New York: Penguin, 1989.

French, Warren. *John Steinbeck's Fiction Revisited* (Twayne's United States Authors, No 638) Twayne, 1994.

Hughes, R. S. *John Steinbeck: A Study of the Short Fiction*. R.S. Hughes. Boston: Twayne, 1989.

Meyer, Michael J. et. al. *The Hayashi Steinbeck Bibliography: 1982-1996* (Scarecrow Author Bibliographies, No 99). Scarecrow Press; 1998.

Railsback, Brian E. *Parallel Expeditions: Charles Darwin and the Art of John Steinbeck*. University of Idaho Press, 1997.

Wyatt, David ed. *New Essays on the Grapes of Wrath*. N.Y.: Cambridge University Press, 1991.

Chapter 24: A Pack of Poets (1900–1960)

Robert Frost

Fleissner, Robert F. *Frost's Road Taken*. N.Y.: Peter Lang, 1996.

Gerber, Philip L., ed. *Critical Essays on Robert Frost*. Boston: G.K. Hall, 1982.

—. *Robert Frost*. Boston: Twayne, 1982.

Ingebretsen, Edward, S.J. *Robert Frost's Star in a Stone Boat: A Grammar of Belief*. Bethesda, Md.: Internat. Scholars, 1996.

Meyers, Jeffrey. *Robert Frost: A Biography*. N.Y.: Houghton Mifflin, 1996.

Monteiro, George. *Robert Frost & the New England Renaissance*. Lexington: University Press of Kentucky, 1988.

Oster, Judith. *Toward Robert Frost: The Reader and the Poet*. Athens: University of Georgia Press, 1991.

Potter, James L. *Robert Frost Handbook*. University Park: Pennsylvania State University Press, 1980.

Pritchard, William H. *Frost: A Literary Life Reconsidered*. N.Y.: Oxford University Press, 1984.

e.e. cummings

Firmage, George J., ed. *e.e. cummings Complete Poems 1904–1962*. N.Y.: Liveright Publishing Corporation, 1991.

Kennedy, Richard S. *e.e. cummings Revisited*. N.Y.: Twayne Publishers, 1994.

—. *e.e. cummings Selected Poems*. N.Y.: Liveright Publishing Corporation, 1994.

McBride, Katherine Winters. *A Concordance to the Complete Poems of e.e. cummings*. Ithaca, N.Y.: Cornell University Press, 1989.

E.A. Robinson

Barnard, Ellsworth. *Edwin Arlington Robinson: Centenary Essays*. Athens: University of Georgia Press, 1970.

Joyner, Nancy Carol. *Edwin Arlington Robinson: A Reference Guide*. Boston: G.K. Hall, 1978.

Carl Sandburg

Callahan, North. *Carl Sandburg: His Life and His Works*. Pennsylvania State University Press, 1987.

Mitchell, Barbara. *Good Morning, Mr. President: A Story About Carl Sandburg*. Carolrhoda Books, 1988.

Niven, Penelope, Carl Fetherling, Dale and Doug Fetherling, eds. *Carl Sandburg at the Movies: A Poet in the Silent Era: 1920 to 1927*. Scarecrow, 1985.

Hacker, Jeffrey H. *Carl Sandburg*. N.Y.: Watts, 1984.

Perry, Lilla. *My Friend, Carl Sandburg: The Biography of a Friendship*. Scarecrow, 1981.

Salwak, Dale. *Carl Sandburg: A Reference Guide*. N.Y.: Macmillan, 1988.

Sandburg, Helga. *Where Love Begins: A Portrait of Carl Sandburg and His Family As Seen Through the Eyes of His Youngest Daughter*. N.Y.: Donald I. Fine, 1989.

Yannella, Philip R. *The Other Carl Sandburg*. Jackson: University Press of Mississippi, 1996.

Chapter 25: The Harlem Renaissance (1915–1929)

General

Baker, Houston A., Jr. *Modernism and the Harlem Renaissance*. Chicago: University of Chicago Press, 1987.

Bassett, John E. *Harlem in Review: Critical Reactions to Black American Writers, 1917–1939*. Selinsgrove: Susquehanna University Press, 1992.

Campbell, Mary S. *Harlem Renaissance: Art of Black America*. N.Y.: Abrams, 1987.

Carby, Hazel. *Reconstructing Womanhood: The Emergence of the Afro-American Woman Novelist*. N.Y.: Oxford University Press, 1987.

Floyd, Samuel A., ed. *Black Music in the Harlem Renaissance: A Collection of Essays*. N.Y.: Greenwood Press, 1990.

Franklin, V.P. *Living Our Stories, Telling Our Truths: Autobiography and the Making of the African-American Intellectual Tradition*. N.Y.: Oxford University Press, 1995.

Gates, Henry L., Jr. *The Signifying Monkey: A Theory of African-American Literary Criticism*. N.Y.: Oxford University Press, 1988.

Greenberg, Cheryl. *"Or Does It Explode?": Black Harlem in the Great Depression*. N.Y.: Oxford University Press, 1991.

Hamalian, Leo and James V. Hatch. *The Roots of African American Drama: An Anthology of Early Plays, 1858–1938*. Detroit: Wayne State University Press, 1991.

Harris, Trudier. *Afro-American Writers Before the Harlem Renaissance. Dictionary of Literary Biography*. Volume Fifty. Detroit: Gale, 1986.

Jones, Gayl. *Liberating Voices: Oral Tradition in African American Literature*. Cambridge: Harvard University Press, 1991.

Richard Wright

Davis, Charles T. and Michel Fabre. *Richard Wright: A Primary Bibliography*. Boston: G.K. Hall, 1982.

Felgar, Robert. *Richard Wright*. Boston: Twayne, 1980.

Hakutani, Yoshinobu. *Critical Essays on Richard Wright*. Boston: G.K. Hall, 1982.

Macksey, Richard and Frank E. Moorer, eds. *Richard Wright, a Collection of Critical Essays*. Englewood Cliffs, N.J.: Prentice-Hall, 1984.

Miller, Eugene E. *Voice of a Native Son: The Poetics of Richard Wright.* Jackson: University Press of Mississippi, 1990.

Langston Hughes

A Meditation on Langston Hughes and the Harlem Renaissance: With the Poetry of Essex Hemphill and Bruce Nugent. Sankofa Film and Video. N.Y.: Water Bearer Films, 1992.

Andrews, William L. *Classic Fiction of the Harlem Renaissance.* N.Y.: Oxford University Press, 1994.

Baker, Houston A., Jr. *Afro-American Poetics: Revisions of Harlem and the Black Aesthetic.* Madison: University of Wisconsin Press, 1988.

—. *Blues, Ideology, and Afro-American Literature: A Vernacular Theory.* Chicago: University of Chicago Press, 1984.

Claude McKay

Cooper, Wayne F. *Claude McKay: Rebel Sojourner in the Harlem Renaissance: A Biography.* N.Y.: Schocken Books, 1990.

Chapter 26: Cult Figures (1945–Present)

The Beats

Bartlett, Lee, ed. *The Beats: Essays in Criticism.* Jefferson, N.C.: McFarland, 1981.

Charters, Ann. "Beat Poetry and the San Francisco Poetry Renaissance." in Parini Jay ed. *The Columbia History of American Poetry.* N.Y.: Columbia University Press, 1993.

Charters, Ann, ed. *The Beats: Literary Bohemians in Prewar America.* Detroit: Gale, 1983.

Stephenson, Gregory. *The Daybreak Boys: Essays on the Literature of the Beat Generation.* Carbondale: Southern Illinois University Press, 1990.

Allen Ginsberg

Ball, Gordon, ed. *Allen Verbatim: Lectures on Poetry, Politics, and Consciousness.* N.Y.: McGraw-Hill, 1974.

Bartlett, Lee. *The Beats: Essays In Criticism.* Jefferson, N.C.: McFarland, 1981.

Bawer, Bruce. "The Phenomenon of Allen Ginsberg." *The New Criterion* 3.6 (Feb 1985): 1–14.

Kraus, Michelle P. *Allen Ginsberg, An Annotated Bibliography 1969–1977.* Metuchen, N.J.: Scarecrow Press, 1980.

Schumacher, Michael. *Dharma Lion: A Critical Biography of Allen Ginsberg.* N.Y.: St. Martin's Press, 1992.

Whitmer, Peter O. *Aquarius Revisited: Seven Who Created the Sixties Counterculture That Changed America: William Burroughs, Allen Ginsberg, Ken Kesey, Timothy Leary, Norman Mailer, Tom Robbins, Hunter S. Thompson.* N.Y.: Macmillan, 1987.

Sylvia Plath

Alexander, Paul. *Ariel Ascending: Writings About Sylvia Plath*. N.Y.: Harper & Row, 1985.

Axelrod, Steven G. *Sylvia Plath: The Wound and the Cure of Words*. Baltimore: Johns Hopkins University Press, 1992.

Bundtzen, Lynda K. *Plath's Incarnations: Woman and the Creative Process*. Ann Arbor: University of Michigan Press, 1983.

Anne Sexton

Colburn, Steven E., ed. *Telling the Tale*. Ann Arbor: The University of Michigan Press, 1988.

Hall, Caroline King Barnard. *Anne Sexton*. Boston: Twayne Publishers, 1989.

Juhasz, Suzanne. *Naked and Fiery Forms: Modern American Poetry by Women, A New Tradition*. N.Y.: Octagon Books, 1978.

Middlebrook, Diane Wood. *Anne Sexton: A Biography*. Boston: Houghton Mifflin Company, 1991.

Robert Lowell

Mariani, Paul. *Lost Puritan: A Life of Robert Lowell*. N.Y.: W.W. Norton, 1994.

Perkins, David. *A History of Modern Poetry: Modernism and After*. Cambridge and London: The Belknap Press of Harvard University Press, 1987.

J.D. Salinger

Bloom, Harold, ed. *J.D. Salinger*. N.Y.: Chelsea, 1987.

French, Warren G. *J.D. Salinger, revisited*. Boston: Twayne Publishers, 1988.

Hamilton, Ian. *In Search of J.D. Salinger*. N.Y.: Random House, 1988.

Salzberg, Joel. *Critical Essays on Salinger's* The Catcher in the Rye. Boston, Mass.: G.K. Hall, 1990.

Wenke, John P. *J.D. Salinger: A Study of the Short Fiction*. Boston: Twayne Publishers, 1991.

Chapter 27: Horror and Humor (1930–1960)

Flannery O'Connor

Asals, Frederick. *Flannery O'Connor, The Imagination Of Extremity*. Athens, Ga.: University of Georgia Press, 1982.

—, ed. *Flannery O'Connor, 'A Good Man Is Hard to Find'*. N.Y.: Rutgers University Press, 1993.

Baumgaertner, Jill P. *Flannery O'Connor: A Proper Scaring*. Wheaton, Ill.: H. Shaw Publishers, 1988.

Bloom, Harold, ed. *Flannery O'Connor.* Chelsea House, 1986.

Brinkmeyer, Robert H., Jr. *The Art and Vision of Flannery O'Connor.* Baton Rouge: Louisiana State University Press, 1989.

Clark, Beverly L. and Melvin J. Friedman, eds. *Critical Essays on Flannery O'Connor.* Boston: G.K. Hall, 1985.

Coles, Robert. *Flannery O'Connor's South.* Louisiana State University Press, 1980.

Desmond, John F. *Risen Sons: Flannery O'Connor's Vision of History.* Athens: University of Georgia Press, 1987.

Driggers, Stephen G., Robert J. Dunn and Sarah Gordon. *The Manuscripts of Flannery O'Connor at Georgia College.* Athens: University of Georgia Press, 1989.

Farmer, David R. *Flannery O'Connor, A Descriptive Bibliography.* N.Y.: Garland Pub., 1981.

Chapter 28: Jewish-American Literature

Saul Bellow

Bach, Gerhard and Jakob J. Kollhofer, eds. *Saul Bellow at Seventy Five: A Collection of Critical Essays.* Tubingen: Narr, 1991.

Bakker, J. *Fiction as Survival Strategy: A Comparative Study of the Major Works of Ernest Hemingway and Saul Bellow.* Amsterdam: Rodopi, 1983.

Bloom, Harold, ed. *Saul Bellow.* N.Y.: Chelsea, 1986.

Bradbury, Malcolm. *Saul Bellow.* N.Y.: Methuen, 1982.

Cronin Gloria L. and Ben Siegel, eds. *Conversations with Saul Bellow.* Jackson: University Press of Mississippi, 1994.

—. and L.H. Goldman, eds. *Saul Bellow in the 1980s: A Collection of Critical Essays.* East Lansing: Michigan State University Press, 1989.

Goldman L.H. et. al, eds. *Saul Bellow: A Mosaic.* N.Y.: Peter Lang, 1992.

Hyland, Peter. *Saul Bellow.* N.Y.: St. Martin's, 1992.

Kiernan, Robert F. *Saul Bellow.* N.Y.: Continuum, 1989.

Newman, Judie. *Saul Bellow and History.* N.Y.: St. Martin's, 1984.

Pifer, Ellen. *Saul Bellow Against the Grain.* Philadelphia: University of Pennsylvania Press, 1990.

Norman Mailer

Begiebing, Robert J. *Toward a New Synthesis: John Fowles, John Gardner, Norman Mailer.* Ann Arbor, Mich.: UMI Research Press, 1989.

Braudy, Leo. *Norman Mailer, a Collection of Critical Essays.* Englewood Cliffs, N.J., Prentice Hall, 1972.

Gordon, Andrew. *An American Dreamer: A Psychoanalytic Study of the Fiction of Norman Mailer.* Rutherford, N.J.: Fairleigh Dickinson University Press, 1980.

Kaufmann, Donald L. *Norman Mailer: the Countdown: the First Twenty Years.* Carbondale, Southern Illinois University Press, 1969.

Lennon, Michael. *Critical Essays on Norman Mailer.* Boston: G.K. Hall, 1986.

Manso, Peter. *Mailer, His Life and Times.* N.Y.: Simon and Schuster, 1985.

Mills, Hilary. *Mailer: A Biography.* N.Y.: Empire Books, 1982.

Poirier, Richard. *Norman Mailer.* N.Y.: Viking Press, 1972.

Wenke, Joseph. *Mailer's America.* Hanover, N.H.: University Press of New England, 1987.

Bernard Malamud

Alter, Iska Sheila. *The Good Man's Dilemma: Social Criticism in the Fiction of Bernard Malamud.* AMS Studies in Modern Literature, no. 5. N.Y.: AMS Press, 1981.

Astro, Richard and Jackson J. Benson, eds. *The Fiction of Bernard Malamud.* Corvallis: Oregon State University Press, 1977.

Bloom, Harold. *Bernard Malamud.* N.Y.: Chelsea House, 1986.

Field, Leslie A. and Joyce W. Field, eds. *Bernard Malamud and the Critics.* N.Y.: New York University Press; London: University of London Press, 1970.

—, eds. *Bernard Malamud: A Collection of Critical Essays.* Englewood Cliffs, N.J.: Prentice-Hall, 1975.

Helterman, Jeffrey. *Understanding Bernard Malamud.* University of South Carolina Press, 1985.

Hershinow, Sheldon J. *Bernard Malamud. Modern Literature Monographs.* N.Y.: Frederick Ungar Publishing Co., 1980.

Kosofsky, Rita Nathalie. *Bernard Malamud: A Descriptive Bibliography.* Westport, Conn.: Greenwood Press, 1991.

Lasher, Lawrence M., ed. *Conversations with Bernard Malamud.* Jackson and London: University Press of Mississippi, 1991.

Ochshorn, Kathleen Gillikin. *The Heart's Essential Landscape: Bernard Malamud's Hero.* N.Y.: Peter Lang, 1990.

Salzberg, Joel. *Bernard Malamud: A Reference Guide.* Boston: G.H. Hall and Co., 1985.

—. *Critical Essays on Bernard Malamud.* Edited by Joel Salzberg. Boston: G.K. Hall and Co., 1987.

Solotaroff, Robert. *Bernard Malamud: A Study of the Short Fiction.* Twayne's Studies in Short Fiction, Series No. 8. Boston: G.K. Hall, 1989.

Chapter 29: Contemporary African–American Literature

James Baldwin

Burt, Nancy V. and Fred L. Standley, eds. *Critical Essays on James Baldwin.* Boston: G.K. Hall, 1988.

Campbell, James. *Talking at the Gates; a Life of James Baldwin.* N.Y.: Penguin Books, 1991.

Gwendolyn Brooks

Kent, George E. *A Life of Gwendolyn Brooks.* Lexington: University Press of Kentucky, 1990.

Kufrin, Joan. "Gwendolyn Brooks." *Uncommon Women,* 35–51. Piscataway, N.J.: New Century Publishers, 1981.

Madhubuti, Haki R., ed. *Say That the River Turns: The Impact of Gwendolyn Brooks.* Chicago: Third World Press, 1987.

Melhem, D.H. *Gwendolyn Brooks: Poetry and the Heroic Voice.* Lexington: University Press of Kentucky, 1987.

Shaw, Harry B. *Gwendolyn Brooks.* Boston: Twayne, 1980.

Wright, Stephen Caldwell. *The Chicago Collective: Poems for and Inspired by Gwendolyn Brooks.* Sanford, Fla.: Christopher-Burghardt, 1990.

—. *On Gwendolyn Brooks: Reliant Contemplation.* Ann Arbor, Mich.: University of Michigan Press, 1996.

Ralph Ellison

Benston, Kimberly W., ed. *Speaking for You: The Vision of Ralph Ellison.* Washington, D.C.: Howard University Press, 1987.

Busby, Mark. *Ralph Ellison.* Boston: Twayne Publishers, 1991.

De Jongh, James. *Vicious Modernism: Black Harlem and the Literary Imagination.* N.Y.: Cambridge University Press, 1990.

Driskell, David C. and others. *Harlem Renaissance: Art of Black America.* N.Y.: Abrams, 1987.

Fabre, Michel. *From Harlem to Paris: Black American Writers in France, 1840–1980.* Urbana: University of Illinois Press, 1991.

Nadel, Alan. *Invisible Criticism: Ralph Ellison and the American Canon.* Iowa City: University of Iowa Press, 1988.

O'Meally, Robert G. *The Craft of Ralph Ellison.* Cambridge: Harvard University Press, 1980.

O'Meally, Robert, ed. *New Essays on Invisible Man.* Cambridge: Cambridge University Press, 1988.

Toni Morrison

Bjork, Patrick B. *The Novels of Toni Morrison: The Search for Self and Place Within the Community*. N.Y.: P. Lang, 1996.

Butler-Evans, Elliott. *Race, Gender, and Desire: Narrative Strategies in the Fiction of Toni Cade Bambara, Toni Morrison, and Alice Walker*. Philadelphia: Temple University Press, 1989.

Carmean, Karen. *Toni Morrison's World of Fiction*. Troy, N.Y.: Whitston, 1993.

McKay, Nellie Y. *Critical Essays on Toni Morrison*. Boston: G.K. Hall, 1988.

Samuels, Wilfred D. and Clenora Hudson-Weems. *Toni Morrison*. Boston: Twayne, 1990.

Chapter 30: Modern Canadian Literature

Margaret Atwood

Davidson, Arnold and Cathy, ed. *The Art of Margaret Atwood: Essays in Criticism*. House of Anansi Press, 1980.

Grace, Sherill. *Violent Duality; A Study of Margaret Atwood*. Vehicule Press, 1980.

Grace, Sherrill and Lorraine Weir, eds. *Margaret Atwood: Language, Text and System*. University of British Columbia Press, 1983.

Ingersoll, Earl G., ed. *Margaret Atwood: Conversations*. Princeton, N.J.: Ontario Review Press, 1990.

Irvine, Lorna. *Collecting Clues: Margaret Atwood's Bodily Harm*. Toronto: ECW Press, 1993.

McCombs, Judith, ed. *Critical Essays on Margaret Atwood*. Boston: G.K. Hall & Co., 1988.

Rao, Eleonora. *Strategies for Identity: The Fiction of Margaret Atwood*. N.Y.: Peter Land Publishing, 1994.

Rosenberg, Jerome H. *Margaret Atwood*. Boston: Twayne, 1984.

Staels, Hilda. *Margaret Atwood's Novels: A Study of Narrative Discourse*. Tubingen, Germany: Francke Verlag, 1995.

Van Spanckeren, Kathryn and Jan Garden Castro, eds. *Vision and Forms*. Southern Illinois University Press, 1988.

Wilson, Sharon Rose. *Margaret Atwood's Fairy-Tale Sexual Politics*. University Press of Mississippi, 1993.

York, Lorraine M., ed. *Various Atwoods: Essays on the Later Poems, Short Fiction, and Novels*. House of Anansi Press, 1995.

Chapter 31: Native-American, Latino-American, and Asian-American Literature

Butcher, Philip. *The Ethnic Image in Modern American Literature*. Washington, D.C.: Howard University Press, 1984.

Dearborn, Mary V. *Pocahontas's Daughters: Gender and Ethnicity in American Culture*. N.Y.: Oxford University Press, 1986.

Enriquez, Evangelina. *Towards a Definition of, and Critical Approaches to Chicanoa Literature*. Thesis Ph.D. Riverside: University of California.

Hoffman, Donald. "Whose Home on the Range? Finding Room for Native Americans, African Americans, and Latino Americans in the Revisionist Western." *Melus* 22.2 (Sumr 1997): 45–61.

Horno-Delgado, Asuncion. *Breaking Boundaries: Latina Writing and Critical Readings*. Amherst: University of Massachusetts Press, 1989.

Lim, Shirley. *The Forbidden Stitch: An Asian American Women's Anthology*. Corvallis, Oreg.: Calyx Books, 1989.

Wardrop, Stephanie. "Last of the Red Hot Mohicans: Miscegenation in the Popular American Romance." *Melus* 22.2 (Sumr 1997): 61–75.

Chapter 32: New Frontiers

Arac, Jonathan, ed. *Postmodernism and Politics*. Minneapolis: University of Minnesota Press, 1986.

Callinicos, Alex. *Against Postmodernism: a Marxist Critique*. N.Y.: St. Martin's Press, 1990.

Caviola, Hugo. *In the Zone: Perception and Presentation of Space in German and American Postmodernism*. Boston: Birkhauser, 1991.

Falck, Colin. *Myth, Truth, and Literature: Towards A True Post-Modernism*. N.Y.: Cambridge University Press, 1989.

McGowan, John. *Postmodernism and Its Critics*. Ithaca: Cornell University Press, 1991.

McHale, Brian. *Postmodernist Fiction*. N.Y.: Methuen, 1987.

Perloff, Marjorie. *Poetic License: Essays on Modernist and Postmodernist Lyric*. Evanston, Ill.: Northwestern University Press, 1990.

Rose, Margaret A. *The Post-Modern and the Post-Industrial: A Critical Analysis*. N.Y.: Cambridge University Press, 1991.

Ruland, Richard and Malcolm Bradbury. *From Puritanism to Postmodernism: A History of American Literature*. N.Y.: Viking, 1991.

John Updike

Gullette, Margaret M. *Safe at Last in the Middle Years: The Invention of the Midlife Progress Novel: Saul Bellow, Margaret Drabble, Anne Tyler, John Updike*. Berkeley: University of California Press, 1988.

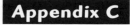

Timeline

1492

Christopher Columbus sights land in the Bahamas, "discovers" the New World

1503

Leonardo da Vinci paints the *Mona Lisa*

1509

Michelangelo paints the ceiling of the Sistine Chapel

1520

Chocolate introduced to Europe

1605

Shakespeare completes *Macbeth*

1607

Jamestown settled

1616

John Smith's *A Description of New England*

1620

Mayflower lands at Plymouth

1621

First Thanksgiving, at Plymouth

1630

John Winthrop delivers the lay sermon *A Model of Christian Charity* while aboard the ship *Arabella*

William Bradford begins writing *Of Plymouth Plantation*

1636

Harvard University established

1640

Bay Psalm Book published, first book printed in the colonies

1644

China's Ming dynasty ends

1650

Anne Bradstreet's *The Tenth Muse*

1667

Milton, the great English writer, publishes *Paradise Lost*

1692

Salem witchcraft trials; by the end of the hysteria, 19 people and three dogs hanged

1735

Great Awakening, a religious revival, sweeps across the colonies

1741

First American magazines appear: Andrew Bradford's *American Magazine* and Benjamin Franklin's *General Magazine, and Historical Chronicle*

Jonathan Edwards delivers his "fire and brimstone" sermon, "Sinners in the Hands of an Angry God"

1749

Sign language invented

1752

Benjamin Franklin conducts his kite and key experiments with lightning

1765

In England, James Watt invents the steam engine

1776

Thomas Paine's *Common Sense* helps spur the movement for American independence

1789

Beginnings of short fiction in American magazines: "Azakia: A Canadian Story" in *Monthly Miscellany* and *Vermont Magazine;* "The Story of the Captain's Wife and an Aged Woman" in *Gentleman* and *Lady's Town and Country Magazine*

1800

In England, Coleridge finishes "Kulba Khan"

1803

Louisiana Purchase extends nation's territory to the Rocky Mountains

1804

Lewis and Clark begin expedition exploring and mapping the vast West

Napoleon proclaims himself emperor

1805

Beethoven's *Third Symphony*

1807

Robert Fulton's steamboat makes first trip

1809

Washington Irving's *A History of New York*

1812

U.S. declares war on Great Britain

1813

In England, Jane Austen's *Pride and Prejudice* published

1814

Francis Scott Key writes "The Star Spangled Banner"

1815

Battle of New Orleans

The *North American Review* established

1817

William Cullen Bryant's "Thanatopsis"

1818

In England, Mary Wollestonecraft Shelley's *Frankenstein*

1819

Washington Irving's *The Sketch Book*

Spain relinquishes Florida

John Keats' "Ode to a Nightingale" and "Ode on a Grecian Urn"

Rene Laennec invents the stethoscope

Sir Walter Scott's *Ivanhoe*

1820

Missouri Compromise balances slave and free states admitted to the Union

James Monroe elected over John Quincy Adams as president

Daniel Boone dies at age 85

U.S. population: 9,638,453

Washington Irving's *The Sketch Book*

1821

Missouri enters Union as 24th state, thus balancing the union at 12 slave and 12 free states

Opening of Santa Fe trail

James Fenimore Cooper gains fame with *The Spy*

First women's college founded

The Saturday Evening Post established

1822

Washington Irving's *Bracebridge Hall: or, The Humorists* published in England

1823

James Fenimore Cooper's *The Pioneers* introduces Natty Bumppo

Monroe Doctrine warns European powers to keep their hands off Latin America

1824

John Quincy Adams elected president (1824–1828)

Washington Irving's *Tales of a Traveler*

1825

Erie Canal finished

Russia: Decembrist uprising crushed by czarist forces

1826

James Fenimore Cooper's *The Last of the Mohicans*

Death of Thomas Jefferson and John Adams on July 4, hours apart

1827

Edgar Allan Poe's first collection of poems, *Tamberlane*

1828

Noah Webster's *An American Dictionary of the English Language*

Andrew Jackson elected president

Birth of Emily Dickinson

1830

"Tom Thumb," was America's first steam-driven locomotive

U.S. population: 12,866,020

Nathaniel Hawthorne's earliest tales ("Provincial Tales" and "Seven Tales of My Native Land") published individually in *Token, Salem Gazette,* and *Atlantic Souvenir.*

1830–1865: Romantic Period

1831

Victor Hugo's *The Hunchback of Notre Dame*

Nat Turner leads slave uprising in which 70 whites are killed; 100 blacks are killed in a search for Turner

1832

Washington Irving's *The Alhambra*

Grimm's *Fairy Tales* translated into English

Andrew Jackson reelected president

Seminole chiefs cede Florida to the U.S. and agree to move west of the Mississippi

The Oregon Trail becomes a main route for settlers

New England Anti-Slavery Society

Nathaniel Hawthorne's "Roger Malvin's Burial"

1833

Edgar Allan Poe's "MS. Found in a Bottle"

First issue of *Knickerbocker Magazine*

Americans in Texas territory vote to separate Texas from Mexico

Britain prohibits slavery in her colonies

Oberlin College opens, the first coeducational college and the first to admit blacks

1834

Cyrus Hall McCormick's mechanical reaper

1835

National debt is paid off

Mob in Charleston, S.C., burns abolitionist literature, and abolitionist writers are expelled from Southern states

Alexis de Tocqueville publishes *Democracy in America* in France

Samuel L. Clemens (Mark Twain) born in Florida, Missouri

1836

The Battle of the Alamo (Santa Anna leads 3,000 men in a siege of the Alamo, killing all 187 Texans inside on March 6; on March 27, his troops kill 300 soldiers defending Goliad. Texans capture Santa Anna at the Battle of San Jacinto.)

Ralph Waldo Emerson's *Nature* kicks off New England Renaissance

Settlers led by Dr. Marcus Whitman reach Walla Walla in present-day Washington

Massachusetts Supreme Court rules that any slave brought within its borders by a master is free

Transcendental Club (1836–1844)

Bret Harte born

1837

Samuel F.B. Morse invents telegraph

Charles Dickens' *Oliver Twist*

Martin Van Buren elected president

Financial Panic of 1837

Birth of William Dean Howells in Ohio

Nathaniel Hawthorne's *Twice-Told Tales* (including "My Kinsman, Major Molineux")

1838

Removal of 15,000 to 17,000 Cherokee Indians from Georgia on the "Trail of Tears" results in 4,000 deaths

Republic of Texas withdraws its offer of annexation with the U.S.

Underground Railroad organized

Ralph Waldo Emerson's "An Address…" (revised in 1841 as "The Divinity School Address")

Alexis De Tocqueville's *Democracy in America* (first American edition)

1839

Edgar Allan Poe's "The Fall of the House of Usher"

Spanish slave ship *Amistad,* carrying 53 slaves, is taken over in a mutiny by their leader, Cinque

Edgar Allan Poe's *Tales of the Grotesque and Arabesque*

1840

William Henry Harrison ("Old Tippecanoe") defeats Martin Van Buren for the presidency

U.S. population: 17,069,453

Transcendentalist Club begins to publish its magazine, *The Dial*

Upper and Lower Canada are united

1841

Supreme Court upholds lower court ruling and allows the Amistad mutineers to return to Africa

William Henry Harrison dies; John Tyler becomes president

Brook Farm Institute is founded (1841–1847)

Ralph Waldo Emerson's *Essays, First Series*

Herman Melville sails on whaler *Acushnet* and jumps ship in the Marquesas in July 1842

1842

Colonel John C. Frémont leads an expedition to explore the Rocky Mountains

Edgar Allan Poe, Reviews of Hawthorne's *Twice-Told Tales*

Hong Kong becomes a British colony

1843

Beginning of large migration westward

Second Seminole War ends

Edgar Allan Poe's "The Gold Bug"; "The Black Cat"

In England, Dickens publishes *A Christmas Carol.*

1844

James K. Polk defeats Henry Clay for the presidency

Ralph Waldo Emerson's *Essays: Second Series* (including "Experience" and "The Poet")

In France, Dumas publishes *The Three Musketeers*

1845

Texas joins the Union as the 28th state

Potato famine in Ireland brings great numbers of Irish immigrants

Edgar Allan Poe's *The Raven and Other Poems*

Margaret Fuller's *Woman in the Nineteenth Century*

Henry David Thoreau begins living at Walden Pond

Frederick Douglass' *Narrative of the Life of Frederick Douglass, an American Slave*

1846

Mexican war begins

Treaty with Great Britain extends the Oregon Territory boundary at latitude 40 degrees to Puget Sound

James Russell Lowell publishes the first of "The Bigelow Papers"

Edgar Allan Poe's "The Philosophy of Composition"

Nathaniel Hawthorne's *Mosses from an Old Manse* (includes "Roger Malvin's Burial" and "Young Goodman Brown")

Herman Melville's *Typee*

1847

Frederick Douglass founds *The North Star*, an abolitionist newspaper

Ralph Waldo Emerson's *Poems* (includes "Hamatreya" and "Each and All")

Henry Wadsworth Longfellow's *Evangeline*

Herman Melville's *Omoo*

In England, Emily Bronte publishes *Wuthering Heights*

1848

Mexican War ends with the Treaty of Guadalupe Hidalgo

Lucretia Mott and Elizabeth Cady Stanton organize the first American women's rights convention in Seneca Falls, New York

1849

James Fenimore Cooper's *The Pathfinder*

1849

Amelia Bloomer begins publishing the *Lily,* a journal supporting temperance and women's rights

First gold seekers arrive at San Francisco

Zachary Taylor inaugurated as 12th president

Henry David Thoreau's *Resistance to Civil Government; A Week on the Concord and Merrimack Rivers*

Edgar Allan Poe's "The Bells"; "Annabel Lee"

Poe dies in Baltimore

Sarah Orne Jewett born

Herman Melville's *Redburn; Mardi*

1850

Fugitive Slave Act provides for the return of slaves brought to free states

Compromise of 1850 admits California as a free state and Texas as a slave state; New Mexico and Utah organized with no restrictions on slavery

U.S. population: 23,191,876

Nathaniel Hawthorne's *The Scarlet Letter*

Ralph Waldo Emerson's *Representative Men*

Herman Melville's *White-Jacket*

1851

Horace Greeley advises, "Go West, young man."

Herman Melville's *Moby Dick*

Nathaniel Hawthorne's *The House of the Seven Gables*

Birth of Kate Chopin

1852

Franklin Pierce elected president

"Know-Nothing" Party opposes Catholics and foreigners

Herman Melville's *Pierre*

Nathaniel Hawthorne's *The Blithedale Romance*

Harriet Beecher Stowe's *Uncle Tom's Cabin*

1853

Nathaniel Hawthorne's *Tanglewood Tales for Girls and Boys*

1854

Kansas-Nebraska Act passes, allowing "popular sovereignty"

Henry David Thoreau's *Walden*

Herman Melville's "The Encantadas"

1855

Frederick Douglass' *My Bondage and My Freedom*

Walt Whitman's *Leaves of Grass*

Henry Wadsworth Longfellow's *Hiawatha*

Herman Melville's "Benito Cereno"

1856

Abolitionist John Brown kills five proslavery men at Pottawatamie River

James Buchanan elected president

Herman Melville's *The Piazza Tales* and "Bartleby, the Scrivener"

1857

Dred Scott decision by the Supreme Court

Herman Melville's *The Confidence Man*

Atlantic Monthly founded

1858

Lincoln-Douglas debates

Financial panic of 1858

Oliver Wendell Holmes' *The Autocrat of the Breakfast-Table*

1859

John Brown leads an armed group of 21 to seize the arsenal at Harpers Ferry, Virginia; is captured; and is executed

Harriet E. Wilson's *Our Nig: or, Sketches in the Life of a Free Black...*, first novel by an African-American woman

1860

Abraham Lincoln elected president

South Carolina votes to secede from the Union

U.S. population: 31,443,321

Nathaniel Hawthorne's *The Marble Fawn*

1861

Attack on Fort Sumter on April 12 signals the beginning of the Civil War

Battle of Bull Run

Henry Wadsworth Longfellow's *Paul Revere's Ride*

1862

President Lincoln signs the Homestead Act, allowing citizens to acquire up to 160 acres after farming it for five years

Robert E. Lee commands the Confederate Armies of Northern Virginia

Birth of Edith Wharton

1863

Henry Wadsworth Longfellow's *Tales of a Wayside Inn*

Abraham Lincoln's "Gettysburg Address"

Nathaniel Hawthorne's *Our Old Home*

1864

Abraham Lincoln reelected

General Sherman takes Atlanta

Nathaniel Hawthorne dies

1865

Civil War officially ends when Robert E. Lee surrenders to Ulysses S. Grant at Appomattox Courthouse

April 14, Lincoln assassinated

Thirteenth Amendment abolishes slavery

Mark Twain's "The Celebrated Jumping Frog of Calaveras County"

Walt Whitman's "When Lilacs Last in the Dooryard Bloom'd" and *Drum-Taps*

1866

Atlantic cable completed

Herman Melville's *Battle-Pieces and Aspects of the War* (poems)

John Greenleaf Whittier's *Snow-Bound*

Ralph Waldo Emerson's "Terminus"

In Russia, Dostoyevsky publishes *Crime and Punishment*

1867

Reconstruction Act

U.S. purchases Alaska from Russia for two cents an acre

1868

Fourteenth Amendment guarantees civil rights

Louisa May Alcott's *Little Women*

Bret Harte's "The Luck of Roaring Camp"

1869

Ulysses S. Grant elected president (1869–77)

Union Pacific–Central Pacific transcontinental railroad completed

Wyoming passes first woman's suffrage act

Mark Twain's *The Innocents Abroad*

Harriet Beecher Stowe's *Oldtown Folks*

Bret Harte's "The Outcasts of Poker Flat"

1870

Franco-Prussian War

John D. Rockefeller founds the Standard Oil Company

Birth of Frank Norris in Chicago

Bret Harte's *The Luck of Roaring Camp and Other Sketches*

1871

Chicago destroyed by fire

Charles Darwin's *The Descent of Man and Selection in Relation to Sex*

Birth of Stephen Crane

Walt Whitman's *Democratic Vistas; A Passage to India*

Louisa May Alcott's *Little Men*

1872

Mark Twain's *Roughing It*

Birth of Paul Laurence Dunbar

1873

Financial Panic of 1873

Birth of Willa Cather

1874

Women's Christian Temperance Union founded

First impressionist painting exhibition in Paris

1875

William Dean Howells' *A Foregone Conclusion*

1876

Alexander Graham Bell invents the telephone

George Armstrong Custer defeated at Little Big Horn

Mark Twain's *Adventures of Tom Sawyer*

Walt Whitman's *Leaves of Grass* (Centennial Edition)

Herman Melville's *Clarel* (poems)

Birth of Jack London and Sherwood Anderson

1877

Chief Joseph's revolt: the Nez Percé war

Henry James' *The American*

Sarah Orne Jewett's *Deephaven*

451

1878

Thomas Edison establishes The Edison Electric Light Co. in New York City

Henry James' *The Europeans*

1879

Thomas Edison invents the lightbulb

Henry James' *Daisy Miller*

1880

James A. Garfield elected president

Joel Chandler Harris' *Uncle Remus His Songs and His Sayings*

1881

Garfield assassinated on July 2, 1881; Chester A. Arthur becomes president

Tuskegee Institute founded by Booker T. Washington

Henry James' *Washington Square; The Portrait of a Lady*

Frederick Douglass' *Life and Times of Frederick Douglass*

1882

Immigration of Chinese labor suspended

John D. Rockefeller organizes the Standard Oil trust

Mark Twain's *The Prince and the Pauper*

Death of Emerson

Walt Whitman's *Specimen Days*

1883

Brooklyn Bridge completed

Mark Twain's *Life on the Mississippi*

A 10-story building in Chicago is the world's first true skyscraper

1884

Sarah Orne Jewett's *A Country Doctor*

Mark Twain's *The Adventures of Huckleberry Finn*

1885

Grover Cleveland elected president

Washington Monument dedicated

William Dean Howells' *The Rise of Silas Lapham*

Birth of Sinclair Lewis and Ezra Pound

In Germany, Karl Benz builds the first car powered by an internal-combustion engine

1886

Haymarket Square Riot: 11 people were killed and more than 100 wounded. Eight anarchists were tried, but no evidence was found to link them to the bomb.

Statue of Liberty dedicated in New York Harbor

Henry James' *The Princess Casamassima; The Bostonians*

Death of Emily Dickinson

1887

Dawes Severalty Act provides for 160 acres to be given to each Indian family, breaking up the system of communal land holdings

1888

Great Blizzard of 1888

Secret ballot system introduced to U.S.

Death of Bronson and Louisa May Alcott

Henry James' *The Aspern Papers*

Walt Whitman's *November Boughs; Complete Poems and Prose*

Edward Bellamy's *Looking Backward* (utopian novel)

Birth of T.S. Eliot and Eugene O'Neill

1889

Benjamin Harrison elected president

Johnstown (Pennsylvania) flood

Oklahoma land rush

Theodore Roosevelt's *The Winning of the West*

Mark Twain's *A Connecticut Yankee in King Arthur's Court*

Jane Addams sets up Hull House, the first of many settlement houses to aid the poor

1890

Sherman Anti-Trust Act

Yosemite Park created by Act of Congress

Battle of Wounded Knee, South Dakota

Henry James' *The Tragic Muse*

1891

First international copyright law

Acres of Indian land in Oklahoma opened to white settlers

Death of Herman Melville in obscurity in New York

Emily Dickinson's *Poems: Second Series* (posthumous)

1892

Homestead (Pennsylvania) steelworkers strike; governor calls in the militia

Death of Walt Whitman

1893

Financial panic of 1893

Stephen Crane's *Maggie: A Girl of the Streets*

Coxey's Army, a group of unemployed men, marches from Ohio to Washington, D.C. A related group, Kelly's Industrial Army, sets out from the West Coast; one of them is Jack London.

Mark Twain's *Pudd'nhead Wilson*

Kate Chopin's *Bayou Folk*

1895

Death of Frederick Douglass

Stephen Crane's *The Red Badge of Courage;* "Black Riders and Other Lines"

1896

Klondike gold rush

William Jennings Bryan gives the "Cross of Gold" speech supporting free silver (instead of the gold standard)

In Plessy v. Ferguson, the Supreme Court upholds the "separate but equal" doctrine

Emily Dickinson's *Poems: Third Series*

Birth of F. Scott Fitzgerald

1897

William McKinley president

Annexation of Hawaii

Birth of William Faulkner

Henry James' *What Maisie Knew; The Spoils of Poynton*

1898

The sinking of the battleship *Maine* results in 260 deaths

Assistant Secretary of the Navy Theodore Roosevelt sends the Pacific fleet to the Philippines

Spanish-American War (April–December)

Henry James' "The Turn of the Screw"

Stephen Crane's "The Open Boat"

1899

Stephen Crane's "The Monster;" "War Is Kind"

Thorstein Veblen's *The Theory of the Leisure Class*

Henry James' *The Awkward Age*

Frank Norris' *McTeague; Blix*

1900

Hawaii granted territorial standing

U.S. population: 75,994,575

Theodore Dreiser's *Sister Carrie*

Jack London's *The Son of the Wolf*

Stephen Crane's *Whilomville Stories*

Death of Stephen Crane

Mark Twain's *The Man Who Corrupted Hadleyburg and Other Stories*

Jack London's *The Son of the Wolf: Tales of the Far North*

1900–1910: Naturalistic Period

1900

Women compete in the Olympics for the first time

1901

Frank Norris' *The Octopus*

Edith Wharton's collection of short stories, *Crucial Instances*

1903

Frank Norris' *The Pit*

Henry James' *The Ambassadors*

1904

Edith Wharton's *The Descent of Man and Other Stories*

Henry James' *The Golden Bowl*

Edith Wharton's *The House of Mirth*

1905

Willa Cather's *The Troll Garden* (including "Paul's Case")

1906

O. Henry's *The Four Million* (including "The Gift of the Magi")

1910–1945: Modernism

1910

Henry James' *The Finer Grain*

1911

Edith Wharton's *Ethan Frome*

Theodore Dreiser's *Jennie Gerhardt*

1912

Theodore Dreiser's *The Financier*

1913

Willa Cather's *O Pioneers!*

Model T Ford produced on assembly line

1915

Edward J. O'Brien begins publishing *The Best American Short Stories* annual series

1916

Edith Wharton's *Xingu and Other Stories*

Carl Sandburg's *Chicago Poems*

1917

Hamlin Garland's *A Son of the Middle Border*

Ring Lardner's *Gullible's Travels*

America enters the first World War

1918

Theodore Dreiser's *Free and Other Stories*

Willa Cather's *My Antonia*

1919

Sherwood Anderson's *Winesberg, Ohio*

Prohibition becomes law

Treaty of Versailles ends World War I

1920

F. Scott Fitzgerald's *Flappers and Philosophers; This Side of Paradise*

Edith Wharton's *The Age of Innocence*

Sinclair Lewis' *Main Street*

Nineteenth Amendment gives women the right to vote

1921

Sherwood Anderson's "The Triumph of the Egg"

1922

F. Scott Fitzgerald's *Tales of the Jazz Age*

Sinclair Lewis' *Babbitt*

T.S. Eliot's *The Waste Land*

Ireland's James Joyce publishes *Ulysses*

1923

Ellen Glasgow's *The Shadowy Third and Other Stories*

Jean Toomer's *Cane*

Willa Cather's *A Lost Lady*

1924

Ring Lardner's *How to Write Short Stories (with Samples)*

1925

Ernest Hemingway's *In Our Time* (including "Big Two-Hearted River")

The *New Yorker* established

Time magazine established

Theodore Dreiser's *An American Tragedy*

F. Scott Fitzgerald's *The Great Gatsby*

Sinclair Lewis' *Arrowsmith*

Ellen Glasgow's *Barren Ground*

1926

Fitzgerald's *All the Sad Young Men*

Lardner's *The Love Nest and Other Stories*

Ernest Hemingway's *The Sun Also Rises*

Langston Hughes' *Weary Blues*

1927

Ernest Hemingway's *Men Without Women* (including "The Killers")

Babe Ruth hits 60 home runs

1929

William Faulkner's *The Sound and the Fury*

The Best of O. Henry

Ring Lardner's *Round Up*

Ernest Hemingway's *A Farewell to Arms*

Thomas Wolfe's *Look Homeward, Angel*

1930

Kay Boyle's *Wedding Day and Other Stories*

Katherine Anne Porter's *Flowering Judas*

1932

William Faulkner's *Light in August*

James T. Farrell's *Young Lonigan*

Ernest Hemingway's *Winner Take Nothing* (including "A Clean, Well-Lighted Place")

1933

Sherwood Anderson's *Death in the Woods and Other Stories*

1934

William Faulkner's *Doctor Martino*

James T. Farrell's *Calico Shoes*

Conrad Aiken's *Among the Lost People*

William Saroyan's *The Daring Young Man on the Flying Trapeze*

Langston Hughes' *The Ways of White Folks*

F. Scott Fitzgerald's *Tender is the Night*

John O'Hara's *Appointment in Samara*

1935

Katherine Anne Porter's *Flowering Judas and Other Stories*

John O'Hara's *The Doctor's Son and Other Stories*

Thomas Wolfe's *From Death to Morning*

Sinclair Lewis' *Selected Short Stories*

F. Scott Fitzgerald's *Taps at Reveille* (including "Babylon Revisited")

Thomas Wolfe's *Of Time and the River*

1936

Edith Wharton's *The World Over* (including "Roman Fever")

Margaret Mitchell's *Gone with the Wind*

William Faulker's *Absalom, Absalom!*

1937

John Steinbeck's *Of Mice and Men*

1938

John Steinbeck's *The Long Valley* (including "The Chrysanthemums")

Richard Wright's *Uncle Tom's Children*

William Faulkner's *The Unvanquished*

Ernest Hemingway's *The Fifth Column and the First Forty-Nine Stories* (including "The Short Happy Life of Francis Macomber;" "The Snows of Kilimanjaro")

1939

Katherine Anne Porter's *Pale Horse, Pale Rider*

Dorothy Parker's *Here Lies: The Collected Stories*

The *Kenyon Review* established

John Steinbeck's *The Grapes of Wrath*

1940

Ernest Hemingway's *For Whom the Bell Tolls*

Thomas Wolfe's *You Can't Go Home Again*

Carson McCullers' *The Heart is a Lonely Hunter*

Richard Wright's *Native Son*

1941

Eudora Welty's *A Curtain of Green and Other Stories* (including "A Worn Path")

Thomas Wolfe's *The Hills Beyond*

America enters World War II

1942

William Faulkner's *Go Down, Moses* (including "The Bear")

James Thurber's *My Life and Welcome to It* (including "Walter Mitty")

James T. Farrell's *$1000 A Week and Other Stories*

1943

John Cheever's *The Way Some People Live*

Dashiell Hammett's *The Adventures of Sam Spade and Other Stories*

1944

Katherine Anne Porter's *The Leaning Tower and Other Stories*

Raymond Chandler's *Five Murderers*

James T. Farrell's *To Whom It May Concern*

1945

Gwendolyn Brooks' *A Street in Bronzeville*

Atomic bombs dropped on Japan

World War II ends

United Nations formed

1946

Robert Penn Warren's *All the King's Men*

1948

James Michener's *Tales of the South Pacific* wins the Pulitzer Prize

Norman Mailer's *The Naked and the Dead*

The state of Israel established

Gandhi assassinated

1949

Shirley Jackson's "The Lottery" published in the *New Yorker* elicits the largest reader response in the magazine's history

Arthur Miller's *Death of a Salesman* wins Pulitzer Prize for drama

NATO established

1950

William Faulkner's *Collected Stories*

William Carlos Williams' *Make Light of It: Collected Stories*

President Harry Truman sends troops to South Korea after North Korea invasion

1951

Carson McCullers' *The Ballad of the Sad Café and Other Stories*

J.D. Salinger's *The Catcher in the Rye*

1952

Flannery O'Connor's *Wise Blood*

Ralph Ellison's *Invisible Man*

Elizabeth II assumes England's throne

1953

John Cheever's *The Enormous Radio and Other Stories*

J.D. Salinger's *Nine Stories*

1954

Supreme Court holds school segregation unconstitutional

1955

Flannery O'Connor's *A Good Man is Hard to Find*

Vladimir Nabokov's *Lolita*

Tennessee Williams' *Cat on a Hot Tin Roof* appears on Broadway

1957

Isaac Bashevis Singer's *Gimpel the Fool and Other Stories*

Bernard Malamud's *The Magic Barrel*

1959

Philip Roth's *Goodbye, Columbus and Five Short Stories*

Grace Paley's *The Little Disturbances of Man*

Alaska and Hawaii admitted to the Union as the 49th and 50th states, respectively

Fidel Castro overthrows the Bastista regime and becomes Cuba's dictator

In Canada, Mordecai Richler publishes *The Apprenticeship of Duddy Kravitz*

1960

John Updike's *Rabbit, Run*

Flannery O'Connor's *The Violent Bear It Away*

1961

Joseph Heller's *Catch-22*

Berlin Wall built

Roger Maris breaks Babe Ruth's record by hitting 61 home runs in one season

1962

Katherine Ann Porter's *Ship of Fools*

John Updike's *Pigeon Feathers and Other Stories*

John Glenn first American to orbit earth

Cuban missile crisis

1963

Thomas Pynchon's *V*

Kurt Vonnegut's *Cat's Cradle*

President John Fitzgerald Kennedy assassinated

1964

Saul Bellow's *Herzog*

1965

Katherine Anne Porter's *Collected Short Stories* wins the National Book Award

Malcolm X assassinated

1966

Bernard Malamud's *The Fixer*

First artificial heart inplanted

1967

Chaim Potok's *The Chosen*

William Styron's *The Confessions of Nat Turner*

1968

Kurt Vonnegut's *Welcome to the Monkey House*

Martin Luther King, Jr. assassinated

Robert Kennedy assassinated

1969

Philip Roth's *Portnoy's Complaint*

Kurt Vonnegut's *Slaughterhouse Five*

N. Scott Momaday's *The Way to Rainy Mountain*

Momaday wins the 1969 Pulitzer for *House Made of Dawn*

John Cheever's *Bullet Park*

First men on the moon, Americans Neil Armstrong and Buzz Aldrin

1970

Saul Bellow's *Mr. Sammler's Planet*

Toni Morrison's *The Bluest Eye*

1971

The Complete Short Stories of Flannery O'Connor (posthumous)

John Updike's *Rabbit Redux*

John Gardner's *Grendel*

1972

Ernest Hemingway's *The Nick Adams Stories* (posthumous)

Toni Cade Bambara's *Gorilla, My Love*

John Gardner's *The Sunlight Dialogues*

1973

Alice Walker's *In Love and Trouble: Stories of Black Women*

Tim O'Brian's *Going after Cacciato*

1974

President Nixon resigns

1975

Saul Bellow's *Humboldt's Gift*

North and South Vietnam united as one country

1976

Rudolpho Anaya's *Bless Me Ultima*

1977

Leslie Marmon Silko's *Ceremony*

Toni Morrison's *Song of Solomon*

1978

The Stories of John Cheever wins the Pulitzer Prize

Isaac Bashevis Singer wins the Nobel Prize

Ann Beattie's *New Yorker* stories collected in *Secrets and Surprises*

1980

The Collected Short Stories of Eudora Welty

Frank O'Connor's *Collected Short Stories*

Polish strike inspires Solidarity movement

1981

Raymond Carver's *What We Talk About When We Talk About Love*

1982

Bobbie Ann Mason's *Shiloh and Other Stories*

Alice Walker's *The Color Purple*

Brief war in the Falklands

1983

Cynthia Ozick's *Art & Ardor*

Jamaica Kincaid's *At the Bottom of the River*

1984

Raymond Carver's *Cathedral*

Louise Erdrich's *Love Medicine*

1985

Alice Adams' *Return Trips*

Anne Tyler's *The Accidental Tourist*

Don DeLillo's *White Noise*

Bobbie Ann Mason's *In Country*

1986

Challenger explodes, all seven crew members killed

AIDS virus identified

1987

Toni Morrison's *Beloved*

1989

Amy Tan's *The Joy Luck Club*

Berlin Wall torn down

1990

Tim O'Brien's *The Things They Carried*

Julia Alvarez' *How the Garcia Girls Lost Their Accents*

1991

Soviet Union dissolved

South African schools integrate

1992

Toni Morrison's *Jazz*

1995

Margaret Atwood's *Morning in the Burned House*

1998

Mark McGwire hits 70 home runs, the most ever in one season

President Bill Clinton impeached

Index

X-Y-Z

Check Out These
Best-Selling
COMPLETE IDIOT'S GUIDES®

Understanding **Catholicism**
SECOND EDITION
Bob O'Gorman, Ph.D. and Mary Faulkner, M.A.
1-59257-085-2
$18.95

Learning **Spanish**
THIRD EDITION
Gail Stein
0-02-864451-4
$18.95

The **Bible**
SECOND EDITION
James S. Bell Jr. and Stan Campbell
0-02-864382-8
$18.95

Being a **Groom**
SECOND EDITION
Jennifer Lata Rung and Mark Rung
0-02-864456-5
$9.95

Grammar and **Style**
SECOND EDITION
Laurie E. Rozakis, Ph.D.
1-59257-115-8
$16.95

Playing the **Guitar**
SECOND EDITION
Frederick Noad
0-02-864244-9
$21.95 w/CD

Personal Finance in Your **20s & 30s**
SECOND EDITION
Sarah Young Fisher and Susan Shelly
0-02-864374-7
$19.95

Knitting and Crocheting
SECOND EDITION
Illustrated
Barbara Breiter and Gail Diven
1-59257-089-5
$16.95

The **Perfect Resume**
THIRD EDITION
Susan Ireland
0-02-864440-9
$14.95

Buying and Selling a Home
FOURTH EDITION
Shelley O'Hara and Nancy D. Lewis
1-59257-120-4
$18.95

Low-Carb Meals
Lucy Beale and Sandy G. Couvillon, M.S., L.D.N, R.D.
1-59257-180-8
$18.95

Calculus
W. Michael Kelley
0-02-864365-8
$18.95

More than *450 titles* in *30 different categories*
Available at booksellers everywhere

ALPHA